Cloud 3.0

Drafting and Negotiating
Cloud Computing Agreements

Lisa R. Lifshitz and John A. Rothchild
Editors

AMERICAN BAR ASSOCIATION
Business Law Section

Contents

Introduction

Prospective readers considering the purchase of this book may wonder: "Who needs a book on contracting with cloud computing vendors? Aren't all cloud contracts basically commoditized, comprised of 'boilerplate' language? And surely no vendor would agree to make any changes to its standard form cloud agreements? It's all just futile, really."

"Dear reader," we would respond, "this book will be very useful if you are (or your client is) considering moving to the cloud." While it is true that in comparison with the earliest one-sided contracts current cloud agreements have begun to (slowly) evolve to meet regulatory and legal environments, not all cloud agreements are created equal or adequately meet customers' increasingly demanding legal and regulatory requirements. This is where lawyers and others can step in to help redress imbalances in so-called "standard" cloud agreements and create agreements that are more clearly expressed and better suited to the needs of cloud customers. Contrary to popular belief, sophisticated cloud vendors are often open to negotiation of their agreements, particularly as needed to comply with regulatory requirements or can offer alternatives that allow customers to lawfully use their services. Choosing the "right" cloud vendor is therefore a critical component of obtaining cloud services and due diligence is key. Moreover, as many businesses operate internationally, both cloud providers and users of cloud services increasingly have to consider the impact of laws from multiple jurisdictions on the provision and use of cloud services.

This book is intended to teach lawyers and others to understand cloud agreements, separating the "buzz" from the cloud. While it is accessible to non-experts, even seasoned technology law veterans will benefit from the authoritative guidance of our authors who are experts in their fields. We strive to offer our readers practical guidance, including "best practices," to drafting and negotiating effective cloud computing agreements, taking into account the technological, business, and legal considerations of an organization's use of cloud computing technologies. The book also explains how to differentiate the good from the bad vendors and how to recognize agreements that heavily favor the vendor. We endeavour to provide readers with practical information and approaches that will help lawyers and others create useful cloud computing agreements that meet their clients' business and legal requirements.

Our first chapter offers a basic cloud technology overview to set the stage before considering the legal issues. In Chapter 2 we dive into a detailed discussion about negotiating the "must-have" representations and warranties, key carve-outs, and vendor cross-indemnities, with a special emphasis on current trends in limiting liability. Chapter 3 offers a detailed analysis of service levels in cloud agreements, with the intention of demystifying them and avoiding the "gotchas." It also explains the differences between service level agreements and service level penalties, explains credits and penalties, exemptions and exceptions, and provides tips about negotiating service level agreements in public and private cloud environments. Chapters 4 and 5 deal with best practices for cloud privacy and security, including U.S. federal and state regulatory requirements, data breach disclosure rules, and other applicable standards.

Recognizing that certain industries require more specialized cloud agreements, Chapter 6 focuses on clouds for financial service providers (such as banks) and Chapter 7 on healthcare providers (such as hospitals), covering in detail the effective due diligence required to choose vendors in these areas, how to meet relevant regulatory requirements, and cross-border data issues.

Chapter 8 looks at what happens when things go wrong in a cloud arrangement, focussing on dispute resolution and litigation issues, including bankruptcy, litigation strategies, and the good and bad of arbitration clauses in cloud agreements. Chapters 9–11 focus on international aspects of cloud computing, looking at differing laws in Canada, Germany and the United Kingdom (including data protection) that impact both the providers of cloud services and the legal requirements of users in those jurisdictions.

While entering a cloud agreement may be as easy as one click, extricating oneself from a cloud services arrangement is never quite so simple. Chapter 12 focusses on negotiating the exit from a cloud contract and ensuring successful transition, whether to another provider or in-house. Topics covered include crafting appropriate transition clauses, ensuring adequate data migration and data destruction, "no-hostage" payment terms, and compliance with records retention requirements.

In Chapter 13 we include a very practical set of tips and best practices for effective cloud negotiations to better arm you to create "win-win" cloud agreements. Lawyers will appreciate guidance on managing client expectations while meeting their ethical and professional obligations, dealing with the difficult "scorched earth" client, disengaged clients, "sharp practices," as well as mitigating contract errors and avoiding "over-lawyering." Chapter 14 is aimed at lawyers and their legal ethics and professional responsibilities while using cloud services.

Lastly and thinking outside of the law, we conclude in Chapter 15 with a timely look at how cyberliability insurance can be used to mitigate certain risks associated with the use of cloud services, including why and when such insurance should be used, understanding potential coverage restrictions, determining how much coverage should be sought, and how to choose the "right" cyberliability policy.

We would like to thank Ted Claypoole, the past chair of the Business Law Section Cyberspace Law Committee, for originally green-lighting (and encouraging) this book, as well as our current Committee chair, Cheryl Balough, for her ongoing support. We also thank the members of the Committee who contributed the chapters that constitute the book, and others who contributed their time and effort to this project.

Lisa R. Lifshitz
John A. Rothchild
Co-editors

Chapter 1

Overview of Cloud Computing Technology

By David Ma[1]

I. Introduction

Since its introduction, cloud computing has rapidly grown to become an important component of the information technologies that businesses use, and although spending on cloud computing constitutes less than five percent of overall spending on information technology, spending on cloud computing has grown at 4.5 times the rate of general information technology spending since 2009, a figure that is projected to rise by a multiple of six in the near future.[2] A 2016 survey of chief information officers revealed that 16 percent of data processing workloads run in the public cloud, which will grow to 41 percent by 2021.[3] Of the *Fortune* Global 50 companies, 48 have announced plans to adopt cloud computing.[4] In other words, the importance of cloud computing to businesses is likely to continue growing.

The objective of this chapter is to provide a brief overview of the technology that enables cloud computing, the general characteristics and types of cloud computing, the models that can be used to deploy them, and some advantages and disadvantages of cloud computing.[5]

II. Technical Elements of Cloud Computing

An oft-cited definition of cloud computing is one developed by the National Institute of Standards and Technology (NIST): "a model for enabling ubiquitous, convenient, on-demand network access to a shared pool of configurable computing resources (e.g., networks, servers, storage, applications, and services) that can be rapidly provisioned and

---

1 The views expressed are solely those of the author. References to vendors are for illustrative purposes only and do not constitute a recommendation or endorsement of such vendors. The author would like to acknowledge and thank Jerry Dawkins, CEO and founder of True Digital Security, for his helpful review and comments on drafts of this chapter. Errors and omissions remain the sole responsibility of the author.

2 John F. Gantz & Pam Miller, The Salesforce Economy: Enabling 1.9 Million New Jobs and $389 Billion in New Revenue Over the Next Five Years 3 (2016), https://www.salesforce.com/content/dam/web/en_us/www/academic-alliance/datasheets/IDC-salesforce-economy-study-2016.pdf.

3 Tiernan Ray, *Amazon Seeing "Momentous" Change of Guard as Public Cloud "Booms," Says JP Morgan*, Barron's, Apr. 14, 2016, http://www.barrons.com/articles/amazon-seeing-momentous-change-of-guard-as-public-cloud-booms-says-jp-morgan-1460669610.

4 Mark Brinda & Michael Heric, *The Changing Faces of the Cloud*, Bain Brief, Jan. 25, 2017, http://www.bain.com/publications/articles/the-changing-faces-of-the-cloud.aspx.

5 This chapter summarizes only some of the more significant technologies used to facilitate cloud computing. There are others not addressed here, such as those related to usage monitoring, metering and billing, automated scaling mechanisms, load balancers, service-level monitors, and identity and security management. For a more comprehensive list of cloud-related technologies, see the list of projects that comprise OpenStack, https://www.openstack.org/software/.

released with minimal management effort or service provider interaction."[6] Although the NIST Definition is helpful in describing the characteristics of cloud computing, it is not quite as helpful in explaining exactly what the cloud is.

Perhaps another useful starting point is the history of the term "cloud." Well before the advent of cloud computing, computer network designers used a pictogram of a cloud in networking diagrams to identify a group of networked computers connected to the network depicted.[7] The purpose of using the pictogram was to keep the diagram simple—the cloud was intended to depict the abstract notion of computing resources that are linked to a network where the details were either unknown or not particularly important. The notion of abstraction is particularly appropriate when it comes to cloud computing. At the conceptual level, cloud computing can perhaps best be thought of as the abstraction of computing resources. The following sections provide further detail on how that abstraction is achieved.

A. Hardware

Cloud computing has always been (and likely always will be) powered by computers and related equipment in some shape or form. For cloud computing, this will typically consist of hundreds or thousands of computers densely packed into data centers, networked together along with storage devices with connectivity to the internet.[8]

B. Network Connectivity

It should come as no surprise that one of the enabling technologies for cloud computing is network connectivity. Although cloud computing services can in theory be provided through various types of network connections, most if not all current cloud computing services are delivered through the internet. As cloud computing often requires the rapid transmission of significant amounts of data between the cloud computing service provider and its users, the rise of broadband and mobile internet connectivity over the past decade has been instrumental in enabling the corresponding rise in cloud computing.[9]

---

6 Peter Mell & Timothy Grance, National Institute of Standards and Technology, The NIST Definition of Cloud Computing (Special Publication 800-145) (2011), at 2, http://nvlpubs.nist. gov/nistpubs/Legacy/SP/nistspecialpublication800-145.pdf [hereinafter NIST Definition].

7 *See* Rebecca J. Rosen, *Clouds: The Most Useful Metaphor of All Time?*, Atlantic, Sept. 30, 2011, https://www.theatlantic.com/technology/archive/2011/09/clouds-the-most-useful-metaphor-of-all-time/245851/. For a more in-depth exploration of the origins of the terms, *see* Antonio Regalado, *Who Coined "Cloud Computing"?*, MIT Technology Review, Oct. 31, 2011, https://www.technologyreview.com/s/425970/who-coined-cloud-computing/.

8 Readers should be cautioned, however, that "typically" does not equate to "necessarily"—the term "cloud" can be used generically to describe any remote computing resources, including far less robust arrangements. Thus, when prospective service providers indicate that they utilize "the cloud," users would be well advised to enquire exactly what that entails.

9 According to the Federal Communications Commission, median download speed in the United States quadrupled between 2011 and 2015 from 10 Mbps (megabits per second) to 41 Mbps. FCC, Measuring Broadband America: Fixed Broadband Report 15 (2016), https://www.fcc.gov/reports-research/reports/measuring-broadband-america/measuring-fixed-broadband-report-2016.

C. Communication Standards

The development and rapid adoption of web, internet, and related technology standards has also played an important role in enabling the rise of cloud computing by setting out standardized formats and protocols for receiving, transmitting, and displaying data and information. Service providers can conform to these uniform standards, knowing that a broad base of users can readily access them, including through browsers that are already installed on their computers, obviating the need to install specialized software.

A subset of such standards that is particularly important for cloud computing are the service standards and protocols that are used to enable applications on two different computers to communicate and interact with each other.[10]

D. Virtualization

There is of course more to cloud computing than just computers. One of the key enabling technologies for cloud computing is virtualization technology. This technology enables simulation of the hardware of an actual computer in software, commonly referred to as a "virtual machine." A somewhat rough analogy[11] is a flight simulator game: the game simulates and presents the experience of flying an airplane, including responding and re-acting to inputs in a manner similar to a real airplane. Virtualization software (sometimes referred to as a "hypervisor") does something similar, except that instead of an airplane, it simulates (or "virtualizes") a computer and does so very accurately—so accurately that almost any software that can be installed on a physical computer can also be installed and operated within that virtual machine. Virtual machines mimic, in software, all the elements of a physical computer, including a central processing unit, memory, storage, and networking interfaces, subject, of course, to the limitations of the physical comput-er (the "host") on which the hypervisor is installed. As a result, one can create a virtual machine running the Linux operating system, for example, even though the underlying host is running Windows.[12] One can even install multiple virtual machines on a single host, each running a different operating system (again, subject to the limits of the physical computer). Moreover, any software running within a virtual machine is isolated within

---

10 These include technologies such as Simple Object Access Protocol, representational state transfer, Web Service Description Language, and Universal Description, Discovery, and Integration, among others.

11 It should perhaps be emphasized that this is a conceptual rather than a technical analogy: the design and architecture of a flight simulator bears little to no resemblance to virtualization software. That being said, one of the earliest implementations of virtual machines on personal computers was developed spe-cifically for a text-based adventure game called Zork, to reduce its size so that it could be run on personal computers (as it had originally been developed on a much larger mainframe computer), and to enable portability across different hardware platforms. *See* P. David Lebling, *Zork and the Future of Computer-ized Fantasy Simulations*, 5 Byte 12, 172 (Dec. 1980), https://archive.org/details/byte-magazine-1980-12.

12 There are a number of software packages that enable one to experience virtualization firsthand on standard desktop computers, such as VirtualBox, https://www.virtualbox.org/ (free and available for Windows, Linux and Mac) or Parallels Desktop, https://www.parallels.com/ca/products/desktop (paid, for Mac only). Microsoft Hyper-V can also be enabled on certain versions of Windows 8 and 10. Anthony Bartolo, *Step-By-Step: Enabling Hyper-V for Use on Windows 10*, Canitpro.net, Sept. 8, 2015, https://blogs.technet.microsoft.com/canitpro/2015/09/08/step-by-step-enabling-hyper-v-for-use-on-windows-10/.

that virtual machine and cannot communicate with or affect either the physical computer or other virtual machines installed on that physical computer.[13]

Because virtual machines are created entirely in software, they provide all of the benefits of software, many of which are key to enabling cloud computing. These include:

1) **Portability and replicability.** Given that a virtual machine is created in software, it can be easily saved as a file and copied or moved to and operated on another host with virtualization software installed, without the need to reinstall and reconfigure the operating system and all applications installed on the virtual machine, making it much faster and easier to move to another host, or to provision a new server by simply copying an existing virtual machine that has already been configured.

2) **Reliability and availability.** Some hypervisors can be configured to automatically move a virtual machine to another host under certain conditions (for example, if it detects a possible failure of the host)[14] or to maintain an identical running copy of the virtual machine on another host and automatically switch to that copy, in both cases enhancing availability and reliability, and enabling easier disaster recovery.

3) **Greater hardware flexibility.** Given that virtualization enables virtual machines to have characteristics independent of the hardware on which they run, there is typically more flexibility when selecting and purchasing physical computers so long as they are compatible with the applicable virtualization software.

4) **Recovery.** Given that multiple images of virtual machines can be saved at any time, periodic "snapshots" can be created. If a virtual machine fails for any reason (for example, after a failed upgrade or patch to the operating system), it can simply be "rolled back" to an earlier snapshot that was working properly.

5) **Security and stability.** Given that virtual machines are isolated from both each other and the host computer, they can be used to enhance security, for example by creating a separate virtual machine to run test environments for new or experimental applications so that failures or crashes of such applications will impact only that separate virtual machine.[15]

6) **Efficiency.** Physical servers are often underutilized. Virtualization can enable greater efficiency by replacing physical computers with virtual machines and consolidating those virtual machines onto fewer physical computers, reducing both hardware and operating costs.

---

13 This is to some extent an overgeneralization. A hypervisor can be configured to enable interaction between a given virtual machine and its host or other virtual machines by, for example, creating virtual network connections between them. Certain types of virtualization technology also allow for (or require) some limited awareness of the underlying physical host within the guest operating system. In addition, vulnerabilities occasionally are discovered that could be used to access the host system from within a virtual machine, typically referred to as virtual machine escape. *See, e.g.,* Dan Goodin, *Extremely Serious Virtual Machine Bug Threatens Cloud Providers Everywhere,* Ars Technica, May 13, 2015, https://arstechnica.com/information-technology/2015/05/extremely-serious-virtual-machine-bug-threatens-cloud-providers-everywhere/.

14 See also Part II.F., *infra.*

15 Security is thereby enhanced as compared to running such applications on the same computer without the use of virtualization. Security would not be improved as compared to running such applications on a separate physical computer, although of course doing so would entail additional cost.

One notable variation of virtualization is containerization.[16] In contrast to "full" virtualization, which runs a completely separate operating system within a virtual machine, a container utilizes some elements of the operating system installed on the host, but still remains isolated from the host. Containers share some traits with full virtualization, such as ease of porting or replicating. However, containers typically require significantly less overhead than full virtualization due to their reliance on elements of the underlying operating system, resulting in lower resource usage and faster creation and execution. Thus, a given physical computer can host a much larger number of containers than virtual machines. Lastly, some container technologies allow for portability across different hosts.[17]

E. Multitenant Technology

"Multitenant technology" is a term used to describe an approach to application development that enables multiple users (or multiple groups of users) to each access the same instance of an application in such a way that the application appears to be customized for each such user and logically isolated from every other user.

Although multitenant architecture can achieve the same result as virtualization, the two technologies are distinct from one other. For example, a service provider could service multiple users by creating a distinct virtual machine for each such user and installing the same non-multitenant application in each virtual machine. Given that virtual machines are isolated from one another, each user would have its own uniquely configured application. In contrast, if the same application were developed using multitenant architecture, each user[18] would access a single instance of the application. The data and configuration stored for each user would be distinct, however, and accessible only by that user through the use of logical controls within the application. Multitenant architecture can also be combined with virtualization. For example, a single instance of a multitenant application could be installed and operated within a virtual machine to serve multiple users. Alternatively, there could be multiple instances in multiple virtual machines, with each instance serving multiple users.[19]

Although multitenant architecture is typically much more complex (and therefore more costly) to develop, it can result in cost savings as it enables resources to be shared more efficiently across users, as compared to creating an individual virtual machine and individual instance of the application for each user. However, it may reduce the flexibility afforded to end-users. For example, given that all users of a multitenant application are accessing the same instance of that application, they typically must all use the same version of the application.

---

16 This is sometimes called container-based virtualization or operating system level virtualization.

17 This was perhaps the primary benefit of Docker (a particular type of container technology; *see What Is Docker*, DOCKER, https://www.docker.com/what-docker) as compared to other container technologies, such as Linux containers, which are to some degree dependent on the configuration of the underlying host. *See* Chenxi Wang, *What is Docker? Linux Containers Explained*, INFOWORLD, June 29, 2017, https://www.infoworld.com/article/3204171/linux/what-is-docker-linux-containers-explained.html.

18 In this context, a "user" could be an organization with multiple individual users, all of whom could access the data and configuration for that organization.

19 *See, e.g.,* THOMAS Y. KWOK ET AL., A SOFTWARE AS A SERVICE WITH MULTI-TENANCY SUPPORT FOR AN ELECTRONIC CONTRACT MANAGEMENT APPLICATION (IBM Research Report RC24537 (W0804-071)) (2008), http://domino.research.ibm.com/library/cyberdig.nsf/papers/B81E880A2CD5B66A852574BF-005092C4/$File/rc23537.pdf. Although somewhat dated, this paper provides a useful overview of the design and architecture of a multitenant SaaS application, including figures that depict the distinction between single-tenant and multitenant approaches.

F. Resource-Pooling, Allocation, and Management Technologies

Another group of technologies that facilitate cloud computing are those that are used to pool, allocate, and manage the underlying physical resources, such as processing power, network communications, and data storage for use by individual users. Such physical resources are typically comprised of hundreds or thousands (or more) computers located in one or multiple data centers, each connected through networking equipment.

One example of such technology is virtual infrastructure managers (VIMs). VIMs are used to manage virtual machines across physical servers. For example, assume that a (quite small) cloud service provider uses two computers. Each has a hypervisor installed on it, which in turn hosts multiple virtual machines. If one computer is nearing the limits of its capacity and a request for a new virtual machine comes in, a VIM can be used to allocate that virtual machine to the second computer. VIMs can also be used to move virtual machines from one physical computer to another, in some cases even while the virtual machine continues to operate.

Along similar lines, various types of cloud storage technologies can be used to allocate, move, and manage storage capacity among multiple virtual machines. Although there are various ways of implementing this approach,[20] such technologies essentially virtualize storage. For example, if a user creates a "virtual drive" within a virtual machine and writes data to it, storage technology will take that data, break it up into chunks, and write it to multiple physical storage devices, such as hard drives, which can be on multiple computers. Even though the chunks are spread across multiple computers and multiple drives, the storage technology keeps track of exactly where each chunk is so that, to an end user, those disparate chunks appear to be on one drive. In addition to keeping track of those chunks, such technologies will also either record multiple copies of the data, or apply an algorithm that generates additional data so that if one or more chunks are lost (for example, due to the failure of a physical hard drive), the data can still be recovered.

Along similar lines, functions that would otherwise be served by physical networking devices, such as firewalls, routers, and switches, can be replicated in software.[21]

---

20 Traditional approaches include, for example, storage area networks—typically proprietary hardware consisting of one or more devices, each containing numerous drives. More recently, software solutions have been developed to implement the same (or better) functionality using generic, nonvendor-specific hardware, some of which is open source. These include, for example, Ceph (http://ceph.com/) and Gluster (https://www.gluster.org/), both open source, as well as proprietary technologies such as VMware vSAN (https://www.vmware.com/products/vsan.html) and a subset of the functionality in Nutanix (https://www.nutanix.com/).

21 Examples of such technologies include virtual switch technology built directly within hypervisors to enable virtual machines on a given host to communicate between each other and to the host machine and elsewhere (for example, virtual switches in VMware's vSphere, https://www.vmware.com/support/ws55/doc/ws_net_component_vswitch.html, or libvert virtual network switches in KVM, https://access.redhat.com/documentation/en-US/Red_Hat_Enterprise_Linux/6/html/Virtualization_Administration_Guide/chap-Virtualization_Administration_Guide-Virtual_Networking.html, as well as software-defined networking technologies, which are typically (but not always) implemented in dedicated physical networking devices and shift control of certain networking functions (typically referred to as the control plane) so that they are programmatically controlled by software and, in some cases, by virtualizing specific network functions such as load balancers or firewalls. Example of the latter include OpenDaylight, https://www.opendaylight.org/, Open vSwitch, http://openvswitch.org/, and VMware NSX, https://www.vmware.com/ca/products/nsx.html.

Perhaps due in part to the burgeoning popularity of cloud computing, a number of groups and companies have created collections of software tools (or "stacks") that can be used to comprehensively implement a cloud computing environment. These include, for example, OpenStack,[22] Apache CloudStack,[23] and vCloud Suite.[24]

G. Recent Developments

As with most other types of information technology, cloud computing continues to develop and evolve at a rapid pace. The following are some examples of recent developments in cloud computing.

1) **Cloud-native applications.** The term "cloud native" is generally used to refer to applications that have been designed and written to run on cloud services, meaning that they can run on various cloud platforms, can be easily copied or moved, and are scalable.[25] They typically will also take a "microservice" approach: instead of one large application performing many functions, those functions are divided into numerous individual applications (or microservices) that can interface with each other, making each easier to maintain and allowing for a more modular approach in that end users can combine microservices as appropriate for the task at hand.[26] One of the primary enabling technologies for cloud-native applications is container technology.[27] Conceptually, cloud-native applications can be thought of as abstraction at the application level in the same way that physical machines are abstracted into virtual machines.[28]

2) **Serverless computing.** A somewhat related concept is that of "serverless computing" where the cloud provider assumes responsibility for dynamically providing whatever resources are required by the application, rather than the end user manually allocating additional resources as required. For example, with a traditional approach, a user would create an application, select an appropriately sized virtual machine, and run it, paying for the use of that virtual machine. If the workload grows, then the user would increase the size of that virtual machine. In contrast, if the same application were implemented using a serverless approach, the end user would pay only for the resources actually used by the application. If, for example, the application were not used for a given period of time, no resources would be used; therefore, no usage fees would be paid.[29]

---

22 https://www.openstack.org/.

23 https://cloudstack.apache.org/.

24 https://www.vmware.com/ca/products/vcloud-suite.html.

25 Libby Clark & Mark Hinkle, Guide to the Open Cloud 6 (2016), https://www.linuxfoundation.org/publications/guide-to-open-cloud-2016.

26 For a more detailed description of microservices architecture, *see* MuleSoft, *Microservices vs Monolithic Architecture,* https://www.mulesoft.com/resources/api/microservices-vs-monolithic.

27 See Part II.D., *supra.*

28 Clark & Hinkle, *supra* note 25, at 7.

29 For a very detailed and helpful overview of serverless computing, *see* Mike Roberts, *Serverless Architectures,* Martinfowler.com, Aug. 4, 2016, https://martinfowler.com/articles/serverless.html. *See also* Carl Osipov, *Composable Architecture Patterns for Serverless Computing Applications—Part 4,* Clouds with Carl, Aug. 15, 2016, http://cloudswithcarl.com/blog/2016/08/15/composable-architecture-patterns-for-serverless-computing-applications-part-4/. Examples of serverless computing services are AWS Lambda, https://docs.aws.amazon.com/lambda/latest/dg/welcome.html, and Google Cloud Functions, https://cloud.google.com/functions/docs/.

3) **Edge computing.** To date, most cloud computing has been enabled through the use of large, centralized data centers hosting thousands of computers. This has resulted in a significant number of users being rather distant from the physical location where processing actually occurs, causing small delays in the processing of information (sometimes referred to as latency). Although in many cases the degree of latency is not critical, for certain applications, such as autonomous vehicles and robotics, it may be. As such applications become more widely implemented, there will be an increasing demand for low-latency cloud computing, resulting in the increased use of decentralized data centers that are more geographically dispersed closer to end users and therefore lower latency.[30] Interestingly, some cloud providers have developed solutions to "extend" their cloud services to operate on an end user's equipment to achieve this objective.[31]

4) **Big computing.** Artificial intelligence and, in particular, deep learning typically require significant amounts of computing power, but for limited periods of time. As such technologies become more widely used, the demand for high-performance computing will increase. As a result, cloud providers have begun to develop "big compute" cloud services to enable end users to utilize deep learning without the need to procure a high-performance data center.[32]

5) **Decentralized cloud computing.** At present, Infrastructure as a Service (IaaS)[33] cloud computing is generally dominated by a small number of large companies, each of which owns and operates multiple, large-scale data centers with millions of computers. This is perhaps to be expected, given the advantages afforded by economies of scale. However, there are still millions of computers and computing devices outside of those owned by cloud providers that, for the most part, are not used to their full capacity.[34] Technologies to harness such unutilized capacity have been used for more than two decades with a fair degree of success, but until recently have largely been limited to volunteer efforts for scientific research.[35] However, a

---

30 Jeremy Hsu, *It's Time to Think Beyond Cloud Computing*, WIRED, Aug. 23, 2017, https://www.wired.com/story/its-time-to-think-beyond-cloud-computing.

31 For example, AWS Greengrass, https://aws.amazon.com/greengrass, and Microsoft Azure IoT Edge, https://azure.microsoft.com/en-ca/services/iot-edge/.

32 Amazon and Microsoft both now offer high-performance cloud computing. *See* High Performance Computing, Amazon, https://aws.amazon.com/hpc/; High Performance Computing, Microsoft, https://azure.microsoft.com/en-us/solutions/high-performance-computing/.

33 For an explanation of Infrastructure as a Service, see Part III.B., *infra*.

34 Smartphones alone constitute a significant portion of this capacity. In 2013, one researcher stated that "there are about a billion Android devices right now, and their total computing power exceeds that of the largest supercomputers." *See* Richard Gray, *How CERN's Grid May Place the Power of the World's Computers in Your Hands*, TELEGRAPH, Aug. 14, 2013, http://www.telegraph.co.uk/technology/news/10242837/How-CERNs-Grid-may-place-the-power-of-the-worlds-computers-in-your-hands.html. As of 2018, there are approximately 2.5 billion active smartphones. *See Number of Smartphone Users Worldwide from 2014 to 2020*, STATISTA, https://www.statista.com/statistics/330695/number-of-smartphone-users-worldwide/.

35 The first such effort was the Great Internet Mersenne Prime Search, https://www.mersenne.org/, launched in 1996 to (as the name suggests) search for Mersenne prime numbers, which takes a significant amount of computing power. The project has discovered 15 prime numbers to date. In 2017, slightly over 1.5 million CPUs participated in the project. Other similar projects include Distributed.net, http://www.distributed.net/Main_Page, which undertakes research projects primarily related to cryptography; SETI@home, https://setiathome.berkeley.edu/, which uses computing power to analyze radio telescope data for signs of extraterrestrial intelligence; and Folding@home, http://folding.stanford.edu/, which focuses on disease research by simulating the folding of proteins and other elements.

number of ventures have recently been launched to offer general IaaS cloud computing services powered by decentralized computing resources, using blockchain technology to assist in accounting for the usage and provisioning of resources.[36] Such an approach has some possible advantages as compared with traditional cloud computing, such as lower cost and higher responsiveness,[37] although it may too early to assess whether those advantages will be realized at any significant scale.

III. Characteristics and Models

While Part II above focused on the elements of technology that are used to create cloud computing solutions, Part III outlines the general characteristics of cloud computing from the perspective of the user, and describes how cloud computing services are characterized both in terms of the nature of the services being provided (the "service model") and who is entitled to use such services (the "deployment model").

A. Characteristics of Cloud Computing Services

Application of the technologies described above results in the availability of computing services that have a specific set of characteristics. The NIST Definition identifies five such characteristics:[38]

1) **On-demand self-service.** End users can easily obtain the computer services through automated means (such as a website) and without human assistance.
2) **Broad network access.** Services are provided through standardized means (for example, the internet and web browsers) and can be accessed and used utilizing a variety of devices, such as mobile phones, tablets, or desktop computers.
3) **Resource-pooling.** Computing resources are pooled together and dynamically assigned (and reassigned) for use by multiple users, generally without knowledge or control on the part of the user regarding where those resources are located.
4) **Rapid elasticity.** The quantity of resources can easily and quickly (and in some cases automatically) increase or decrease on demand in almost any quantity and at any time.
5) **Measured service.** Billing is metered and delivered as a utility service.

B. Service Models

The NIST Definition also sets out three service models under which cloud services are categorized based on the nature of the services provided:[39]

---

36 Examples include *Blockchain-Based Decentralized Cloud Computing*, iExec, http://iex.ec/, and Dfinity, https://dfinity.network/, both of which offer (or plan to offer) general IaaS services. Storj, https://storj.io/, focuses on distributed cloud storage.

37 For further details on how such advantages could be realized, *see* Storj Labs, *THERE IS NO CLOUD: It's Just Someone Else's Computer*, Medium, Mar. 16, 2016, https://medium.com/@storjproject/there-is-no-cloud-it-s-just-someone-else-s-computer-6ecc37cdcfe5; and Gilles Fedak, *How Can Blockchain Improve Cloud Computing*, Medium, Sept. 1, 2016, https://medium.com/iex-ec/how-blockchain-can-improve-cloud-computing-1ca24c270f4f.

38 Paraphrased from Mell & Grance, *supra* note 6, at 2.

39 Paraphrased from *id.* at 2–3.

1) **Software as a Service (SaaS).** The provision of application services running on a cloud infrastructure,[40] typically accessed by end users through a web browser, without any ability on the part of the end user to manage or control the infrastructure used to provide such services. Examples include e-mail services (such as Google Gmail[41]) and customer relationship management applications (such as Salesforce[42]). SaaS generally comprises the largest proportion of spending on cloud computing.[43]

2) **Platform as a Service (PaaS).** The provision of programming languages and tools to enable end users to create applications and deploy those applications on a cloud platform for use by the user or by others. As with SaaS, the end user does not manage or control the underlying infrastructure. Examples include Heroku[44] and Google App Engine.[45]

3) **Infrastructure as a Service (IaaS).** The provision of fundamental computing resources such as processing, storage, and networking to enable users to run any software they choose, including operating systems or applications, but with no control or management of the underlying infrastructure other than the specific computing resources provisioned. Examples include Amazon EC2[46] (computing), Amazon S3[47] (storage), and Microsoft Azure.[48]

A given cloud service provider does not necessarily own or control all the resources used to provide its services. For example, a SaaS vendor may decide to implement its application using the services provided by a separate IaaS vendor so that the SaaS vendor can focus on its strengths (namely, the development of the application) rather than non-core competencies, such as building and managing data centers and physical servers.[49] That IaaS vendor may, in turn, decide to use a third-party vendor to provide data centers and hardware.[50]

---

40 The NIST Definition defines a cloud infrastructure as one that meets the five characteristics described in Part III.A., *supra.*

41 https://www.google.com/gmail/about/.

42 https://www.salesforce.com/.

43 SaaS represented approximately 73 percent of worldwide spending on public cloud computing in 2015. IaaS represented 16 percent, and PaaS represented 11 percent. *See* Gantz & Miller, *supra* note 2, at 4.

44 https://www.heroku.com/.

45 https://cloud.google.com/appengine/.

46 https://aws.amazon.com/ec2/.

47 https://aws.amazon.com/s3/.

48 https://azure.microsoft.com/. Both Amazon AWS and Microsoft Azure include many different offerings, some of which are IaaS in nature, whereas others are more properly described as PaaS or SaaS.

49 *See, e.g.*, Barb Darrow, *Welcome to the Era of Great Data Center Consolidation*, Fortune, Feb. 15, 2017, http://fortune.com/2017/02/15/data-center-consolidation-cloud/. The article explains that software developers are increasingly relying on IaaS vendors to deliver the functionality of their software. Jeff Bezos, CEO of Amazon, has compared this to the evolution of the power industry: "You go back in time a hundred years, if you wanted to have electricity, you had to build your own little electric power plant, and a lot of factories did this. As soon as the electric power grid came online, they dumped their electric power generator, and they started buying power off the grid. It just makes more sense. And that's what is starting to happen with infrastructure computing." Brad Stone, The Everything Store: Jeff Bezos and the Age of Amazon (2013).

50 Most IaaS vendors, however, own and control their own physical infrastructure.

C. Deployment Models

The NIST Definition also sets out four different deployment models that describe who is permitted to use the infrastructure powering the cloud service:[51]

1) **Private cloud.** The infrastructure can be used by only a single organization (which may be comprised of multiple end users). It may be owned, managed, or operated by the organization itself, a third party, or a combination thereof, and the physical infrastructure may be located on the premises of that organization or elsewhere. Private clouds are typically implemented where isolation of the physical resources is required—for example, to facilitate higher security or for regulatory compliance.[52] The trade-off is that private clouds are more costly and less flexible as compared to public clouds.[53] The end user typically will pay for all the dedicated physical resources comprising the private cloud and, if the capacity of the private cloud is reached, must pay for additional physical resources to be installed and added to the cloud.[54]

2) **Community cloud.** Similar to private cloud except that use is limited to a specific community whose members have shared concerns, interests, or needs.

3) **Public cloud.** A cloud service that is available for use by the general public.[55] The infrastructure may be owned, managed, and operated by a business, governmental, or other organization (or a combination thereof). The physical infrastructure is typically located on the premises of the provider.

4) **Hybrid cloud.** A combination of two or more of the above, with technology that enables data and applications to be moved or shared between or among them. Although the NIST Definition only contemplates the use of this term to reference combinations of different cloud types, the term "hybrid" also is often used to describe offerings that enable on-premise computing resources to access cloud services, such as additional storage. End users can install either an appliance or software on premises, which will then enable them to access cloud storage as if it were an on-site physical storage device.[56]

---

51 Paraphrased from MELL & GRANCE, *supra* note 6, at 3.

52 Some vendors use the term "private cloud" to mean something different. In some cases, offerings marketed as private clouds do, in fact, involve shared resources that are logically (but not physically) segregated. Care should be taken in investigating offerings described as private clouds to ensure the degree and nature of isolation meets the requirements of the end user.

53 For a useful summary of trade-offs between private and public clouds, *see Comparing Private and Public Clouds*, RACKSPACE, https://www.rackspace.com/library/cloud-computing-difference.

54 Some vendors have begun to offer utility pricing (i.e., pricing based on use) for private clouds—*see, e.g.*, Arturo Suarez, *Introducing Utility Pricing to Your Managed Private Cloud*, UBUNTU, July 9, 2015, https://insights.ubuntu.com/2015/07/09/introducing-utility-pricing-to-your-managed-private-cloud/, but such pricing is only for management and operation services and does not include the underlying hardware, which the end user must purchase separately.

55 Availability to the general public does not necessarily mean that the public cloud services purchased by a given user are made available to the general public, or that they are made freely available to the general public.

56 Examples include Microsoft Azure StorSimple, https://azure.microsoft.com/en-us/services/storsimple/, and Amazon AWS Storage Gateway, https://docs.aws.amazon.com/storagegateway/latest/userguide/WhatIsStorageGateway.html.

Some cloud providers have developed slight variations on the above models. One example is a virtual private cloud, a pool of computing resources created within a public cloud infrastructure but subject to a higher degree of isolation than usual to ensure the pool is available to only the user creating the virtual private cloud.[57]

Virtual private clouds should not be confused with virtual private servers. Despite the similar name and the use of some of the same underlying technology, virtual private servers are distinct from virtual private clouds, or cloud computing generally for that matter. A virtual private server is essentially a virtual machine created and hosted on a computer that is allocated for the exclusive use of a given user. In other words, the end user is purchasing a portion of the resources of a physical computer that has been divided up into multiple virtual machines. In contrast to cloud computing, there are typically limits to the scalability of a given virtual private server, and if there is a failure of the host computer, all virtual private servers on that computer will also fail.

Another variation of the above models is a multicloud approach, where the services of two or more cloud service providers are used in tandem. For example, an end user could configure a primary virtual server with one service provider and a backup server with another, and then configure them to allow the backup server to automatically take over in the event the primary virtual server fails. Some organizations have developed solutions that facilitate the implementation of and help manage multicloud approaches.[58]

In addition, some organizations have begun working toward the development of cloud interoperability—an approach sometimes referred to as "intercloud." In contrast to a multi-cloud approach, where the end user or its service provider assumes the responsibility for developing solutions to address the specific standards of each different cloud service vendor (which may change over time), an intercloud approach focuses on the development of standardized interfaces to be adopted by cloud service providers to enable interoperability among themselves, and to allow users to easily access multiple cloud service providers though that same interface.[59] To this end, the Institute of Electrical and Electronics Engineers has begun developing standards to help facilitate the adoption of intercloud computing.[60] However, to date, intercloud does not appear to have gained much traction with cloud providers.[61]

---

57 This is typically accomplished through the use of a separate virtual network along with additional security measures. *See, e.g., Amazon Virtual Private Cloud*, AMAZON, https://aws.amazon.com/vpc/.

58 *See, e.g.,* Cloud Foundry, https://www.cloudfoundry.org/multi-cloud/; interCloud, https://www.intercloud.com/; and RightScale, https://www.rightscale.com/. *See also* James Sanders, *Multicloud: A Cheat Sheet*, TECHREPUBLIC, May 4, 2017, http://www.techrepublic.com/article/multicloud-the-smart-persons-guide/.

59 CLOUD STRATEGY PARTNERS, LLC, IEEE INTERCLOUD INTEROPERABILITY AND FEDERATION FRAMEWORK 6–8, https://cloudcomputing.ieee.org/images/files/education/studygroup/IEEE_Intercloud_Interoperability_and_Federation_Framework.pdf (suggesting that cloud computing interoperability is inevitable, following similar trends toward uniform standards in various other industries, such as electric power, financial markets, telephony, and the internet).

60 *See* IEEE Project P2302—Standard for Intercloud Interoperability and Federation, IEEE, https://standards.ieee.org/develop/project/2302.html; IEEE Project P2301—Guide for Cloud Portability and Interoperability Profiles, IEEE, http://standards.ieee.org/develop/project/2301.html.

61 For example, Cisco shut down its intercloud offering in early 2017. Simon Sharwood, *Cisco to Kill Its Intercloud Public Cloud on March 31, 2017*, REGISTER, Dec. 13, 2016, https://www.theregister.co.uk/2016/12/13/cisco_to_kill_its_intercloud_public_cloud_on_march_31st_2017/. Although one possible advantage of intercloud would be to enable smaller cloud providers to present themselves collectively as a much larger network, it is less clear why market-dominant cloud providers would be interested in intercloud. Some vendors, however, do continue to market intercloud connectivity. *See, e.g., Multi-Cloud Connectivity with RackConnect Global*, RACKCONNECT, https://www.rackspace.com/hybrid/rackconnect/global.

IV. Advantages of Cloud Computing

Although the technology that enables cloud computing is critical, business considerations are of equal importance. Innovative technology is unlikely to be adopted if doing so does not make business sense. This section outlines some of the business advantages of cloud computing.

A. Costs and Cash Flow

Many cloud providers, particularly those offering IaaS, price their services on a utility basis: there are no up-front costs, and fees are charged only as and when the services are used.[62] This enables end users to more precisely align their expenses with their requirements.[63] For example, a small business can begin with a small virtual machine provisioned at a low cost. As its business grows, it can increase the size of the virtual machine in small increments or purchase additional virtual machines fairly quickly and easily. If there is a downturn in business, the company can also quickly scale down its usage, and therefore its costs, accordingly. If there is a significant project that requires an unusually high level of computing resources, it can temporarily procure as much as it may require through the cloud provider. Given that costs incurred are based on the needs of the business at a given point in time, expenditures are more likely to align with revenue.

Compare this to the more traditional model in which an organization must purchase a server and license software at a significant up-front cost. Given that the quantity of resources purchased must be sufficient for peak usage, and given that those resources (depending on the business) may not be used on a 24/7 basis, the resources will typically be underutilized. As its business grows, it must buy a minimum of one additional server, even if it does not require all of the capacity of an additional server. It must also factor in room for growth because the process of purchasing, installing, and configuring an additional server takes substantial time. If there is a downturn in business, the company is unlikely to realize much value when it disposes of unneeded servers. Given that the initial capital outlays do not necessarily align with revenue, financing may also be required. On-premise hardware will also require other costs, such as supporting hardware (for example, uninterruptible power supplies), space, staff, electricity, and possibly support and maintenance contracts requiring long-term financial commitments.[64]

B. Efficiency—Economies of Scale and Commodification

Of course, hardware must still be purchased to enable cloud computing, and although end users who purchase cloud services are relieved of those capital expenditures, cloud

---

62 This is less likely to be the case for SaaS providers. Although some SaaS providers will allow for a degree of flexibility in increasing or decreasing usage, there will typically be some limitations, such as a minimum subscription period or minimum usage requirements, and the offering will therefore not be as flexible as most public cloud IaaS offerings.

63 This may not be true for private cloud deployments. See Part III.C., *supra*.

64 For a more in-depth economic analysis of cloud versus on-premise equipment, *see Cloud Economics— Are You Getting the Bigger Picture?*, CLOUD TECHNOLOGY PARTNERS, https://www.cloudtp.com/doppler/cloud-economics-getting-bigger-picture/.

providers (and in particular IaaS providers)[65] are not. Even though they face the same challenges as end users regarding capital expenditures, cloud providers have been able to maintain competitive pricing by becoming more efficient in their delivery of services in a number of ways:

1) **Hardware Costs.** Cloud providers can rely on economies of scale to realize savings due to the volume of their purchases. In addition, rather than purchasing the brand-name, premium-priced equipment that enterprises typically purchase, cloud providers purchase lower-priced commodity hardware because resiliency and redundancy is built into the enabling technology they use. Some cloud providers have developed their own custom hardware designs to maximize the cost efficiency of their hardware purchases.[66]

2) **Software Costs.** Many IaaS cloud providers make extensive use of open source software, thus eliminating (or greatly reducing) the cost of software.[67] In addition, certain information technology functions that were traditionally performed by hardware are now handled through the use of software.[68]

3) **Efficient Resource Usage.** An inherent function of the technology used to enable the provision of cloud computing is efficient resource allocation and utilization across physical resources.[69] IaaS providers can also balance peaks and valleys in resource usage over time and geography across their customer base. The net result is that IaaS providers can operate much more efficiently than enterprises do—by some estimates up to three times more efficiently.[70]

C. Elasticity and Scalability

IaaS users can provision one or many virtual server in minutes and can add or remove resources within similar timeframes. In many cases, resources can be configured to

---

65 SaaS providers can, of course, run their applications using an IaaS provider rather than building out their own physical infrastructure—and many do. *See* Julie Bort, *Netflix, Juniper, and Intuit Explain How Amazon Is Eating the $3.5 Trillion IT Industry*, Business Insider, Jan. 13, 2016, http://www.businessinsider.com/netflix-intuit-juniper-go-all-in-on-amazon-cloud-2016-1.

66 *See, e.g.,* Dan Richman, *Amazon Web Services' Secret Weapon: Its Custom-Made Hardware and Network*, GeekWire, Jan. 19, 2017, https://www.geekwire.com/2017/amazon-web-services-secret-weapon-custom-made-hardware-network/.

67 For example, Amazon Web Services appears to make extensive use of Linux. Steven J. Vaughan-Nichols, *Amazon EC2 Cloud Is Made Up of Almost Half-a-Million Linux Servers*, ZDNet, Mar. 16, 2012, http://www.zdnet.com/article/amazon-ec2-cloud-is-made-up-of-almost-half-a-million-linux-servers/. More than 20 public cloud providers use OpenStack, an open-source cloud computing platform. Barb Darrow, *HPE and Cisco Moves Hurt OpenStack's Public Cloud Story*, Fortune, Dec. 19, 2016, http://fortune.com/2016/12/19/openstack-public-cloud/. Google uses open-source code such as Ganeti, https://opensource.google.com/projects/ganeti, and Kubernetes, https://kubernetes.io/, both originally developed by Google, although the extent to which they are used in its cloud computing offerings is unclear. Google has, however, indicated that it uses Linux extensively in its cloud offerings. *See* Cade Metz, *Google Shaman Explains Mysteries of "Compute Engine,"* Wired, July 3, 2012, https://www.wired.com/2012/07/google-compute-engine/.

68 See Part II.F., *supra.*

69 See Part II.D., *supra.*

70 *See* Larry Dignan, *AWS Cloud Computing Ops, Data Centers, 1.3 Million Servers Creating Efficiency Flywheel*, ZDNet, June 7, 2016, http://www.zdnet.com/article/aws-cloud-computing-ops-data-centers-1-3-million-servers-creating-efficiency-flywheel/.

automatically scale based on workloads. Compare this to a typical process to procure a physical server, which would likely involve several days at a minimum. Unlike physical hardware, there is no need to install or remove servers, nor are there concerns about hardware failures. In brief, cloud computing is more flexible and convenient for end users.

D. Increased Functionality and Reliability

One aspect of cloud computing that has often been cited by Amazon in relation to its cloud offerings is what it has dubbed the "flywheel effect" or the "virtuous circle." Cloud computing features significant economies of scale. As a cloud provider signs on more customers, there is more usage; more usage leads the cloud provider to roll out more infrastructure; more infrastructure leads to greater economies of scale, resulting in lower infrastructure costs; lower infrastructure costs lead to additional innovations and reduced prices, both of which in turn lead to more customers, and so on. The net result for Amazon has been an exponential increase in new features over time—for example, it launched a total of 24 new services in 2008, but in 2015 it launched 516.[71] Amazon's early emphasis on developing its cloud computing business has given it a substantial lead in this efficiency race, which some believe is unlikely to be matched by any other provider.[72]

The adoption of a SaaS as a delivery mechanism, as compared to more traditional software licensed for on-premise use,[73] has given SaaS providers unprecedented insight into the usage of their applications. SaaS vendors can gather great quantities of data on how their applications are used, who is using them, when they are used, what features are used (and which are not), problems encountered, and so on, all in real time.[74] As a result, SaaS providers are able to identify and fix bugs sooner and identify and improve the features and functionality of their application more rapidly. In addition, SaaS users have fewer concerns about patches, version management, and compatibility and interoperability with hardware, operating systems, and other software.

E. Additional Revenue Streams

Cloud computing approaches also open up the possibility of realizing additional revenue streams for providers, particularly for SaaS providers. Although this is of course primarily of benefit to providers, it may indirectly benefit users by enabling the cloud provider to lower fees charged to end users for the cloud provider's services. The following are a few examples:

---

71 Matt Weinberger, *The Cloud Wars Explained: Why Nobody Can Catch Up with Amazon*, Business Insider, Nov. 7, 2015, http://www.businessinsider.com/why-amazon-is-so-hard-to-topple-in-the-cloud-and-where-everybody-else-falls-2015-10.

72 *Id.*

73 Collection of usage information is also possible with on-premise software (often referred to as "telemetry") and has become more prevalent over time. However, it is subject to certain challenges, e.g., the blocking of telemetry transmissions by an end user's security measures, such as firewalls.

74 The rise of analytics has resulted in the growth of service providers that enable SaaS vendors to implement monitoring more easily. Examples include AppDynamics, https://www.appdynamics.com/info/service-saas/, KISSmetrics, https://blog.kissmetrics.com/saas-guides/, and Mixpanel, https://mixpanel.com/solutions/saas/.

1) **Data monetization.** In contrast to on-premise software, with SaaS the service provider will typically have some degree of access to the data of its users. This opens up the possibility of utilizing the data for purposes other than the provision of services to the end user in order to generate additional revenue. Although the topic is not without controversy and often raises the hackles of prospective SaaS users, data monetization is not a novel concept and is a strategy that has been employed by other types of service providers since before the advent of cloud computing.[75] In some cases, the potential value in data monetization could exceed the revenue generated from the service itself.[76] It is not difficult to envision how this could be applied to various types of SaaS applications across numerous industries.[77] Of course, end users may have concerns regarding privacy, confidentiality, and security of their data, particularly in the case of highly sensitive data such as personal health information.

2) **Networks, ecosystems, and marketplaces.** Although not necessarily exclusive to cloud offerings, cloud providers are to some extent better positioned to enable integration with third-party software or solutions, due in part to the use of industry standard interfaces and protocols.[78] Cloud providers can further encourage this by developing interfaces and protocols to enable third parties to easily integrate with the cloud provider's offerings, or offer PaaS solutions to enable the development or migration of their applications.[79] Doing so allows the cloud provider to earn additional revenue by charging for the privilege of integrating with the cloud provider's platform, for example, or acting as a reseller or distributor and earning

---

75 For example, ADP, a payroll service provider, leverages the information it collects in the course of providing such services to develop analytics and statistical reports and related services. *See* Tom Davenport, *How ADP Gives Data Value Back To Its Customers*, FORBES, Mar. 12, 2018, https://www.forbes.com/sites/tomdavenport/2018/03/12/how-adp-gives-data-value-back-to-its-customers/#2d4830a5732c. American Express has used transaction information from its 90 million cards to create Business Insights, "a global information, analytics and consulting organisation that combines real behavioural information—based on actual aggregated purchasing data—with sophisticated analytics to reveal unique insights about your customers, competitive set and marketplace." *Attract Customers/Business Insights*, AMERICAN EXPRESS, https://www.americanexpress.com/uk/content/merchant/business-insights.html. Financial institutions and credit bureaus have a long history of sharing and aggregating data to produce credit reports.

76 One possible example, albeit not from the SaaS world, is Nest, a maker of smart thermostats. Nest collects and aggregates information on energy consumption from those thermostats to provide aggregated energy consumption data to energy companies to enable them to better plan their energy production. The founder of Nest believes that the sale of such data will eventually earn more than the sales of the thermostats. *See* Matthew Mobrea, *Google's Real Plan Behind the Purchase of the Nest Thermostat*, ITWORLD, Apr. 25, 2014, https://www.itworld.com/article/2833423/big-data/google-s-real-plan-behind-the-purchase-of-the-nest-thermostat.html.

77 For example, an online sales or e-commerce platform (e.g., Shopify) could develop analytics on retail sales and pricing strategy; an online accounting services provider could develop analytics on financial information and lending. *See also* Leo Polovets, *The Value of Data, Part 3: Data Business Models*, CODING VC, Mar. 12, 2015, https://codingvc.com/the-value-of-data-part-3-data-business-models. The article discusses other companies that currently use such strategies.

78 See Part II.D., *supra*. *See also* Rossey Charleston, *Cloud vs On-Premise Software Integrations*, B2B COMMERCE DIGITAL, Nov. 6, 2015, https://www.handshake.com/blog/cloud-vs-on-premise-integrations/.

79 *See, e.g., AWS SaaS Partner Program*, AMAZON, https://aws.amazon.com/partners/saas/.

a margin when its users purchase third-party solutions.[80] The availability of an ecosystem comprised of the cloud provider's offerings integrated with third-party solutions may be attractive to end users insofar as it offers one-stop shopping and may reduce the efforts otherwise needed to integrate disparate solutions. This, of course, may make it difficult for end users to transition to another cloud provider—a benefit for the cloud provider, but perhaps a detriment to the end user.

3) **Advertising.** Cloud providers can also potentially earn revenue through the placement of advertisements within their offerings, but at the risk of alienating users. In contrast to passive, content-only websites, SaaS providers may be in a position to leverage the context of the offered services or end user data to target ad placements much more precisely. For example, users of an online accounting solution could be presented with advertisements for loans or tax-return preparation.[81]

V. Disadvantages of Cloud Computing

Cloud computing entails certain disadvantages and risks. The following are some of the more typical concerns:

1) **Reliance on internet connectivity.** Given that cloud services are almost always accessed through the internet, continued access will be dependent on the reliability of both the internet and the end user's internet service provider. If either fails, cloud services cannot be used. Although the risk of a failure of a given internet service provider may be mitigated by using multiple service providers, doing so would come at an additional cost and does not address widespread internet outages. Lastly, given the nature of cloud services, additional bandwidth will likely be required, which will increase costs.

2) **Privacy and security.** The use of cloud services will in almost all cases result in the transfer of data to the cloud service provider, which may raise concerns about the cloud provider's ability to protect against data breach. Cloud providers will typically implement a standard set of security measures, which may or may not meet the requirements of a given user. Although larger providers may implement a fairly robust set of security measures,[82] users must nonetheless evaluate the extent

---

80 One example of this is Amazon's AWS Marketplace, https://aws.amazon.com/marketplace/, which offers thousands of software options that can be deployed on its cloud platform, including operating systems, security software, databases, and business intelligence applications. At the SaaS level, Salesforce's AppExchange, https://appexchange.salesforce.com, offers thousands of applications and services that can be used seamlessly within its platform. Note that the possibilities are not limited to software applications. For example, a SaaS provider offering supply-chain management applications could integrate with providers of shipping or warehousing services. Nor are they limited to providers. For example, a SaaS provider could offer sales solutions for insurance agents as well as services for insurance companies, both of whom would benefit from the interoperability of a common platform.

81 Perhaps one of the earliest examples of this was introduction of advertisements in Google's Gmail. Google displayed targeted advertising by scanning e-mail contents, although only for users of the free consumer version. However, this practice was not without controversy, and ultimately Google decided to discontinue the practice. *See* Daisuke Wakabayashi, *Google Will No Longer Scan Gmail for Ad Targeting*, N.Y. Times, June 23, 2017, https://www.nytimes.com/2017/06/23/technology/gmail-ads.html.

82 *See, e.g.,* the rather lengthy lists of privacy and security certifications for Amazon Web Services, https://aws.amazon.com/compliance/, Microsoft Azure, https://azure.microsoft.com/en-ca/support/trust-center/, and Salesforce, https://trust.salesforce.com/en/compliance/.

to which such measures are adequate for their specific needs, and the extent to which providers contractually commit to responsibility for such measures. The question of security should also be considered in comparison to what security measures a given end user would take in the alternative—for example, if an end user were to set up its own on- premises equipment instead of using a cloud provider, would it implement security measures that are more robust than those implemented by the cloud provider?[83] Lastly, end users may wish to consider adding their own security measures to those offered by the cloud service provider, such as encrypting data before transmitting it to the cloud.[84]

3) **Reliance on the cloud provider.** The use of a cloud provider will necessarily result in some degree of reliance on the provider. If there is a failure in the cloud provider's service, an end user's business operations will likely be impacted. This can be mitigated to some extent by using multiple redundant service providers, though typically only for IaaS and at additional cost and complexity. However, as with security considerations, this question should also be considered in comparison with the alternatives. For example, if an end user were to set up its own on-premise equipment instead of using a cloud provider, it would still be reliant on the vendor of that equipment to address a failure.

VI. Conclusion

This chapter is an admittedly cursory overview of the more significant technologies used in cloud computing. It is by no means comprehensive, but will equip business lawyers with a basic technological understanding of cloud computing to counsel more effectively when advising on cloud computing transactions.

---

83 Some have argued that, in general terms, cloud providers will be better positioned to implement robust security than their end users due, in part, to economies of scale. For example, cloud providers can design and build physically secure data centers and employ teams of security experts and spread that cost across their user base; given that they can monitor a much greater amount of internet traffic, they may be able to detect malware and similar threats sooner, and the larger scale of a cloud provider's infrastructure may be less susceptible to distributed denial of service attacks. *See* Andrew Froehlich, *Why Cloud Security Beats Your Data Center*, INFORMATION WEEK, July 21, 2015, https://www.informationweek.com/cloud/infrastructure-as-a-service/why-cloud-security-beats-your-data-center/d/d-id/1321354; Brandon Butler, *Public Cloud vs. On-Premises, Which Is More Secure?*, NETWORKWORLD, Dec. 17, 2015, https://www.networkworld.com/article/3016673/public-cloud/public-cloud-vs-on-premises-which-is-more-secure.html. It is notable that U.S. intelligence agencies concluded that Amazon Web Services could maintain adequate security when they awarded it a contract for the provision of cloud services, *see* Frank Konkel, *The Details About the CIA's Deal With Amazon*, ATLANTIC, July 17, 2014, https://www.theatlantic.com/technology/archive/2014/07/the-details-about-the-cias-deal-with-amazon/374632/, although that, of course, is not necessarily indicative of the security measures that all end users can expect. Lastly, many recent data breaches that involve cloud services resulted from end user misuse or misconfiguration. *See, e.g.*, Dan O'Sullivan, *The RNC Files: Inside the Largest US Voter Data Leak*, UPGUARD, Dec. 20, 2017, https://www.upguard.com/breaches/the-rnc-files.

84 *See* Stephen Lawton, *Cloud Encryption: Using Data Encryption in the Cloud*, TOM's IT PRO, Apr. 30, 2015, http://www.tomsitpro.com/articles/cloud-data-encryption,2-913.html. User-controlled security measures may be more easily implemented for IaaS than for SaaS because end users will have a greater degree of control over infrastructure for the former. Some vendors have developed resources that enable end users to control encryption in connection with SaaS services. *See, e.g.*, Vaultive's solution for Microsoft Office 365, https://vaultive.com/for-your-technology/office-365-security/.

Chapter 2

Warranties, Indemnities, and Limitations of Liability in Cloud Contracts

By William R. Denny[1]

I. Introduction

Many public cloud-computing services contracts include broad disclaimers that reject any express or implied warranties. Indemnification provisions in these contracts vary somewhat among providers, but most do include an agreement to indemnify the customer should the provider's services allegedly infringe on a third-party's intellectual property rights. Most providers, however, choose also to include an indemnification clause wherein the customer agrees to indemnify the provider for any expenses the provider incurs in relation to the customer's use of its services. Most cloud contracts limit liability as well, excluding all types of damages except direct damages and capping direct damages at a low level, such as what the customer has paid for the previous month of services.

Part II of this chapter lays out reoccurring themes and practices in today's cloud contracts, focusing in turn on warranty, indemnification, and limited liability provisions. Part III addresses cases involving breaches of cloud contracts, specifically what such litigation may reveal about risks that cloud customers accept when entering such contracts. Finally, Part IV describes the possible role of regulation on the ability of cloud customers to negotiate more favorable risk-allocation provisions in their cloud contracts.

II. The Current State of Warranty, Indemnification, and Limited Liability Provisions in Cloud Contracts

A. Warranty Provisions

Warranty provisions today largely favor the cloud service provider over the customer.[2] Issues that are particularly relevant to cloud contracts and that concern customers the most include: the possible infringement of intellectual property rights by the cloud service provider; the actual performance and reliability of cloud services; the risk of and response

---

1 Partner, Potter Anderson & Corroon LLP, Wilmington, Delaware. Mr. Denny's practice focuses on cyber security, data privacy, and information governance.

2 Regina M. Faulkenberry, *Reviewing and Negotiating Cloud Computing Vendor Contracts*, 6 J. HEALTH & LIFE SCI. L. 119, 138 (2013) ("Cloud contracts typically provide a complete disclaimer of warranties related to the cloud vendor's services, including a complete disclaimer of any express or implied warranties (including the warranties of non-infringement, merchantability, title, or fitness for a particular purpose). Also, a disclaimer may be included specifically stating that the provider is not warranting the services will be provided uninterrupted or error or virus free.").

to data-security breaches suffered by the cloud provider that affect customer data; and compliance with customers' data-security and privacy obligations.[3]

A majority of the largest, most popular cloud service providers, including Apple, Amazon, and IBM (among others),[4] disclaim most (if not all) warranties and provide that the customer use their services "as is." Consider the following disclaimer from Amazon's Customer Agreement for its cloud services:

> THE SERVICE OFFERINGS ARE PROVIDED "AS IS." EXCEPT TO THE EXTENT PROHIBITED BY LAW, OR TO THE EXTENT ANY STATUTORY RIGHTS APPLY THAT CANNOT BE EXCLUDED, LIMITED OR WAIVED, WE AND OUR AFFILIATES AND LICENSORS (A) MAKE NO REPRESENTATIONS OR WARRANTIES OF ANY KIND, WHETHER EXPRESS, IMPLIED, STATUTORY OR OTHERWISE REGARDING THE SERVICE OFFERINGS OR THE THIRD-PARTY CONTENT, AND (B) DISCLAIM ALL WARRANTIES, INCLUDING ANY IMPLIED OR EXPRESS WARRANTIES (I) OF MERCHANTABILITY, SATISFACTORY QUALITY, FITNESS FOR A PARTICULAR PURPOSE, NON-INFRINGEMENT, OR QUIET ENJOYMENT, (II) ARISING OUT OF ANY COURSE OF DEALING OR USAGE OF TRADE, (III) THAT THE SERVICE OFFERINGS OR THIRD-PARTY CONTENT WILL BE UNINTERRUPTED, ERROR FREE OR FREE OF HARMFUL COMPONENTS, AND (IV) THAT ANY CONTENT WILL BE SECURE OR NOT OTHERWISE LOST OR ALTERED.[5]

This language is typical among cloud contracts.[6] Warranties of this sort leave many customers vulnerable to bearing the financial responsibility for events that are relatively common in the world of off-site computing, such as the inability to access data in the wake of a cloud service provider malfunction, or corruption or misappropriation of data by hackers.[7] Typically, the only solace that a cloud customer has by way of warranty is that the cloud service provider will "use reasonable skill and due care in providing the [cloud computing] service," and even this vague and unsubstantial warranty is not promised by all cloud service providers.[8]

---

3 Daniel Carmeli, *Keep an I on the Sky: E-Discovery Risks Forecasted for Apple's Icloud*, 2013 B.C. INTELL. PROP. & TECH. F. 1, 2 ("Some employers have already implemented cloud computing entity-wide. Other employers have expressed concern, however, by citing issues like security, data loss, performance, and loss of control."); *see also* Faulkenberry, *supra* note 2, at 128 ("The main areas of concern business representatives must consider when negotiating a cloud computing contract involve the contractual language regarding data, security, disclaimers/indemnification, service, and termination.").

4 These include Joyent, Salesforce, Navisite, GoDaddy, and Google.

5 Amazon Web Services Customer Agreement, § 10. Disclaimers, https://aws.amazon.com/agreement (last updated May 14, 2018).

6 *See, e.g.,* the warranty provisions in the service contracts for the providers listed in note 4.

7 Consider, for example, the failure of Amazon's cloud service in 2012, which caused Netflix to be unusable for nearly an entire day. Brian X. Chen, *"The Cloud" Challenges Amazon*, N.Y. TIMES, Jan. 27, 2009, http://www.nytimes.com/2012/12/27/technology/latest-netflix-disruption-highlights-challenges-of-cloud-computing.html. Similarly, the 2016 disruption in the services of cloud service provider SalesForce left its customers without access to their accounts for a full day. *RCM for NA14 Disruptions of Service*, SALESFORCE, May 16, 2016, 8:00 a.m., https://help.salesforce.com/articleView?id=Root-Cause-Message-for-Disruption-of-Service-on-NA14-May-2016&language=en_US&type=1.

8 iCloud Terms and Conditions, § IX. DISCLAIMER OF WARRANTIES; LIMITATION OF LIABILITY, Apple, https://www.apple.com/legal/internet-services/icloud/en/terms.html (last updated Sept. 19, 2017).

Customers who attempt to seek more favorable warranty terms are hampered by the fact that most cloud service providers refuse to apply significant warranties to any of their services and are largely unwilling to negotiate on the matter, instead operating on a "take it or leave it" basis. This is the case even for larger customers that could provide significant business for the cloud service provider.[9]

B. Indemnification Provisions

Indemnification provisions in cloud contracts are also somewhat unfavorable to customers. In some cases, such as in the Terms of Service agreement for GoDaddy's cloud services, the only indemnification provision is the customer's agreement to indemnify GoDaddy for *any* suit brought against it in relation to the customer's "use of and access to" GoDaddy's cloud services.[10] It should be noted, however, that GoDaddy's indemnification terms are particularly harsh, given that many cloud service providers (including Amazon, IBM, and SalesForce) agree to indemnify customers for costs incurred when a third party brings a claim alleging that use of the cloud provider's services infringes on the third-party's intellectual property rights. Take, for example, the indemnification provision in the Google Cloud Platform Terms of Service:

> Google will defend and indemnify Customer and its Affiliates against Indemnified Liabilities in any Third-Party Legal Proceeding to the extent arising solely from an Allegation that use of (a) Google's technology used to provide the Services or (b) any Google Brand Feature infringes or misappropriates the third party's patent, copyright, trade secret, or trademark.[11]

And consider the section titled "Remedies" that follows it:

> a. If Google reasonably believes the Services might infringe a third party's Intellectual Property Rights, then Google may, at its sole option and expense: (a) procure the right for Customer to continue using the Services; (b) modify the Services to make them non-infringing without materially reducing their functionality; or (c) replace the Services with a non-infringing, functionally equivalent alternative.

> b. If Google does not believe the remedies in Section 14.5(a) are commercially reasonable, then Google may suspend or terminate Customer's use of the impacted Services.[12]

Note that Google's mutual indemnification provision, although more favorable to customers than GoDaddy's unilateral indemnification, still contains pitfalls for its customers. For example, one of the "remedies" Google proposes, should the client be confronted with a third-party infringement suit for Google's services, is to "suspend or terminate

---

9 W. Kuan Hon, Christopher Millard & Ian Walden, *Negotiating Cloud Contracts: Looking at Clouds from Both Sides Now*, 16 STAN. TECH. L. REV. 79, 88–89 (2012) ("Large providers generally decline any changes to their standard terms, insisting their services are only on a 'take it or leave it' basis—even when requested by large users, such as integrators.").
10 Universal Terms of Service Agreement, § 20. INDEMNITY, GoDaddy, https://www.godaddy.com/agreements/showdoc.aspx?pageid=UTOS (last revised May 23, 2018).
11 Google Cloud Platform Terms of Service, §14 Indemnification, Google, https://cloud.google.com/terms/ (last modified June 15, 2018).
12 *Id.*

[the] Customer's use of the impacted Services." This allows Google to decide unilaterally whether to fix the service so that it no longer infringes, replace it, or remove the service entirely. Given that section "b." does not state that Google must provide any notice to the customer before it terminates or suspends its services, this contract allows for a situation where a customer is confronted with a lawsuit for services it does not own or run one day, and then is suddenly deprived of those services without warning the next.

C. Limited Liability Provisions

In addition to warranty and indemnity provisions that are unfavorable to customers, cloud contracts also contain sections that limit the cloud service provider's liability in case of breach. As Part III will address further, even in instances where customers are able to establish a contract breach in court, the limited liability provisions that dictate the terms of their relief are especially unyielding and can often leave customers with a remedy that is wholly inadequate to address the harm that they have suffered.[13]

Many cloud service providers include limited liability provisions that cap the cloud service provider's liability to the amount paid by the customer to the cloud service provider in the 12 months (or less) after the event that gave rise to such liability. Consider the following limitation of liability provision from cloud service provider Joyent:

> JOYENT'S MAXIMUM LIABILITY FOR ANY DAMAGES ARISING OUT OF OR RELATED TO THIS TOS OR THE CLOUD SERVICES, WHETHER BASED ON CONTRACT, WARRANTY, TORT (INCLUDING NEGLIGENCE), STRICT LIABILITY OR OTHERWISE, SHALL BE LIMITED TO THE AMOUNT YOU PAID TO JOYENT DIRECTLY ATTRIBUTABLE TO THE JOYENT CLOUD SERVICE PROVIDED UNDER THIS TOS DURING THE TWELVE (12) MONTHS IMMEDIATELY PRECEDING THE FIRST EVENT GIVING RISE TO LIABILITY UNDER THIS TOS. JOYENT SHALL HAVE NO LIABILITY OR RESPONSIBILITY FOR ANY CUSTOMER DATA OR THIRD PARTY SOFTWARE. THE FOREGOING LIMITATION OF LIABILITY IS INDEPENDENT OF, AND SHALL NOT BE DEEMED TO MODIFY JOYENT'S OBLIGATION UNDER ANY EXCLUSIVE REMEDIES FOR BREACH OF WARRANTY SET FORTH IN THIS TOS.[14]

Joyent, like many other cloud service providers, limits its liability to direct damages only, specifically excluding damages that a customer would most commonly experience, such as loss of profits that customers would face if their cloud services were interrupted or broke down.

---

13 *See* Stuart L. Pardau, *But I'm Just a Lawyer: Do Cloud Ethics Opinions Ask Too Much?*, 22 PROF. LAW. 4, 37, 41 (2014) (the context here is a data breach, but the principle applies equally to a breach of contract claim):

> [C]ommonly in the SaaS environment, the end-user is subject to limitation of liability clauses that purport to absolve the provider of significant financial liability in the event of such [data] breaches. Here, in the context of Azure, Microsoft standard contract terms would cap direct damages at a mere $5,000 per party, and preclude "indirect, special, incidental, consequential, punitive, or exemplary damages, or damages for lost profits, revenues, business interruption, or loss of business information." An Azure user, therefore, is highly unlikely to recoup anything that remotely approximates the likely losses that would be suffered in the event of a significant data breach . . . .

14 Joyent Terms of Service, § 17. LIMITATION OF LIABILITY, Joyent, https://www.joyent.com/about/policies/terms-of-service (last revised June 1, 2017).

III. Recent Cases on Breaches of Cloud Contracts Illustrating Contractual Risks

A. *CareOne*: A Breach with a Very Limited Remedy

In *CareOne Management, LLC v. Navisite, Inc.*, CareOne, a company that managed nursing homes, sued its cloud service provider NaviSite for breach of contract after NaviSite failed to provide the services promised to CareOne in its cloud agreement.[15] Although NaviSite appeared to have breached the terms of its agreement, the court did not address the substantial merits of the breach claim. Instead, the court held that the claim could not be sustained because NaviSite's cloud agreement prevented CareOne from seeking damages in court for such a breach.[16]

NaviSite's conduct in this case was particularly egregious because it failed to provide CareOne with any cloud services that CareOne deemed satisfactory. A month after missing the deadline to implement its services, NaviSite contacted CareOne asking it to "accept four of the promised systems."[17] CareOne immediately responded that because of the incompleteness of the systems offered, it would not be able to accept and use them. After CareOne rejected NaviSite's initial systems, the cloud service provider attempted again, months later, to unload faulty services on CareOne, which found "material problems with all of them."[18] Even after an amendment to the original contract and an agreement to provide CareOne with credit for the months that it had paid for services that NaviSite never rendered, NaviSite never implemented the CareOne systems, and CareOne terminated the agreement.

The NaviSite agreement was somewhat unusual among cloud agreements in that NaviSite agreed to be paid monthly, and CareOne had no obligation to pay NaviSite for any service provided until after CareOne had accepted that service. Under this arrangement, NaviSite bore "much of the risk that it may not be able to deliver systems acceptable to CareOne."[19] However, CareOne had made a number of upfront payments that ended up totaling almost $3 million. Under the terms of the agreement, CareOne's *exclusive* remedy for breach was the following:

> (1) CareOne or Partners could give NaviSite notice of the breach, which would trigger a contractual obligation by NaviSite to work diligently to cure the breach at its expense; (2) CareOne or Partners could obtain a credit against monthly recurring fees for any services affected by the breach of contract; or (3) CareOne or Partners could terminate the contract for any uncured material breach, which would cut off any further obligations by CareOne and Partners to make any payments or doing anything else under the contract. The right to terminate the contract for an uncured material breach by the other side is spelled out in [Master Services Agreement] § 7.4, which provides that a party could only

---

15 CareOne Mgmt., LLC v. Navisite, Inc., No. 1484CV00378BLS2, 2017 WL 2803060, at *1 (Mass. Super. Apr. 25, 2017).

16 *Id.* at *7.

17 *Id.* at *2.

18 *Id.*

19 *Id.* at *3.

terminate for an uncured material breach after giving the other side written notice of the claimed breach and at least thirty days to cure the breach.[20]

The agreement between NaviSite and CareOne also included the following disclaimers and limitations on liability that, as noted in Part II, are fairly standard in cloud contracts:

> Section 6.3 bars any claim that NaviSite breached any kind of implied warranty, by specifying that NaviSite did not make and expressly disclaimed any implied warranty of any kind. And § 9.1 provides that neither NaviSite, CareOne, nor Partners shall be liable "for any indirect, consequential incidental, special or punitive damages—including, without limitation, loss of use, interruption of business, loss of data or loss of profits—arising out of, or in any way connected with" the parties' contract.[21]

As a result of these provisions, CareOne was unable to recoup the $3 million in upfront payments that it had made.

Here, although the breach by NaviSite was not a breach of warranty—it disclaimed any possible warranties—it is still illustrative of the ways in which cloud service providers are currently crafting agreements that allocate much of their financial risk to their customers. CareOne's risk in this agreement was dramatically increased by the inclusion of provisions (most notably the limited liability sections quoted above) that left it with limited forms of redress.

B. *Mill-Run*: A Breach with No Remedy, Despite Damages

In *Mill-Run Tours v. Windstream Services,* Mill-Run sued Windstream for breach of warranty and breach of contract.[22] Mill-Run supplied airline tickets to travel agents and engaged Windstream, "a provider of voice and data network communications, including cloud computing and managed services," to provide it with voice and data communications services. The court ruled in favor of Windstream's motion to dismiss both claims.[23]

Before Mill-Run executed an agreement with Windstream, it let Windstream know that it was having problems with its current voice and data communications provider. Windstream then, according to Mill-Run, assured Mill-Run that "it understood the reputational and financial damages [Mill-Run] would suffer if there was an interruption of service, and that it would never happen with Windstream as the provider."[24] After four years of service, Mill-Run's telephone and data services from Windstream "completely failed."[25] According to Mill-Run, Windstream refused to respond to numerous calls and e-mails about the problem, and the service interruption lasted for a total of six days. Mill-Run asserted that, as a result of this interruption of service, it incurred "reputational damages, loss of sales, and loss of existing and new clients calculated to be in the millions of dollars."[26]

In addressing the breach-of-contract claim first, the court (as was the case in *CareOne*) homed in on the limited liability provisions of the Windstream Service Agreement, which

---

20 *Id.* at *4.

21 *Id.*

22 Mill-Run Tours, Inc. v. Windstream Servs. LLC, No. 16 CIV. 7052 (ER), 2017 WL 2930932, at *1 (S.D.N.Y. July 7, 2017).

23 *Id.*

24 *Id.*

25 *Id.* at *2.

26 *Id.*

expressly barred "special, incidental, and/or consequential damages."[27] Mill-Run argued that the court should not enforce this limited liability clause because it gave Windstream "an unfair and unreasonable advantage over Mill-Run."[28] The court was unpersuaded by this argument, noting that both parties were "highly sophisticated" business entities and that there was "no disparity" between their respective bargaining powers.[29] Therefore, it reasoned, the provision was enforceable and, as a result, Mill-Run could not seek consequential damages for the alleged millions it lost due to Windstream's service interruption.

Mill-Run asserted its breach-of-warranty claim under the theory that it relied on Windstream's oral assurance that its services were superior to that of its competitors. Specifically, Mill-Run argued that Windstream's statement constituted a warranty that Windstream breached when its services failed and it did not restore them within a reasonable time. The court dismissed this claim on a somewhat technical basis, not stating whether the Service Agreement contained any warranty provisions or disclaimers, and instead relying on New York law, which does not allow for causes of action for "breach of warranty in the performance of a service."[30] The court further noted, however, that even had the oral statement pertained to goods and not services, Mill-Run's breach of warranty claim would still not be viable because Windstream's alleged assurances constituted only "nonactionable puffery."[31]

Here, as in *CareOne*, it was not the lack of warranty or inadequacy of indemnification provisions that dealt the hardest blow to the cloud service provider's customer, but rather the limitations on liability that rendered Mill-Run virtually helpless in the aftermath of Windstream's service breakdown. Just as in *CareOne*, the risk that Mill-Run assumed came significantly from these limited liability clauses.

C. *Corizon Health*: A Break for Customers on Misrepresentation and Limitation of Liability

Corizon Health, Inc. v. CorrecTek, Inc.,[32] a decision favorable to the customer, provides an example of a cloud services customer relying on the representations of a provider to that customer's detriment and, similarly to *Mill-Run*, the cloud provider attempting to rely on the protections of the limitation of liability provision. Corizon, a healthcare provider, sued CorrecTek, a medical records software licensing company that provides cloud services. Corizon brought several claims against CorrecTek, including negligent misrepresentation and breach of contract. Corizon alleged that before contracting with CorrecTek, CorrecTek made numerous misrepresentations about its cloud software. For example, CorrecTek spoke highly of its technology and assured Corizon that the software was fully configurable to Corizon's needs, contained state-of-the-art "required form field technology," and could store prescription data in ways that allowed for "automatic medication renewal."[33] Corizon alleged that the software did not perform any of these functions adequately.

---

27 *Id.* at *3.
28 *Id.*
29 *Id.*
30 *Id.* at *4.
31 *Id.*
32 Corizon Health, Inc. v. CorrecTek, Inc., No. 5:17-CV-00035-TBR, 2018 WL 2768883 (W.D. Ky. June 8, 2018).
33 *Id.* at *3.

After CorrecTek made these representations and the parties contracted, Corizon, in collaboration with CorrecTek, entered into a subsequent deal with the Idaho Department of Corrections (IDOC) to implement certain aspects of Corizon's own system in IDOC facilities using CorrecTek technology. Corizon claimed that it relied on CorrecTek's assurances when it decided to enter a schedule agreement with the IDOC, and that "[i]f CorrecTek had accurately represented the functionality and limitations of the CorrecTek [technology] . . . Corizon could have recovered 90% of the license fee paid under the IDOC Schedule."[34]

Corizon requested compensatory damages of not less than $1,500,000, punitive damages, statutory damages including treble damages, and reimbursement of all amounts it paid to CorrecTek. CorrecTek moved for summary judgment on the negligent misrepresentation and breach-of-contract claims. First, the court denied CorrecTek's motion for summary judgment on the misrepresentation claims. The court reasoned that, although most of CorrecTek's representations were likely just "sales talk" or "puffing," some of the representations may have been material facts about software capabilities such that a jury issue existed.[35]

The court did not address the breach-of-contract claim head on, but instead focused on damages. CorrecTek argued that Corizon's damages should be capped at the amount agreed to in the software contract. The Limitation of Liability clause read:

> [E]ach Party's liability to the other Party, regardless of the form of action, shall be limited to the amount that is equal to the total amount to be paid by CUSTOMER to CORRECTEK under the Schedules to this Master Agreement but not to exceed $250,000 per incident. In no event will either Party be liable to the other for . . . (ii) lost profits, incidental or consequential damages, even if advised of the possibility of such damages . . . .[36]

Corizon, in turn, argued that the limitation of liability clause did not apply because the contract was void for fraud. Alternatively, Corizon believed the "per incident" language was ambiguous.[37] Corizon also argued that the IDOC Schedule deal it entered in collaboration with CorrecTek contradicts the limitation of liability clause. The IDOC Schedule deal stated that if CorrecTek fails to resolve the problems after receiving written notification from Corizon, then Corizon has the right to terminate and that "[u]pon such termination, CORRECTEK shall *provide a full refund*."[38]

The court decided that it needed more information from the parties in order to properly rule on the damages issue. The court asked the parties for further briefing on the meaning of "incident" under the limitation of liability clause and on the applicability of the conflicting language in the IDOC Schedule deal.[39] As of this writing, these issues are pending (the opinion and request for further briefing was issued in June 2018).

The basic pattern of misrepresentations and the reliance on a limitation of liability provision is similar to that in *Mill-Run*.[40] In *Mill-Run*, however, the representations and warranties were deemed "nonactionable puffery,"[41] whereas in *Corizon*, the customer survived

---

34 *Id.*
35 *Id.* at *8.
36 *Id.* at *10.
37 *Id.* at *11.
38 *Id.* (emphasis added).
39 *Id.*
40 *See* Mill-Run Tours, Inc. v. Windstream Servs. LLC, No. 16 CIV. 7052 (ER), 2017 WL 2930932, at *3, 4 (S.D.N.Y. July 7, 2017).
41 *Id.* at *4.

summary judgment in part because some of the assurances made by CorrecTek could have been material factual representations related to the function of the cloud software.

No mention of indemnification or warranty disclaimers is found in *Corizon*. Even so, this case shows an example of a court potentially siding with a cloud customer, despite a limitation on liability provision, in part because the provision is ambiguous and because the representations related to the cloud technology's specific functions. Of course, more definite takeaways can only be drawn from *Corizon* once the court rules on the damages issue and provides final holdings. *Corizon* demonstrates that, generally, customers are perhaps more likely to prevail on breach-of-warranty claims under cloud computing contracts when misrepresentations made by the provider are like those in *Corizon*, rather than the mere "puffery" statements made in *Mill-Run*.

IV. Predicting Regulatory Impact on Ability to Negotiate Warranty Terms

As more sensitive data is moved into cloud environments, ensuring compliance with various regulations could become a paramount concern. For example,

> customers whose services involve the handling, processing or storage of payment card information may need to ensure compliance with the Payment Card Industry Data Security Standard, and customers who are subject to the Gramm-Leach-Bliley Act or the Health Insurance Portability and Accountability Act need to consider their obligations to include certain safeguards for personal information in their service provider agreements.[42]

Customers may demand more sophistication and expertise from providers, and will need assurances that regulations will not be violated. Prioritizing compliance could translate into more customer-friendly warranties and representations. As customers who are subject to regulatory schemes embrace cloud computing technology, providers could be forced to be more open-minded and negotiate terms that make these customers feel comfortable. Said differently, these customers might demand warranties and representations that their data is secure and will not be breached or shared. Given the importance of security to these customers, and given the severe consequences[43] that could result from cloud malfunction or breach, these customers may also demand that providers bear liability for the damages stemming from breaches and regulatory violations.

---

42 Andrew Geyer & Melinda McLellan, *Strategies for Evaluating Cloud Computing Agreements*, 3 Bloomberg Law Reports—Technology Law 13, 3 (2011), https://www.huntonak.com/en/insights/strategies-for-evaluating-cloud-computing-agreements-bloomberg.html.
43 *See* Vic Winkler, *Cloud Computing: Legal and Regulatory Issues*, TechNet, May 2012, https://technet.microsoft.com/en-us/library/hh994647.aspx:

> Failure to adequately protect your data can have a number of consequences, including the potential for fines by one or more government or industry regulatory bodies. Such fines can be substantial and potentially crippling for a small or midsize business. For example, the Payment Card Industry (PCI) can impose fines of up to $100,000 per month for violations to its compliance [requirements].

The General Data Protection Regulation of the European Union (GDPR)[44] adds additional urgency to customers of cloud services to include more favorable risk allocation provisions into their contracts. A company that is subject to the GDPR is deemed a "controller" if that company "determines the purposes and means of the processing of personal data."[45] A controller hiring a cloud provider to process its personal data is obligated to use only processors that provide "sufficient guarantees" to implement appropriate data security that will meet the requirements of the GDPR.[46] The GDPR requires that a written contract be in place to govern all processing of personal data,[47] prescribes multiple elements that must be included in the contract, imposes obligations on data processors that can be enforced directly by data subjects,[48] and makes controllers fully liable for any damage caused by processing that infringes the GDPR.[49]

Although the GDPR does not prescribe the allocation of risk between the controller and processor, its provision making the controller fully liable for all conduct of the processor that infringes the GDPR creates a powerful incentive to put contractual provisions in place making the processor, which frequently may be a cloud service provider, responsible for the consequences of its own conduct. A customer of cloud services may thus seek to include the following provisions in its cloud contracts:

> **Compliance with Data Protection Requirements.** Vendor hereby represents and warrants that it will (1) inform itself regarding, and comply with, all applicable Data Protection Requirements; (2) at all times comply with and treat Company Data in accordance with the requirements of this Agreement and the Data Protection Requirements, (3) not take any actions that will compromise the Company's ability to comply with the Data Protection Requirements; and (4) notify the Company in the event that Vendor believes that the Company's instructions concerning Company Data, including, without limitation, the requirements of this Agreement, would cause Vendor to violate any Data Protection Requirement. In the event of such notification, the Company will then instruct Vendor on appropriate compensating controls by which to abide.

> **Indemnification.** Vendor shall indemnify, hold harmless, and defend the Company, Company Entities, and its officers, directors, stockholders, employees, agents, successors, assigns and subcontractors from and against any and all Claims and any and all threatened claims, losses, liabilities, damages, settlements, expenses and costs arising from, in connection with, or based on allegations of, in whole or in part, any of the following: (a) any violation of the requirements of this Agreement or the Data Protection Requirements; (b) any Breach; (c) any negligence or willful misconduct of Vendor or any third party to whom Vendor provides access to Company Data or systems, with respect to security or confidentiality of

---

44 Regulation (EU) 2016/679 of the European Parliament and of the Council of 27 April 2016 on the protection of natural persons with regard to the processing of personal data and on the free movement of such data, and repealing Directive 95/46/EC (General Data Protection Regulation).

45 *Id.* Art. 4(7).

46 *Id.* Art. 28(1).

47 *Id.* Art. 28(2).

48 *Id.* Art. 28(3).

49 *Id.* Art. 82(2).

Company Data; (d) remedial action taken by the Company as a result of a Breach; and (e) any other costs incurred by the Company with respect to the Company's rights in this Agreement.

In using the foregoing clauses, the phrase "Data Protection Requirements" should be defined to encompass all applicable laws relating to the manner in which the cloud provider is processing data, which may include, in addition to the GDPR, such laws as California's Consumer Privacy Act of 2018[50] or sector-specific laws or regulations dealing with privacy and security of data.

Cloud users "have significant and persistent concerns relating to the risks inherent in cloud computing,"[51] but unfortunately, "those concerns are not adequately addressed in the standard contract terms offered by most cloud computing vendors,"[52] and users "lack sufficient bargaining power to negotiate more balanced agreements."[53] There is little indication that bargaining power has begun to shift in favor of customer empowerment.

From the perspective of providers, customers cannot "have their cake and eat it too" by demanding the cheapest services and also demanding warranties and the reduction of liability exclusion provisions.[54] Part of what makes these services affordable is their standardization. Little incentive exists, especially for large cloud providers, to create and offer more customer-friendly contracts. So long as customers continue to agree to liability exclusions, unfavorable indemnity terms, and disclaimed warranties, cloud providers have no reason to give in on those fronts. One proposed solution is for "industry sectors to form buying coalitions and thereby increase their bargaining power for concessions in contracts with cloud providers."[55] However, possible solutions or fixes should not be confused with actual changes to the risk allocation acceptable to cloud providers. As of now, support is lacking for the conclusion that more customer-friendly cloud computing contracts are on the horizon.

V. Conclusion

Cloud computing contracts continue to favor providers. Providers will utilize a "take it or leave it" approach in negotiating so long as customers continue to agree to unfavorable terms. No evidence suggests that cloud computing contracts have shifted to become more favorable to customers, but the cloud computing industry is still young, and as the industry grows and cloud services become ever more popular, it seems unlikely that customers will continue to be content with cloud agreements as they are currently drafted. Customers relying on cloud technology are unlikely to continue tolerating large losses from cloud service failures (like those Mill-Run experienced in the six days its services went offline). To prevent the sort of losses that both CareOne and Mill-Run endured under the terms of their cloud service provider agreements, customers may push back and demand more

---

50 CAL. CIV. CODE §1798.100 *et seq.*
51 T. Noble Foster, *Navigating Through the Fog of Cloud Computing Contracts*, 30 J. MARSHALL J. INFO. TECH. & PRIVACY L. 13, 24 (2013).
52 *Id.* at 24–25.
53 *Id.* at 25.
54 *See* Hon, Millard & Walden, *supra* note 9, at 93.
55 Foster, *supra* note 51, at 30.

favorable terms. Forces such as industry competition, government regulation, and insurance products that help alleviate some risk for all the parties may facilitate a shift toward more customer-centric agreements. If these forces take effect and a shift in bargaining power occurs, cloud providers will be more likely to offer stronger warranties and accept greater potential liability in their services agreements.

Chapter 3

Demystifying Service-Level Agreements and Avoiding the "Gotchas"

By Michael J. Dunne[1]

I. Introduction

This chapter describes the importance of services level agreements to both the users of cloud services and to the providers of those services and, using the three most common service levels or "metrics," suggests and explains approaches to address many of the issues that arise in reviewing and negotiating services level agreements. This chapter ends with a list of general suggestions to avoid typical "gotchas" in the review and negotiation of service level agreements.

II. Cloud Services Service-Level Agreements in General

Cloud services are a continuing and often time-sensitive type of service for which a simple warranty of performance in substantial accordance with the documentation and a corresponding obligation to reperform unsatisfactory services do not always provide appropriate protection for the client utilizing the cloud services (the Client). Although warranties regarding certain aspects of cloud services are appropriate, when it comes to performance or nonperformance of the cloud services, covenants regarding the level of performance with corresponding remedies provisions offer important and necessary protections when properly drafted, implemented, monitored, and enforced.

The below discussion is applicable mainly to "private" cloud services arrangements in which the Client has the ability to require and negotiate performance standards. It should also prove helpful in evaluating performance standards, if any, provided in the terms and conditions of "public" cloud services. Additionally, as discussed at the end of this chapter, the below discussion should be useful with those "public" cloud arrangements where there is an ability to obtain deal-specific performance standards.

Performance covenants also offer an excellent method for the provider of services (the SP) and its Client to work together as a team to ensure a win-win cloud services relationship. Unfortunately, taking a "team" or "win-win" approach to service-level agreements (SLAs) is the exception among SPs and their Clients. In most circumstances, neither the SP nor the Client takes the time or makes the effort to realize the value of such an approach. Instead, they default into taking the same adversarial approach to SLAs as they take to negotiating other arms-length agreements between them—that is, the SP strives to

---

1   Michael J. Dunne is a partner with Day Pitney LLP in the Mergers, Acquisitions, and Joint Venture Practice Group; the Technology, Telecommunications, and Outsourcing Practice Group; and the Emerging Companies and Venture Finance Practice Group. He is a frequent lecturer and has written numerous articles regarding technology, outsourcing, and mergers and acquisitions topics.

structure each SLA to limit any possibility that the SLA won't be met and ensure that the Client will not have any meaningful remedy if the SLA is not met. In that regard, see the service-level objectives (SLO) discussion below. Clients then respond adversarially by attempting to maximize their ability to claim a SLA failure and obtain painful remedies for the SP, believing that such a threat will force the SP to stay focused on providing top-level services to the Client. Given that the adversarial approach to SLAs is the most common approach taken by SPs, their Clients, and their respective counsels, the below analysis is premised on that approach.

SLAs, which are covenants governing the level of service performance by SPs, may be referred to by other terms such as "performance standards" or "performance measures." Regardless of the moniker, properly drafted SLAs provide a means of measuring the SP's performance against agreed-upon expectations and moving forward together when such performance does not meet those expectations, without requiring the Client to declare a breach and seek standard contract remedies for breach. A concomitant benefit for the SP is a reduced likelihood that a Client experiencing difficulties with the SP's cloud services will allege a breach, the mere allegation of which could adversely affect the SP in a variety of ways.

The importance of SLAs for Clients has not been lost on regulators. For example, in the financial services industry, principal federal regulators have consistently advised banks and other financial institutions to ensure they consider and, where appropriate, enter into SLAs with their service providers.[2]

Properly drafted SLAs will, at a minimum, include four separate elements: (1) measurable standards of the promised services (often referred to as the "metrics"); (2) how the metrics or the performance of the metrics will be measured, including, where appropriate, over what time periods; (3) measuring and reporting responsibilities; and (4) ramifications or remedies. Each element must be carefully reviewed, considered, and drafted to ensure effective SLAs. The omission of an important metric, lack of clarity in the definition of a metric or how it is measured, or the failure to include meaningful remedies are mistakes that could undermine the usefulness of the SLAs and lead to dissatisfaction in the cloud service relationship.

Equally important from the SP's perspective are the exceptions to or exclusions from the SLAs. It is in the SP's interest to exclude events, conditions, and circumstances that may adversely affect its performance, such as the performance of third parties. The question for the Client is whether the risk and ramifications of any such event, condition, or circumstance should be borne by the SP or by the Client. Therefore, from the Client's perspective, the exceptions and exclusions must be carefully reviewed, considered, and drafted to ensure not only that the exception does not become the rule and are appropriately limited, but that the risk-shifting is both appropriate and the rules clearly stated so as

---

2   *See* Office of the Comptroller of the Currency, OCC Bulletin 2013-29, Description: Risk Management Guidance, Oct. 30, 2013, at 8, *available at* https://www.occ.gov/news-issuances/bulletins/2013/bulletin-2013-29.html; Federal Financial Institutions Examination Council: Information Technology Examination Handbook Sept. 2016, at 12–15, *available at* https://www.ffiec.gov/press/PDF/FFIEC_IT_Handbook_Information_Security_Booklet.pdf; Board of Governors of the Federal Reserve System, SR 13-19/CA 13-21, Guidance on Managing Outsourcing Risk, Dec. 5, 2013, at 6, *available at* https://www.federalreserve.gov/supervisionreg/srletters/sr1319a1.pdf; Federal Deposit Insurance Corporation, FIL-44-2008, Third-Party Risk Guidance for Managing Third-Party Risk, June 6, 2008, at 7, *available at* https://www.fdic.gov/news/news/financial/2008/fil08044a.html.

not to be overly broad or open to dispute. For example, if a third party is retained by the SP as a subcontractor to provide a portion of the cloud service, should the SP be allowed to exclude from its failure to perform the cloud service any and all such failures caused by such third-party's failure to perform? This is a commonly negotiated issue, the outcome of which will depend on the facts at hand and the bargaining power of the parties, and is discussed more fully below.

III. SLOs—Not the Same as SLAs

Before delving more deeply into service-level agreements, a note of caution: many SPs will offer service-level objectives (SLOs) to Clients in lieu of SLAs. Many SPs will even argue that there is no substantive difference between SLOs and SLAs. In fact, from the Client's perspective, SLOs are vastly different from and, in many ways, vastly inferior to true SLAs. Both will include metrics and descriptions of levels of performance of those metrics. Both may also include obligations to monitor and report. There may even be ramifications for the SP if the services fall below the SLO objectives, such as the obligation to conduct a root-cause analysis to determine how the failure occurred and to take corrective action based on that analysis. However, as the name implies, SLO metrics are only *objectives*. There is no assurance, covenant, or promise that the "objectives" of any metric will be met, and no meaningful repercussions for the SP or agreed-upon remedies for the Client if the objective is not met—it's just an "objective," a "target," after all, not an agreed level of performance with an agreed-upon remedy.

IV. Metrics—The Core of SLAs

Metrics form the core of SLAs. Consequently, the first step in reviewing SLAs proposed by an SP, or in preparing SLAs, is to determine what metrics should be included. The proper metrics will depend upon the services to be provided by the SP and the aspects of those services that are measurable.

However, the determination of what metrics to include must be made in consultation with the Client and, in particular, the individuals who will use or in some manner rely on the proposed services. To be useful and meaningful for the Client, the SLAs must focus on the business objectives and needs of the Client in obtaining the cloud services. The individuals who will use or otherwise rely on the services will be in the best position to define and explain to counsel those objectives and needs and the promised aspects of the SP's services that were key to the Client's decision to engage the SP. Those individuals will also know how the degradation of various aspects of the SP's services will affect the Client and its business, and of those aspects, the ones that are measurable in a meaningful way. Stated another way, the business users will be best positioned to know which failures in the SP's services will cause the most pain and disruption for the Client, and therefore which metrics should be included in the SLAs.

Equally important will be discussions with and assistance from the Client's chief information or chief technology officer and the applicable member(s) of such officer's team. Often an organization's technical team has significant experience working with and negotiating SLAs and can use that experience to help achieve appropriate SLAs. Additionally, an organization's technical staff can be key to explaining to the organization's business users the importance and impact of appropriate SLAs.

A. Defining and Measuring Metrics—Some Typical Metrics and Some Typical "Gotchas" to Avoid

Unfortunately, no standard set of metrics exists that should be included in all cloud services agreements. As noted above, metrics should be tailored to the particular transaction, to the particular objectives and needs of the Client, and of course to the particular services. However, three fairly common metrics for cloud services can be referred to as (1) "availability"; (2) "responsiveness" or "response times"; and (3) "incident response and resolution." These three metrics can also serve as the basis for describing how SLAs should be structured and how to avoid traps for the unwary.

1. Availability

The concept of the "availability" service level is at first blush simple and understandable: What percentage of the time is a cloud service available to the Client? However, an "availability" service level can be and often must be a definition-driven covenant based on the cloud services to be provided. At a minimum, the parties must agree upon: (1) what "available" means; and (2) what time periods are covered. Within those two points, other parameters must be addressed, including exceptions or exclusions.

Depending upon the nature of the service, the SP will likely wish to limit the time during each day that the availability of the service is monitored for purposes of the availability service level. For example, if the users of the cloud services are employees of the Client who will only use the services during normal business hours, then the Client may agree to limit the "availability" metric to the Client's normal business hours on days that it is open for business. However, if the cloud services will support or provide services used on an external-facing website intended to be used by the Client's customers, then having an availability metric of 24 hours per day, seven days a week may be critical to the Client.

As noted above, carefully defining "available" is critical. To simply state that the SP's services will be available 24 hours per day may sound fine; however, in actual practice, such a statement should be seen as ambiguous. What if all but one function of 10 total functions of the cloud service are accessible and may be used by the Client's employees or customers? Is that "available" for purposes of measuring the availability service level? What if that one function is a key function from the Client's perspective that must be functioning for the other nine to be of any use to the Client's employees or customers? What if the Client's employees can access and use all 10 functions, but it takes multiple attempts to enter data and have the data properly processed by some or all of the functions? The point is that for those and other reasons, it is best that the parties define exactly what they mean by "available." A Client would be best served by its counsel conferring with the Client's business users to understand how to define "available" with respect to the particular cloud service to be provided.

Counsel should closely review any calculation proposed by the SP (and independently check such calculations proposed by the SP) to determine with the Client how the calculation will work in practice and whether the results are acceptable to the Client.

A typical approach used by SPs is to lengthen the measurement period over which its performance is measured. Consider that a 10-hour problem spread over a longer period has a lesser proportional or percentage effect on a performance measure than the same problem occurring within a shorter period. Consequently, be wary of measurement periods greater than one month. Another favorite "gotcha" is to take advantage of a limited period during which the cloud service must be available. For example, if the measurement period for the availability service level will be tested as a percentage over each calendar month, and the SP and Client have agreed that the critical period of availability is a set period each day, such as 6:00 a.m. to 10:00 p.m. (the Critical Hours), there are numerous ways for the SP to manipulate the calculation.

First, the calculation for "availability" can be set so a 10-hour problem period during the Critical Hours is deducted from the numerator but not the denominator, while any problem period outside the Critical Hours is not deducted because the Client is not using the service during those hours. This may appear appropriate. However, if the denominator is set at the total hours in the month, such approach will give the SP a "free pass" on the hours between 10:00 p.m. and 6:00 a.m. Instead, the calculation should compare apples-to-apples. Thus, the denominator in the above example would be reduced to the number of hours in the applicable 6:00 a.m. to 10:00 p.m. period during the given month, and the numerator would be the number of hours of availability during the hours of 6:00 a.m. to 10:00 p.m. in such month. There are other tactics to manipulate time in the given example, but the above gives a fair idea of why the Client's counsel must carefully review and perhaps work through a few examples of the proposed service-level calculations.

As noted above, exclusions or exceptions are the SP's means of avoiding responsibility for what might otherwise be failures to comply with SLAs. Some SPs even refer to them as "performance exclusions." Below is an example of how an SP may define performance exclusions:

> SP will not be responsible for, and may exclude from the calculation of compliance with any performance metric, any failure to meet the performance metric if and to the extent that such failure to meet a performance metric is related to or caused by (any of the following being referred to as a "Performance Exclusion"):
>
> (i) prescheduled downtime, downtime during maintenance windows, or downtime during any preventative maintenance, provided advance notice has been given to Client for such downtime;
> (ii) acts or omissions of Client or third-party providers;
> (iii) an event, condition, or other circumstance beyond the reasonable control of SP; or
> (iv) failure of the data communications carrier lines between Client and SP's System.

Again, at first blush, the above may appear reasonable and acceptable. However, even without knowing the exact cloud services to be provided, considered more closely, the above will be seen as ambiguous and heavily in favor of the SP. For example, in subsection (iii) above, it would be better to rely upon a clear, agreed-upon definition of force majeure. The cloud services agreement between the SP and the Client should have a force majeure provision that, among other things, provides some parameters (think restrictions and obligations) around when the SP may rely on an event truly beyond its control to excuse its performance under the cloud services agreement. The better approach, therefore, would be to replace subsection (iii) above with something like "the occurrence of a Force Majeure Event (as defined in the Services Agreement)." The force majeure exculpatory provision in a SLA should also include a right to terminate if the excused performance extends past a set point (e.g., 20 days).

Similarly, consider subsection (ii) in the above sample: "acts or omissions of Client or third-party providers." Subsection (ii) addresses and treats in the same manner two distinct types of actors: first, the Client, and second, "third-party providers." Again, from the Client's perspective, a strong argument may be made that the acts or omissions of third parties, especially those retained by the SP, should be run through the test of the definition of the term "Force Majeure Event." The type of service provided by the third-party provider may affect the strength of the argument for the application of a Force Majeure test. If the third-party service provider is providing a service that falls well within the service expected directly from the SP, the argument for Force Majeure treatment is greatly enhanced. A second way of addressing the point without relying on the Force Majeure reference is to simply revise the wording to focus on which party retains the third-party provider by adding the word "its" or "Client's" before "third-party providers," for example, so that the provision would read: "acts or omissions of Client or Client's third-party providers."

One can make a similar argument with respect to subsection (iv) in the above sample. The argument would be that the exclusion in subsection (iv) is acceptable only if the SP is not responsible for such communication carrier lines. The Client's argument would be that, if the SP is responsible for such carrier lines, then the adverse effect on any SLA caused by a failure of such lines should only be excluded from the measurement of the SLA's performance, if such failure falls within a Force Majeure exclusion. Again, in most cases, a failure to perform does not fall within a Force Majeure exclusion unless it meets certain express conditions.

Next consider subsection (i) above, which provides various exclusions from SLA performance measurements for various types of maintenance services. Addressing the effects of maintenance services on SLA obligations and measurements can, at times, be difficult. The difficulties often stem from the fact that the SP wants to maximize its ability to schedule and perform maintenance, whereas the Client wants to minimize any adverse effects the performance of maintenance may have on its operations or business. As a general principle, from the Client's perspective, maintenance that impinges upon the Client's business operations or needs should not be excluded from the measurement of any SLA. A Client may, however, agree to certain exceptions to that general principle. For example, a Client may be willing to allow its use of the SP's service to be interrupted during the Client's normal working hours solely for the purpose of installing a critical security patch, and to agree that the time to install the patch would not be included with the measurement of any SLA.

Keeping these general principles and exceptions in mind while reviewing subsection (i) in the above sample, the Client would benefit from defining the terms "prescheduled downtime," "downtime," "maintenance windows," and "preventative maintenance." The intent would be to define those terms such that their meanings and application within the cloud services agreement are clear, and not subject to unilateral interpretation by the SP or its service department in a manner that could impinge upon the Client's operations. For example, the Client would want to consider defining "prescheduled downtime" and ensure that such time is excluded from SLA performance measures only if it falls outside of the time periods during which use of the services is critical to the Client's operations.

As shown in the above example, one component of the computation of availability is often the time that the relevant service or system is scheduled to be down and unavailable or not fully available. The goal for the Client is to ensure that the definition of scheduled downtime does not for all practicable purposes make the "availability" metric meaningless, which can occur in many ways within the definition. Given that Scheduled Downtime reflects time that the service or system can be unavailable or not fully available without negatively affecting the SP's performance under the Availability service level, it is important to address restrictions on what may fall within the definition of "Scheduled Downtime." For example, if Scheduled Downtime is excluded from the measurement of SLAs, it would be helpful to the Client to limit (1) the hours during which Scheduled Downtime may occur, (2) how long any one specific period of Scheduled Downtime may occur, and (3) how frequently Scheduled Downtime may occur. The below sample clause[3] provides examples of some of the restrictions that should be considered in defining Schedule Downtime:

> **"Scheduled Downtime"** means any scheduled outage in Availability of which SP notifies the Client at least X (x) business days in advance, provided that such scheduled outage (a) lasts no longer than ___ (_) hour(s); (b) is scheduled between the hours of [X] a.m. and [X] a.m., [TIME ZONE/LOCATION] Time; and (c) occurs no more frequently than [X] per [week] [month]. [Service Provider may request Client's approval for extensions of Scheduled Downtime above one (1) hour [, which approval may [be granted in Client's sole discretion] [not be unreasonably withheld or delayed].]

As noted above, SLAs must be viewed in light of the cloud services provided. If the parties agreed upon a "Critical Hours" approach to measuring the availability service level, then the Client should seek to limit the "maintenance windows" and any other maintenance (prescheduled, emergency, etc.) that may affect availability to the period outside the Critical Hours. In that case, the above "Performance Exclusions" may be reduced to something like "SP shall be excused for a Service Level Failure to the extent the Service Level Failure is caused by a Force Majeure Event or caused solely by Client's acts or omissions."

2. Responsiveness/Response Times

An important aspect of performance for certain cloud services is responsiveness or response time. The concern is perhaps best understood in terms of the answers to the following questions: When a user is logging onto the cloud service, how much time will pass from the time the user has clicked "enter" with the user name and password inserted before the user is actually logged on and the service is available? Or, after logging on, how much time will pass from the time the user makes an inquiry of the cloud service until the user has the response displayed on the user's screen? Will the cloud service's response

---

3   The sample provisions in this chapter are not recommended provisions. They are provided only for purposes of explaining or demonstrating points made within the discussion. Each SLA must be tailored for the specifics of the particular cloud service(s) provided.

speed meet the needs and expectations of the user, or will it be frustrating or useless to the user because of its delays?

Responsiveness can be affected, however, by many forces, some within the control of the SP, some within the control of the Client, and some within neither party's control. An example of an event that could fall within any one of those three categories is the telecommunications connection. The nature of the event may also affect responsiveness. For example, will the telecommunications connection be a dedicated line, a VPN, a plain-old internet browser connection by the user, or some combination of the above depending on the specific aspect of the cloud service accessed/provided?

Again, the nature of the cloud service must be understood and considered in connection with a response time service level. SPs that provide only cloud storage may be unwilling to provide any assurance on responsiveness or any meaningful assurances. Their position is often that they are not providing any processing and that availability is the only appropriate metric. If, however, the SP is providing more than just storage, such as the underlying application, or if the cloud storage provider is also responsible for the telecommunications connection, then that SP should be more willing to provide an appropriate response time service level.

Similar to the availability metric, a service level for response times will normally be based on some type of average percentage (e.g., 99.99 percent) over a set period of time (e.g., a calendar month) and may be measured $24 \times 7 \times 365$ or only during Critical Hours on defined business days. Depending upon the nature of the cloud service, however, there may be other aspects of responsiveness that are critical to the Client that may be measured, such as ensuring that no response takes longer than a specified time during the Critical Hours. In that regard, consider the importance of responsiveness to a high-speed securities or commodities trading platform where the phrase "he who hesitates is lost" has real meaning. In that industry, seconds can make the difference between making and missing a trade, and any trade can be significant. Consequently, there could be a need for multiple response time metrics for the same cloud service.

Below is a sample response time metric offered by a SP that was providing its software as a cloud service (SaaS). The "metric" is the defined term "Response Time." The other terms are used to measure the metric.

"**Average Response Time**" means the average Response Time of the Services during the Responsive Hours, calculated over the course of a calendar month.

"**Response Time**" means the number of seconds required for the Services to fully render the initial login page, log into the application, and fully render the End User's account home page.

"**Responsive Hours**" means the hours between 6 a.m. Eastern Time and 11 p.m. Eastern Time.

Recall that one of the four principal elements of effective SLAs is "measuring and reporting responsibilities." Measuring "response time" can be complicated, and the Client must understand the process that will be used and who will be responsible for monitoring, measuring, and reporting (i.e., the Client or the SP).

Consider how "Response Time" would be (or could be) measured under the above sample provision if the cloud service at issue was an internet banking web site for retail customers of a bank. The Client (i.e., the bank) will be concerned with its customers' experience with the bank's website. The website's responsiveness to the customer's actions will be a big part of that experience. For example, the bank will be concerned with how long it takes the website to display the customer's initial page after the customer has gone through the log-on process and submitted its access information and password. The bank will also be concerned with how long it takes for the website to display the customer's checking or other account information after the customer clicks on the icon for the appropriate account. It is important to understand how those response times are measured and by whom.

Such a situation does not lend itself to direct measurements of the actual experience of each customer. You could not, for example, expect each customer to make the measurements, nor could you expect the bank's customers to allow the bank or the SP to place measuring and reporting software on the customers' computers. Additionally, in such situations, multiple parties are responsible for the telecommunication connections that could affect responsiveness. Nevertheless, responsiveness is a key metric for such websites, and the bank will want some way to measure the metric and its customer's experience. Often in such circumstances where measuring actual performance is not practical or not fully within the SP's control, the SP will propose use of a software tool that, in essence, simulates the customer's actions, such as logging on, and measures the corresponding Response Time.

The measurements resulting from the tool can be used for purposes of the service level. Typically, to avoid adversely affecting Response Time due to network latency, the software tool will be located within the same data center as the servers hosting the Client application or website. Such an approach may be acceptable to a Client if the functioning of the tool is understood and other approaches are not practicable.

3. Incident Response and Resolution

With any cloud service, as with any service based on computers and software, there will be problems or failures to perform as promised, and a properly drafted cloud services agreement should include support and maintenance obligations to remediate such problems or failures. However, an obligation to fix a service deficiency may be insufficient if not coupled with a timeliness obligation. An incident response and resolution service level focuses on the timeliness obligation.

The timeliness obligation can be broken down into its four component aspects: (1) the time until the initial response or acknowledgement from the SP that it is aware a problem has occurred; (2) the effort that will be exerted to fix the problem; (3) the time until an acceptable work-around is provided; and (4) the time until a final resolution or fix is provided.

Not all problems are equal. Some are more catastrophic for the Client than others. In that regard, "severity levels" are often defined on a scale from the most severe (e.g., "Severity Level 1" or "Sev 1") to least troublesome (e.g., "Severity Level 4" or "Sev 4"), with different levels of obligations for the above four components. As the time periods to respond (think time between problem discovery and problem resolution) become longer for each lower level of severity, the severity level definitions can be critical to the success or failure of the Incident Response and Resolution service levels from the Client's perspective.

Equally important can be which party determines the severity level assigned to each problem. Often when pressed, the SP will suggest that the assignment be as "mutually agreed," and many Clients consider "mutually" an acceptable compromise. Unfortunately, when it comes to agreeing upon whether a problem is addressed as a Severity Level 1 or Severity Level 2 incident, many of the advantages of having the problem treated as a Severity Level 1 will have been lost by the time the parties are able to "mutually agree."

Additionally, any stalemate on the decision will favor the SP unless addressed in some manner in the SLA. It is best to avoid the "mutually agreed" approach and allow either party the right to initially designate the severity level, but to give the Client a right to override and make the definitive assignment of severity level based upon the impact to the Client. The logic to such an override right is that the problem is affecting the Client's business, and if there is an ambiguity in the definition of the two levels, the Client should make the business decision as to how much effort must be exerted by the SP to remediate the situation. Protections can be provided to the SP against a Client that constantly cries wolf or that the sky is falling by designating everything as a Severity 1.

The first and probably most important protection is clear and sufficiently detailed definitions for the top severity levels inclusive of the aspects that separate those levels. Such clarity and detailed definitions help avoid disputes and help keep the Client honest in its designation of severity levels for the issues that may arise. As a second protection, establish a standard (e.g., three disagreements on Severity 1 designations by the Client within one month) that allows the SP to bring in an agreed independent third party to review those disagreements. If the independent third party agrees with the SP's lower severity level designation on those issues, then there can be remedies for the SP. Such remedies could include the Client paying for the independent third-party review, and paying the SP at its standard time and material rates with a premium for the services provided in responding to the underlying issues.

Below is a sample incident response and resolution metric service level. The below does not include the definitions of the severity levels, which are necessarily service-specific.

> When Errors are reported, SP will [make commercially reasonable efforts to promptly] meet the applicable acknowledgement and status update requirements as set forth in the table below, whether SP is responsible for the Error or not. For Errors for which SP is responsible, SP shall also meet the resolution requirements set forth in the table below.

Incident Severity Level	Acknowledgement/ Initial Response	Status Update Frequency	Target Resolution
SL-1	30 Minutes	Hourly	2 Hours
SL-2	2 Hours	Every 3 Hours	1 Bus. Day
SL-3	1 Bus. Day	Once Per Bus. Day	5 Bus. Days
SL-4	2 Bus. Days	Once Per Month	Next Release

Using the above as an example, the Client must, at a minimum, (1) define all terms such as "Error"; (2) have an understanding or definition of the Errors for which the SP is responsible; (3) include a detailed description of how the Client reports Errors; and (4) clarify the meaning of "Target" and whether "Resolution" involves a permanent fix or a mere work-around. In addition, consider how the phrase in brackets above waters down the SP's obligations.

B. Ramifications or Remedies—Not Having Specified SLA Remedies Is a Major "Gotcha"

As important as proper metrics and measuring for effective SLAs are the "remedies" for failure. Without specified remedies tied to SLA failures, the Client is, *at best*, back to being required to declare a breach and seek standard contract remedies. *At worst*, the Client has, in essence, lost all effective remedies.

In arguing against providing specific remedies, especially against a right to terminate, SPs and their counsel will often state that the remedy is to terminate the services agreement for breach. However, accepting such a statement may be stepping into one of the worst "gotchas" in SLA negotiations.

In order to understand why accepting the breach approach may be a major "gotcha" for the Client, the terms and conditions of the applicable service levels and of the right to terminate must be reviewed and considered. For example, if the service levels are drafted with wording such as that contained in the brackets in the last sample, the Client may not even have a right to claim a breach, and will hence have no remedy for the SP's failure to meet its service levels. The SP will simply argue that all it was required to do was "make commercially reasonable efforts to" meet the metrics, and given that it had made those efforts, there was no breach.

If the SLA is more specific regarding the SP's obligation to perform at the level or levels set forth in the SLA, such that failure to perform at the level set forth in the SLA is a clear breach of the SP's obligations, then the Client may still be left with no satisfactory or truly effective remedy.

First, consider whether it is clear under the cloud services agreement that a failure to meet a service level is a breach that would allow for remedies. For example, must a breach be "material" for the Client to have remedies? Second, if a service level contains various levels, at what level would the failure be "material?" For example, if there are four severity levels of incidents and the SP constantly fails to meet the response times for Severity 3 incidents, but generally meets the response times for Severity 1 and 2 incidents, is there a "material" breach? Clearly, without more, the use of the term "material" could have a chilling effect on the Client's willingness to exercise any right based on a "breach" under certain service levels. The "more" that would be needed is to ensure a direct coordination between the SLA provisions and what constitutes a material breach under the breach termination provision. A simple fix is to set forth expressly the SLA failures that will be considered a "material breach entitling the Client to the remedies provided by" the breach termination provision.

A second problem with accepting the breach termination approach often suggested by cloud providers is that beach termination provisions usually include a notice and cure period. Again, if the breach termination approach is accepted by the Client, counsel must ensure the SLA provisions and the breach termination provisions are properly coordinated. Consider, for example, if the cure period in the breach termination provision should be omitted for SLA failure because the SLA provisions by their very nature or express terms already provide a type of cure period. For example, SLA provisions often contain the concept that a SLA failure has not occurred until the SP's performance has been below a minimum acceptable level for multiple months or quarters. Allowing a "cure period" for unacceptable SLA performance could easily result in never ending alternating periods of failed performance following by a cure period of minimally satisfactory performance, followed by a period of failed performance leading to another cure period. If the Client is willing to accept the termination for breach remedy, then the applicable provisions must be coordinated to avoid such a result.

Even if the Client is comfortable that a SLA failure is a "breach" that entitles it to exercise its remedies for breach without delay of a cure period or otherwise, such a remedy may not be one that the Client wants or is willing to exercise. In most cloud service agreements, the remedy for any material breach is the right to terminate the cloud services agreement or the service, subject to a right to cure. Of course, for most cloud service agreements, what the Client really wants is proper performance, not a right to terminate and incur the time and expense of switching to a new cloud service. Consequently, the Client could find itself in a situation where performance is unsatisfactory in some measurable manner, but the Client has no effective remedy because, for practical purposes, it cannot terminate the relationship.

For cloud services agreements, SLAs should include two basic types of remedies. First are remedies that provide meaningful incentives for the SP to perform at the desired level. Second is a right to terminate when the performance becomes so poor that the pain of transitioning the services to a new SP or back to the Client is exceeded by the pain of continuing with the present SP.

Specific "incentive" remedies are typically some type of financial credit against fees due, often with an increase in the percentage of the credit for increased levels of failures. The general thought is that the financial credits to the Client will help motivate the SP to perform at an acceptable level to avoid the obligation to provide such credits.

In certain circumstances, especially long-term arrangements, it may be advantageous to the Client to agree to a method for the SP to gain back credits. For example, enhanced performance by the SP with no SLA failures over a set period may negate the SP's obligation to provide the Client with the service level credit previously earned. Similarly, in long-term agreements, it may be equally or more important to the Client that the SP promptly conduct a thorough analysis of the cause of the service level failure, take steps to minimize the likelihood of repeated failures, and report to the Client the results of such analysis and the steps undertaken.

If, however, the Client does want to terminate the cloud service agreement or cloud services because of a SLA failure or chronic SLA failures, relying on the standard contractual right to terminate may be ineffective for the Client. As noted above, such right is often contingent upon the provision of notice of breach and an opportunity to cure. From Client's position, that is unsatisfactory because it allows the SP to "cure" after already failing on numerous occasions or in a material manner. In many cases it would, in essence, be placing a right to cure on top of a prior right to cure. Such a right to cure before termination could result in rolling service-level defaults (i.e., chronic poor performance over several months) separated only by the rolling cure periods (e.g., 30 days) during which the SP performs at the minimum acceptable level.

Below is a sample termination provision for "chronic" service level failures:

> Without limiting Client's remedies under the Agreement or applicable law, if a Service Level Failure occurs: (i) in any three (3) consecutive months or (ii) in any five (5) separate months in any rolling twelve (12) month period, Client shall have the right to terminate the Agreement at any time thereafter upon prior written notice to SP (which notice shall reference this Section and shall describe such failures) without any penalty or liability, and shall receive a prorated refund of all amounts prepaid by Client and unearned by SP as of the date of termination.

In such a provision, counsel must ensure the phrase "Service Level Failure" was properly and clearly defined. Note also that the provision includes a clause to ensure the right to terminate is not interpreted as an exclusive remedy.

V. General Suggestions to Avoid Typical "Gotchas"

1. A major mistake in preparing a SLA is a lack of focus on the business objectives of the Client in retaining the cloud service. The Client is relying upon the SP to meet its business needs. Ensure those business needs and objectives are well understood, the expectations around them are set, and they are properly addressed within the service levels. That will require the descriptions of the services (which will likely be outside the SLA provisions) to be clearly written with the appropriate detail to meet the Client's business objectives.

2. Another major mistake is to place the Client in a position where it has no ability to adapt to changes in its business objectives and needs with respect to the cloud services. Especially in long-term arrangements with SPs, counsel for the Client should consult the business side about the importance of and need to require periodic (e.g., annual) reviews by the Client and the SP of the services and the associated service levels, including the process to revise, add to, and replace the service levels based on the SP's performance to that point and changes in technology and the relevant industry. This could be tied into a requirement in the main agreement for the SP to continuously improve its cloud services and the performance of its cloud services.

3. Similarly, in long-term agreements there should be a requirement to include new service levels for any new service that may be added to the cloud services agreement. The cloud services agreement or SLA provisions should include an understanding of minimum service level requirements, including credits or liquidated damages, and a right to terminate for chronic failures and/or severe underperformance.

4. All SLAs should include a savings clause to ensure that remedies available with respect to the performance standards are *not* the exclusive remedies available to the Client for SLA failures. Counsel for the Client should ensure that the payment of credits will not limit the Client's right to recover other damages and losses, whether pursuant to other provisions in the agreement or applicable law or equitable remedies.

5.   Clarify that the credits or liquidated damages are not "penalties," given that provisions in commercial contracts that are viewed as penalties under the law are often unenforceable. Rather, such credits should be intended and seen as a genuine estimate of reduced value to the Client resulting from the SP's failure to meet the agreed service levels or performance measures in that such reduced value to the Client is difficult or impossible to calculate in advance.

6.   Whether the SLA has a specific termination right, counsel for the Client should seek to ensure that nothing in the SLA provisions (the credits or otherwise) will be deemed to limit or obviate the Client's right to terminate the cloud services agreement or seek and obtain remedies under other portions of the Agreement or applicable law, even if the SP issues the appropriate service-level fee credits to the Client.

7.   Keep the service levels simple and clear. Avoid SLAs with complicated and intertwined provisions, such as weighting provisions. "Weighting" provisions look at numerous metrics and their possible failures or reduced levels of performance and give different "weights" to the different metrics based on the concept that some metrics are more important than others. A numerical value based on the weighting is then calculated for each metric, which numeric values are then added together to determine whether there has been a service level failure. Such weighting provisions can become so complicated it is nearly impossible to understand how they will function. If you believe examples are needed to ensure the metrics or measurements are understood, then the SLA is likely too complicated and must be rewritten so it is clear. Remember, the service levels must be focused on the Client's objectives and needs, and those are usually easy to state and define. The users of the cloud services are unlikely to find it useful, or in any way meaningful, to have complicated, weighted service levels. They have specific objectives and goals they need met. Those objectives and needs are what the metrics should be measuring. In most instances, complicated metrics serve only the goal of the SP to avoid SLA failures rather than focusing on ensuring the service meets the needs of the business user.

8.   Consider including a requirement for periodic meetings (monthly, quarterly) to review performance of the cloud service and an escalation process to address problems in managing the SLAs.

9.   Consider placing the service levels in a separate document or attachment to the services agreement. Such an arrangement makes the service levels accessible and more easily used by the users of the cloud service and by those managing the ongoing relationship with the SP.

10.   Finally, in reviewing and drafting SLAs, keep in mind the differences among "public" and "private" cloud services delivery models. A public cloud service assumes a shared service platform for all of the SP's customers, whereas a private cloud service assumes a dedicated service platform for each separate SP customer. Typically, this means that the Client will have greater flexibility establishing the Client's specific service levels in the private cloud environment than in the public cloud environment, but don't let SPs tell you that the SP has no ability to negotiate regarding SLAs for pubic cloud services. SPs often offer fairly modest

public cloud service levels with no (or minimal) service level credits or remedies. Experience shows, however, that many SPs are willing to offer enhanced service levels and service level credits as an incentive to win business or as part of a higher cost support package. Always remember that you will never get enhanced service levels or remedies if you don't ask!

VI. Conclusion

Properly structured service level agreements can be and often are the key to ensuring a successful cloud service arrangement for both the Client and the SP. Consequently, it is well worth the time and effort to carefully work through with your client and negotiate the appropriate and well-defined metrics, service levels, monitoring, and remedies.

Chapter 4

Best Practices for Cloud Privacy

By Richard C. Balough and Della M. Hill[1]

I. Introduction

The concept of privacy is not new.[2] There has long been a recognition that certain types of information about individuals should remain private. At one time, privacy was conceptualized as simply the right to be left alone. Those who violated a person's right to privacy were held liable under tort law, including actions for intrusion upon one's seclusion.

With today's sophisticated technology, information about individuals is collected from multiple sources and assembled in massive databases, which in turn are combined with other databases, giving database owners a tremendous amount of information, both in the aggregate and individually, about specific individuals.

Growing concern over this expansive collection of information and, more importantly, over the potentially unchecked use and disclosure of this information, has led to a shift in the concept of privacy. No longer simply the right to be left alone, today's concept of privacy encompasses an individual's right to know, and to some degree to control, what information is collected, to whom it is disclosed, and how it is used. This broader conception of privacy and of what the law should do to protect it is reflected in the growing body of legislation addressing privacy.[3]

Information privacy (also referred to as data privacy) and related information (or data) security is regulated in the United States by a complex and ever-growing patchwork of laws and regulations at both the federal and state levels. Any company collecting and using data has almost certainly triggered, and is required to comply with, at least one (but most likely several) of these laws.

Shifting the control or management of a company's data to a third party, in this case a cloud service provider, will not relieve the company of its obligations to comply with applicable privacy and security laws. Indeed, a company that contracts with a cloud provider to manage its trove of data remains ultimately responsible for compliance, and may

---

1 Richard C. Balough is a partner at Balough Law Offices, LLC, Chicago; Della M. Hill is an associate at MacDonald Weiss PLLC, New York City.

2 The seminal scholarly treatment of privacy is Samuel D. Warren & Louis D. Brandeis, *The Right to Privacy*, 4 HARV. L. REV. 193 (1890).

3 In 1973, the U.S. Department of Health, Education, and Welfare issued its report of the Secretary's Advisory Committee on Automated Personal Data Systems, the result of the committee's study on recordkeeping in the "computer age." U.S. DEP'T OF HEALTH, EDUC. & WELFARE, RECORDS, COMPUTERS, AND THE RIGHTS OF CITIZENS (1973). That report advocated "fair information practices" and led to enactment of the Privacy Act of 1974, 5 U.S.C. § 552a. In the ensuing years, Congress passed laws to protect privacy in various sectors, including the Electronic Communications Privacy Act of 1986, 18 U.S.C. §§ 2510–2522, 2701–2709, the Driver's Privacy Protection Act of 1994, 18 U.S.C. §§ 2721–2725, the Health Insurance Portability and Accountability Act of 1996, Pub. L. No. 104-191 (codified as amended in scattered sections of 29 U.S.C.), the Children's Online Privacy Protection Act of 1998 (COPPA), 15 U.S.C. §§ 6501–6506 (2018), and the Gramm-Leach-Bliley Act of 1999 (GLBA), 15 U.S.C. §§ 6801–6809.

be liable for any breaches of these laws by the cloud provider. For this reason, an effective cloud agreement is essential. The privacy and security of a company's data stored in the cloud depends upon the safeguards contractually required from the cloud provider under the cloud agreement.

The goal of this chapter is to provide attorneys with an overview of general best practices for satisfying U.S. privacy and security obligations through an adequate and effective cloud agreement. Part II provides an overview of the legal framework for privacy and security in the United States. It also includes a discussion of a few examples of U.S. laws that might be triggered by a cloud customer's use of data. Part III sets out some key provisions that an attorney should seek to include in a cloud agreement, regardless of the industry of the cloud customer. Finally, Part IV provides an overview of additional security considerations for cloud agreements.

II. Framework for U.S. Privacy and Security Laws

Unlike Europe or Canada, the United States does not have a comprehensive law regulating information privacy and security; rather, information privacy and security is regulated on a "sectoral" basis—that is, on both the federal and state levels, legal privacy and security obligations may be triggered by sector or industry (e.g., health or financial sectors), by types of information (e.g., personally identifiable information, especially particularly sensitive information such as biometric information or information about children), and by location of data subjects (e.g., the state in which a company's data subjects reside).

A. Determining Applicable Laws for a Cloud Customer

Prior to the engagement of a cloud service provider, or even the review of a cloud service provider's contract, an attorney must understand the collection, use, and processing of data by the company (soon-to-be cloud customer) and inventory the data the company intends to move to the cloud. This data-mapping process is necessary for identifying and analyzing the privacy and security laws and regulations applicable to the cloud customer and is the crucial first step toward compliance with such obligations in a cloud agreement.

A threshold question the attorney should consider is whether the relevant data involves personal information. Personal information, which is also referred to in some contexts as personally identifiable information (PII), is a central concept in U.S. privacy and security regulation.[4] The involvement of PII serves as the trigger for application of many U.S. privacy laws.[5] There is no single definition for PII; rather, PII is defined and categorized in various ways depending on the applicable law.[6] Generally speaking, PII is information that may be used to identify an individual. Depending on the particular law or regulation, PII may include first and last names, initials, Social Security numbers, driver's license numbers, state identification card numbers, bank account information, home addresses, e-mail addresses, telephone numbers, and passport numbers. PII can also be a combination

---

4 Daniel J. Solove & Paul M. Schwartz, Privacy Law Fundamentals 154 (IAPP 4th ed. 2017).

5 *Id.*

6 *See, e.g.,* the difference in definitions of "PII" under COPPA, GLBA, and the California Consumer Privacy Act of 2018 (each discussed elsewhere in this chapter).

of data items that, together, may be used to identify an individual. For example, even if the name from an individual's data file is removed, that individual may still be identified using as few as three data points, such as zip code, date of birth, and gender. The combination of those "anonymous" data points together may be considered PII. Inappropriate or unauthorized disclosure of PII will violate a multitude of federal and state laws, so any cloud contract must address PII privacy and protection. As a first step, therefore, if there is no business or legal reason to keep the PII, then it should be deleted. If the PII must be retained, the attorney should inquire as to whether there is a way to mask the PII before it goes to the cloud without negatively impacting the service provided in the cloud.

Another question an attorney should consider is whether the company has made any promises or representations to its data subjects in a privacy policy or notice posted on its website or otherwise distributed to its data subjects regarding (1) the collection, use, and disclosure of PII, or (2) any of its privacy and security practices. Although most states do not require privacy policies to be posted on websites, it is common practice (and in some contexts, required)[7] for companies to do so. Any promises made in such policies must also be upheld by a cloud provider. The FTC has brought enforcement actions against companies that violate their privacy policies.[8]

Other questions for an attorney include whether the data involves financial- or health-related information, and questions relating to the data subjects of the company, including who they are (e.g., students or children under the age of 13) and where they are located (in a single state or throughout the country).

All of these questions and many more in the data-mapping process will enable the attorney to analyze and identify the applicable state and federal laws and regulations that must be addressed in a cloud agreement. In all likelihood, a company's responses to these questions will trigger multiple, often overlapping laws.

B. Note on General FTC Regulation

In addition to the federal and state laws described in Part II.C. below, it is important to note that the Federal Trade Commission (FTC) has some information data and privacy enforcement authority under the Federal Trade Commission Act (the FTC Act). Indeed, the FTC may bring enforcement actions against cloud customers for the failings of their third-party service providers (which may include cloud providers). In *In re GMR Transcription Services Inc.*, for example, the FTC concluded that the respondent company's failure to properly oversee the security practices of its contractors to ensure implementation of reasonable and appropriate security measures for customers' personal information was an unfair and deceptive trade practice under section 5 of the FTC Act.[9]

C. Examples of U.S. Privacy and Security Laws

The following laws include privacy and security provisions and may be applicable in any given scenario. When these laws are triggered, a cloud agreement should require

---

7 Most prominently, California law requires commercial websites that collect PII from California residents to post a privacy policy including specified elements. CAL. BUS. & PROF. CODE § 22575.

8 *See, e.g., In re* Uber Technologies, Inc., No. C-4662 (F.T.C. Oct. 25, 2018); FTC v. Toysmart.com, LLC, No. 00-11341-RGS, 2000 WL 34016434 (D. Mass. July 21, 2000).

9 *In re* GMR Transcription Servs., No. C-4482 (F.T.C. Aug. 14, 2014).

compliance with such laws by the cloud provider. It is important to note, however, that each of the laws below may be only one of several laws triggered by a company's use of certain data. For example, although the federal Children's Online Privacy Protection Act described below may be triggered by the collection and processing of an audio file containing the voice of a child under the age of 13, the Illinois Biometric Information Privacy Act (also described below) may be simultaneously triggered if that child is an Illinois resident and the audio file is converted into a voiceprint. Similarly, although the Gramm-Leach-Bliley Act described below may be triggered by use of (among other data items) an individual's Social Security number, that individual's state of residence may also have a state law compliance requirement triggered by use of that Social Security number.

Given the complexity of the patchwork sectoral nature of U.S. privacy and security regulation and the often overlapping laws triggered, the discussion below includes a few key recommendations for cloud agreement provisions, but reference should also be made to the complete list of best-practice provisions for privacy and security compliance of a cloud agreement in Parts III and IV, *infra*.

1. State Laws Regulating Biometric Data

Several states have laws concerning collecting, storing, and using biometric data. The laws are not uniform and may apply only to data collected or manipulated in the particular state. As data may have a connection to multiple states, more than one law may apply.

Regulation of biometric data originated in 2008 when Illinois passed its Biometric Information Privacy Act.[10] Originally designed to address business and security screening, the act notes that "an overwhelming majority of members of the public are weary of the use of biometrics when such information is tied to finances and other personal information."[11] Unlike other forms of identity such as Social Security numbers, which may be changed if compromised, biometrics "are biologically unique to the individual; therefore, once compromised, the individual has no recourse, is at heightened risk for identity theft, and is likely to withdraw from biometric-facilitated transactions."[12] The act recognized a decade ago that, "[t]he full ramifications of biometric technology are not fully known."[13] Since the Illinois statute was passed, other states have adopted biometric data laws in various forms, including Texas and Washington.[14] Legislation is pending in other states. At present, only the Illinois law provides a private cause of action as opposed to the requirement of the state attorney general bringing an action for a violation.

Illinois prohibits a private entity from possessing, collecting, purchasing, or selling biometric identifiers or biometric information unless it first (1) informs the subject in writing that a biometric identifier is being collected or stored, (2) informs the subject of the specific purpose and length of term for which it is being collected, stored, and used, and (3) receives a written release executed by the subject of the identifiers or information.[15]

---

10 740 ILL. COMP. STAT. 14/1–14/25.

11 *Id*. at 14/5(d).

12 *Id*. at 14/5(c).

13 *Id*. at 14/5(f).

14 TEX. BUS. & COM. CODE ANN. § 503.001; WASH. REV. CODE ANN. § 19.375.010–.900.

15 740 ILL. COMP. STAT. 14/15(b).

The lengthy definition of "biometric identifier" in the Illinois act begins by stating that the term means "a retina or iris scan, fingerprint, voiceprint, or scan of hand or face geometry."[16] The definition excludes "writing samples, written signatures, photographs, human biological samples used for valid scientific testing or screening, demographic data, tattoo descriptions, or physical descriptions such as height, weight, hair color, or eye color." It also excludes donated organs, tissues, or blood.[17] "Biometric information" includes "any information, regardless of how it is captured, converted, stored, or shared, based on an individual's biometric identifier used to identify an individual."[18]

Even though photographs are excluded from the definition of biometric identifier, a photograph may nonetheless constitute "biometric information" if the photograph reveals a biometric identifier. When Shutterfly scanned an uploaded photograph, analyzed the geometric data relating to unique face contours, and used the data to extract a person's face geometry, its conduct was held to be within the scope of the statute.[19] As another court explained:

> The affirmative definition of "biometric information" does important work for the [Illinois Biometric Information] Privacy Act; without it, private entities could evade (or at least arguably could evade) the Act's restrictions by converting a person's biometric identifier into some other piece of information, like a mathematical representation or, even simpler, a unique number assigned to a person's biometric identifier. So whatever a private entity does in manipulating a biometric identifier into a piece of information, the resulting information is still covered by the Privacy Act if that information can be used to identify the person.[20]

By contrast, the definition of "biometric identifier" under Washington's biometrics law is more restrictive, and is limited to:

> data generated by automatic measurements of an individual's biological characteristics, such as a fingerprint, voiceprint, eye retinas, irises, or other unique biological patterns or characteristics that is used to identify a specific individual. "Biometric identifier" does not include a physical or digital photograph, video or audio recording or data generated therefrom, or information collected, used, or stored for health care treatment, payment, or operations under the federal health insurance portability and accountability act of 1996.[21]

Although state laws control actions within the state, they still may apply extraterritorially. In *Rivera v. Google*, photos taken on a droid device in Illinois were automatically uploaded to Google Photos, a cloud-based service.[22] Google then scanned the photographs to create a unique face "template" that was then used to find and group together other photographs. Plaintiffs contended Google was collecting biometric information in violation of the Illinois statute.[23] Google filed a motion to dismiss, contending (among other things) that its actions relating to the photos did not occur in Illinois; therefore, the Illinois statute did

---

16 *Id.* at 14/10.
17 *Id.*
18 *Id.*
19 Monroy v. Shutterfly, Inc., 2017 WL 4099846 (N.D. Ill. Sept. 15, 2017).
20 Rivera v. Google Inc., 238 F. Supp. 3d 1088, 1095 (N.D. Ill. 2017).
21 WASH. REV. CODE ANN. § 19.375.010(1).
22 *Rivera*, 238 F. Supp. 3d at 1090.
23 *Id.*

not apply.[24] Noting that there is no "bright line" to determine whether an action "in the cloud" (such as uploading information) would invoke jurisdiction, the court denied Google's motion to dismiss on the grounds that a fact-intensive review was required.[25]

In addition to notice to the data subjects, the statutes require "reasonable" measures to protect the identifiers and information, and restrict the dissemination of the information. For example, the Illinois statute prohibits disclosure unless (1) the subject gives consent, (2) the initial disclosure or redisclosure completes a financial transaction requested by the subject, (3) the disclosure or redisclosure is required by law, or (4) disclosure is required pursuant to a valid warrant or subpoena.[26]

The data may be retained "no longer than is reasonably necessary" under the Washington statute,[27] or in the case of the Illinois law, must be destroyed "when the initial purpose for collecting or obtaining such identifiers or information has been satisfied or within 3 years of the individual's last interaction with the private entity, whichever occurs first."[28] The Texas law requires destruction "within a reasonable time, but not later than the first anniversary of the date the purpose for collecting the identifier expires."[29]

For a cloud customer moving biometric information into the cloud, an attorney should consider all of the best-practice provisions detailed in Parts III and IV. It is worth noting, however, that for this type of data in particular, a cloud provider should be contractually obligated to provide to the cloud customer detailed and specific information regarding the physical, organizational, and technical safeguards for the protection of the biometric data. The agreement should further require that the cloud provider restrict access to the data by any third parties, specify that the cloud provider can use the data only as specifically and strictly required to provide the agreed-upon services in the agreement, and provide that the data be returned or destroyed by the cloud provider upon request or as specified in the agreement.

2. Children's Online Privacy Protection Act

Any cloud service that includes information collected from children must comply with the Children's Online Privacy Protection Act (COPPA),[30] which governs the collection of personal information from children under 13 and is enforced by the FTC.[31] COPPA applies not only to collection of information via a website, but also mobile apps that send or receive information online (games and social networking apps); internet-enabled gaming platforms; plug-ins; advertising networks; internet-enabled, location-based services; VoIP services; and connected toys.[32] In other words, COPPA is not just for websites.

---

24 *Id.* at 1100.

25 *Id.* at 1102 (noting that much of the case revolved around "conduct occurring online or on a 'cloud,'" the court concluded that although the plaintiffs sufficiently alleged facts that would deem Google's asserted violations as having happened within the state, further factual discovery was required).

26 740 Ill. Comp. Stat. 14/15(d)(1)–(4).

27 Wash. Rev. Code Ann. § 19.375.020(4)(b).

28 740 Ill. Comp. Stat. 14/15(a).

29 Tex. Bus. & Com. Code Ann. § 503.001(c)(3).

30 15 U.S.C. §§ 6501–6506.

31 *See* 16 C.F.R. pt. 312.

32 *Id.* pt. 312.2.

For example, if an internet-enabled toy such as a doll or toy dinosaur uses speech-recognition technology and collects personal information about children under 13, the toy manufacturer must comply with COPPA. In *United States v. VTech Electronics Limited*,[33] VTech settled an FTC complaint alleging that the company violated COPPA with its Kid Connect app, which was used with some of the company's electronic toys. VTech collected personal information of children under 13 but failed to provide direct notice of its information collection and use practices to parents in each area where the information was collected. In addition, the FTC charged that the company failed to take reasonable steps to protect the information it collected, such as implementing adequate safeguards and security measures to protect transmitted and stored information, and implementing an intrusion prevention or detection system to alert the company of a hack.

Personal information under COPPA includes (1) first and last name, (2) home or other physical address including street name and name of city or town, (3) online contact information like an e-mail address or other identifier that permits someone to contact a person directly, (4) a screen or user name when it functions as an identifier, (5) a telephone number, (6) Social Security number, (7) a persistent identifier that can be used to recognize a user over time and across different sites, including a cookie number, (8) a photograph, video, or audio file of a child, (9) geolocation information sufficient to identify street and city, and (10) information concerning the child or child's parents that can be combined with other information.[34]

A person whose actions are within the scope of COPPA, called an "operator," must post a clear and comprehensive privacy policy that describes how the information is collected and used.[35] The operator must also obtain verifiable parental consent prior to collecting, using, or disclosing a child's personal information.[36] An operator must make reasonable efforts, taking into account available technology, to ensure that the parent receives direct notice concerning the collection, use, or disclosure practices to which the parent consents.[37] A parent has the right to review the information collected, such as name, address, telephone number, e-mail address, hobbies, and extracurricular activities.[38] The operator must "establish and maintain reasonable procedures to protect the confidentiality, security, and integrity of personal information collected from children."[39]

As with the laws relating to biometric data, a cloud agreement involving data governed by COPPA should contain all of the best-practice provisions detailed in Parts III and IV. A key provision in particular to include is a description of what constitutes "personal information" as defined under COPPA. This meets the best-practice requirement for transparency and communication between the cloud provider and the cloud customer regarding the exact data that must be kept confidential. Moreover, a cloud agreement involving data governed by COPPA must include a provision relating to access of and restrictions to use of the data because parents have the right to review the data collected about their children and also to prohibit the disclosure of such data to third parties.

---

33 No. 18-cv-114, 2018 WL 317978 (N.D. Ill. Jan. 8, 2018).
34 16 C.F.R. § 312.2.
35 *Id.* § 312.4(d).
36 *Id.* § 312.5(a)(1).
37 *Id.* § 312.5(b)(1).
38 *Id.* § 312.6(a).
39 *Id.* § 312.8.

3. Gramm-Leach-Bliley Act

The Gramm-Leach-Bliley Act protects disclosure of "nonpublic personal information" of customers and consumers of financial institutions via the FTC's Privacy of Consumer Financial Information Rule.[40] The FTC has also published standards for safeguarding consumer information, including data on the cloud (Privacy Rules).[41]

The Privacy Rules cover entities that are "significantly engaged" in "financial activities," which are defined in section 4(k) of the Bank Holding Company Act.[42] These activities include lending; exchanging; transferring; investing for others; providing financial, investment, or economic advisory services; brokering loans; servicing loans; debt collection; providing real estate settlement services; and career counseling.[43] "Nonpublic personal information" includes any information an individual provides for a financial product or service (name, address, income, Social Security number, or other information on an application).[44] The act requires that a privacy notice be given to consumers and customers.

The standards for safeguarding consumer information apply to anyone handling nonpublic personal information regardless of whether the entity has a relationship with the customer, merely receives the information from another financial institution, or is handling or maintaining the information on behalf of a financial institution. It also covers a "service provider" that "receives, maintains, processes, or otherwise is permitted access to customer information through its provision of services directly to a financial institution" covered by the rule,[45] including cloud-based providers. The rule requires development, implementation, and maintenance of a "comprehensive information security program."[46]

The elements of the security program include overseeing service providers by (1) taking reasonable steps to select and retain service providers that are capable of maintaining appropriate safeguards for the customer information, (2) requiring the service providers by contract to implement and maintain such safeguards, and (3) evaluating and adjusting the security program in light of results and testing and monitoring via risk assessment the key controls, systems, and procedures.[47]

A cloud customer moving financial information to a cloud provider should choose a provider with experience in the financial industry, given the heavy regulatory requirements. The cloud agreement ultimately must contractually obligate the cloud provider to implement and maintain high-level safeguards for customer information. Moreover, the cloud agreement must include a provision requiring the cloud provider to continually evaluate and adjust the security program as needed. The cloud agreement should also contain the best-practice provisions described in Parts III and IV.

---

40 16 C.F.R. pt. 313.

41 16 C.F.R. pt. 314.

42 16 C.F.R. § 313.3(k)(1) (citing the Bank Holding Company Act, 12 U.S.C. § 1843(k)).

43 12 U.S.C. § 1843(k)(4).

44 16 C.F.R. § 313.3(n).

45 *Id.* § 314.2(d).

46 *Id.* § 314.3(a).

47 *Id.* § 314.4.

4. HIPAA and HITECH

The Health Insurance Portability and Accountability Act (HIPAA),[48] as expanded by the Health Information Technology for Economic and Clinical Health Act (HITECH),[49] protects personally identifiable health information (PHI) by imposing regulations on its disclosure by covered entities and their business associates. HIPAA is discussed in more detail in Chapter 7. HIPAA-covered entities and business associates are moving PHI to cloud solutions and in fact are mandated by HITECH to digitize and electronically share information with patients and doctors. The cloud service providers engaged by either covered entities or their business associates to create, maintain, or transmit PHI are business associates themselves under HITECH and must comply with HIPAA regulations regardless of the cloud solution provided. In particular, a cloud customer that is required to comply with HIPAA must contractually obligate a cloud provider to: conduct risk analysis and risk management;[50] implement written privacy and security policies and procedures;[51] designate a privacy official responsible for developing and implementing privacy policies and procedures;[52] provide workforce training;[53] maintain data safeguards;[54] and notify individuals when there is a breach of PHI.[55] Moreover, the cloud agreement must specify that the cloud service provider may use and disclose PHI only as permitted by a business associate agreement and HIPAA privacy rules, or as otherwise required by law.[56]

5. The General Data Protection Regulation

Although not a U.S. law, the European Union's General Data Protection Regulation (GDPR)[57] may be applicable to entities located in the United States. The GDPR applies to companies established anywhere in the world that offer goods or services to European Union residents or that monitor the activities of people located in the EU.[58] The regulation imposes stringent requirements on the handling of "personal data," a term that is broadly defined.[59] Applicability of the GDPR to cloud services is addressed in Chapters 10 and 11.

6. Family Educational Rights and Privacy Act

The Family Educational Rights and Privacy Act protects the privacy of student education records.[60] "Education records" are records that are: (1) directly related to a student; and

---

48 Pub. L. No. 104-191 (1996) (codified as amended in scattered sections of 29 U.S.C.).
49 Pub. L. No. 111–5, tit. XIII (2009).
50 45 C.F.R. § 164.308(a).
51 *Id.* §§ 164.316, 164.530(i).
52 *Id.* § 164.530(a).
53 *Id.* § 164.530(b)(1).
54 *Id.* § 164.530(c).
55 42 U.S.C. § 17932.
56 45 C.F.R. § 164.504.
57 Regulation (EU) 2016/679 of the European Parliament and of the Council of 27 April 2016 on the protection of natural persons with regard to the processing of personal data and on the free movement of such data, and repealing Directive 95/46/EC (General Data Protection Regulation), 2016 O.J. (L 119) 1.
58 *Id.* art. 3(2).
59 *Id.* art. 4(1).
60 20 U.S.C. § 1232g.

(2) maintained by an educational agency or institution, or by a party acting for the agency or institution.[61] It applies to all schools receiving funds from the U.S. Department of Education.

　　If the storage or maintenance of the records is in the cloud, the provider may be considered a "school official" so that it may store or maintain the records. The educational institution must ensure that the provider uses "reasonable methods" to control access to the records.[62] The cloud agreement must therefore include provisions contractually obligating the cloud provider to restrict access to the records to only authorized parties. The agreement should also contain the best-practice provisions set out in Parts III and IV.

7. California Consumer Privacy Act

In 2018, California adopted the California Consumer Privacy Act (CalCPA),[63] which finds that the "unauthorized disclosure of personal information and the loss of privacy can have devastating effects for individuals, ranging from financial fraud, identity theft, and unnecessary costs to personal time and finances, to destruction of property, harassment, reputational damage, emotional stress, and even potential physical harm."[64] Consumers have the right to request a copy of their personal information and to have the information deleted; thus, contractual provisions relating to ownership and access to the data are key. PII under CalCPA is defined broadly as any "information that identifies, relates to, describes, is capable of being associated with, or could reasonably be linked, directly or indirectly, with a particular consumer or household."[65]

8. State Breach Notification Laws

Most of the laws listed above have provisions regarding notice to individuals whose PII has been exposed as the result of a breach. In addition, all 50 states have individual breach notification laws. The definition of what constitutes a breach varies by state, as do the timeframes for sending the notice, the content of the notice, and any exemptions from the notice requirements.[66] Given that a cloud customer could hold PII of individuals in any number of states, a cloud agreement should generally require that if a breach occurs, the cloud provider is obligated to promptly inform the cloud customer directly, and that the cloud customer will have exclusive control over the procedures for notification to data subjects under any applicable breach notification law, including timing, method, and content of such notifications. Moreover, the parties may include in the cloud agreement that if the cloud provider is responsible for the breach, it must reimburse the cloud customer for reasonable costs incurred by the cloud customer in providing the notification to the data subjects.

61　*Id.* § 1232g(a)(4).
62　34 C.F.R. § 99.31.
63　Cal. Civ. Code § 1798.100–.199.
64　California Consumer Privacy Act § 2(f).
65　Cal. Civ. Code § 1798.140(o).
66　A state-by-state listing of breach laws is available at http://www.ncsl.org/research/telecommunications-and-information-technology/security-breach-notification-laws.aspx.

III. Summary of Best Practices for Cloud Privacy and Security Compliance

Navigation of U.S. privacy laws is complex, but failure to protect customer information may have disastrous consequences. A breach of private information may violate federal and state laws that protect privacy, and may require costly notifications to customers. This cost is in addition to the costs of responding to and remedying the breach. Additionally, a breach may severely damage a company's reputation.

When third parties perform some, if not all, of the services previously provided in-house, privacy policies and practices must be included in the third-party contracts and terms of service because there are differences in how data is handled by each cloud-based provider.

A crucial step toward compliance with U.S. privacy and data security laws is the attorney's review of the potential cloud service provider's contract. Attorneys must understand the privacy and security provisions in cloud agreements—whether expressed in individually negotiated contracts or standard terms of service. If the necessary provisions are not in the agreements offered by the cloud service provider, then the contracting attorney should add such provisions.

The provisions below provide a summary of some of the best practices today for cloud privacy and security compliance.[67] Of course, protecting privacy in the cloud is a dynamic process; today's adequate protections are tomorrow's inadequate safeguards. The summary is not exhaustive, and an attorney should consider the facts and circumstances of each cloud customer to determine which provisions may (or may not) be necessary.

Generally, attorneys reviewing a cloud agreement should look for, and if needed, negotiate for, the following provisions:

A. Compliance with Privacy and Security Standards Set by the Cloud Customer

- The cloud provider must comply with all laws, regulations, and industry standards relating to both privacy and security that are applicable to the cloud customer's data.
  - In this connection, transparency and clarity are key. Legal obligations and responsibilities may be understood or interpreted differently between the parties. The cloud agreement should therefore include specific and detailed information regarding the cloud provider's obligations to protect the cloud customer's data under applicable laws, regulations, and standards. The agreement should further provide that the obligations are subject to change, and that the cloud customer has the right to update the obligations as needed.

---

67 MANAGING PRIVACY AND DATA SECURITY RISKS IN VENDOR RELATIONSHIPS, Practical Law Practice Note w-001-8814, Practical Law Intellectual Prop. & Tech.; Edward R. McNicholas, William RM Long, Yuet Ming Tham, Mark L. Kaufmann & Colleen T. Brown, *Privacy and Security Issues in Cloud Computing*, Part V(B), CONTRACTING WITH CLOUD VENDORS 515 (Privacy & Data Security Practice Portfolio Series (Bloomberg Law)); Michael R. Overly, *Drafting and Negotiating Effective Cloud Computing Agreements*, LEXIS PRACTICE ADVISOR J. 56 (2015), https://www.lexisnexis.com/lexis-practice-advisor/the-journal/b/lpa/archive/2015/11/30/drafting-and-negotiating-effective-cloud-computing-agreements.aspx.

- The cloud provider must comply with requirements set out in a cloud customer's privacy policy, which may be attached to as an exhibit to, and made part of, the agreement.
  - o Ideally, a company should have in place a robust privacy policy even before considering a cloud-based data solution. However, policies developed for in-house hosted data, although a good starting point, may not be sufficient for the cloud. When moving to the cloud from an in-house hosted environment, existing privacy policies should be reviewed to determine whether the policies should be strengthened or modified before they are transmitted to the cloud provider.
  - o As with provisions relating to the cloud provider's compliance with laws, regulations, and industry standards, the cloud agreement should provide that the cloud customer's privacy policy is subject to change and that the cloud customer has the right to update the policy (and thus, the cloud provider's obligations) as needed.

B. Use and Disclosure of Data

- The cloud provider may access and use the data only to the extent strictly necessary to perform the services agreed upon in the contract.
- The cloud provider is prohibited from disclosing the cloud customer's data to any third party (including subcontractors) unless specifically authorized in writing in advance by the cloud customer.
- The cloud provider is obligated to inform its subcontractors and service providers of the privacy and security obligations to which it is subject, and must require them in writing to meet those same obligations. The provider must agree to be legally responsible for compliance by such third parties.

C. Ownership of and Access to Data

- The cloud agreement must explicitly acknowledge the cloud customer's ownership of the data.
  - o This provision will permit a cloud customer to avoid any disputes as to ownership of data in the event that the data subject requests the return of his or her data under applicable laws.
  - o The attorney should carefully review the cloud provider's agreement for any language that might grant license rights or other interests in the data to the cloud provider.
- The cloud agreement should acknowledge and address data subjects' rights to access data.
  - o This is crucial under COPPA. Additionally, in light of the GDPR, the trend is to allow data subjects the right to review and delete their PII. Cloud agreements need to specify how the data is kept, and how individual data may be tracked and retrieved, and, if necessary, deleted at the data subject's request.

- The cloud provider agrees to return or destroy, at the cloud customer's request, or upon a date specified in the contract (but at a minimum upon termination of the agreement), all copies of the cloud customer's data.
- The cloud agreement should specifically provide that the cloud customer shall be in full control of the data, and shall have the right to specify how it is used and with whom it may be shared.

D. Reporting, Allocation of Responsibilities, and General Monitoring

- The cloud agreement should address the cloud provider's responsibilities for reporting security incidents to the cloud customer.
  - o Even if a security incident does not rise to the level of a data breach under the various applicable state laws, the cloud customer should be informed of any issues to ensure that security requirements in the cloud contract are being satisfied.
- The cloud provider should be obligated to notify the cloud customer immediately of any known or suspected data breaches and cooperate with the cloud customer to allow the cloud customer to meet its data breach notification responsibilities under applicable laws.
- The cloud agreement should include provisions relating to allocation of responsibilities between the cloud provider and cloud customer for handling data breaches, and for any related costs, such as the cost of notifying data subjects, as well as for any related liabilities.
- The cloud agreement should include a provision permitting the cloud customer to periodically perform audits of the cloud provider's practices relating to privacy and security of the cloud customer's data. Such audits may be conducted either (1) directly by the cloud customer or its contractors; (2) through self-assessment and self-certification by the cloud provider; (3) by independent third-party audits or certifications; or (4) a combination of these methods.
- The cloud agreement should include specific details relating to the cloud provider's security processes, practices, and procedures.

IV. Additional Security Considerations for Cloud Agreements

As the previous sections addressed, privacy should not be an afterthought but rather must be designed into a company's cloud presence from the beginning. Privacy goes hand-in-hand with security because a company's data cannot remain private if it is not secure. This part provides a summary of additional considerations relating specifically to data security in the cloud.

PII must be protected from unauthorized disclosure or hacking regardless of whether it is located on a company's private server or in the cloud. A key question to consider before moving PII to the cloud is, "Does the cloud offer the same or greater security to protect PII as an in-house solution?"

A. Data Transmission

Data must be transmitted from the source to the cloud environment. The transmission may be directly to the intended cloud server or it may be temporarily stored in transit as it passes through other servers. The agreement should specify whether the company is connecting to the cloud via a secured network, a virtual private network, or TLS/SSL security. When data is "in transit," it must be protected from being hacked, diverted, or altered. Encryption is one way to protect the data. A cloud agreement should include provisions as to which encryption method will be used. (The data should remain encrypted after it is stored.) Encrypted data is accessed via an encryption key. The agreement should detail who has access to the key and explain under what circumstances the key will be provided to others, including law enforcement.

B. Storing Data in the Cloud

The cloud offers the potential for unlimited storage of data. This data is stored at massive server facilities, or farms. Providers might state that the facilities are protected by fences, alarm systems, limited physical access, and the like. It is important to know what physical security protects the cloud servers, but physical security is only a small part of guarding data. Data breaches occur more often than not by hacking and online intrusion, and not infrequently hackers may have access to a system undetected for months downloading data. A cloud contract should include representations as to physical security as well as internet security. For example, the contract should specify which security standard the cloud provider builds into its system. The Cloud Security Alliance maintains a Security, Trust and Assurance Registry,[68] which permits customers to compare the security compliance of various cloud providers, so it is important to know how the cloud provider scores.

C. Location of the Data

For cloud-based solutions, data normally will be in more than one location. A cloud agreement should identify where the data will primarily be housed and explain where the backup or failover servers are located, including which country or countries. If the data is stored in another country, the company should know what access the foreign government may have to the data. For example, some non-U.S. entities do not want their data stored or mirrored in the United States because the data may be subject to a U.S. national security letter or other subpoena. Likewise, if a U.S.-based entity obtains personal information about a resident of the European Union, the entity will have to take additional measures to comply with the GDPR. The Canadian Personal Information Protection and Electronic Documents Act requires adequate contractual and security measures be in place for personal data of Canadians processed and stored outside Canada.

---

68 *See CSA STAR: The Future of Cloud Trust and Assurance*, Cloud Security Alliance, https://cloudsecurityalliance.org/star.

D. Access to the Data

A cloud agreement also should address the issue of who has access to the data residing in the cloud. If the agreement specifically authorizes the cloud provider to give access to sub-contractors, then there must be restrictions on the access. Is the shared access solely for processing the data? Does the cloud provider collect and track usage patterns? If so, the agreement should specify what data may be collected and to whom the data are given. All contacts should contain some language regarding access to the data in response to a lawful subpoena or other law enforcement request. The language should not be too vague. For example, language that the data are provided pursuant to a governmental request is not sufficient. The cloud provider should be required to give the company adequate notice of a request to turn over data and give the company an opportunity to contest the request.[69]

E. Type of Cloud Structure

A company should be aware of the type of cloud used to house the data because it can affect the level of security. In a public cloud, a company shares the server on which its data is stored with other companies, whereas in a private cloud, data resides only on a dedicated infrastructure. A community cloud is a private cloud shared by a group of companies with similar interests. Finally, a hybrid cloud is a private cloud that has links to a public cloud. Unless the company knows which cloud structure is used, it is difficult to implement appropriate privacy and security safeguards.

F. Rights Management

Rights management is both a company and cloud provider function that should be detailed in a cloud agreement. Rights management defines who can open, modify, print, forward, or take other action with the data in the cloud. It should specify whether two-factor authentication is required, set the password strength and parameters, and include a requirement to change passwords on a regular basis. The cloud agreement should explain the credential revocation process and time required to revoke access. A good rights-management protocol also includes detailed logs to review who may access the data and when.

V. Conclusion

In summary, an attorney should remember that moving a company's data to the cloud does not relieve the company of its obligations to protect PII and to comply with applicable statutes and regulations. The cloud agreement should include provisions to ensure that these obligations are met.

---

69 Of course, if the request is pursuant to a national security letter, the cloud provider is prevented from providing any notice or even acknowledging to the company that such a request for its data has been made.

Chapter 5

Legal Obligations and Best Practices for Maintaining Security in the Cloud

By William R. Denny[1]

In today's business environment, companies often rely on cloud service providers to handle much of their data. Although the use of cloud computing provides the business with tremendous economic benefits, including reduced costs and increased productivity, it also creates significant potential vulnerabilities that can adversely affect the business, its customers, and other entities with whom it interacts. When company or customer data is in the possession or under the control of a third party, this presents special security challenges. Thus, it is important to address the security of the company's data in the possession of such third parties.

When discussing cybersecurity risks anticipated in 2019, Deloitte's chief of risk and financial advisory practice noted that third-party partners can introduce security flaws and risks into your organization, and company leaders must manage these risks. A majority of CEOs do not hold their extended enterprise to the same security standards as their own organizations, Deloitte research found.[2]

To that end, laws and regulations imposing information security obligations on businesses often expressly extend those risk management practices to the use of cloud providers. Such rules and regulations make clear that, regardless of who performs the work, the legal obligation to provide the security itself remains with the business. As it is often said, "you can outsource the work, but not the responsibility." Thus, cloud relationships should be subject to the same risk management, security, privacy, and other protection policies that would be expected if a company were conducting the activities directly.[3]

To limit the risk of unauthorized access, use, disclosure, alteration, loss, or destruction of data in the cloud, businesses must consider cloud providers as part of their own enterprise risk management. Generally, the legal standard for security imposes three basic requirements on businesses that give cloud providers access to their data: (1) they must exercise due diligence in selecting service providers, (2) they must contractually require outsource providers to implement appropriate security measures, and (3) they must monitor the performance of the outsource providers.[4] Cloud service providers, in turn, must establish and implement their own information security program in compliance with industry standards and with the laws and regulations that apply to them as well as to their

---

1 Partner, Potter Anderson Corroon LLP, denny@potteranderson.com. This chapter is adapted from Thomas J. Smedinghoff & Ruth Hill Bro, *Chapter 4: Lawyers' Legal Obligations to Provide Data Security* to Jill D. Rhodes & Robert S. Litt, The ABA Cybersecurity Handbook: A Resource for Attorneys, Law firms and Business Professionals (2d ed. 2018), with the generous permission of the authors.

2 Tech Republic, *7 Tips for CXOs to Combat Cybersecurity Risks in 2019 and Beyond*, Dec. 7, 2018, https://www.techrepublic.com/article/7-tips-for-cxos-to-combat-cybersecurity-risks-in-2019-and-beyond/.

3 *See, e.g.*, Mass. Standards for the Protection of Personal Info., 201 Mass. Code Regs. 17.02(2)(f).

4 *Id.*

customers. This chapter will provide an overview of the legal obligations with which businesses, and by extension their cloud providers, must comply.

I. Overview

A. What Is Data Security?

The concept of "security" refers to an entity's implementation and maintenance of security controls to protect one or more of its assets (such as buildings, equipment, cargo, inventory, and people) from threats. Information security (also referred to as cyber security or data security) involves the implementation of security controls to protect a business's digital assets. It has been generally described as "the protection of *information and information systems* from unauthorized access, use, disclosure, disruption, modification, or destruction in order to provide confidentiality, integrity, and availability."[5] Thus, information security involves the protection of both (1) information systems—that is, computer systems, networks, and software and (2) the electronic records, data, messages, and other information that are typically recorded on, processed by, communicated via, stored in, shared by, or received from such information systems.

The objectives of using security measures can be defined in terms of either the positive results to be achieved or the negative consequences to be avoided. The positive results to be achieved are typically described as ensuring the *confidentiality, integrity,* and *availability* of information.[6] The harms to be avoided, as noted above, are often described as unauthorized access, use, disclosure, disruption, modification, or destruction.[7]

Achieving these objectives involves implementing security measures designed to protect systems and information from the various threats they face and ensuring that cloud service providers and other vendors with access to confidential data do the same. The kinds of threats, where they come from, the nature of the risk, and the seriousness of the consequences will, of course, vary greatly from case to case, but responding to the threats a business faces with appropriate security measures is the focus of the duty to provide security.

Measures designed to protect the security of information systems and data are generally grouped into the following three categories (based on the nature of the control):

- **Physical security controls.** These security measures are designed to protect the tangible items that comprise the physical computer systems, networks, and storage devices that process, communicate, and store the data, including servers, devices used to access the system, storage devices, and the like. Physical security controls are intended to prevent unauthorized persons from entering that environment and to help protect against natural disasters. One regulation defines physical safeguards as "physical measures, policies, and procedures to protect a

---

5   NIST, NISTIR 7298, Rev. 2, Glossary of Key Information Security Terms 94 (May 2013) (definition of "information security") (emphasis added). *See also* Federal Information Security Management Act (FISMA), 44 U.S.C. § 3542(b)(1) (definition of "information security").

6   *See, e.g.,* FISMA, 44 U.S.C. § 3542(b)(1); Health Insurance Portability and Accountability Act of 1996 (HIPAA) Security Regulations, 45 C.F.R. § 164.306(a)(1).

7   *See supra* note 5.

covered entity's or business associate's electronic information systems and related buildings and equipment, from natural and environmental hazards, and unauthorized intrusion."[8] Examples of physical security controls include fences, walls, and other barriers; locks, safes, and vaults; armed guards; sensors; and alarm bells.

- **Technical security controls.** These security measures typically involve the use of software and data safeguards incorporated into computer hardware, software, and related devices. These measures are designed to ensure system availability, control access to systems and information, authenticate persons seeking access, protect the integrity of information communicated via, and stored on, the system, and ensure confidentiality where appropriate. Examples include firewalls, intrusion detection software, access control software, antivirus software, passwords, PIN numbers, smart cards, biometric tokens, and encryption processes.

- **Administrative security controls.** Sometimes referred to as "procedural" or "organizational" controls, these security measures consist of written policies, procedures, standards, guidelines, and supplemental administrative controls to guide conduct, prevent unauthorized access, and provide an acceptable level of protection for computing resources and data. Administrative security measures frequently include personnel management, employee use policies, training, discipline, and informing people how to conduct day-to-day operations.

Within each of these three categories, security measures are further classified into the following three separate categories (based on their timing regarding the risks and threats they are designed to address):

- **Preventive** security measures are designed to prevent the occurrence of events that compromise security. Examples include a lock on a door (to prevent access to a room containing computer equipment) or a firewall (to prevent unauthorized online access to a computer system).

- **Detective** security measures are designed to identify security breaches after they have occurred. Examples include a smoke alarm (to detect a fire) or intrusion detection software (to detect and track unauthorized online access to a computer system).

- **Reactive** security measures are designed to respond to a security breach and typically include efforts to stop or contain the breach, identify the party or parties involved, and allow recovery of information that is lost or damaged. Examples include calling the police (after an alarm detects that a burglary is in process) or shutting down a computer system (after intrusion detection software determines that an unauthorized user has obtained access to the system).

B. Security Law: The Basic Security Obligations

Concerns about individual privacy, accountability for financial information, the authenticity and integrity of transaction data, and the need to protect the confidentiality and security of sensitive business and customer data are driving the enactment of new laws and

---

8   HIPAA Security Regulations, 45 C.F.R. § 164.304.

regulations designed to ensure that all businesses adequately address the security of the data in their possession or under their control, including data in the hands of their cloud service providers. Taken as a group, those laws and regulations impose two fundamental obligations on most businesses:

- the duty to provide security for their data; and
- the duty to warn of security breaches that occur.

The thesis of this chapter is that all businesses, whether regulated or not, are generally subject to these legal duties regarding the security of the data in their possession or under their control. The following sections explain the source and scope of those duties.

II. The Duty to Provide Data Security

A. What Is the Duty?

The law often simply refers to the basic legal duty to provide data security as an obligation to implement "reasonable" or "appropriate" security measures designed to achieve the security objectives noted above (i.e., to ensure the *confidentiality*, *integrity*, and *availability* of information). For example, several state security laws, such as in California, generally impose a duty to implement "*reasonable* security procedures and practices."[9] At the federal level, the Health Insurance Portability and Accountability Act of 1996 (HIPAA) requires "*reasonable and appropriate*" security,[10] and the Gramm-Leach-Bliley (GLB) security regulations require security "*appropriate* to the size and complexity of the bank and the nature and scope of its activities."[11]

The focus on the reasonableness or appropriateness of security makes clear that the law recognizes that security is a relative concept: what qualifies as reasonable or appropriate security varies with the situation. Thus, the law typically provides little or no guidance on what specific security measures are required or on how much security a business should implement to satisfy those legal obligations. Although some laws include specific requirements for particular security measures that must be implemented,[12] the laws generally provide no safe harbors. Accordingly, the choice of security measures and technology can vary depending on the situation.

One exception is Ohio, which passed the first data security law in the United States that provides a limited safe harbor against liability for those who comply with the law.[13] Effective as of November 2018, it applies to businesses that process personal information. The law requires that organizations implement safeguards, which shall be determined

---

9   Cal. Civ. Code § 1798.81.5(b) (emphasis added).

10 42 U.S.C. § 1320d-2(d)(2) (emphasis added).

11 12 C.F.R. pt. 208, app. D-2, pt. II.A (Federal Reserve System) (emphasis added). *See also* other GLB-implementing security regulations: 12 C.F.R. pt. 30, app. B, pt. II.A (OCC); 12 C.F.R. pt. 364, app. B, pt. II.A. (FDIC); and 16 C.F.R. § 314.3(a) (FTC) (adding "sensitivity of any customer information at issue" to the other factors in determining what is "appropriate").

12 For example, the Massachusetts security regulations require implementation of firewalls, the use of virus software, and in certain cases, the use of encryption. *See* 201 Mass. Code Regs.

13 Ohio Data Protection Act, S. 220 (2018).

based on the sensitivity of the data retained and the size and complexity of the business. For those businesses that implement one of 10 industry-recognized cybersecurity frameworks, it provides an affirmative defense from civil liability for tort claims brought under Ohio law or in Ohio courts alleging that failure to implement reasonable security resulted in a data breach.[14]

B. To Whom Does the Duty Apply?

The duty to provide security applies generally to all businesses. Certain sectors of the U.S. economy are, of course, subject to extensive regulations regarding data security. The most obvious examples are the financial sector,[15] the healthcare sector,[16] the federal government sector,[17] and other critical infrastructure sectors.[18] However, there also is no doubt that nonregulated businesses are subject to data security obligations.

One need look no further than the last 18 years of Federal Trade Commission (FTC) enforcement actions, as well as recent state attorneys general enforcement actions, to see that numerous, nonregulated businesses have been targeted for failing to provide appropriate data security for their own data. Examples include software vendors (Oracle, Microsoft, Guidance Software), consumer electronics companies (ASUS, TRENDnet, HTC America, Genica/Computer Geeks), mobile app developers (Snapchat, Fandango, Credit Karma), clothing/shoe retailers (Guess, Life is Good, DSW), music retailers (Tower Records), animal supply retailers (Petco), general merchandise stores (Target, BJ's Wholesale, TJX Companies), restaurant and entertainment establishments (Dave & Busters, Briar Group), social media and networking sites (Twitter, Facebook, and Ashley Madison), transcription services (GMR), bookstores (Barnes & Noble), property management firms (Maloney Properties, Inc.), and hotels (Wyndham).[19]

In addition to the federal- and state-level unfair or deceptive trade practice statutes that often support these enforcement actions, many state security laws and regulations expressly apply to "any business" or "any person" that maintains certain types of data.

Moreover, as discussed below, many sector-specific security regulations may be imposed on cloud service providers through their customer relationships. For example, the HIPAA regulations in the health care sector and the GLB regulations in the financial sector both require that entities governed by those regulations push down certain security obligations to their service providers who access the protected data. In addition, the HIPAA regulations have been revised to impose security obligations directly on "covered entities" providing services to healthcare companies.

---

14 *Id.*

15 Subject to GLB, Pub. L. No. 106-102, §§ 501 and 505(b), 15 U.S.C. §§ 6801, 6805, and implementing security regulations; *see supra* note 11.

16 Subject to HIPAA, 42 U.S.C. § 1320d-2, and HIPAA Security Regulations, 45 C.F.R. pt. 164.

17 Subject to FISMA, 44 U.S.C. §§ 3541–3549.

18 *See* Exec. Order No. 13,636, Improving Critical Infrastructure Cybersecurity, 78 Fed. Reg. 11,739 (Feb. 19, 2013), *available at* https://www.whitehouse.gov/the-press-office/2013/02/12/executive-order-improving-critical-infrastructure-cybersecurity.

19 *See, e.g.*, FTC, Data Security, https://www.ftc.gov/datasecurity (for list of all FTC data security cases and enforcement actions); May 2017 state attorney general settlement agreement with Target Corp., http://www.illinoisattorneygeneral.gov/pressroom/2017_05/17-AVC-0008TargetCorporation.pdf.

C. What Is the Source of the Duty?

There is no single law, statute, or regulation that governs the obligations of a business to provide security for the information in its possession or under its control. Instead, legal obligations to implement data security measures are found in an ever-expanding patchwork of state, federal, and international laws, regulations, and enforcement actions, as well as in common-law duties and other express and implied obligations to provide "reasonable" or "appropriate" security for business data.

Some laws seek to protect the business and its owners, shareholders, investors, and business partners. Other laws focus on the interests of employees, customers, and prospects. In some cases, governmental regulatory interests or evidentiary requirements are at stake. Many of the requirements are industry-specific (e.g., focused on the financial sector or the healthcare sector) or data-specific (e.g., focused on personal information or financial data). Some laws focus only on public companies.

When viewed as a group, however, such laws and regulations provide ever-expanding coverage of most business activity. The most common sources of obligations to provide security include the following:

Statutes and regulations.[20] Numerous statutes and regulations impose obligations to provide data security. Sometimes they use recognizable terms such as "security" or "safeguards," but in many cases they are subtler by using attributes of security, such as "authenticate," "integrity," "confidentiality," "availability of data," and the like. Such statutes and regulations include the following:

- Privacy laws and regulations, which typically include provisions governing the security of the personal data covered by the applicable law.
- Security laws and regulations, such as the state-level security laws that impose a general obligation on businesses to protect the security of certain personal data they maintain about individuals and/or that regulate the communication or destruction of certain data;
- E-transaction laws, which are designed to ensure the enforceability and compliance of electronic documents generally;
- Corporate governance legislation and regulations, which are designed to protect public companies and their shareholders, investors, and business partners;
- Unfair business practice laws at both the federal and state level, and precedent set by related government enforcement actions; and
- Sector-specific regulations, such as the HIPAA security regulations and the GLB Safeguard Rules, which impose security obligations regarding specific data in the healthcare and financial sectors respectively.

Common-law obligations.[21] Commentators have argued for years that there is a common-law duty to provide appropriate security for corporate and personal data, the breach of which constitutes a tort. Courts are beginning to accept that view. In one case,

---

20 See Appendices A (Federal Statutes), B (State Statutes), C (Federal Regulations), and D (State Regulations) to this chapter for examples of such statutes and regulations. See also Appendices H (CFPB Decision and Consent Decree), I (FTC Decisions and Consent Decrees), and J (SEC Decision and Consent Decree) for government enforcement actions under certain statutes and regulations.

21 See, e.g., selected cases listed in Appendix G (Court Decisions Re: Duty to Provide Data Security) to this chapter.

for example, the court held that "defendant did owe plaintiffs a duty to protect them from identity theft by providing some safeguards to ensure the security of their most essential confidential identifying information."[22] In another case, the court allowed plaintiffs to proceed on a "negligent misrepresentation" claim based on the theory that the defendants made implied representations that they had implemented the security measures required by industry practice to safeguard personal and financial information.[23]

Rules of evidence. Providing appropriate security to ensure the integrity of electronic records (and the identity of the creator, sender, or signer of the record) can be critical to securing the admission of an electronic record in evidence in a dispute. This conclusion is supported by the form requirement for an "original" in electronic transaction laws,[24] the evidence rules regarding authentication,[25] and case law addressing evidentiary authentication requirements.[26]

Contractual obligations. Businesses frequently try to satisfy (at least in part) their obligation to protect data by entering contracts with third parties who will possess, or have access to, their business data. This is particularly common in cloud service agreements where the data will be processed by a third party. Several laws, such as the generally applicable Massachusetts data security regulations[27] or the financial sector's GLB Safeguard Rules, mandate that the business impose appropriate security obligations on the third party with access to its data. In other cases, businesses must comply with the requirements of certain technical security standards. Examples include the Payment Card Industry Data Security Standard (PCI Standard),[28] to which merchants must agree as a condition of accepting credit cards.

Self-imposed obligations. In many cases, security obligations are self-imposed. Through statements in privacy notices, on websites, in advertising materials, or elsewhere, businesses often make representations regarding the level of security they provide for their data (particularly personal data collected from persons to whom the statements are made). By making such statements, businesses impose on themselves an obligation to comply with the standard they have told the public that they meet. If those statements are not true or are misleading, they may become deceptive trade practices under section 5 of the FTC Act or equivalent state laws.

Obligations pushed to cloud service providers from customers. In some cases, data security laws and regulations do not apply directly to cloud service providers, but might apply indirectly (e.g., because of the cloud service providers' customers who themselves are subject to certain sector-specific security regulations). Such regulations frequently

---

22 Bell v. Mich. Council, 205 Mich. App. LEXIS 353, at *16 (Mich. App. Feb. 15, 2005).

23 *In re* TJX Cos. Retail Sec. Breach Litig., 524 F. Supp. 2d 83 (D. Mass. 2007).

24 *See, e.g.*, Unif. Electronic Transactions Act (UETA) § 12(d), *available at* http://www.uniformlaws.org/shared/docs/electronic%20transactions/ueta_final_99.pdf; Electronic Signatures in Global and National Commerce Act (E-SIGN) 15 U.S.C. § 7001(d)(3), *available at* https://www.gpo.gov/fdsys/pkg/PLAW-106publ229/pdf/PLAW-106publ229.pdf.

25 *See, e.g.*, Fed. R. Evid. 901(a).

26 *See, e.g.*, Am. Express v. Vinhnee, 336 B.R. 437 (B.A.P. 9th Cir. 2005); Lorraine v. Markel, 241 F.R.D. 534 (D. Md. May 4, 2007).

27 Standards for the Protection of Personal Information of Residents of the Commonwealth, 201 Mass. Code Regs. 17.00 *et seq.* (2012) [hereinafter Mass. Standards for the Protection of Personal Info], *available at* http://www.mass.gov/ocabr/docs/idtheft/201cmr1700reg.pdf.

28 *See* PCI Sec. Standards Council, https://www.pcisecuritystandards.org.

impose on covered businesses an obligation to push certain security requirements to third parties with whom they do business or who otherwise are involved in processing their data. This approach is increasingly becoming a source of data security obligations for cloud service providers. For example, a cloud service provider must comply with security requirements imposed on its financial or health care sector customers where those requirements must be passed down to the cloud service provider. In many such cases, customer requirements to satisfy certain security regulations motivate customer audits of cloud service provider security measures.

Thus, the duty of any business to provide security may come from several different sources and several different jurisdictions—each perhaps regulating a different aspect of the business's information—but the net result is a general obligation to provide security for all business data and information systems. In other words, information security is not just good business practice; it is a legal obligation.

D. What Data Is Covered?

All types of business information should be protected by appropriate security when in the possession of cloud service providers, including financial information, personal information, tax-related records, employee information, transaction information, information obtained from or produced for customers, litigation information (including what is obtained in discovery), and other confidential information.

When examining particular security laws that may apply to a business, it is important to note that such laws and regulations will frequently focus on a certain category of information. Commonly addressed categories include the following:

- **Personal data.** The obligation to provide adequate security for personal data collected, used, communicated, or stored by a business is a critical component of all privacy laws as well as sector-specific privacy regulations, such as those governing healthcare or personal financial records.
- **Financial data.** Corporate governance laws designed to protect the company and its shareholders, investors, and business partners (such as Sarbanes-Oxley and implementing regulations) require public companies to ensure that they have implemented appropriate information security controls for their financial information.[29] Similarly, Securities and Exchange (SEC) regulations impose various requirements for internal controls over information systems.
- **Transaction records.** Both the federal and state electronic transaction statutes—E-SIGN (Electronic Signatures in Global and National Commerce Act) and UETA (Uniform Electronic Transactions Act, now enacted in 47 states, the District of Columbia, and the U.S. Virgin Islands)—require security for storage of electronic records relating to online transactions.
- **Tax records.** Internal Revenue Service (IRS) regulations require businesses to implement information security to protect electronic tax records and as a condition of engaging in certain electronic transactions.

---

29 *See generally* Bruce H. Nearon et al., *Life after Sarbanes-Oxley: The Merger of Information Security and Accountability*, 45 JURIMETRICS: J.L., SCI. & TECH. 379–412 (Summer 2005).

- **E-mail.** SEC regulations address security in a variety of contexts, and Food and Drug Administration (FDA) regulations require security for certain records.

Most laws do not differentiate based on the format of the data involved. Data kept in databases, e-mails, text documents, spreadsheets, voicemail messages, pictures, video, sound recordings, and other formats are typically treated the same.

In some cases, however, statutes and regulations governing data security differ based upon the media on which the data reside. Many laws focus only on electronic forms of data. Some, however, also address paper-based information (e.g., including those regulating proper data destruction). Some rules also can become very media-specific. For example, under some regulations, data kept on "removable media" is subject to additional encryption requirements that do not apply to data stored on other forms of electronic media.

E. What Level of Security Is Required?

Defining the scope of a business's security obligations begins with understanding that the law views security as a relative concept. Thus, as noted above, the basic standard for compliance is typically that security must be "reasonable"[30] or "appropriate."[31]

In some cases, statutes and regulations define that standard in terms of positive results to be achieved, such as ensuring the *confidentiality*, *integrity*, and *availability* of systems and information.[32] In other cases, that standard is defined in terms of the harms to be avoided—for example, to protect systems and information against unauthorized access, use, disclosure, and so on. In some cases, the standard is not defined.

Regardless of approach, meeting this standard and achieving these objectives involves implementing appropriate physical, technical, and administrative security measures to protect both information systems and information from the various threats they face. What those threats are, where they come from, what is at risk, and the seriousness of the consequences will vary greatly from business to business. Thus, laws and regulations rarely specify or provide guidance about what specific security measures or technology a

---

30 *See, e.g.*, HIPAA, 42 U.S.C. § 1320d-2, and HIPAA Security Regulations, 45 C.F.R. § 164.306; COPPA, 15 U.S.C. § 6502(b)(1)(D), and COPPA regulations, 16 C.F.R. § 312.8; I.R.S. Rev. Proc. 97-22, § 4.01(2); SEC regulations, 17 C.F.R. § 257. *See also* U.C.C. art. 4A, § 202 ("commercially reasonable" security procedure). Although HIPAA requires "reasonable *and* appropriate" security, 42 U.S.C. 1320d-2(d)(2) (emphasis added), some state personal information security laws require only that security procedures and practices be "reasonable"—*see, e.g.*, Cal. Civ. Code § 1798.81.5(b). See also Appendix B.1 (State Laws Imposing Obligations to Provide Security for Personal Information) to this chapter.

31 HIPAA requires "reasonable and appropriate" security, 42 U.S.C. § 1320d-2(d)(2). GLB requires covered financial institutions to "implement a comprehensive written information security program that includes administrative, technical, and physical safeguards *appropriate* to the size and complexity of the bank and the nature and scope of its activities." 12 C.F.R. pt. 208, app. D-2, pt. II.A (Federal Reserve System) (emphasis added); *see also* GLB-implementing security regulations, *supra* note 11. The Massachusetts data security regulations require a comprehensive written security program that contains safeguards that are "appropriate" to the size of the business, the resources available, the amount of stored data, and the need for security. Mass. Standards for the Protection of Personal Info., 201 Mass. Code Regs. 17.03(1).

32 *See, e.g.*, FISMA and HIPAA Security Regulations, *supra* note 6. *See also* GLB Security Regulations (OCC), 12 C.F.R. pt. 30, app. B, pt. II.B; Mass. Standards for the Protection of Personal Info., 201 Mass. Code Regs. 17.00; N.Y. Dep't of Fin. Servs., Cybersecurity Requirements for Financial Services Companies, N.Y. Comp. Codes R. & Regs. tit. 23, § 500.02.

business should implement,[33] but instead require establishing and maintaining internal security "procedures," "controls," "safeguards," or "measures"[34] designed to achieve the objectives identified above.

F. The Legal Requirements for "Reasonable Security"

Although security is relative, a legal standard for "reasonable" security is emerging. That standard rejects requirements for specific security measures (such as firewalls, passwords, or the like) and instead adopts a fact-specific approach to business security obligations that requires a "process" to assess risks, identify and implement appropriate security measures responsive to those risks, verify that the measures are effectively implemented, and ensure that they are continually updated in response to new developments.

This "process-oriented" legal standard for information security has been widely adopted:

- It was first outlined in a series of financial industry security regulations required under GLB titled Interagency Guidelines Establishing Standards for Safeguarding Consumer Information. They were issued by the Federal Reserve, the Office of the Comptroller of the Currency (OCC), the Federal Deposit Insurance Corporation (FDIC), and the Office of Thrift Supervision on February 1, 2001,[35] and later were adopted by the FTC in its Safeguards Rule on May 23, 2002.[36]

- The same approach was incorporated in the Federal Information Security Management Act of 2002[37] (FISMA) and in the HIPAA Security Standards issued by the Department of Health and Human Services on February 20, 2003.[38]

- The FTC has since adopted the view that the "process-oriented" approach to information security outlined in these regulations is a "best practice" for legal compliance that should apply to all businesses in all industries. The FTC has, in effect, implemented this "process-oriented" approach in all of its decisions and consent decrees relating to alleged failures to provide appropriate information security.[39]

---

33 Laws and regulations, however, do often focus on categories of security measures to address. *See, e.g.,* HIPAA Security Regulations, 45 C.F.R. pt. 164. See also Appendices E (Best Practice Guidelines Issued by Federal Government Agencies) and F (Best Practices Guidelines Issued by State Government Agencies) to this chapter.

34 *See, e.g.,* FDA regulations at 21 C.F.R. pt. 11 (procedures and controls); SEC regulations at 17 C.F.R. 257.1(e)(3) (procedures); SEC regulations at 17 C.F.R. 240.17a-4 (controls); GLB regulations (FTC) 16 C.F.R. pt. 314 (safeguards).

35 12 C.F.R. pt. 30, app. B (OCC), 12 C.F.R. pt. 208, app. D-2 and 12 C.F.R. pt. 25, app. F (Federal Reserve System); 12 C.F.R. pt. 364, app. B (FDIC); 12 C.F.R. pt. 568 and 570, app. B (Office of Thrift Supervision, which merged with the OCC as of July 21, 2011).

36 FTC, Standards for Safeguarding Customer Information, 67 Fed. Reg. 36,484 (May 23, 2002) (FTC Safeguards Rule); 16 C.F.R. pt. 314.

37 44 U.S.C. § 3544(b).

38 45 C.F.R. pt. 164.

39 *See, e.g.,* FTC, Data Security, https://www.ftc.gov/datasecurity (for list of FTC data security cases and corresponding decisions and consent decrees implementing this approach).

- The National Association of Insurance Commissioners (NAIC) has recommended the same approach, and several state insurance regulators have adopted it.[40]
- The Illinois attorney general[41] endorsed this approach in 2012; the California attorney general[42] likewise endorsed in 2016.
- Some courts are taking the same approach.[43]
- The Massachusetts Office of Consumer Affairs and Business Regulation adopted the approach in 2008 when it released its "Standards for Protection of Personal Information of Residents of the Commonwealth"[44] (Massachusetts Regulations), as required by the 2007 Massachusetts security breach and data destruction law.[45] By specifically requiring businesses to implement a risk-based, process-oriented, *"comprehensive, written information security program"* in accordance with a detailed list of requirements, the Massachusetts Regulations created one of the most comprehensive sets of general data security obligations imposed on businesses by a state.
- The 2017 cybersecurity regulations released by the New York State Department of Financial Services also adopted a similar approach.[46]

Thus, the trend in the law is to recognize what security consultants have been saying for some time: "security is a process, not a product."[47] Legal compliance with security obligations involves applying a "process" to the facts of each case to achieve an objective (i.e., to identify and implement the security measures appropriate for that situation), rather than implementing specific security measures in all cases. Thus, cloud service providers and their customers cannot simply implement a standard set of security controls but rather must look more closely at their own individual situation.

This process-oriented approach to security compliance generally requires all businesses to take several steps, as outlined below.

1. Identify Information Assets

To protect something, you must know what it is, where it is, how it is used, how valuable it is, and so forth. Thus, when addressing information security, the first step is to identify the information assets to be protected and define the scope of the effort. This involves taking an inventory of the data and information that the business creates, collects,

---

40 *See, e.g.*, Nat'l Ass'n of Ins. Comm'rs, ST-673-1, Standards for Safeguarding Customer Information Model Regulation (Apr. 2002), http://www.naic.org/store/free/MDL-673.pdf. *See* other NAIC cybersecurity resources at http://www.naic.org/cipr_topics/topic_cyber_risk.htm.
41 Ill. Att'y Gen., Information Security and Security Breach Notification Guide 5 (Jan. 2012), http://www.illinoisattorneygeneral.gov/consumers/Security_Breach_Notification_Guidance.pdf.
42 Cal. Att'y Gen., California Data Breach Report 2016, at 29 (Feb. 2016), https://oag.ca.gov/breachreport2016.
43 *See, e.g.*, Guin v. Brazos Higher Educ. Serv., 2006 U.S. Dist. LEXIS 4846 (D. Minn. Feb. 7, 2006).
44 Mass. Standards for the Protection of Personal Info., 201 Mass. Code Regs. 17.00 *et seq.*
45 Mass. Gen. Laws ch. 93H, § 2(a).
46 N.Y. Dep't of Fin. Servs., Cybersecurity Requirements for Financial Services Companies, N.Y. Comp. Codes R. & Regs. tit. 23. § 500.02.
47 Bruce Schneier, Secrets & Lies: Digital Security in a Networked World xii (2000). See also Appendices E (Best Practice Guidelines Issued by Federal Government Agencies) and F (Best Practices Guidelines Issued by State Government Agencies) to this chapter.

receives, uses, processes, stores, and communicates to others. It also requires examining the systems, networks, and processes by which such data is created, collected, received, used, processed, stored, and communicated.

Sensitive data files are often found in a variety of places within the company. Data also is often in the possession and control of a third party, such as a cloud service provider, yet the business is still responsible for the security of its (or its customers') data in the possession of third parties.

Identifying information assets also will help to determine the data security laws and regulations applicable to specific assets that must be addressed. This includes, for example, protected health information regulated under HIPAA, personally identifiable financial information regulated under GLB, information about children regulated under the Children's Online Privacy Protection Act (COPPA), and other types of personal information regulated under state security laws, the Fair Credit Reporting Act, or section 5 of the FTC Act.

Many security laws, regulations, and guidance documents expressly require identification of information assets. Examples include the following:

- An FTC business guidance document states what should be obvious but is often overlooked: "Effective data security starts with assessing what information you have and identifying who has access to it. Understanding how personal information moves into, through, and out of your business and who has—or could have—access to it is essential to assessing security vulnerabilities. You can determine the best ways to secure the information only after you've traced how it flows."[48]
- A California attorney general guidance document states that organizations should "[i]dentify information assets and data to be secured."[49]
- Identification of information assets is a key component of the Cybersecurity Framework of the National Institute of Standards and Technology (NIST) and is included in the "Identify" function and "Asset Management" category of the Framework Core.[50]

2. Conduct Periodic Risk Assessments

Just as you cannot implement security until you identify what you have that must be protected, you also cannot implement security until you know what risks you must protect against. Thus, implementing reasonable security to protect the information assets of a business requires a thorough assessment of the potential risks to the entity's information systems and data.

A risk assessment is the process of identifying vulnerabilities and threats to the information assets used by the business and assessing the potential impact and harm that

---

48 FTC, PROTECTING PERSONAL INFORMATION: A GUIDE FOR BUSINESS 2 (Oct. 2016), https://www.ftc.gov/tips-advice/business-center/guidance/protecting-personal-information-guide-business.

49 *See* CAL. ATT'Y GEN., CALIFORNIA DATA BREACH REPORT 2016, at 29 (Feb. 2016), https://oag.ca.gov/breachreport2016.

50 NIST FRAMEWORK FOR IMPROVING CRITICAL INFRASTRUCTURE CYBERSECURITY, VERSION 1.1 (Apr. 16, 2018) [hereinafter CYBERSECURITY FRAMEWORK], Framework Core at app. A, https://www.nist.gov/cyberframework. The Cybersecurity Framework is discussed in Part II.H, *infra*.

would result if a threat materializes. This forms the basis for determining what counter-measures (i.e., security controls), if any, should be implemented to reduce risk to an acceptable level. Thus, a risk assessment requires:

- conducting a threat assessment to identify all reasonably foreseeable internal and external threats to the information and system assets to be protected;[51]
- conducting a vulnerability assessment to identify the organization's vulnerabilities;
- assessing the likelihood that each of the threats will materialize and, if so, the probability that one or more of the vulnerabilities will be exploited to cause harm—that is, identifying the likelihood that threat sources with the potential to exploit weaknesses or vulnerabilities in the system will actually do so;
- evaluating the potential damage that will result; and
- assessing the sufficiency of the security controls in place to guard against the threat.[52]

A threat is anything that has the potential to cause harm. It can be an act of nature (such as a fire, flood, or tornado) or man-made, such as a computer virus, a hacker's actions, or an employee's negligent mistake. Threats should be considered in each area of relevant operation, including information systems; network and software design; information processing, storage, and disposal; prevention, detection, and response to attacks, intrusions, and system failures; and employee training and management.

Assessing risks also requires consideration of vulnerabilities. A vulnerability is a flaw or weakness that can be accidentally triggered or intentionally exploited by the threat to endanger or cause harm to an information asset. A vulnerability might be a hole in the roof, a system with easy-to-guess passwords, unencrypted data on a laptop computer, disgruntled employees, or employees who simply do not understand what steps they must take to protect the security of their company's data.

The likelihood that a threat will exploit a vulnerability to cause harm creates a risk. In other words, "risk" is the likelihood that something bad will happen that causes harm to an information asset. Somewhat more precisely, "[r]isk is a measure of the extent to which an entity is threatened by a potential circumstance or event, and is typically a function of: (i) the adverse impacts that would arise if the circumstance or event occurs; and (ii) the likelihood of occurrence."[53] Risk is present wherever a threat intersects with a vulnerability. For example, if the threat is rain, and the vulnerability is a hole in the roof, risk is the likelihood that it will rain, causing water to enter the building through the hole in the roof and doing damage to the building and/or its contents. Similarly, if the threat is a hacker, and the vulnerability is open internet access to a server containing sensitive data, risk is the likelihood that a hacker will enter the system and view, copy, alter, or destroy the sensitive data.

This process will be the baseline against which security controls can be selected, implemented, measured, and validated. The goal is to understand the risks that the company faces and determine what level of risk is acceptable in order to identify appropriate and

---

51 *See, e.g.*, GLB Security Regulations, 12 C.F.R. pt. 30, app. B, pt. III.B.1.

52 *See, e.g.*, FISMA, 44 U.S.C. § 3544(a)(2)(A) and 3544(b)(1); GLB Security Regulations, 12 C.F.R. pt. 30, app. B, pt. III.B.2.

53 NIST Spec. Publ'n 800-30, Rev. 1, Guide for Conducting Risk Assessments 8 (Sept. 2012).

cost-effective safeguards to combat that risk. Thus, such risks should be evaluated in light of the nature of the business and its customers, its transactional capabilities, the sensitivity and value of the stored information to the business and its trading partners, and the size and volume of its transactions.[54]

Numerous security laws and regulations expressly require a risk assessment as part of a comprehensive security program. Laws and regulations that do not expressly include such a requirement often do so implicitly.

- Various federal security statutes and regulations, including GLB,[55] HIPAA,[56] and FISMA,[57] expressly require a risk assessment.
- The consent decrees entered in FTC enforcement actions have expressly required "the identification of material internal and external risks to the security, confidentiality, and integrity of covered information that could result in the unauthorized disclosure, misuse, loss, alteration, destruction, or other compromise of such information."[58]
- State security laws (e.g., in Oregon[59]) and regulations in Massachusetts[60] and New York[61] expressly require a risk assessment.
- Risk assessment is a key component of the NIST Cybersecurity Framework and is included in the "Identify" function and "Risk Assessment" category of the Framework Core.[62]
- The California attorney general's office released a report stating that "[i]nformation security laws and regulations generally require a risk management approach. In essence, this means organizations must develop, implement, monitor, and regularly update a comprehensive information security program [under which organizations must] assess risks to the assets and data."[63]
- Similarly, guidance issued by the Illinois attorney general recommends that businesses and government agencies should "[i]dentify reasonably foreseeable internal and external risks to the security, confidentiality, and integrity of customer information that could result in the unauthorized disclosure, misuse, alteration, destruction, or other compromise of such information, and assess the sufficiency of any safeguards in place to control these risks."[64]

54 *See, e.g.*, Fed. Fin. Insts. Examination Council, Authentication in an Electronic Banking Environment 3 (July 30, 2001), https://www.ffiec.gov/pdf/authentication_guidance.pdf.

55 16 C.F.R. § 314.4(b).

56 45 C.F.R. § 164.308(a)(1)(ii)(A).

57 44 U.S.C. § 3554(b)(1).

58 *See* FTC, Data Security, https://www.ftc.gov/datasecurity (for list of FTC cases and enforcement actions alleging failure to provide reasonable security).

59 Or. Rev. Stat. § 646A.622(2)(d)(A).

60 Mass. Standards for the Protection of Personal Info., 201 Mass. Code Regs. 17.03(2)(b).

61 N.Y. Dep't of Fin. Servs., Cybersecurity Requirements for Financial Services Companies, N.Y. Comp. Codes R. & Regs. tit. 23, § 500.02.

62 *See* Cybersecurity Framework, *supra* note 50, § 1.2 and Framework Core at app. A.

63 Cal. Att'y Gen., California Data Breach Report 2016, at 29 (Feb. 2016), https://oag.ca.gov/breachreport2016.

64 Ill. Att'y Gen., Information Security and Security Breach Notification Guide 5 (Jan. 2012), http://www.illinoisattorneygeneral.gov/consumers/Security_Breach_Notification_Guidance.pdf.

- In addition, several U.S. courts have held that a risk assessment plays a key role in determining whether a duty will be imposed and liability found. Where injury is foreseeable and preventable, a business has a duty to provide appropriate security to address the potential harm.[65] On the other hand, where a proper risk assessment was done, but a particular harm was not reasonably foreseeable, the defendant would not be liable for failure to defend against it.[66]

The following publications provide general information and guidance on conducting a risk assessment:

- NIST Special Publication 800-30, Rev. 1, *Guide for Conducting Risk Assessments*[67]
- Massachusetts's *A Small Business Guide: Formulating A Comprehensive Written Information Security Program*[68]
- *Interagency Guidelines Establishing Information Security Standards: Small-Entity Compliance Guide*[69]
- Federal Financial Institutions Examination Council (FFIEC) *IT Examination Chapter* and *Information Security Booklet*[70]

3. Develop and Implement an Appropriate Security Program

Based on the results of the risk assessment, the law requires a business to design and implement a security program consisting of reasonable physical, technical, and administrative security measures to manage and control the risks identified during the risk assessment.[71] The security program should be designed to provide reasonable safeguards to control the identified risks[72]—that is, to reduce the risks and vulnerabilities to a reasonable and appropriate level.

---

65 *See, e.g.,* Wolfe v. MBNA Am. Bank, 485 F. Supp. 2d 874, 882 (W.D. Tenn. 2007); Bell v. Mich. Council, 2005 Mich. App. LEXIS 353 (Mich. App. Feb. 15, 2005).

66 *See* Guin v. Brazos Higher Educ. Serv., 2006 U.S. Dist. LEXIS 4846, at *13 (D. Minn. Feb. 7, 2006) (finding that where a proper risk assessment was done, the inability to foresee and deter a specific burglary of a laptop was not a breach of a duty of reasonable care).

67 *See* NIST Spec. Publ'n No. 800-30, Rev. 1, Guide for Conducting Risk Assessments (Sept. 2012), http://nvlpubs.nist.gov/nistpubs/Legacy/SP/nistspecialpublication800-30r1.pdf.

68 *See* Mass. Office of Consumer Affairs, A Small Business Guide: Formulating A Comprehensive Written Information Security Program, http://www.mass.gov/ocabr/docs/idtheft/secplan-smallbiz-guide.pdf. *See also* Ill. Att'y Gen., Information Security and Security Breach Notification Guidance (2012), http://illinoisattorneygeneral.gov/consumers/Security_Breach_Notification_Guidance.pdf.

69 Fed. Reserve Bd. et al., Interagency Guidelines Establishing Information Security Standards: Small-Entity Compliance Guide (Dec. 14, 2005), https://www.federalreserve.gov/boarddocs/press/bcreg/2005/20051214/attachment.pdf.

70 FFIEC, IT Examination Chapter InfoBase, IT Booklets, http://itChapter.ffiec.gov/it-booklets.aspx (links to booklets).

71 *See, e.g.,* FTC, Data Security, https://www.ftc.gov/datasecurity (for list of FTC data security decisions and consent decrees imposing such requirements); GLB Security Regulations (OCC), 12 C.F.R. pt. 30, app. B, pt. II.A; HIPAA Security Regulations, 45 C.F.R. § 164.308(a)(1)(i); FISMA, 44 U.S.C. § 3544(b).

72 *See, e.g.,* FTC, Data Security, https://www.ftc.gov/datasecurity (for list of FTC data security decisions and consent decrees imposing such requirements); GLB Security Regulations, 12 C.F.R. pt. 30, app. B, pt. II.B.

The presence or absence of specific security measures says little about the status of a business's legal compliance with its information security obligations. The security measures implemented by a business must respond to the particular threats it faces and address its specific vulnerabilities. Posting armed guards around a building sounds impressive as a security measure, but it is of little value if the primary threat the business faces is unauthorized remote access to its data via the internet. Likewise, firewalls and intrusion detection software are often effective ways to stop hackers and protect sensitive databases, but if a business's major vulnerability is careless (or malicious) employees who inadvertently (or intentionally) disclose passwords or protected information, then even those sophisticated and important technical security measures will not adequately address the problem.

a. Relevant Factors to Consider

Virtually all of the existing precedent recognizes that there is no "one size fits all" approach when determining what security measures to implement within a particular business. Such a determination will depend upon a variety of factors.

Traditional negligence law suggests that the relevant factors are: (1) the probability of the identified harm occurring (i.e., the likelihood that a foreseeable threat will materialize); (2) the gravity of the resulting injury if the threat does materialize; and (3) the burden of implementing adequate precautions.[73] In other words, the standard of care to be exercised in any particular case depends upon the circumstances of that case and the extent of foreseeable danger.[74]

Security regulations take a similar approach and indicate that the following factors are relevant in determining what security measures should be implemented:

- the probability and criticality of potential risks;
- the size, complexity, and capabilities of the business;
- the nature and scope of the business activities;
- the nature and sensitivity of the information to be protected;
- the organization's technical infrastructure, hardware, and software security capabilities;
- the state of the art of technology and security; and
- the cost of the security measures (cost was the factor mentioned most often, which suggests that businesses are not required to do everything theoretically possible).

b. Categories of Security Measures to Consider

Most laws do not require businesses to implement specific security measures or use a particular technology, but instead provide flexibility to use measures reasonably designed to achieve the objectives specified in the regulations.[75] This focus on flexibility means that, like the obligation to use "reasonable care" under tort law, determining compliance

---

73 *See, e.g.*, United States v. Carroll Towing, 159 F.2d 169, 173 (2d Cir. 1947).

74 *See, e.g.*, DCR Inc. v. Peak Alarm Co., 663 P.2d 433, 435 (Utah 1983); *see also* Glatt v. Feist, 156 N.W.2d 819, 829 (N.D. 1968) (the amount or degree of diligence necessary to constitute ordinary care varies with the facts and circumstances of each case).

75 *See, e.g.*, HIPAA Security Regulations, 45 C.F.R. § 164.306(b)(1).

may ultimately become more difficult because there are unlikely to be any safe harbors for security.

Nonetheless, statutes and regulations[76] consistently focus on physical, technical, and administrative security measures and, within those areas, often mention certain categories of security measures that businesses should consider (although how a business must address the categories is typically not specified). Those categories of security measures include

- **Physical facility and device security controls.** Measures to safeguard the facility; measures to protect against destruction, loss, or damage of information due to potential environmental hazards (such as fire and water damage or technological failures); procedures that govern the receipt and removal of hardware and electronic media into and out of a facility; and procedures that govern the use and security of physical workstations;
- **Physical access controls.** Access restrictions at buildings, computer facilities, and records storage facilities to permit access only to authorized individuals;
- **Technical access controls.** Software, policies, and procedures to ensure that authorized persons who need access to the system have appropriate access and that those who should not have access are prevented from getting it, including procedures to determine access authorization, grant and control access, verify that a person or entity seeking access is the one claimed (i.e., authentication), and terminate access;
- **Intrusion detection procedures.** Software, policies, and procedures to monitor log-in attempts and report discrepancies; system monitoring and intrusion detection systems and procedures to detect actual and attempted attacks on, or intrusions into, the organization's information systems; and procedures for preventing, detecting, and reporting malicious software (e.g., virus software);
- **Employee procedures.** Job control procedures, segregation of duties, and background checks for employees with responsibility for or access to protected information, and controls to prevent employees from providing information to unauthorized individuals who may seek to obtain this information through fraudulent means;
- **System modification procedures.** Procedures designed to ensure that system modifications are consistent with the business's security program;
- **Data integrity, confidentiality, and storage.** Procedures to protect information from unauthorized access, alteration, disclosure, or destruction during storage or transmission, including storage of data in a format that cannot be meaningfully interpreted if accessed (e.g., encrypted), or in a location that is inaccessible to unauthorized persons and/or protected by a firewall;
- **Data destruction and hardware and media disposal.** Procedures regarding final disposition of information and/or hardware on which it resides, and procedures for removal of data from media before reuse of the media;
- **Audit controls.** Maintenance of records to document repairs and modifications to the physical components of the facility related to security (walls, doors, locks,

76 See Appendix C.2 (Federal Regulations Imposing Authentication Requirements) to this chapter.

etc.) and hardware, software, and/or procedural audit control mechanisms that record and examine activity in the systems;

- **Contingency plan.** Procedures designed to ensure the ability to continue operations in an emergency, such as a data backup plan, disaster recovery plan, and emergency mode operation plan;

- **Incident response plan.** A plan for taking responsive actions if the business suspects or detects that a security breach has occurred, including ensuring that appropriate persons are promptly notified of the breach and that prompt action is taken in responding to the breach (e.g., to stop further information compromise and work with law enforcement), and in notifying appropriate persons who may be injured by the breach.

4. Provide Training and Education

Training and education for employees is a critical component of any security program. Even the best physical, technical, and administrative security measures are of little value if employees do not understand their roles and responsibilities regarding security. For example, installing heavy-duty doors with state-of-the-art locks (whether physical or virtual) will not provide the intended protection if the employees authorized to have access leave the doors open or unlocked for unauthorized persons to pass through.

Security education begins with communicating applicable security policies, procedures, standards, and guidelines to employees. It also includes implementing a security awareness program, providing periodic security reminders, and developing and maintaining relevant employee training, such as user education on virus protection, password management, and how to report discrepancies. It is also important to impose appropriate sanctions against employees who fail to comply with security policies and procedures.

5. Monitor and Test the Security Controls

Merely implementing security measures is not sufficient. A business also must ensure that the security measures have been properly put in place and are effective. This includes conducting an assessment of the sufficiency of the security measures in place to control the identified risks, and conducting regular testing or monitoring of the effectiveness of those measures. Existing precedent also suggests that a business must monitor compliance with its security program. To that end, a regular review of records of system activity, such as audit logs, access reports, and security incident tracking reports, is also important.

6. Review and Adjust the Security Program

The legal standard for information security recognizes that security is a moving target. Businesses must continually keep up with ever-changing threats, risks, and vulnerabilities as well as the security measures available to respond to them. This requires conducting periodic internal reviews to evaluate and adjust the information security program in light of:

- the results of the testing and monitoring;
- any material changes to the business or customer arrangements;
- any changes in technology;

- any changes in internal or external threats;
- any environmental or operational changes; and
- any other circumstances that may have a material impact.[77]

In addition to conducting periodic internal reviews, it also may be appropriate to obtain a periodic review and assessment (audit) by qualified, independent, third-party professionals. Such professionals would use procedures and standards generally accepted in the profession to certify that the security program meets or exceeds applicable requirements and that the program is operating with sufficient effectiveness to provide reasonable assurances that the security, confidentiality, integrity, and availability of information are protected. The business should then adjust the security program in light of the findings or recommendations that come from such reviews.

G. Rules Governing Specific Data Elements and Controls

1. Special Rules for Specific Data Elements or Activities

In addition to imposing a general obligation to provide data security, some laws and regulations require protection of specific data elements, such as Social Security numbers, credit card transaction data, and other sensitive data.

The various state security breach notification laws (discussed in Part III below) have created a de facto category of sensitive information in the United States. These laws require special action (i.e., disclosure) upon a breach of security for a subcategory of personal data generally considered to be sensitive because it can facilitate identity theft.

The security of Social Security numbers has been the particular focus of numerous state laws enacted in recent years.[78] The scope of these laws ranges from restrictions on the manner in which Social Security numbers can be used to requirements for security when communicating and/or storing such numbers. For example, several states have enacted laws that prohibit requiring an individual to transmit his or her Social Security number over the internet unless the connection is secure or the number is encrypted.[79]

For businesses that accept credit card transactions, the PCI Standard[80] imposes significant security obligations for credit card data captured as part of any credit card transaction. The PCI Standard, jointly created by the major credit card associations, requires

---

77 *See, e.g.*, GLB Security Regulations, 12 C.F.R. pt. 30, app. B, pt. II.E; HIPAA Security Regulations, 45 C.F.R. § 164.308(a)(8).

78 See, e.g., Appendix B.6 (State SSN Laws) and Appendix B.9 (State Laws Requiring SSN Policies) to this chapter.

79 *See* U.S. Gov't Accountability Office, GAO-05-1016T, Social Security Numbers: Federal and State Laws Restrict Use of SSNs, yet Gaps Remain, at app. III (Sept. 15, 2005), http://www.gao.gov/assets/120/112174.pdf (list of state laws). Many federal agencies are making efforts to reduce collection, use, and display of SSNs, but have had mixed success given a number of factors (including statutes and regulations that mandate collection of SSNs); *see* U.S. Gov't Accountability Office, GAO-17-655T, Social Security Numbers: OMB and Federal Efforts to Reduce Collection, Use, and Display (May 23, 2017), https://www.gao.gov/products/GAO-17-655T.

80 *See* PCI Sec. Standards Council, Document Library, https://www.pcisecuritystandards.org/document_library.

businesses that accept MasterCard, Visa, American Express, Discover, and Diners Club cards to comply. State law obligations also may apply.[81]

2. Duty to Encrypt Data

Some laws and regulations impose obligations to use encryption in certain situations. Initially this included state laws that mandate encryption of Social Security numbers for communication over the internet.[82] More recently, however, some state laws prohibit the electronic transmission of any personal information to a person outside of the secure system of the business unless the information is encrypted. Most notable are the Massachusetts Regulations, which require businesses to encrypt personal information if it is stored on "laptops or other portable devices," "will travel across public networks," or will "be transmitted wirelessly."[83]

3. Duty to Destroy Data Properly

Several laws and regulations impose security requirements regarding the way that data is destroyed.[84] Such statutes and regulations generally require businesses to properly dispose of personal information by taking reasonable measures to protect against unauthorized access to, or use of, the information in connection with its disposal. For information in paper form, this typically requires implementing and monitoring compliance with policies and procedures that require the burning, pulverizing, or shredding of papers containing personal information so that it cannot be read or reconstructed. For information in electronic form, such regulations typically require implementing and monitoring compliance with policies and procedures that require the destruction or erasure of electronic media containing consumer personal information so that it cannot be read or reconstructed.

H. Frameworks for Reasonable Security

The Cybersecurity Framework is one of the deliverables contemplated by President Barack Obama's Executive Order 13,636, Improving Critical Infrastructure Cybersecurity, which was issued on February 12, 2013, and revised on April 16, 2018.[85] Recognizing that the national and economic security of the United States depends on the reliable functioning of the nation's critical infrastructure, the executive order directed NIST to work with the private sector to develop a voluntary framework—based on existing standards, guidelines, and practices—for reducing cyber risks to critical infrastructure.

---

81 See, e.g., Appendix B.2 (State Laws Imposing Obligations to Provide Security for Credit Card Information) to this chapter.

82 See, e.g., ARIZ. REV. STAT. § 44-1373; CAL. CIV. CODE § 1798.85; CONN. GEN. STAT. § 42-470; MD. CODE ANN., COM. LAW § 14-3402(4). See also Appendix B.6 (State SSN Laws) to this chapter; many state SSN laws mandate use of encryption when transmitting Social Security numbers.

83 Mass. Standards for the Protection of Personal Info., 201 MASS. CODE REGS. 17.04(3) and (5).

84 See, e.g., Appendix B.3 (State Data Disposal/Destruction Laws) and Appendix C.3 (Federal Data Disposal/Destruction Regulations) to this chapter.

85 Exec. Order No. 13,636, supra note 21.

Consistent with the requirements of the executive order, the Cybersecurity Framework was created through collaboration between industry and government[86] and "provides a consensus description of what's needed for a comprehensive cybersecurity program." "It reflects the efforts of a broad range of industries that see the value of and need for improving cybersecurity and lowering risk."[87] According to NIST, the Cybersecurity Framework "allows organizations—regardless of size, degree of cyber risk or cybersecurity sophistication—to apply the principles and best practices of risk management to improve the security and resilience of critical infrastructure."[88]

The Cybersecurity Framework references several generally accepted domestic and international security standards, and the participants generally agree that it constitutes a best practice for cyber security.[89] It might be argued that the Cybersecurity Framework is little more than a compilation of established industry security practices, but even so it collates such practices into a framework of activities that arguably establishes a set of requirements for the development of "reasonable" security practices. Moreover, it carries the weight of a government-issued framework that was the result of a year-long collaboration between industry and government to develop a voluntary "how to" guide for organizations to enhance their cyber security.[90]

Technically, the Cybersecurity Framework was originally written only for businesses in the 16 critical infrastructure sectors,[91] but the practical reality goes much farther. Version 1.1 explicitly expanded the applicability of the framework outside of critical infrastructure. Version 1.1 provides that the framework is useful for addressing cyber security for any company relying on technology, "whether their cybersecurity focus is primarily on information technology (IT), industrial control systems (ICS), cyber-physical systems (CPS), or connected devices more generally, including the Internet of Things."[92] The Cybersecurity Framework is written as a generally applicable document that is in no way unique to critical infrastructure industries. It is not industry-specific, nor is it country-specific. Consistent with existing law, the Cybersecurity Framework adopts a risk-based approach to managing cybersecurity risk. As such, it appears to fit quite well

---

86 The "framework is the culmination of a year-long effort that brought together thousands of individuals and organizations from industry, academia and government." Press Release, NIST, NIST Releases Cybersecurity Framework Version 1.0 (Feb. 12, 2014), https://www.nist.gov/itl/csd/launch-cybersecurity-framework-021214.cfm.

87 *Id.* (quoting Undersecretary of Commerce for Standards and Technology and NIST Director Patrick D. Gallagher).

88 *Id.*

89 "Over the past year, individuals and organizations throughout the country and across the globe have provided their thoughts on the kinds of standards, best practices, and guidelines that would meaningfully improve critical infrastructure cybersecurity. The Department of Commerce's National Institute of Standards and Technology (NIST) consolidated that input into the voluntary Cybersecurity Framework that we are releasing today." Press Release, White House, Launch of the Cybersecurity Framework (Feb. 12, 2014), https://www.whitehouse.gov/the-press-office/2014/02/12/launch-cybersecurity-framework.

90 *Id.*

91 According to Presidential Policy Directive 21 (PPD-21), the 16 critical infrastructure sectors are chemical, commercial facilities, communications, critical manufacturing, dams, defense industrial base, emergency services, energy, financial services, food and agriculture, government facilities, health care and public health, information technology, nuclear reactors, materials and waste, transportation systems, and water and wastewater systems.

92 Cybersecurity Framework, *supra* note 50, at iv.

with the approach of existing legal requirements for cybersecurity obligations. It provides general approaches and activities to address cyber security for all businesses.

Version 1.1 of the framework provides enhanced guidance for supply-chain risk management, including the management of risk associated with cloud service providers. It indicates that the primary objective of supply-chain risk management (SCRM) is to identify, assess, and mitigate the risk of products and services that "may contain potentially malicious functionality, are counterfeit, or are vulnerable due to poor manufacturing and development practices within the cyber supply chain." [93] The Framework describes supply chains as "[beginning] with the sourcing of products and services and [extending] from the design, development, manufacturing, processing, handling, and delivery of products and services to the end user. Given these complex and interconnected relationships, supply chain risk management (SCRM) is a critical organizational function."[94]

"The Framework is designed to complement existing business and cybersecurity operations. It can serve as the foundation for a new cybersecurity program or a mechanism for improving an existing program."[95] The drafters of the Cybersecurity Framework contemplated that "[o]rganizations can use the framework to determine their current level of cybersecurity, set goals for cybersecurity that are in sync with their business environment, and establish a plan for improving or maintaining their cybersecurity. It also offers a methodology to protect privacy and civil liberties to help organizations incorporate those protections into a comprehensive cybersecurity program."[96]

NIST noted that "an organization without an existing cybersecurity program can use the Framework as a reference to establish one"[97] or to improve an existing program.[98]

Other cybersecurity frameworks are often used as a methodology to implement reasonable security in an organization. Two of the more commonly used are: (1) the ISO/IEC 27001 framework, which was developed by the International Organization for Standardization (ISO) and the International Electrotechnical Commission (IEC),[99] and (2) the Control Objectives for Information and Related Technologies (COBIT) framework, which was created by ISACA (previously known as the Information Systems Audit and Control Association).[100]

III. Duty to Notify of Security Breaches

Legal and regulatory requirements do not stop at obligations to *implement* security measures to protect data. Now there is a global trend to enact laws and regulations that impose an obligation to *disclose* security breaches to the persons affected.

---

93   *Id.* at 16.

94   *Id.*

95   *Id.* at 13. *See generally id.* § 3.2, Establishing or Improving a Cybersecurity Program, at 13–15.

96   *See* Press Release, NIST, NIST Releases Cybersecurity Framework Version 1.0 (Feb. 12, 2014), https://www.nist.gov/itl/csd/launch-cybersecurity-framework-021214.cfm.

97   Cybersecurity Framework, *supra* note 50, at 4.

98   *See id.* § 3.2.

99   ISO/IEC 27001, Information Technology—Security Techniques—Information Security Management Systems—Requirements (2013), *available for purchase at* https://www.iso.org/isoiec-27001-information-security.html.

100   *See* ISACA, http://www.isaca.org/cobit/pages/default.aspx.

A. What Is the Source of the Duty?

All U.S. states and territories have enacted security breach notification laws, generally based on a 2003 California law, and such obligations can also be triggered at the federal level.[101] The HIPAA regulations require breach notification,[102] as do the requirements of the federal banking regulatory agencies.[103] The IRS also has imposed a disclosure requirement with respect to taxpayers whose electronic tax records are the subject of a security breach.[104]

These laws impose an obligation similar to the common-law "duty to warn" of dangers, which is often based on the view that a party who has superior knowledge of a danger of injury or damage to another posed by a specific hazard must warn those who lack such knowledge. By requiring notice to persons who might be adversely affected (e.g., those whose compromised personal information may be used to facilitate identity theft), such laws seek to warn such persons that personal information has been compromised and provide an opportunity to take steps to self-protect against the consequences of identity theft.

B. What Is the Statutory Duty?

The statutory duty, as embodied in the state and federal security breach notification laws, generally requires that any business that possesses or controls certain sensitive personal information about a covered individual must disclose any breach of such information to the affected person.[105] Several statutes also require notification to the state attorney general or other regulatory agency. In some cases, notification requirements also extend to informing credit reporting agencies and the press.

The key elements of the breach notification statutes can be summarized as follows:

Type of information. The breach notification statutes generally apply to unencrypted, sensitive, personally identifiable information—for example, information consisting of first name or initial and last name, plus one of the following: Social Security number, driver's license or state ID number, or financial account number or credit or debit card number (along with any PIN or other access code where required to access the account). In some states, this list is longer and may also include, for example, medical information, insurance policy numbers, passwords by themselves, biometric information, professional license or permit numbers, telecommunication access codes, mother's maiden name,

---

101 *See, e.g.,* Appendix B.4 (State Security Breach Notification Laws) and Appendix C.4 (Federal Security Breach Notification Regulations) to this chapter.

102 45 C.F.R. § 164.314(a)(2)(1)(C), 45 C.F.R. § 164.410.

103 Interagency Guidance on Response Programs for Unauthorized Access to Customer Information and Customer Notice, 12 C.F.R. pt. 30, app., supp. A, pt. III (OCC), 12 C.F.R. pt. 208 (Federal Reserve System), and 12 C.F.R. pt. 364 (FDIC), and 12 C.F.R. pt. 568 (Office of Thrift Supervision, which merged with the OCC as of July 21, 2011), 70 Fed. Reg. No. 59, Mar. 29, 2005, at 15,736 [hereinafter Interagency Guidance].

104 *See* I.R.S. Rev. Proc. 98-25, § 8.01. See Appendix C.4 (Federal Security Breach Notification Regulations) to this chapter.

105 Exception: Where the business maintains computerized personal information that the business does not own, the laws require the business to notify the owner or licensee of the information, rather than the individuals themselves, of any breach of the security of the system.

employer ID number, electronic signatures, and descriptions of an individual's personal characteristics.[106]

Triggering event. The event that triggers the obligation to provide individuals with notice of a breach involving their personal information is typically referred to in the breach statutes as a "breach of the security of the system." This term is often defined as: "unauthorized acquisition of unencrypted computerized data that compromises the security, confidentiality or integrity of personal information maintained by the person or business."[107] The requirements of this definition, in combination with certain other exclusions available in many states (e.g., an exclusion for security breaches that the custodian of the exposed data determines will not likely cause harm),[108] allow for more than one approach to determining when factors are present that impose an obligation to notify under the breach notification statutes.

Who must be notified. Notice must be given to, at a minimum, any residents of the state whose unencrypted personal information was the subject of the breach. In some cases, the state's attorney general (or other enforcement agency) and/or the media must also be notified.

When notice must be provided. Generally, persons must be notified in the most expedient time possible and without unreasonable delay (although some states specify a certain number of days). In most states, the time for notice may be extended for the legitimate needs of law enforcement, if notification would impede a criminal investigation, or to take necessary measures to determine the scope of the breach and restore reasonable integrity to the system.

Form of notice. Notice may be provided in writing (e.g., on paper and sent by mail), in electronic form (e.g., by e-mail, but only in compliance with E-SIGN[109]), or by substitute notice. If the cost of providing individual notice is greater than a certain amount (e.g., $250,000), or if more than a certain number of people would have to be notified (e.g., 500,000), the business may use substitute notice, consisting of e-mail, when the e-mail address is available; conspicuous posting on the entity's website; and publishing notice in all major statewide media.

Requirements vary from state to state, however, and some requirements have become controversial. One of the biggest issues concerns the nature of the triggering event. In California, for example, notification is required whenever there has been unauthorized access that compromises the security, confidentiality, or integrity of electronic personal data.

---

106 *See, e.g.,* Ark. Code §§ 4-110-101 *et seq.*; La. Rev. Stat. §§ 51:3071 *et seq.*; Md. Code Ann., Com. Law §§ 14-3501 *et seq.*; Neb. Rev. Stat. §§ 87-801 *et seq.*; N.J. Stat. 56:8-163; N.C. Gen. Stat. § 75-65; N.D. Cent. Code §§ 51-30-01 *et seq.*; Or. Rev. Stat. § 646A.600–.628. The Federal Banking Interagency Guidance, *see supra* note 100, also includes any combination of components of customer information that would allow someone to log onto or access the customer's account, such as user name and password, or account number and password.

107 *See, e.g.,* Cal. Civ. Code § 1798.82(d).

108 For example, Iowa's breach notification statute stipulates that notification is not required if "after an appropriate investigation or after consultation with the relevant federal, state, or local agencies responsible for law enforcement, the person determined that no reasonable likelihood of financial harm to the consumers whose personal information has been acquired has resulted or will result from the breach. Such a determination must be documented in writing and the documentation must be maintained for five years." *See* Iowa Code § 715C.2(6).

109 15 U.S.C. §§ 7001 *et seq.* This generally requires that entities comply with the requisite consumer consent provisions of E-SIGN at 15 U.S.C. § 7001(c).

In other states, unauthorized access does not trigger the notification requirement unless there is a reasonable likelihood of harm to the individuals whose personal information is involved or unless the breach is material.

C. When Does a Contract-Based Duty Arise?

It is increasingly common for contracts with business partners of all types, including cloud service providers, to require the recipient or processor of a business's data to notify that party in the event of a breach. Customers (particularly in regulated industries such as financial or health care) are requiring that their business partners provide prompt notice of any security breach. For example, breach reporting is a key requirement of the Model Information Protection and Security Controls for Outside Counsel Processing Company Confidential Information, released in 2017 by the Association of Corporate Counsel.[110]

IV. Practical Considerations: A Top-10 List

Businesses and their cloud service providers have many legal obligations to provide data security that arise from generally applicable law. Below is a list of practical tips regarding compliance with those obligations:

1. Take appropriate steps to ensure that your cloud service providers and other out-source vendors adequately protect the security of the data you entrust to them.
2. Identify the data that you have (obtained during due diligence) and understand where it is stored, how it can be accessed, and how it is used.
3. Evaluate the risks to the data you have.
4. Develop a security program to protect that data against the identified risks.
5. On a regular basis, reevaluate the risks you face and the adequacy of your security program, and adjust the program as necessary.
6. Determine which data (obtained during due diligence or discovery) are subject to which laws and regulations (including special sector-specific regulations such as GLB or HIPAA), and ensure that you handle it in accordance with any special requirements in those laws and regulations.
7. Recognize that other employees within the business can be a weak link and provide appropriate training and awareness-raising reminders for all employees.
8. Develop an incident response plan that covers the data you have.
9. Keep in mind that laws and regulations governing data security may apply to all of the data in your possession.
10. Remember that security is a process and is never complete, so you must remain vigilant for new threats.

---

110 Ass'n of Corporate Counsel, Model Information Protection and Security Controls for Outside Counsel Processing Company Confidential Information (Jan. 2017), http://www.acc.com/advocacy/upload/Model-Information-Protection-and-Security-Controls-for-Outside-Counsel-Jan2017.pdf.

Appendices to Chapter 5

Legal Obligations and Best Practices for Cloud Security

Appendix A

Federal Statutes

1. COPPA: Children's Online Privacy Protection Act of 1998, 15 U.S.C. §§ 6501 *et seq.*

2. CFPA: Consumer Financial Protection Act of 2010, 12 U.S.C. §§ 5531(a), 5536(a)(1) (prohibits unfair, deceptive, or abusive acts or practices in connection with a transaction for, or offer of, a consumer financial product or service).

3. E-SIGN: Electronic Signatures in Global and National Commerce Act, 15 U.S.C. § 7001(d).

4. FCRA/FACTA: Fair Credit Reporting Act, as amended by the Fair and Accurate Credit Transaction Act, 15 U.S.C. §§ 1681 *et seq.*

5. FISMA: Federal Information Security Management Act of 2002, 44 U.S.C. §§ 3541–3549.

6. FTC Act: Federal Trade Commission Act, 15 U.S.C. § 45(a)(1) (prohibits unfair or deceptive acts or practices in or affecting commerce).

7. GLB Act: Gramm-Leach-Bliley Act, Pub. L. No. 106-102, §§ 501 and 505(b), 15 U.S.C. §§ 6801, 6805.

8. HIPAA: Health Insurance Portability and Accountability Act, 42 U.S.C. §§ 1320d-2, 1320d-4. See also Subtitle D of Title XIII of the American Recovery and Reinvestment Act of 2009 (ARRA), Pub. L. No. 111-5, 123 Stat. 115, at §§ 13401 *et seq.*

9. Homeland Security Act of 2002: 44 U.S.C. § 3532(b)(1).

10. Privacy Act of 1974: 5 U.S.C. § 552a.

11. Sarbanes-Oxley Act: Pub. L. No. 107-204, §§ 302, 404; 15 U.S.C. § 7241 (corporate responsibility for financial reports) and § 7262 (management assessment of internal controls).

12. Federal Rules of Evidence 901(a). See *American Express v. Vinnie*, 336 B.R. 437 (B.A.P. 9th Cir. 2005), *Lorraine v. Markel*, 241 F.R.D. 534 (D. Md. 2007).

Appendix B

State Statutes

1. State Laws Imposing Obligations to Provide Security for Personal Information

Arkansas	Ark. Code Ann. § 4-110-104(b)
California	Cal. Civ. Code §§ 1798.81.5, 56 *et seq.* (medical information)
Colorado	Colo. Rev. Stat. § 6-1-713.5 (private entity), § 24-73-102 (gov't entity)
Connecticut	Conn. Gen. Stat. §§ 42-471, 4e-70 (state contractors)
Delaware	Del. Code Ann. tit. 6, § 12B-100
Florida	Fla. Stat. §§ 501.171(2), 282.318 (state agency)
Illinois	815 Ill. Comp. Stat. Ann. 530/45; 740 Ill. Comp. Stat. Ann. 14/1 (Biometric Information Privacy Act)
Indiana	Ind. Code § 24-4.9-3-3.5
Kansas	Kan. Stat. Ann. §§ 50-6, 139b
Maryland	Md. Code Ann., Com. Law § 14-3503
Massachusetts	Mass. Gen. Laws ch. 93H, § 2(a); 201 Mass. Code Regs. 17.00 *et seq.*
Minnesota	Minn. Stat. § 325M.05
Nevada	Nev. Rev. Stat. § 603A.210
New York	Stop Hacks and Improve Electronic Data Security (SHIELD) Act (proposed), S. S6993B
Ohio	Ohio Data Protection Act, 2018 S. 220
Oregon	Or. Rev. Stat. § 646A.622
Rhode Island	R.I. Gen. Laws 11-49.3-2
Texas	Tex. Bus. & Com. Code Ann. § 521.052
Utah	Utah Code Ann. § 13-44-201
Vermont	9 V.S.A. §§ 2430 *et seq.* (data brokers)

2. State Laws Imposing Obligations to Provide Security for Credit Card Information

Minnesota	Minn. Stat. § 325E.64
Nevada	Nev. Rev. Stat. § 603A.215
Washington	Wash. Rev. Code § 19.255.010

3. State Data Disposal/Destruction Laws

Alaska	Ala. Stat. §§ 45.48.500–45.48.590
Arizona	Ariz. Rev. Stat. § 44-7601*
Arkansas	Ark. Code Ann. § 4-110-104(a)

California	Cal. Civ. Code § 1798.81
Colorado	Colo. Rev. Stat. § 6-1-713
Connecticut	Conn. Gen. Stat. § 42-471
Delaware	Del. Code Ann. tit. 6, §§ 5001C *et seq.*; tit. 19, § 736 (employers)
Florida	Fla. Stat. § 501.171(8)
Georgia	Ga. Code Ann. § 10-15-2
Hawaii	Haw. Rev. Stat. § 487R-2
Illinois	815 Ill. Comp. Stat. 530/40 (all), 530/30 (state agencies) 20 Ill. Comp. Stat. 450/20 (state computers); 740 Ill. Comp. Stat. Ann. 14/15 (Biometric Information Privacy Act)
Indiana	Ind. Code §§ 24-4-14-8, 24-4.9-3-3.5(c)
Kansas	Kan. Stat. Ann. § 50-7a03
Kentucky	Ky. Rev. Stat. Ann. § 365.725
Maryland	Md. Code Ann., Comm. Law § 14-3502; Md. Code Ann., State Gov't §§ 10-1301–1303 (government unit)
Massachusetts	Mass. Gen. Laws ch. 93I, § 2
Michigan	Mich. Comp. Laws § 445.72a
Montana	Mont. Code Ann. § 30-14-1703
Nevada	Nev. Rev. Stat. § 603A.200
New Jersey	N.J. Stat. § 56:8-162
New York	N.Y. Gen. Bus. Law § 399-H
North Carolina	N.C. Gen. Stat. § 75-64
Oregon	Or. Rev. Stat. § 646A.622
Puerto Rico	2014 P.R. Laws #234-2014
Rhode Island	R.I. Gen. Laws § 6-52-2
South Carolina	S.C. Code §§ 37-20-190, 30-2-310
Tennessee	Tenn. Code § 39-14-150(g)
Texas	Tex. Bus. & Com. Code Ann. §§ 48.102(b), 72.004, 521.052
Utah	Utah Code Ann. § 13-44-201
Vermont	Vt. Stat. Ann. tit. 9, §§ 2445 *et seq.*
Washington	Wash. Rev. Code Ann. § 19.215.020
Wisconsin	Wis. Stat. § 134.97**

*Applies to paper documents only.

**Applies to financial institutions, medical businesses, and tax preparation businesses.

4. State Security Breach Notification Laws

Alabama	Ala. Code § 8-38-1 *et seq.*
Alaska	Alaska Stat. §§ 45.48.010–45.48.090
Arizona	Ariz. Rev. Stat. § 18-545
Arkansas	Ark. Code Ann. §§ 4-110-101 *et seq.*
California	Cal. Civ. Code §§ 1798.82 (person or business), 1798.29 (state agency)
Colorado	Colo. Rev. Stat. § 6-1-716
Connecticut	Conn. Gen Stat. §§ 36a-701(b), 4e-70 (state contractors)
Delaware	Del. Code Ann. tit. 6, §§ 12B-101 *et seq.*
District of Columbia	D.C. Code §§ 28-3851 *et seq.*
Florida	Fla. Stat. § 501.171 (all); Fla Stat. § 282.0041 and § 282.318 (state agency add'l requirements)
Georgia	Ga. Code Ann. §§ 10-1-910 *et seq.** Ga. Code Ann. § 46-5-214 (telephone records)
Guam	9 Guam Code Ann. §§ 48.10 *et seq.*
Hawaii	Haw. Rev. Stat. § 487N
Idaho	Id. Code §§ 28-51-104 to 28-51-107
Illinois	815 Ill. Comp. Stat. 530/1 *et seq.*
Indiana	Ind. Code §§ 24-4.9, 4-1-11 *et seq.* (state agency)
Iowa	Iowa Code § 715C
Kansas	Kan. Stat. Ann. §§ 50-7a01 *et seq.*
Kentucky	Ky. Rev. Stat. Ann. §§ 365.732, 61.931–61.934 (state)
Louisiana	La. Rev. Stat. Ann. §§ 51:3071 *et seq.*; La. Admin. Code tit. 16, pt. 3, § 701 (reporting requirements)
Maine	Me. Rev Stat. Ann. tit. 10 §§ 1346 *et seq.*
Maryland	Md. Code Ann., Com. Law §§ 14-3501 *et seq.* Md. Code Ann., State Gov't §§ 10-1301 *et seq.* (government unit)
Massachusetts	Mass. Gen. Laws ch. 93H
Michigan	Mich. Comp. Laws §§ 445.61 *et seq.* (see § 445.72)

Minnesota	Minn. Stat. §§ 325E.61, 325E.64, 609.891
Mississippi	Miss. Code Ann. § 75-24-29
Missouri	Mo. Rev. Stat. § 407.1500
Montana	Mont. Code Ann. §§ 30-14-1701 *et seq.*; § 33-19-321 (insurance-related); §§ 2-6-1501 *et seq.* (state agency)
Nebraska	Neb. Rev. Stat. §§ 87-801 *et seq.*
Nevada	Nev. Rev. Stat. §§ 603A.010 *et seq.* (see § 603A.220), 242.183
New Hampshire	N.H. Rev. Stat. Ann. §§ 359-C:19 *et seq.*
New Jersey	N.J. Stat. Ann. § 56:8-163
New Mexico	2017 H.B. 15, Ch. 36 (Data Breach Notification Act, eff. 6/16/17)
New York	N.Y. Gen. Bus. Law § 899-aa; N.Y. State Tech Law § 208 (state entity)
North Carolina	N.C. Gen. Stat. § 75-65
North Dakota	N.D. Cent. Code §§ 51-30-01 *et seq.*
Ohio	Ohio Rev. Code Ann. §§ 1349.19, 1349.191, 1349.192; Ohio Rev. Code Ann. §§ 1347 *et seq.* (state/local agency)
Oklahoma	Okla. Stat. tit. 24, §§ 161 *et seq.*; tit. 74, § 3113.1 (state unit)
Oregon	Or. Rev. Stat. § 646A.600–.628
Pennsylvania	73 Pa. Cons. Stat. §§ 2301 *et seq.*
Puerto Rico	P.R. Laws Ann. tit. 10 §§ 4051 *et seq.*
Rhode Island	R.I. Gen. Laws §§ 11-49.3-1 *et seq.*
South Carolina	S.C. Code Ann. § 39-1-90; § 1-11-490 (state agency)
South Dakota	SDCL §§ 22-40-19–22-40-26
Tennessee	Tenn. Code Ann. §§ 47-18-2107, 8-4-119 (state agency)
Texas	Tex. Bus. & Com. Code Ann. § 521.053
Utah	Utah Code Ann. §§ 13-44-101 *et seq.*
Vermont	Vt. Stat. Ann. tit. 9, §§ 2430 *et seq.*
Virgin Islands	V.I. Code Ann. tit. 14, §§ 2209 (person or business), 2208 (agency)
Virginia	Va. Code. Ann. §§ 18.2-186.6, 32.1-127.1:05 (gov't entities, medical info.)

Washington	Wash. Rev. Code §§19.255.010, 42.56.590 (state/local agencies)
West Virginia	W. Va. Code §§ 46A-2A-101 to 46A-2A-105
Wisconsin	Wis. Stat. § 134.98
Wyoming	Wyo. Stat. Ann. §§ 40-12-501 to 40-12-502

* Applies only to "information brokers" and "data collectors" as defined in Ga. Code Ann. § 10-1-911. Draft legislation (most recently 2017–2018 Regular Session—H.B. 499, titled "Georgia Personal Data Security Act") proposes to expand applicable scope.

5. State Social Security Number Laws*

Alabama	Ala. Code § 41-13-6
Alaska	Alaska Stat. § 45.48.400
Arizona	Ariz. Rev. Stat. § 44-1373
Arkansas	Ark. Code Ann. §§ 4-86-107, 6-18-208
California	Cal. Civ. Code § 1798.85; Cal. Fam. Code § 2024.5; Cal. Lab. Code § 226
Colorado	Colo. Rev. Stat. §§ 6-1-715, 13-21-109.5, 23-5-127, 24-72.3-102
Connecticut	Conn. Gen. Stat. §§ 42-470, 8-64b
Delaware	Del. Code Ann., tit. 7 § 503
Florida	Fla. Stat. § 97.0585
Georgia	Ga. Code Ann. §§ 50-18-72, 10-1-393.8
Guam	5 Guam Code Ann. §§ 32704, 32705
Hawaii	Haw. Rev. Stat. §§ 487J-1–487J-4, 12-3
Idaho	Idaho Code § 28-52-108(1)
Illinois	815 Ill. Comp. Stat. 505/2QQ, 505/2RR
Indiana	Ind. Code §§ 4-1-10-1 *et seq.*, §§ 4-1-8 *et seq.*, § 9-24-9-2
Kansas	Kan. Stat. Ann. § 75-3520
Louisiana	La. Rev. Stat. Ann. §§ 17:440, 18:154, 32:409.1, 37:23, 44:11; La. Civ. Code Ann. art. 3352 § 3352
Maine	Me. Rev. Stat. Ann. tit. 10, §§ 1272, 1272-B
Maryland	Md. Code Ann., Com. Law § 14-3402
Massachusetts	Mass. Gen. Laws ch. 167B, §§ 14, 22
Michigan	Mich. Comp. Laws §§ 445.81 *et seq.*, 565.452, 565.491

Minnesota	Minn. Stat. § 325E.59
Mississippi	Miss. Code Ann. § 25-1-111
Missouri	Mo. Rev. Stat. § 407.1355
Montana	Mont. Code Ann. §§ 32-6-306, 30-14-1702, 30-14-1703
Nebraska	Neb. Rev. Stat. § 48-237
Nevada	Nev. Rev. Stat. §§ 239, 239B, 603
New Jersey	N.J. Stat. Ann. §§ 47:1-16, 56:8-164
New Mexico	N.M. Stat. Ann. §§ 57-12B-1 *et seq.*
New York	N.Y. Gen. Bus. Law § 399-dd; N.Y. Lab. Law § 203-d**
North Carolina	N.C. Gen. Stat. § 75-62
North Dakota	N.D. Cent. Code §§ 39-33-01, 39-33-02
Ohio	Ohio Rev. Code Ann. § 1349.17
Oklahoma	Okla. Stat. tit. 40, § 173.1
Oregon	Or. Rev. Stat. §§ 107.840, 646A.620
Pennsylvania	74 Pa. Stat. Ann. §§ 201–204
Rhode Island	R.I. Gen. Laws §§ 6-13-15, 6-13-17, 6-13-19
South Carolina	S.C. Code Ann. §§ 7-5-170, 37-20-180, 30-2-310
South Dakota	S.D. Codified Laws §§ 32-12-17.10, 32-12-17.13
Tennessee	Tenn. Code Ann. § 47-18-2110
Texas	Tex. Bus. & Com. Code Ann. §§ 501.001–501.002, §§ 501.101–501.102; Tex. Elec. Code Ann. § 13.004; Tex. Bus. & Com. Code § 20.02
Utah	Utah Code Ann. §§ 31A-21-110, 13-45-301, 35A-4-312.5, 76-6-1102
Vermont	9 Vt. Stat. Ann. §§ 2440, 2430
Virginia	Va. Code Ann. §§ 2.2-3808, 59.1-443.2
Washington	Wash. Rev. Code Ann. § 19.146.205
West Virginia	W. Va. Code §§ 17E-1-11, 16-5-33, 18-2-5f
Wisconsin	Wis. Stat. § 36.32

* Many state SSN laws mandate use of encryption when transmitting Social Security numbers.

** Applies to employers.

6. State Laws Requiring SSN Policies

Connecticut	Conn. Gen. Stat. § 42-471
Massachusetts	201 Mass. Code Regs. §§ 17.01–17.04 (broader than just SSNs)
Michigan	Mich. Comp. Laws § 445.84
New Mexico	N.M. Stat. §§ 57-12B-2 to 57-12B-3
New York	N.Y. Gen. Bus. Law § 3990dd(4)
Texas	Tex. Bus. & Com. Code Ann. §§ 501.051–501.053 (also covers driver's license)

Appendix C

Federal Regulations

1. Federal Regulations Imposing an Obligation to Provide Security

    (a) COPPA Regulations: 16 C.F.R. § 312.8.

    (b) DHS Regulations: Electronic Signature and Storage of Form 1-9, Employment Eligibility Verification, 8 C.F.R. § 274a.2 (e), (f), (g), and (h) (requiring an effective records security program).

    (c) FCC Order re Pretexting, In the Matter of Implementation of the Telecommunications Act of 1996: Telecommunications Carriers' Use of Customer Proprietary Network Information and Other Customer Information IP-Enabled Services, CC Docket No. 96-115, WC Docket No. 04-36, Apr. 2, 2007, at ¶¶ 33–36; https://apps.fcc.gov/edocs_public/attachmatch/FCC-07-22A1.pdf.

    (d) FDA Regulations: 21 C.F.R. pt. 11.

    (e) FFIEC Guidance: *Authentication in an Internet Banking Environment*, Oct. 12, 2005, https://www.ffiec.gov/pdf/authentication _guidance.pdf. See also *Frequently Asked Questions on FFIEC Guidance on Authentication in an Internet Banking Environment*, Aug. 15, 2006, at 5, https://www.ffiec.gov/pdf/authentication_faq.pdf; and *Supplement to Authentication in an Internet Banking Environment*, June 28, 2011, https://www.ffiec.gov/press/pr062811.htm.

    (f) GLB Security Regulations: Interagency Guidelines Establishing Standards for Safeguarding Consumer Information (to implement §§ 501 and 505(b) of the Gramm-Leach-Bliley Act), 12 C.F.R. pt. 30, Appendix B (OCC); 12 C.F.R. pt. 208, Appendix D-2; 12 C.F.R. pt. 225, Appendix F (Federal Reserve System); 12 C.F.R. pt. 364, Appendix B (FDIC); 12 C.F.R. pt. 570, Appendix B (Office of Thrift Supervision, which merged with the OCC as of July 21, 2011).

    (g) GLB Security Regulations (FTC): FTC Standards for Safeguarding Customer Information (Safeguards Rule) (to implement §§ 501 and 505(b) of the Gramm-Leach-Bliley Act), 16 C.F.R. pt. 314 (FTC).

    (h) HIPAA Security Regulations: Final HIPAA Security Regulations, 45 C.F.R. pt. 164.

    (i) IRS Regulations: Rev. Proc. 97-22, 1997-1 C.B. 652, 1997-13 I.R.B. 9 and Rev. Proc. 98-25.

    (j) IRS Regulations: IRS Announcement 98-27, 1998-15 I.R.B. 30 and Tax Regs. 26 C.F.R. § 1.1441-1(e)(4)(iv).

    (k) SEC Guidance: SEC CF Disclosure Guidance: Topic No. 2, Cyber-security (Oct. 13, 2011), https://www.sec.gov/divisions/corpfin/guidance/cfguidance-topic2.htm.

    (l) SEC Regulation S-P: 17 C.F.R. § 248.

    (m) SEC Regulations: 17 C.F.R. § 240.17a-4 and 17 C.F.R. § 257.1(e)(3).

    (n) SEC Regulations: 17 C.F.R. § 248.30 (procedures to safeguard customer records and information; disposal of consumer report information (applies to any broker, dealer, and investment company, and every investment advisor registered with the SEC)).

(o) SEC Regulation SCI, Rule 1002(b) (upon any responsible SCI personnel having a reasonable basis to conclude that an SCI event has occurred, the SCI entity must provide the Commission with notifications pertaining to such event and regular updates until the event is resolved).

(p) DEARS: 48 C.F.R. § 204.7300 (applies to contractors and subcontractors to safeguard covered unclassified defense information and also requires reporting of cyber incidents within 72 hours).

2. Federal Regulations Imposing Authentication Requirements

(a) ACH Operating Rules (2013) § 2.5.2.5(d) (Verification of Receiver's Identity)

(b) Banking Know-Your-Customer Rules

    i. 31 C.F.R. § 103.121, Customer Identification Programs for Banks, Savings Associations, Credit Unions, and Certain Non-Federally Regulated Banks

    ii. 31 C.F.R. § 103.122, Customer Identification Programs for Broker-Dealers

    iii. 31 C.F.R. § 103.123, Customer Identification Programs for Futures Commission Merchants and Introducing Brokers

    iv. 31 C.F.R. § 103.131, Customer Identification Programs for Mutual Funds

(c) FCC Order re Pretexting, Apr. 2, 2007—In the Matter of Implementation of the Telecommunications Act of 1996: Telecommunications Carriers' Use of Customer Proprietary Network Information and Other Customer Information IP-Enabled Services, CC Docket No. 96-115, WC Docket No. 04-36, Apr. 2, 2007, at ¶¶ 13–25, https://apps.fcc.gov/edocs_public/attachmatch/FCC-07-22A1.pdf.

(d) FFIEC Guidance: Authentication in an Internet Banking Environment, Oct. 12, 2005, http://wvvw.ffiec.gov/pdf/authentication_guidance.pdf. *See also* Supplement to Authentication in an Internet Banking Environment, http://wwwv.fdic.gov/news/news/press/2011/pr11111a.pdf.

(e) USA PATRIOT Act

    i. 31 U.S.C. § 5318 (Verification of Identification)

    ii. Know-your-customer rules

3. Federal Data Disposal/Destruction Regulations

(a) FCRA Data Disposal Rules: 12 C.F.R. pt. 334, 364.

(b) SEC Regulations: 17 C.F.R. § 248.30 (procedures to safeguard customer records and information; disposal of consumer report information—applies to any broker, dealer, and investment company, and every investment advisor registered with the SEC).

4. Federal Security Breach Notification Regulations

(a) FCC Order re Pretexting, In the Matter of Implementation of the Telecommunications Act of 1996: Telecommunications Carriers' Use of Customer Proprietary Network Information and Other Customer Information

IP-Enabled Services, CC Docket No. 96-115, WC Docket No. 04-36, Apr. 2, 2007, at ¶¶ 26–32, https://apps.fcc.gov/edocs_public/attachmatch/FCC-07-22A1.pdf.

(b) GLB Security Breach Notification Rule: Interagency Guidance on Response Programs for Unauthorized Access to Customer Information and Customer Notice (Mar. 29, 2005), 12 C.F.R. pt. 30 (OCC), 12 C.F.R. pt. 208 and 225 (Federal Reserve System), 12 C.F.R. pt. 364 (FDIC), and 12 C.F.R. pt. 568 and 570 (Office of Thrift Supervision, which merged with the OCC as of July 21, 2011), available at https://www.occ.treas.gov/news-issuances/federal-register/70fr15736.pdf.

(c) IRS Regulations: Rev. Proc. 98-25, § 8.01.

(d) HIPAA Breach Notification Rules: 45 C.F.R. §§ 164.400–164.414.

(e) SEC Guidance: SEC CF Disclosure Guidance: Topic No. 2, Cybersecurity (Oct. 13, 2011); https://www.sec.gov/divisions/corpfin/guidance/cfguidance-topic2.htm.

Appendix D

State Regulations

1. Insurance: NAIC Model Regulations: National Association of Insurance Commissioners, Standards for Safeguarding Consumer Information, Model Regulation.

2. Massachusetts: Standards for the Protection of Personal Information of Residents of the Commonwealth, 201 Mass. Code Regs. 17.00 *et seq.* New York: N.Y. Department of Fin. Servs., Cybersecurity Requirements for Financial Services Companies, N.Y. Comp. Codes R. & Regs. tit. 23, §§ 500 *et seq.*

3. New York: N.Y. Department of Fin. Servs., Cybersecurity Requirements for Financial Services Companies, N.Y. Comp. Codes R. & Regs. tit. 23, §§ 500 *et seq.*

Appendix E

Best Practice Guidelines Issued by Federal Government Agencies

1. NIST Special Publications (SP), 800 Series, Computer Security, http://csrc.nist. gov/publications/PubsSPs.html#SP 800.

2. NIST Cybersecurity Framework, Version 1.1 (Apr. 16, 2018), https://www.nist. gov/cyberframework.

3. U.S. Department of Justice, *Best Practices for Victim Response and Reporting of Cyber Incidents,* Version 1.0 (Apr. 2015), http://www.justice.gov/sites/default/files/ opa/speeches/attachments/2015/04/29/criminal_division_guidance_on_best_ practices_for_victim_response _and_reporting_cyber_incidents2.pdf.

Appendix F

Best Practices Guidelines Issued by State Government Agencies

1. **California**: California Attorney General, California Data Breach Report (Feb. 2016), https://oag.ca.gov/breachreport2016.

2. **Illinois**: Illinois Attorney General, Information Security and Security Breach Notification Guidance, *available at* http://www.illinoisattorneygeneral.gov/consumers/Security_Breach_Notification_Guidance.pdf.

3. **Massachusetts**: Massachusetts Office of Consumer Affairs and Business Regulation, *A Small Business Guide: Formulating a Comprehensive Written Information Security Program*, http://www.mass.gov/ocabr/docs/idtheft/sec-plan-smallbiz-guide.pdf.

Appendix G

Court Decisions Regarding Duty to Provide Data Security

1. *In re* Target Corp. Customer Data Sec. Breach Litig., 64 F. Supp. 3d 1304, 1310 (D. Minn. 2014) ("adequately pled that Target owed them a duty of care").

2. *In re* Sony Gaming Networks & Customer Data Sec. Breach Litig., 996 F Supp. 2d 942 (S.D. Cal. 2014) (recognized legal duty to "safeguard a consumer's confidential information entrusted to a commercial entity"; failing to use "industry-standard" encryption breached legal duty of care).

3. Patco Construction Co. v. People's United Bank, 684 F.3d 197 (1st Cir. 2012).

4. Lone Star Nat'l Bank v. Heartland Payment Systems, Inc. 729 F.3d 421 (5th Cir. 2013) (recognizing negligence claim and finding economic loss doctrine not applicable).

5. Experi-Metal, Inc. v. Comerica Bank, No. 09-14890, 2011 WL 2433383 (E.D. Mich. June 13, 2011).

6. Cooney v. Chicago Public Schools, 2010 Ill. App. LEXIS 1424 (Dec. 30, 2010) (no common-law duty to provide security).

7. Prudential Ins. Co. of America v. Dukoff, No. 07-1080, 2009 U.S. Dist. LEXIS 117843 (E.D.N.Y. Dec. 18, 2009) (must authenticate identity of signer of insurance application in order to enforce signature).

8. Kerr v. Dillard Store Services, Inc., 2009 U.S. Dist. LEXIS 11792 (D. Kan. Feb. 17, 2009) (electronic signature not enforceable due to lack of security re attribution of signer to signature).

9. *In re* TJX Companies Retail Security Breach Litigation, 524 F. Supp. 2d 83 (D. Mass. 2007) (rejecting a negligence claim due to the economic loss doctrine, but allowing a negligent misrepresentation claim to proceed).

10. Wolfe v. MBNA America Bank, 485 F. Supp. 2d 874, 882 (W.D. Tenn. 2007).

11. Lorraine v. Markel, 241 F.R.D. 534 (D. Md. 2007).

12. Guin v. Brazos Higher Education Service, 2006 U.S. Dist. LEXIS 4846 (D. Minn. Feb. 7, 2006).

13. American Express v. Vinhnee, 336 B.R. 437 (B.A.P. 9th Cir. 2005).

14. Bell v. Michigan Council, 2005 Mich. App. LEXIS 353 (Mich. App. Feb. 15, 2005) (unpublished opinion).

15. Inquiry Regarding the Entry of Verizon-Maine into the InterLATA Telephone Market Pursuant to Section 271 of Telecommunication Act of 1996, Docket No. 2000-849, Maine Public Utilities Commission, 2003 Me. PUC LEXIS 181, Apr. 30, 2003, http://www.steptoe.com/assets/attachments/1670.pdf.

Appendix H

CFPB Decision and Consent Decree

In re Dwolla, Inc., File No. 2016-CFPB-0007, Consent Order (C.F.P.B. Mar. 2, 2016), http://files.consumerfinance.gov/f/201603_cfpb_consent-order-dwolla-inc.pdf. *See also* Press Release, Consumer Financial Protection Bureau, CFPB Takes Action against Dwolla for Misrepresenting Data Security Practices (Mar. 2, 2016), https://www.consumerfinance.gov/about-us/newsroom/cfpb-takes-action-against-dwolla-for-misrepresenting-data-security-practices/.

Appendix I

FTC Decisions and Consent Decrees

List of FTC data security cases and enforcement actions are available at Federal Trade Commission, Data Security, https://www.ftc.gov/datasecurity.

Appendix J

SEC Decision and Consent Decree

Press Release, U.S. Sec. Exch. Comm., SEC: Morgan Stanley Failed to Safeguard Customer Data (June 8, 2016) (relating to *In re* Morgan Stanley Smith Barney LLC, Administrative Proceeding, File No. 3-17280), https://www.sec.gov/news/pressrelease/2016-112.html; https://www.sec.gov/litigation/admin/2016/34-78021.pdf (Order); IAPP July 20, 2016 analysis article at https://iapp.org/news/a/not-unfair-may-still-be-unreasonable-the-ramifications-of -the-secs-morgan-stanley-settlement/.

Chapter 6

Cloud Computing Legal Issues for Financial Services

By Erin Fonte and Jesse Moore[1]

I. Introduction

One of the industry verticals where there has been a lot of development and innovation in cloud computing is in financial services technology products and services. Cloud computing in the financial services sector is now a high-stakes business with serious risks and rewards—the delivery of cloud-computing-related services to the financial services sector has become a multibillion-dollar industry.[2] Industry experts have predicted that a security breach will cause the failure of a major financial institution (FI) sometime within the next 10 years,[3] and the recent Equifax data breach showed how many individuals a major data security incident can affect. Cloud computing attracts financial service innovators for the same reasons that cloud computing draws pioneers in other industries; by offering increased flexibility and efficiency at lower costs than on-premises computing solutions, cloud-based computing environments seem to be inevitable in the further development of large-scale, multiuser computing platforms in the financial services industry. However, cloud computing for financial vendors creates increased security risks and regulatory and legal scrutiny. After briefly reviewing the many advantageous ways that FIs use cloud computing, this chapter will discuss the unique legal and regulatory standards, guidance, and concerns (including the New York Department of Financial Services Cybersecurity Regulation)[4] that FI advisors should consider regarding cloud computing in general and in negotiating and drafting effective cloud-computing-related agreements in particular.

---

1   Erin Fonte is Co-Leader of Hunton Andrews Kurth's Financial Institutions Corporate and Regulatory Group and focuses on FinTech, payments, and digital commerce. She is resident in the firm's Austin office, where she assists clients with a broad range of matters related to banking and financial services, including financial services vendor agreements, third-party vendor management, FinTech, payments/payment systems, digital commerce, and cybersecurity, privacy, and data asset management matters, with increasing emphasis on blockchain, AI, Big Data and connected devices/Internet of Things issues. Jesse Moore is an Associate General Counsel at the Texas Department of Banking in Austin, Texas. He previously clerked for the Hon. Barbara J. Houser, Chief U.S. Bankruptcy Judge for the Northern District of Texas, and then worked at Hunton & Williams and Dykema Cox Smith in Dallas and Austin.

2   *See Silver Linings: Banks Big and Small Are Embracing Cloud Computing*, THE ECONOMIST, July 20, 2013, *available at* http://www.economist.com/news/finance-and-economics/21582013-banks-big-and-small-are-embracing-cloud-computing-silver-linings.

3   Matthew Wall, *2017 Tech Trends: "A Major Bank Will Fail,"* BBC NEWS, Jan. 6, 2017, *available at* http://www.bbc.com/news/business-38517517 (quoting Prof. Richard Benham, chairman of the National Cyber Management Centre, Ltd.).

4   N.Y. COMP. CODES R. & REGS. tit. 23.

II. What Do Financial Institutions Want and Need in Cloud Computing Services?

The proliferation of cloud computing in the financial services sector arises from two trends: the increased efficiency and practicality of cloud-based computing systems, and the increased efficiency and practicality of outsourcing to third-party vendors. These trends are related—as cloud computing becomes faster and more secure, it increasingly facilitates third-party outsourcing of various business functions by FIs. Functions subject to outsourcing include both FI-specific activities (e.g., servicing the needs of depositors, borrowers, and other customers) and normal functions that apply to any FI as a business (e.g., human resource management and technical support).

Although these outsourcing trends are not unique to the FI sector, FIs do bear increased regulatory burdens with regard to their activities, which tend to reflect a risk-based, common-sense approach that should apply to any industry with a heightened security profile; nevertheless, professional advisors to FIs should be aware of FI-specific requirements and expectations. Advisors must also accurately recognize third-party arrangements that give rise to cloud-computing-related issues in order to provide proper guidance. Before discussing the ins and outs of FI-specific considerations for cloud-computing-related contracts, this chapter will briefly discuss how FIs are using cloud computing either now or in the near-term future. Although not yet ubiquitous, cloud-computing-related concepts have become quite common in the financial services sector.

A. Advent of Cloud Computing for FIs

As with companies in many other sectors, FIs first began using cloud computing in the 1990s or earlier, long before the term "cloud computing" became fashionable. For instance, FIs have been utilizing internal-facing cloud-based services like limited, remote employee access to e-mails or other systems for decades. Basic external-facing, cloud-based services like remote customer account access through third-party-hosted systems are also not new within the industry.

However, these earlier systems were typically private systems hosted by the FIs themselves. Given that dedicated private systems require FIs to make considerable direct investments, the systems lack some of the flexibility and efficiency that third-party cloud solutions offer. Nevertheless, FIs traditionally preferred the perceived increased security of limited private clouds over the increased flexibility and decreased costs of external hybrid public-private cloud services.[5] This reluctance has recently been eroding in the industry, especially among smaller FIs that have never been able to afford private systems.

---

5   Nomenclature regarding "public clouds," "private clouds," and "hybrid clouds" remains somewhat unsettled. The authors of this chapter prefer these definitions: (1) a "public cloud" is "based on shared physical hardware which is owned and operated by a third-party provider"; (2) a "private cloud is "infrastructure dedicated entirely to your business that's hosted either on-site or in a service provider's data center"; and (3) a "hybrid cloud" will "combine public cloud with private cloud or dedicated hosting and leverage the best of what each has to offer to meet your needs—use the public cloud for non-sensitive operations, the private cloud for business-critical operations, and incorporate any existing dedicated resources to achieve a highly flexible, highly agile and highly cost-effective solution." Rackspace, *The Difference Between Private and Public Cloud*, https://www.rackspace.com/en-us/cloud/cloud-computing/difference (last visited Mar. 24, 2017).

Continued innovation is leading many FIs to hybrid cloud services that aim to combine the security benefits of an internal private cloud system with the cost advantages and expertise of a third-party-hosted cloud system. The popularity of these arrangements grows as hybrid third-party-hosted cloud systems offer ever-increasing benefits with ever-improving security measures and decreasing security risks.[6]

B. Benefits of Cloud Computing for FIs

Cloud computing provides considerable benefits for FIs. FIs have often been leaders of technological innovation. Financial institutions deal with a tremendous quantity of data and distance—each institution has thousands of customers using financial accounts to conduct millions of routine transactions across many states or countries, or even the entire planet. Properly tracking, analyzing, verifying, and recording these transactions requires considerable resources. Cloud computing is ideal for these challenges—centrally located and maintained systems that process this data in bulk, and that can be accessed remotely from a simple terminal, are superior to systems developed in-house.[7]

Although larger financial institutions tend to have the resources needed to develop private clouds, the efficiency of outsourcing these functions to third-party vendors attracts FIs both large and small. This may reflect the trend mentioned above toward outsourcing various business functions to third parties rather than performing those functions in-house. Just as an FI may not want to hire its own experts to build a private cloud specifically for the FI, FIs also are moving away from staffing in-house loan servicers, customer support personnel, professional advisors, and technical support consultants, and instead contracting with third-party vendors to provide these functions.

Many of these outsourced services already involve some sort of cloud computing arrangements. Vendors often interface with their multiple clients through a commonly accessible computer platform where FI clients can log in remotely to exchange information with the vendor and provide it with instructions. For example, these platforms will permit employee information to be exchanged with a vendor that will process the payroll, or permit borrower information to be exchanged with a loan servicer. The services provided by modern vendors are often so intertwined with the software interface that this sort of arrangement even has its own acronym: "SaaS," which stands for software-as-a-service. This proliferation of vendors in general, and SaaS vendors in particular, is remarkable. In some instances, certain FI vendors chiefly interact with other FI vendors rather than FI personnel. Some smaller FIs have through outsourcing cut their payrolls to a surprisingly small handful of direct employees. The competitive advantages for these low-cost, tech-savvy FIs cannot be ignored. The cost benefits by reducing an FI's traditional brick-and-mortar presence in favor of online, cloud-related services are considerable—a cloud does not require a ground lease, premises liability insurance, or nice plants and a custodial staff.

More importantly, FIs that do not match increased consumer expectations for online, mobile, and omni-channel services are also falling behind their competitors.[8] Customers

---

6   *Id.*

7   *See* Penny Crosman, *Why Banks Are Finally Embracing Cloud Computing*, AM. BANKER, Aug. 12, 2013, *available at* https://www.americanbanker.com/news/why-banks-are-finally-embracing-cloud-computing.

8   Irving Wladawsky-Berger, *Is FinTech Forcing Banking to a Tipping Point?*, WALL ST. J.: CIO J., Apr. 15, 2016, *available at* http://blogs.wsj.com/cio/2016/04/15/is-fintech-forcing-banking-to-a-tipping-point/.

have become accustomed to monitoring accounts, depositing checks, and initiating transactions from the convenience of their computer, smart phone, or other mobile device. The rapid proliferation of nontraditional financial technology (fintech) companies in the financial services sector is only increasing this competition. For instance, companies like PayPal, Venmo (bought by PayPal), and Amazon.com have created systems for providing financial services (e.g., payment services offered by Amazon Pay) that invade traditional FI territory using cloud-based technology. Customers may now expect their preferred traditional FI to match up to these cloud-based services from non-FI fintech companies. In many instances, an FI can provide these services most quickly and efficiently through a third-party vendor.

C. Cloud Computing Concerns for FIs

FIs must treat any arrangement involving a remote computing platform that is hosted by or accessible to a third party, and that receives sensitive or nonpublic information[9] from the FI, as a "cloud" and negotiate and document that arrangement accordingly. Fortunately, along with offering ever-increasing benefits to FIs, cloud computing vendors also offer ever-increasing security measures and protections. For cloud-computing or any remote-access system, the lack of location-dependent access will always be a potential security problem—FIs have long relied on physical barriers (such as safes, locked doors, or in-person identification by a teller) to reduce the risks of intrusion and theft. Moving services to a cloud-based environment means that the FI itself does not have direct control over physical security or systems security and must trust that the cloud computing vendor is maintaining physical and systems security to the same level the FI would itself, which can potentially create increased security risks if the cloud computing vendor is not meeting its security commitments.

However, ever-improving security measures such as encryption, multifactor authentication, penetration testing, and distributed databases (blockchain) are steadily improving and reducing risks for hybrid cloud computing compared to the security risks for internal systems and private clouds. Indeed, some analysts argue that the expertise of third-party vendors makes private clouds riskier than properly hosted hybrid clouds.[10] As these security risks for cloud and noncloud computing options approach parity, the regulatory and legal environment has become more favorable and conducive for FIs utilizing cloud-based computing services.

Lawyers, consultants, and employees providing advice to FIs should keep in mind that laws, rules, and regulations, as well as regulator standards and formal guidance, also often inform good business judgment and practices for FI management. The risks from the security breaches that these regulations are designed to minimize go far beyond the risks of a regulatory enforcement actions—security breaches threaten FIs with quick, catastrophic, and irreversible losses from theft, fraud, and the loss of customer confidence and trust (i.e., reputational risks). From the FI regulatory agency perspective, regulatory guidance for FIs regarding cloud computing is not and should not be viewed as static

---

9   15 U.S.C. § 6801(a).

10   Neil Munshi, *Data Security Concerns Force Banks Up into the Cloud*, FIN. TIMES, Oct. 10, 2016, *available at* https://www.ft.com/content/e4667fe2-7522-11e6-bf48-b372cdb1043a (interview with Neil Munshi, CEO of Trading Technologies, Ltd.).

guidance. FI personnel and professional FI advisors should always be looking for ways to improve their clients' security measures and systems to exceed the basic standards set forth in the laws and regulations discussed below, as well as countering an ever-evolving security threat landscape.

III. Understanding and Meeting FI Regulatory Requirements for Cloud Computing

As participants in a regulated industry, FIs must consider laws, rules, and regulations first and foremost in their activities. Such laws, rules, and regulations, along with guidance from federal and state functional regulators, will instruct FIs and their professional advisors of many important issues in dealing with third-party vendors, including cloud-related vendors. Any agreement with a cloud-based vendor must require the vendor to comply with the applicable laws, rules, and regulations. Some detail may be needed—in some instances, a mere broad promise to comply with all applicable law will not suffice, and instead the FI should spell out what actions are needed for compliance by the cloud vendor.

In addition, the FI will endeavor to compel its third-party cloud vendor (and its agents and contractors) to perform their obligations in accordance with those laws, rules, and regulations applicable to the FI (although some cloud vendors will attempt to push back on this). For instance, if the FI must provide ongoing training to its personnel, the vendor must do so as well. If the FI is required to implement certain security measures, such as encryption or multifactor authentication, then vendors are also required to implement those measures (and vendors must require their own vendors to do so—the concept of "fourth-party due diligence"). If the FI must conduct audits for security issues, it must require its vendors to cooperate with such audits. If an FI uses a third-party vendor to audit its other vendors, these cloud vendors must agree to cooperate with each other. The next portion of this chapter will discuss some of the federal and state legal and regulatory requirements that FIs should consider when doing business with a vendor that relates to cloud computing.

A. Federal Legal and Regulatory Requirements

Federal law on FI use of cloud computing is still somewhat minimal; however, the requirements for cloud computing vendors arise out of the federal laws, rules, and regulations already applicable to third-party FI vendors in general. There are federal laws relating to employee or customer privacy, which will be discussed in this section. There are also plenty of other federal laws that are relevant to cloud computing, such as tax laws, laws on patents and intellectual property, laws restricting unauthorized access to computer systems, or laws relating to trade and competition. In addition, any FI should consider whether its vendor arrangements comply with broader applicable federal laws and regulations for FIs, such as the limits on the activities of national banking associations.[11] Last but certainly not least, there is extensive guidance from federal FI regulators that generally

---

11 *See, e.g.,* 12 U.S.C. § 24 (listing the corporate powers that a national banking association may exercise).

should be followed with the same attentiveness accorded to formal laws and regulations. Federal regulatory guidance on cloud computing will be discussed in Part III.

Many federal laws are important to FIs who use cloud-based, third-party services, yet are not unique to FIs. For instance, any FI that transmits health-related employee information to a cloud (particularly protected health information (PHI)) should heed the Health Insurance Portability and Accountability Act of 1996 and its related rules (HIPAA).[12] In some instances, the FIs may be themselves considered "business associates" as defined under HIPAA. These considerations are not unique to FIs and are discussed in depth elsewhere in this book.

The federal Gramm-Leach-Bliley Act of 1999 (GLBA) provides that "[i]t is the policy of the Congress that each financial institution has an affirmative and continuing obligation to respect the privacy of its customers and to protect the security and confidentiality of those customers' nonpublic personal information."[13] FIs must comply accordingly with various limits on disclosing nonpublic personal information about their customers.[14] Applicable federal FI regulators have been given rulemaking authority to "establish appropriate standards" for maintaining the security of this information.[15]

In 2000, a number of federal regulatory agencies published the Security Rule and the Privacy Rule under the GLBA in the *Interagency Guidelines Establishing Information Security Standards* (Interagency Security Guidelines), which set forth mandatory standards for privacy and data security under GLBA for various FIs.[16] These guidelines have relatively routine requirements; in a nutshell, for data security, FIs must develop an appropriate security program with the involvement of the FI's board of directors that includes training, intrusion detection, and an incident response plan, and this security program must be implemented properly, revisited for potential improvements, and reviewed by the FI's board at least once per year.[17]

The Interagency Security Guidelines do have a short but specific section on vendor management. Each FI must do the following:

1) exercise appropriate due diligence in selecting its vendors;

2) require its vendors *by contract* to implement appropriate measures designed to meet the objectives of these guidelines; and

3) where indicated by the [FI's] risk assessment, monitor its vendors to confirm that they have satisfied their obligations as required by paragraph [2], and as part of this monitoring, an FI should review audits, summaries of test results, or other equivalent evaluations of its vendors.[18]

---

12 *See* 45 C.F.R. pt. 160, and subparts A and E of pt. 164.

13 15 U.S.C. § 6801(a).

14 *Id.* § 6802(a).

15 *Id.* § 6801(b).

16 *See Interagency Guidelines Establishing Information Security Standards* as adopted by the following federal banking regulatory agencies: Federal Reserve Board (12 C.F.R. pt. 208, App. D-2 and 12 C.F.R. pt. 225, App. F); Office of the Comptroller of the Currency (12 C.F.R. 30, App. B); and Federal Deposit Insurance Corporation (12 C.F.R. pt. 364, App. B and 12 CFR pt. 391, subpart B, App. B). Note that the content of the *Interagency Guidelines Establishing Information Security Standards* is identical as adopted by each federal banking agency within their respective regulatory section of the C.F.R.

17 *Id.*

18 *Id.*

This brief guidance does touch on two important subjects—pre-engagement due diligence and post-engagement monitoring—that will be discussed in other parts of this chapter. For negotiating the actual cloud vendor agreement, the main takeaway from the Interagency Security Guidelines is that vendor contracts must permit the FI to comply with the guidelines, including appropriate monitoring and auditing of all third parties (and vendors to the third parties, i.e., fourth-party due diligence).

Another GLBA-related point for FIs might be that federal Regulation P requires an FI to provide its individual customers with a privacy notice that states the FI's "policies and practices with respect to protecting the confidentiality and security of nonpublic personal information."[19] Detail is not necessary—an FI may merely "[d]escribe in general terms who is authorized to have access to the information" and "[s]tate whether [it has] security practices and procedures in place to ensure the confidentiality of the information in accordance with [its] policy." [20] FIs "are not required to describe technical information about the safeguards [they] use."[21] Compliance is simple—FIs must comply with the terms of the privacy notice unless and until the notice is changed, and the customer is given reasonable notice of the change and an opportunity to opt out prior to implementation of the change but does not do so.[22] Entities that do not live up to the promises in their applicable privacy notice may face serious monetary penalties.[23] FIs should ensure that their arrangements with vendors, cloud-based or not, involving private consumer information are accurately represented on the FI's privacy notices.

B. State Law Requirements

Although federal law is the chief source of law and regulation for FIs, state law and regulation cannot be overlooked. FIs formed under state law or otherwise subject to state FI regulation must always comply with applicable state and federal requirements. These requirements can be specific to FIs or broadly apply to activities in which the FI engages, such as the handling of nonpublic customer information. FI cloud-based vendor contracts must both require compliance with applicable regulations and contain provisions that facilitate this compliance. To understand these minimal requirements, applicable laws, rules, and regulations must be understood.[24]

Step one of this analysis—determining what law applies—can be complicated. FIs must consider both their own physical locations and their customers' state of residency and current locations when determining what state laws apply. Some state regulators will take the position that certain regulations will apply to FIs with no physical location in the

---

19 12 C.F.R. § 1016.6(a)(8).

20 *Id.* § 1016.6(c)(6).

21 *Id.*

22 *Id.* § 1016.8.

23 *See, e.g.,* Consent Order, *In re* Dwolla, Inc., No. 2016-CFPB-0007 (Consumer Fin. Protection Bureau, Mar. 20, 2016), *available at* http://files.consumerfinance.gov/f/201603_cfpb_consent-order-dwolla-inc.pdf (issuing $100,000 fine to FI that exaggerated its security practices in its notices, including falsely promising consumers that its practices "exceed" or "surpass" industry standards and that all data would be encrypted).

24 This chapter does not discuss the plethora of other legal issues that should be considered when reaching an agreement with a vendor implicating cloud computing, such as basic contract and property law, local and state tax law, agency law, intellectual property law, etc.

state in question if those FIs are doing business with residents of that particular state.[25] In addition, cities, counties, or other local governments may at some point enact regulations that must be considered as well.

New York seems to be the sole state as of this writing that has passed its own specific cybersecurity regulations for FIs (the New York DFS Cybersecurity Regulations), which went into effect on March 1, 2017.[26] Subject to certain smaller FI exemptions, these regulations apply to any FI "operating under or required to operate under a license, registration, charter, certificate, permit, accreditation or similar authorization under the Banking Law, the Insurance Law or the Financial Services Law."[27] On the whole, the New York DFS Cybersecurity Regulations are stricter than corresponding federal laws, rules, regulations, and guidance.

An important aspect of the New York DFS Cybersecurity Regulations for professional advisors is that its requirements are basic and reflect sound risk-management principles for an FI. An FI must first conduct a "risk assessment" that will be sufficient to inform the design of a cybersecurity program to protect the FI's information systems, nonpublic information, and business operations.[28] Written policies and procedures are required for this risk assessment.[29] Based on this risk assessment, the FI must develop a cybersecurity program that identifies cybersecurity risks, deploys defenses, detects intrusions, responds to intrusions, and fulfills regulatory reporting requirements.[30] A written cybersecurity policy must be drafted, and a chief information security officer must be appointed to oversee and implement this policy and the program (including data breach response measures).[31] Penetration testing and regular document audits are required.[32] Individual user access privileges should be narrowly and appropriately tailored and periodically reviewed.[33] Appropriate cybersecurity personnel must be utilized and provided with ongoing training.[34]

The New York DFS Cybersecurity Regulations do mandate specific security measures, such as multifactor authentication for remote external access and encryption of sensitive nonpublic information.[35] Training of personnel and monitoring for breaches is required, and an incident response plan must also be established.[36] Reports of security incidents must be made to the New York state regulators along with annual compliance certifications.[37]

Moreover, policies for managing third-party vendors must also be created and implemented.[38] In short, these policies for vendors must repeat the requirements for the FI itself

---

25 *See, e.g.,* N.Y. State Banking Dept., *Letter re: Section 340 of the New York Banking Law* (Dec. 21, 2006), *available at* http://www.dfs.ny.gov//legal/interpret/lo061221.htm (holding that lender based in Nevada with no physical presence in the State of New York must be licensed under New York law to lend to New York residents solely over the internet).

26 N.Y. Comp. Codes R. & Regs. tit. 23. § 500.01*et seq.*

27 N.Y. Comp. Codes R. & Regs. tit. 23, § 500.01(c). *See also id.* § 500.19 (listing exemptions).

28 *Id.* § 500.09(a).

29 *Id.* § 500.09(b).

30 *Id.* § 500.02.

31 *Id.* §§ 500.03–04.

32 *Id.* §§ 500.05–06.

33 *Id.* § 500.07.

34 *Id.* § 500.10.

35 *Id.* § 500.13 & 500.15.

36 *Id.* § 500.14 & 500.16.

37 *Id.* § 500.17.

38 *Id.* § 500.11.

under the New York DFS Cybersecurity Regulations. This reflects a good cloud-based vendor management rule of thumb: what goes for the FI goes for the vendor. Any standard, protocol, or expectation that applies to an FI itself should also apply to the vendor.

Although other states may not yet have cybersecurity-specific laws, most states do have privacy laws that will apply to an FI, all customer information that it chooses to host in the cloud, and the FI's third-party vendors who have access to such systems or information. An FI must have cybersecurity policies that enable it to comply with these applicable laws. This chapter will not discuss each and every potentially applicable state or local privacy law, but here are some examples:

1) Under Texas law, an FI with a Texas presence must adhere to the limits on disclosing customer data in response to a subpoena.[39]

2) Massachusetts has requirements for any "owner of personal information" of Massachusetts residents that create a duty to develop and implement an appropriate security program, including reasonable computer security systems.[40] Security measures such as authentication, firewalls, and encryption are mandated in certain circumstances.[41]

3) California requires that any FI with "personal information about a California resident shall implement and maintain reasonable security procedures and practices appropriate to the nature of the information, to protect the personal information from unauthorized access, destruction, use, modification, or disclosure," and that any FI entrusting such information to a third party have a contract requiring such third party to adhere to those same standards.[42] The California attorney general has opined that failing to implement the 20 critical security controls of the Center for Internet Security "constitutes a lack of reasonable security."[43]

Again, these are just examples of potentially applicable laws, not an exhaustive survey. Practitioners should consult treatises or other materials that attempt to list all potentially applicable laws regarding states in which their FI clients operate.[44]

IV. Federal Regulatory Guidance on Contract Formation

Federal regulatory guidance on outsourced cloud computing for FIs sets forth both regulatory expectations for forming contracts with vendors and thoughtful risk-management advice. It should be noted that FIs are expected to have a comprehensive risk-management

---

39 *See* TEX. FIN. CODE § 59.006.

40 201 MASS. CODE REGS. §§ 17.01–05.

41 *Id.* § 17.04.

42 CAL. CIV. CODE § 1798.81.5.

43 Kamala D. Harris, California Data Breach Report (Feb. 2016), *available at* https://oag.ca.gov/breachreport2016. The critical controls are available at https://www.cisecurity.org/critical-controls/index.cfm.

44 *See, e.g.,* DANIEL SOLOVE & PAUL SCHWARTZ, PRIVACY LAW FUNDAMENTALS, 2D ED. (Int'l Assoc. of Privacy Profs. 2013); BLOOMBERG LAW: PRIVACY & DATA SECURITY, *available at* https://www.bna.com/bloomberg-law-privacy-data-security/; RONALD WEIKERS & MEGAN COSTELLO, DATA SECURITY AND PRIVACY LAW, 2016 ED. (Thompson Reuters 2016).

program for all vendors and third-party servicers, from custodial and cafeteria vendors all the way through sophisticated cloud-based SaaS providers. Any contract negotiation process with a cloud-based vendor should follow this risk-management program, and the risk-management program should address the issues discussed in this chapter.

The Federal Financial Institutions Examination Council (FFIEC) issued in 2012 a document on outsourced cloud computing that discusses cloud computing risk management.[45] Most of this document is routine—due diligence is needed, as is ongoing auditing and monitoring and business continuity planning/disaster recovery. These will be discussed in this chapter, along with the important comment that risks increase "where the cloud computing service provider processes and stores data overseas or comingles the [FI's] data with data from other customers that operate under diverse legal and regulatory jurisdictions[.]"[46] This document highlights the need for the FI to be able to switch vendors or find different solutions if changing regulations requires changing vendors.[47]

The best source of federal regulatory guidance for FIs and third-party cloud computing services is the Federal Financial Institutions Examination Council (FFIEC) examination handbook entitled *Outsourcing Technology Services*.[48] The examination procedures in Appendix A of this handbook state that for cloud computing, it is important whether:

1) resources are shared within a single organization or across various clients of the vendor;
2) the [FI] has the ability to increase or decrease resources on demand without involving the vendor (on-demand self-service);
3) massive scalability in terms of bandwidth or storage is available to the [FI];
4) the [FI] can rapidly deploy or release resources; and
5) the [FI] pays only for those resources that are actually used (pay-as-you-go pricing).[49]

It is worth observing that some of these considerations mostly relate to the economic justification for the arrangement, rather than customer or privacy-/data-security-oriented concerns.

Specific contractual considerations expected by the FFIEC for outsourcing vendors include issues ranging from pricing, to appropriate legal review, to security issues:

1) The contract contains adequate and measurable service-level agreements;
2) Allowed pricing methods do not adversely affect the institution's safety and soundness, including the reasonableness of future price changes;
3) The rights and responsibilities of both FI and vendor are sufficiently detailed;
4) Required contract clauses address significant issues, such as financial and control reporting, financial statements and financial audits of vendor, right to audit, ownership of data and programs, confidentiality, subcontractors, continuity of service, etc.;

---

45 FFIEC, Outsourced Cloud Computing (July 10, 2012), *available at* http://ithandbook.ffiec.gov/media/153119/06-28-12_-_external_cloud_computing_-_public_statement.pdf.
46 *Id.* at 4.
47 *Id.* at 2–3.
48 FFIEC, Outsourcing Technology Services (June 2004), *available at* http://ithandbook.ffiec.gov/IT-Booklets/FFIEC_ITBooklet_OutsourcingTechnologyServices.pdf.
49 *Id.* at A-2.

5) Legal counsel reviewed the contract and legal issues were satisfactorily resolved; and

6) Contract inducement concerns are adequately addressed.[50]

It should be noted that the main text of the *Outsourcing Technology Services* provides plenty of information and insight into reasons behind these action items. For instance, it explains that "contract inducement concerns" may include "extended terms (up to 10 years), significant increases in costs after the first few years, and/or substantial cancellation penalties."[51]

The FI must show that it has evaluated cloud-computing risks and implemented appropriate control mechanisms. According to the handbook, examiners will expect the following:

1) Action plans are developed and implemented in instances where residual risk requires further mitigation.

2) [FI] [m]anagement updates the risk assessment as necessary.

3) The types of data in the cloud have been identified (Social Security numbers, account numbers, IP addresses, etc.) and have established appropriate data classifications based on the [FI's] policies.

4) The controls are commensurate with the sensitivity and criticality of the data.

5) The effectiveness of the controls are tested and verified.

6) Adequate controls exist over the hypervisor if a virtual machine environment supports the cloud services.

7) All network traffic is encrypted in the cloud provider's internal network and during transition from the cloud to the [FI's] network.

8) All data stored on the vendors' systems are being encrypted with unique keys that only authenticated users from this institution can access.

9) Unless the [FI] is using a private cloud model, determine what controls the [FI] or vendor established to mitigate the risks of multitenancy.

10) If a [FI] is using the Software as a Service (SaaS) model, determine whether regular backup copies of the data are being made in a format that can be read by the [FI]. (Backup copies made by the vendor may not be readable.)

11) Ensure that the [FI's] business continuity/disaster recovery plan addresses contingencies for the cloud computing service. Determine whether the [FI] has an exit strategy and de-conversion plan or strategy for the cloud services.

12) Determine whether the cloud vendor has an internal IT audit staff with adequate knowledge and experience or an adequate contractual arrangement with a qualified third-party audit firm.[52]

This mentions several issues that go beyond the scope of this book, such as business continuity planning/disaster recovery and vendor deconversion issues. These concerns are important and worth mentioning briefly. FIs must have adequate plans in place for responding to a natural disaster that could potentially disrupt the delivery of services from the cloud-based vendor, and such plans must be formulated and tested in advance of any

---

50 *Id.* at A-4 to A-5.
51 *Id.* at 17.
52 *Id.* at A-5 to A-6.

disaster occurring. FIs must also have adequate plans in place for terminating a vendor relationship prior to the time when termination becomes necessary.

The FFIEC expects contracts and other written agreements with FI vendors to appropriately address the following items:

1) scope of services
2) performance standards
3) pricing
4) controls
5) financial, financial statements, and control reporting
6) right to audit
7) ownership of data and programs
8) confidentiality and security
9) regulatory compliance
10) indemnification
11) limitation of liability
12) dispute resolution
13) contract duration
14) restrictions on, or prior approval for, vendor subcontractors
15) termination and assignment, including timely return of data in a machine-readable format
16) insurance coverage
17) prevailing jurisdiction (where applicable)
18) choice of law (foreign outsourcing arrangements)
19) regulatory access to data and information necessary for supervision
20) business continuity planning/disaster recovery[53]

In addition, the FFIEC requires consideration of whether service-level agreements sufficiently provide the following:

1) Significant elements of the service are identified and based on the FI's requirements;
2) Objective measurements for each significant element are defined;
3) Reporting of measurements is required;
4) Measurements specify what constitutes inadequate performance; and
5) Inadequate performance is met with appropriate sanctions, such as reduction in contract fees or contract termination.[54]

See Chapter 3 of this book for additional information on service-level agreements in particular.

It is worth noting that the FFIEC even provides guidance for selecting the proper vendor of legal services to perform the expected legal review of the vendor contract prior to closing. FIs must "[e]nsure that the legal counsel is qualified to review the contract particularly if it is based on the laws of a foreign country or other state" and "[e]nsure that the legal review includes an assessment of the enforceability of local contract provisions and

---

53 *Id.* at A-9 to A-10.
54 *Id.* at A-10.

laws in foreign or out-of-state jurisdictions."[55] FI counsel should ensure that their delivery of legal services meets these standards.

Another point worth emphasizing is contractual restrictions on, or prior approval for, subcontractors. An FI should treat potential subcontractors with the same caution that it treats vendors. Adding an intermediary contractor does not relieve the FI from its duty to properly monitor and supervise all persons and entities acting directly or indirectly on behalf of the FI. If a cloud vendor wants to bargain for the ability to assign or subcontract its responsibilities to the FI to a subcontractor, the FI must engage in due proper diligence on the subcontractors before entering a contract with a vendor permitting such assignment or subcontracting (fourth-party due diligence). At a minimum, the cloud contract should permit the FI to immediately terminate its contract with a vendor prior to the vendor assigning some or all of its material duties under the contract to a new party. For more important functions, an FI should expect to have the services provided by the actual vendor that initially promised to do the services—unlimited assignability is not acceptable for a third-party cloud provider of important FI services. As discussed below, preagreement diligence is essential, and that diligence becomes meaningless if the vendor that was subject to the diligence is not the vendor providing the services.

Given that federal FI regulators have provided a 94-page handbook that extensively discusses all of these regulatory expectations for cloud- and noncloud-based outsourcing arrangements (and this book itself provides additional information about general considerations for these arrangements), this chapter will conclude by briefly discussing some additional vendor selection and management considerations that go beyond the contract itself.

V. Choosing the Right Cloud Computing Vendor— Effective Due Diligence

The FFIEC *Outsourcing Technology Services* examination handbook also provides ample guidance on best practices for conducting due diligence regarding a potential cloud-based vendor. The FFIEC identifies a number of relevant issues. The first set of issues on which the FFIEC focuses is the financial stability of the prospective vendor, which can become quite important when an FI expects to be indemnified by a vendor for risks that the vendor was entrusted to avoid (and is especially important with regard to vendors that are fintech startups):

1) the prospective vendor's audited financial statements and annual reports;
2) the prospective provider's length of operation and market share;
3) the size of the FI's contract in relation to the size of the prospective vendor;
4) the prospective vendor's level of technological expenditures to ensure ongoing support; and
5) the impact of economic, political, or environmental risk on the prospective vendor's financial stability.[56]

---

55 *Id.* at A-9.
56 FFIEC, *supra* note 48.

Additional diligence items to consider are:

1) references from current users or user groups about a particular prospective vendor's reputation and performance;
2) the prospective vendor's experience and ability in the industry;
3) the prospective vendor's experience and ability in dealing with situations similar to the institution's environment and operations;
4) the quality and effectiveness of any cost/benefit analyses, including incremental costs of the additional monitoring, operations responsibilities, and protections that may be required by the FI of the prospective vendor;
5) the cost for additional system and data conversions or interfaces presented by the various prospective vendors;
6) shortcomings in the prospective vendor's expertise that the institution would need to supplement in order to fully mitigate risks;
7) the prospective vendor's proposed use of third parties, subcontractors, or partners to support the outsourced activities;
8) the prospective vendor's ability to respond to service disruptions;
9) the prospective vendor's key personnel that would be assigned to support the institution;
10) the prospective vendor's ability to comply with appropriate federal and state laws, particularly federal laws (including GLBA and the USA PATRIOT Act); and
11) country, state, or local risk.[57]

In addition, the FFIEC gives a nod to other factors that are equally important but perhaps more abstract:

> Other important elements include probing for information on intangibles, such as the third party's service philosophies, quality initiatives, and management style. The culture, values, and business styles should fit those of the financial institution.[58]

Although reputation, history, and culture may be somewhat intangible or subjective, these measures are often among the most important aspects of vendor due diligence. Along with contacting references provided by candidates, FI personnel should reach out to contacts at peer institutions to see what can be learned through unofficial sources that are not favored by the vendor. Given the unique challenges and risks for FIs that deal with hybrid clouds, vendor history is also especially important—prospective vendors that are not familiar with the increased regulatory requirements of FIs may not be prepared to properly serve their customers in the financial-services sector.

Along with assessing the financial stability of a prospective vendor based on its balance sheet and other financial statements, an FI should consider whether the vendor has appropriate cyberliability insurance for the services it provides and associated risks, and whether the FI should purchase additional coverage in case the vendor is unable to fulfill its obligations to hold the FI harmless from losses caused by the vendor's breach of contract.[59] It should be noted that even vendors that are not thinly capitalized often have

---

57 *Id.*
58 *Id.* at 11.
59 See Chapter 15, *infra* this volume.

significant risk exposure to certain sorts of problems. For example, a cloud-based data storage vendor may have considerable remediation and restitution obligations to an FI arising from a data breach or intellectual property legal action. The vendor will often have similar obligations to its other FI clients and may quickly find itself insolvent. Cyberliability insurance either for the vendor or the FI as named beneficiary (if not outright policy holder) may be necessary to adequately mitigate these risks. When reviewing the adequacy of such coverage, an FI must keep in mind that a vendor may have a number of other clients with similar claims in a worst-case scenario.

A final point is that due diligence should never cease. As the FFIEC has stated, "throughout the life of the relationship, [FIs] should ensure the service provider's physical and data security standards meet or exceed standards required by the institution."[60] Ongoing monitoring and auditing of any third-party relationship, including relationships with cloud vendors, must be conducted.

VI. Cross-Border Issues

Despite the delocalized nature of cloud computing, the physical location of any FI cloud-based vendors and their subcontractors, servers, and equipment remains an important issue for FIs. The FFIEC's *Outsourcing Technology Services* handbook contains an entire appendix on the subject.[61] The guidance here can be simplified: FIs should proceed with extra caution when dealing with vendors that may be subject to the laws of non-U.S. jurisdictions.

FIs should always remember that the physical locations of vendors and subcontractors can be of paramount importance in data security. If local governments can seize computer servers and hard drives, or if local governments cannot prevent extrajudicial misappropriation (i.e., theft), then all of the cybersecurity considerations become moot. These considerations likewise become irrelevant if local law permits such confidential information to be obtained through judicial processes, such as subpoenas, without appropriate protective mechanisms.

FIs that do conduct business with cloud vendors that may be subject to non-U.S. law must apprise themselves of both the currently applicable legal and regulatory environment in those foreign jurisdictions and potential upcoming changes to that environment. This additional diligence goes beyond mere legal issues:

> Managing country risk requires organizations to gather and assess information regarding foreign political, social, and economic conditions and events, and to address the exposures introduced by the relationship with a foreign-based provider. Risk management procedures should include the establishment of contingency, service continuity, and exit strategies in the event of unexpected disruptions in service.[62]

An FI must ensure that the applicable local laws permit compliance with applicable U.S. laws. For instance, U.S. law requires FIs to maintain the secrecy of anti-money laundering

---

60 FFIEC, *supra* note 48, at 25.
61 *Id.* at Appendix C.
62 *Id.* at C-2.

reports, certain regulatory exam-related items, and certain customer and employee information. If the confidentiality of these items cannot be protected under applicable non-U.S. law, then an FI cannot permit those items to be subject to such foreign law. Similarly, regulators must be able to examine the services provided by FI vendors regardless of the location of those vendors—FIs "must maintain, in the files of a U.S. office, appropriate English language documentation to support all arrangements with service providers."[63]

> An organization's use of a foreign-based third-party service provider (and the location of critical data and processes outside of U.S. territory) must not compromise the ability of U.S. regulatory authorities to effectively examine the organization. Thus, organizations should not establish servicing arrangements with entities where local laws or regulations would interfere with U.S. regulatory agencies' full and complete access to data or other relevant information. Any analysis of foreign laws obtained from counsel should include a discussion regarding regulatory access to information for supervisory purposes.[64]

Although this regulatory guidance by no means prohibits U.S. FIs from contracting with overseas vendors for cloud-based services, FIs must be aware of and satisfactorily address the increased risks and burdens of such arrangements. Chapters 9–12 discuss some considerations regarding negotiating international cloud agreements and provides an excellent place to begin to understand these issues further.

VII. Conclusion

The proliferation of cloud computing services and providers continues to expand and FIs are exploring and deploying multiple cloud computing services to save costs, increase efficiency, expand customer products, services and offering, and the financial services industry verticals will continue to be a robust area of cloud computing offerings and vendors. As this chapter has discussed, however, the benefits of cloud computing are tempered by the potential for increased security risks, and face growing and evolving regulatory and legal scrutiny. As highlighted in this chapter, there are unique legal and regulatory standards, guidance, and concerns that FIs and their consultants, attorneys and advisors must consider and address regarding cloud computing in general, and in particular in the negotiation and drafting cloud computing third party vendor agreements. With good due diligence, a comprehensive strategy for negotiation, and effective oversight and partnerships with qualified and responsive third party vendors, FIs can utilize and deploy new and cutting-edge technology while still protecting customers and maintaining the safety and soundness of the institution.

---

63 *Id.* at C-4.
64 *Id.* at C-5.

Chapter 7

Clouds for Health Care Providers

By Kathrin E. Kudner and Janet A. Stiven[1]

I. Introduction

Congress established the Health Care Industry Cybersecurity Task Force in 2015 to evaluate cybersecurity attacks focused on the health care industry, including data breaches, medical identity theft, and ransomware.[2] In May 2017 the task force issued a report concluding that "healthcare cybersecurity is in critical condition," in part due to aging equipment and technology, lack of qualified IT personnel, and a rush to develop systems to comply with "meaningful use."[3] As health care organizations are grappling with the challenges of providing high-quality care in a cost-effective manner while ensuring the privacy and security of patient data, many have looked to cloud computing as the solution.

Cloud computing has extensive implications in the health care industry, not only for health care providers, but also for other organizations directly and even indirectly involved with providers. Organizations such as pharmaceutical and medical device manufacturers, medical research organizations, insurance companies and managed care organizations, benefit managers, and health information exchanges all touch health care data as part of their day-to-day operations. In today's world, the delivery of high-quality and cost-effective care requires effective and secure digital systems and connections. Many health care providers and other health care organizations have invested significant resources in information technology (IT) systems and data analytics programs to enable them to better serve their patients and customers. Smaller health care providers with fewer resources are looking to alternative solutions, such as cloud computing.

In a 2014 survey conducted by HiMSS Analytics (the HiMSS Survey), an affiliate of the Healthcare Information and Management Systems Society, more than 80 percent of the survey respondents reported that they use cloud services. Another significant percentage of respondents is planning to begin using cloud computing in the future.[4] Although cloud migrations are growing among health care organizations, the transition to cloud computing remains tentative as these organizations evaluate cloud computing efficiencies, costs of implementation and maintenance, data governance, performance and complexity in hybrid cloud environments, and most importantly, the impact on quality of patient care and privacy and security of data. This cautious approach to cloud computing is a

---

1   Kathrin E. Kudner is a Member of Dykema Gossett PLLC. Janet A. Stiven is Vice President and General Counsel of The Moody Bible Institute of Chicago.

2   *See* Cybersecurity Act of 2015, Division N of the Consolidated Appropriations Act of 2016, Pub. L. No. 114-113, 129 Stat. 2242 (2015).

3   Health Care Industry Cybersecurity Task Force, Report on Improving Cybersecurity in the Health Care Industry 1 (May 2017), https://wwww.phe.gov/Preparedness/planning/CyberTF/Documents/report2017.pdf.

4   HiMSS Analytics, 2014 HiMSS Analytics Cloud Survey 4 (2014), https://www.himss.org/2014-himss-analytics-cloud-survey-full-results?ItemNumber=41958.

prudent one because health care organizations must learn to track and manage risks and performance in a virtual or cloud environment and ensure cloud implementations are compliant with the requirements of the Health Insurance Portability and Accountability Act of 1996 (HIPAA),[5] as amended by the Health Information for Economic and Clinical Health Act enacted as Title XIII of the American Recovery and Reinvestment Act of 2009 (HITECH), and promulgated regulations[6] (when used herein, the term HIPAA includes reference to HITECH).

The fact that a cloud service provider (CSP) is popular or well developed does not mean it is suitable for handling sensitive health care data, nor are cloud services like fine wines that improve with age—the mere fact that a CSP is large or has been operating for a long period of time does not necessarily ensure that the cloud services it provides are suited for your health care organization's business process and regulatory requirements. Invest the time to conduct appropriate due diligence and risk management activities before contracting for cloud services.

Given that much has already been written on the basics of cloud computing generally, the focus of this chapter is to identify unique and emerging issues involving cloud use by health care organizations.

II. Wants and Needs of Health Care Providers

Attitudes toward the health care cloud are rapidly changing due, in part, to an aging population, increased interest in wellness, a shift to a more customer-focused health care model that treats patients as consumers, expanded telemedicine, and a growing quantity of health care data combined with rising costs of on-premises data centers.[7] From 2012 to 2017, the percentage of medical providers using electronic health records rose from 40 percent to 67 percent.[8] Driven primarily by government payor requirements, higher costs related to the delivery of care, and lower reimbursement rates, the health care market is moving from volume-based to value-based care, with an emphasis on increasing quality and decreasing costs. Government payors, in particular, are encouraging this transition through innovative models of care and incentives tied to quality and shared responsibility for costs. The market is also moving from institution-based care to outpatient and home-based care. This involves more creative thinking on how to reach and communicate with patients effectively with no loss of quality. As a result, the health care industry is looking for ways to maximize quality and minimize costs and, to the extent applicable, increase reimbursement for services. As an example, the Centers for Medicare and Medicaid Services (CMS) is encouraging more sophisticated data analytics for everything from reimbursement, quality control, and the identification of fraud and abuse to support of clinical research. This increases the need for communication among providers and between providers and their patients. Health care providers are searching for effective, secure, and

---

5   Pub. L. No. 104-191, 110 Stat. 1936.
6   Pub. L. No. 111-5, 123 Stat. 226. See *infra* notes 23–25.
7   Cloud Standards Customer Council, Impact of Cloud Computing on Healthcare (Version 2.0), Feb. 2017, at 5–6, http://www.cloud-council.org/deliverables/CSCC-Impact-of-Cloud-Computing-on-Healthcare.pdf.
8   *EHR adoption rates: 20 must-see stats*, PRACTICE FUSION, Mar. 1, 2017, https://www.practicefusion.com/blog/ehr-adoption-rates/.

low-cost technology to facilitate these communications and are increasingly looking to the cloud for solutions.

Health care organizations are at various stages in the adoption of cloud computing. Some have not yet begun; others are well along the road of making use of cloud computing in various aspects of their business. Health care providers in particular are gradually using the cloud for treatment, operations, and innovative models for strategy and delivery of care. The following are examples of areas where health care providers are currently, or will be, using the cloud.

A. Electronic Health Records

Most health care providers currently use or are in the process of adopting electronic health records (EHR) systems. These systems contain not only the standard medical and clinical data gathered by the provider (referred to as the electronic medical record), but also additional information such as the patient's complete medical history and information from other providers who have treated the patient. All of the information in the EHR is likely to be subject not only to HIPAA, but also to state and common-law privacy protections.[9] An EHR system permits more data storage and access to and sharing of the data across health care providers and from various locations. EHR systems also permit providers to track data over time as well as evaluate how patients compare to other patients with similar conditions and their treatment outcomes. One of the most significant examples of the digitalization of health care is electronic prescribing and computerized provider order entry systems (CPOE). These systems are in place in many hospitals and long-term care facilities and permit prescribing professionals to directly interface with pharmacies. Use of CPOE permits the prescribing professional to be notified immediately with flags of drug interactions, thus improving quality and safety.

EHR systems have advantages for providers trying to comply with "meaningful use" criteria. Under HITECH, CMS implemented the EHR Incentives Programs to authorize incentive payments to eligible professionals, eligible hospitals, critical access hospitals, and Medicare Advantage organizations to move from paper records and demonstrate "meaningful use" of certified EHR technology.[10] Health care professionals, hospitals, and Medicare Advantage organizations can qualify for incentive payments by showing "meaningful use" of certified EHR technology (1) in a meaningful way (such as with e-prescribing), (2) for electronic exchange of health information to improve quality of care, and (3) to submit clinical quality and other measures.[11] A CSP that complies with certified EHR technology requirements can supply the provider with the platform and tools needed to demonstrate "meaningful use" and qualify for the incentive. Since implementation of the program, many providers have learned to their disadvantage that not all CSPs offer cloud-based services that meet the rigorous HITECH requirements.

EHR systems may be used in a conventional IT setting where EHR software is licensed to the provider to operate on the provider's own equipment, or a provider may contract with an EHR vendor that operates the EHR on its equipment and makes the data

---

9   Individual states have data privacy and security laws, including laws specific to health care information. *See* CAL. CIV. CODE §56.10; FLA. STAT. §456.057; N.Y. COMP. CODES R. & REGS. tit. 8, §292.
10   *See supra* note 6.
11   42 C.F.R. pt. 495.

in the EHR available to the provider through a cloud service. Internally based EHR systems often are designed for local storage and do not have the capability to integrate with other systems or patients.

Cloud-based EHR may offer more functionality, flexibility, and interoperability. A significant amount of EHR data in the United States is expected to be moved to the cloud because cloud computing has the potential to offer the provider greater storage and access to the data at any time and from any location without the cost of equipment acquisition or additional IT staff. However, simply moving an on-premises EHR system to the cloud does not necessarily guarantee the same results and protections as may be available in the on-premises system.

B. Collaborative Care and Clinical Integration

1. Provider Communication

Consultation and cooperation among a patient's health care providers is essential to high-quality care. Historically, this collaboration required a constant flow of paper. With cloud computing, providers can share patient information more quickly and efficiently, not only for development and monitoring of treatment and care plans, but also for predictive clinical modeling and evidenced-based population health-management programs. Hospitals can use cloud-based systems to access analytics to develop strategic plans focused on anticipated patient needs based on data analysis from existing patients, other providers, and community dashboards; emergency-room doctors can quickly access medical history and prescription information for patients in the ER and avoid costly and harmful medical errors and drug interactions; and primary care and mental health providers can share information about patients they have in common in real-time, just to name a few examples. The cloud permits access to data from anywhere and through a variety of devices.

2. Patient Portals

Health care providers and health care payors are encouraging patient involvement in decision-making. Access through a portal increases the likelihood that the patient will communicate with his or her provider in a timelier, efficient, and cost-effective manner. Portals can be used not only for disease management, preventive care, and education, but also for timelier responses by providers to patients. Most large health care systems and larger providers host and manage their own private patient portals, whereas smaller providers generally contract with a CSP to manage and operate a cloud platform as the patient portal.

3. Outcome Prediction

Cloud computing offers opportunities for providers to conduct analysis of disease and patient trends to predict outcomes. Providers can use these tools to develop treatment protocols or care plans to better meet the needs of the individual patient. Cloud computing facilitates cross-industry services through information sharing, knowledge management, and predictive analytics across the health care system. Recent studies have found that the health care cloud is focusing on location- and time-independent, collaborative, consistent, and real-time cognitive support to provide evidence-based, predictive analytics for medical diagnosis and treatment planning.[12]

C. Innovative Models of Care

1. Telemedicine

Providers are increasingly using telemedicine to consult with, diagnose, and treat patients in off-site locations. Telemedicine permits the provider to view, question, and treat the patient using electronic media, saving the patient a trip to the provider. It also permits the rural provider to consult with a specialist while the patient is in the office. Telemedicine presents several challenges to the provider and the patient, including heterogeneity of devices, data security, simplicity of operation, and flexibility to meet the specific needs of individual patients. Providers also complain that the systems are slow, images are unclear, and data capacity is limited. Cloud computing may offer solutions to certain of these challenges by storing large amounts of data in the cloud, making the data accessible to both the provider and the patient and permitting the provider to address the patient's needs in real-time.

2. Home-Based Care

Government payors are focusing on the importance of patient-centered care and home-based care and are providing incentives to encourage health care providers to offer treatment outside the facility setting. This requires use of technology to ensure that the provider and patient are able to communicate effectively. Hospitals in particular are using cloud computing to enable providers and patients to communicate "face-to-face." Providers are using cloud-based home care management systems to monitor patients in their homes and communicate the results to the patient's providers in real time.

D. Medical Devices and Internet of Things (IoT)

Medical devices and mobile medical devices are an inherent part of the delivery of health care. The use of mobile medical devices is increasing. Mobile medical devices include software programs that run on smartphones, other mobile communication devices or accessories, or a combination of accessories and software that meet the definition of a medical device.[13] This equipping of physical assets with digital data is part of a larger framework known as the Internet of Things (IoT).[14] According to a recent survey, 87 percent of health

---

12 Cloud Standards Customer Council, *supra* note 7, at 6.

13 FDA, Mobile Medical Applications, https://www.fda.gov/medicaldevices/digitalhealth/mobilemedicalapplications/default.htm.

14 "The Internet of Things (IoT) is the network of physical devices, vehicles, home appliances, and other items embedded with electronics, software, sensors, actuators, and connectivity which enables these things to connect and exchange data, creating opportunities for more direct integration of the physical world into computer-based systems, resulting in efficiency improvements, economic benefits, and reduced human exertions." https://en.wikipedia.org/wiki/Internet_of_things (citations omitted) (last visited July 20, 2018).

care organizations will adopt IoT technology by 2019.[15] Mobile devices permit users to participate in a variety of medical applications that extend use of the health care system beyond traditional medicine. Cloud computing makes it possible to use mobile medical devices, smart phones, and other technologies in the growing IoT, such as by transmitting data relating to a health condition to a provider and receiving information, including test results or recommended treatment back from the provider. Currently, an estimated 60 percent of health care organizations are already using IoT technology for such purposes as collecting, logging, tracking, and trending data about blood glucose levels, blood pressure, heart rate, or weight; viewing and analyzing images of skin lesions; controlling settings for neuromuscular stimulators and other therapeutic devices; monitoring internal and external Holter monitors, pacemakers, and other medical devices; and enabling interactive communication between smart medical spaces (e.g., clinics, patients' homes) and remote users (e.g., physicians, medical staff).[16] Benefits of IoT include improved innovation, cost savings, and improved workflow productivity. Challenges facing medical IoT include low bandwidth; heterogeneous networks; lack of availability due to network congestion; lack of signal, quality of service, or network failure; and privacy and security.[17]

The Food & Drug Administration (FDA) regulates medical devices, including mobile medical devices, under the Food, Drug and Cosmetic Act (FDCA).[18] CSPs may be considered medical device manufacturers subject to the FDCA and regulated by the FDA if they manufacture hardware or software used in cloud services and it performs functions that make the hardware or software a medical device as defined in the FDCA.[19] Consider, for example, cloud-based SaaS software and applications, including a certified EHR, a radiological image viewing application, and other software that performs CDS analysis. The SaaS software and applications (in this example EHR software, a radiological viewing application, and CDS software) could each be deemed a medical device depending on their intended uses.

The use of cloud computing with medical devices presents challenges for both the security of the device itself and the security of the data in the cloud. Many medical devices in use today lack basic security. Medical devices are vulnerable to cyber attacks because

---

15 *87% of Healthcare Organizations Will Adopt Internet of Things Technology by 2019*, HIPAA J., Mar 1, 2017, https://www.hipaajournal.com/87pc-healthcare-organizations-adopt-internet-of-things-technology-2019-8712/ (last visited Aug. 22, 2018).

16 Ray Parker, *Internet of Things in Healthcare: What are the Possibilities and Challenges?*, Jan. 13, 2018, https://readwrite.com/2018/01/13/internet-things-healthcare-possibilities-challenges/. *See also*, Cloud Standards Customer Council, *supra*, note 7 at 18.

17 HIT Infrastructure, Addressing Healthcare Network Connectivity Challenges, https://hitinfrastructure.com/features/addressing-healthcare-network-connectivity-challenges (last visited Aug. 22, 2018).

18 21 U.S.C. §§ 301–399(d). A medical device is defined within the FDCA as "an instrument, apparatus, implement, machine, contrivance, implant, in vitro reagent, or other similar or related article, including a component part or accessory which is: recognized in the official National Formulary, or the United States Pharmacopoeia, or any supplement to them, intended for use in the diagnosis of disease or other conditions, or in the cure, mitigation, treatment, or prevention of disease, in man or other animals, or intended to affect the structure or any function of the body of man or other animals, and which does not achieve its primary intended purposes through chemical action within or on the body of man or other animals and which is not dependent upon being metabolized for the achievement of any of its primary intended purposes." 21 U.S.C. § 321(h). *See also* https://www.fda.gov/forindustry/importprogram/importbasics/regulatedproducts/ucm510630.htm (last visited July 20, 2018).

19 See also Part IV.B., *infra*.

they often lack endpoint protection and processes for ensuring that operating systems are properly maintained and patched for security.

The FDA has recognized that medical devices using the Internet, the cloud, or radio frequencies present potential safety issues for the patient due to cybersecurity vulnerabilities. The FDA has issued safety communications to different manufacturers regarding potential cybersecurity vulnerabilities in medical devices.[20] In late 2016, the FDA issued *Guidance on Postmarket Management of Cybersecurity in Medical Devices*, encouraging device manufacturers and users to address cybersecurity risks in medical devices.[21] The FDA has also taken action concerning at least one specific medical device manufacturer, requesting that it address cybersecurity concerns about a particular line of medical devices.[22]

E. Clinical Research

Cloud computing offers several advantages for those involved in clinical research. Use of a cloud-based system permits medical researchers to store and analyze massive amounts of data from a variety of sources at a lower cost and in less time. Cloud systems facilitate the sharing of research data among medical research organizations, private organizations, health care providers, and other sources. Researchers can now directly access patient data, including medical images, from the providers' EHR systems. Clinical investigators can use cloud-based systems to manage the clinical trial, including evaluating subject enrollment, obtaining informed consents, accessing data in real time, generating data directly from the system for reports, and identifying and providing immediate notification of and response to serious adverse events during the trial.

Before using cloud services for clinical research, researchers must first address serious privacy and security concerns to avoid jeopardizing the integrity of the clinical investigation or violating HIPAA or similar state laws. HIPAA includes specific requirements for using, disclosing, or accessing patient information for research purposes, including a requirement in certain circumstances that a patient provide a HIPAA-compliant authorization. Health care systems are concerned about the use of cloud computing by individual clinical investigators because of the lack of control by the health care system over the investigator's use of the cloud, the investigator's understanding of the risks inherent in the cloud, and the investigator's compliance with the health care system's privacy and security policies.

---

20 Safety Communication issued by FDA on January 9, 2017, relating to St. Jude Medical's Implantable Cardia Devices and Merlin@home transmitters; Safety Communication issued by FDA on July 31, 2015, relating to Symbiq Infusion System access to the device through hospital network; and Safety Communication issued by FDA on May 13, 2015, related to Hospira's LifeCare PCA3 and PCA5 Infusion Pump Systems. *See* www.fda.gov/medicaldevices/safety/alertsandnotices/.
21 Guidance for Industry and Food and Drug Administration Staff, U.S. Food & Drug Administration, Guidance on Postmarket Management of Cybersecurity in Medical Devices, (Dec. 28, 2016), www.fda.gov/downloads/MedicalDevices/DeviceRegulationandGuidance/GuidanceDocuments/UCM482022.pdf. *See also* Changes to Existing Medical Software Policies Resulting from Section 3060 of the 21st Century Cures Act, www.fda.gov/downloads/MedicalDevices/DeviceRegulationandGuidance/GuidanceDocuments/UCM587820.pdf.
22 FDA Safety Communication, Cybersecurity Vulnerabilities Identified in St. Jude Medical's Implantable Cardia Devices and Merlin@home Transmitter (Jan. 9, 2017), https:www.fda.gov/MedicalDevices/Safety/Alertsand Notices/ucm535843.htm.

F. Back Office Services

Cloud computing can facilitate support services for providers in the day-to-day operation of their business.

Administrative support. Health care providers use the cloud for a variety of support operations. Generally, any administrative function that involves gathering or retaining data can be performed in the cloud, including materials management, billing applications, personnel, regulatory survey and corrective action plans, payroll, and purchasing.

Clinical support. Providers can use cloud-based systems to establish an infrastructure that supports the delivery of care. For example, the cloud can be used for nurses station monitoring, nurse call systems, scheduling, and information exchange.

Data storage. Cloud systems make it easier to hold a substantial amount of data at a lower cost and to access that data at any time and from any place.

Disaster recovery and business continuity. Access to patient health care data is critical to the operations of health care providers. IT systems must be available at all times to ensure continuity of care in the event of a disaster or other interruption in business. In addition, health care providers subject to HIPAA are required to have data backup and disaster recovery systems in place. Cloud-based recovery systems are a means to address this need.

Data analysis. Cloud computing enables the health care industry to analyze large amounts of data to evaluate patient demographics, disease trends, diagnostic measures, provider utilization, and specific areas of community need. Providers can use this data to meet payor reporting requirements and to develop treatment plans individualized to the patient. Cloud computing can also be used for marketing to target populations with a potential need for the provider's services.

III. Data Privacy and Security

One factor that has slowed adoption of cloud computing by health care providers is concern about the privacy and security of the data, including concerns about inappropriate access, disclosure, and loss of data. Health care providers, in addition to state and common-law privacy requirements, are subject to HIPAA and its Privacy Rule,[23] Security Rule,[24] and Breach Notification Rule.[25]

A. Background and the Law

HIPAA was enacted in 1996[26] and amended with passage of HITECH.[27] HIPAA establishes, among other things, national minimum standards for privacy and security of

---

23 45 C.F.R. pt. 160 and Subparts A and E of Part 164, discussed at https://www.hhs.gov/hipaa/for-professionals/privacy/index.html.

24 45 C.F.R. pt. 160 and Subparts A and E of Part 164, discussed at https://www.hhs.gov/hipaa/for-professionals/security/index.html.

25 45 C.F.R. § 164.400–.414, discussed at https://www.hhs.gov/hipaa/for-professionals/breachnotification/index.html. Similar breach notification provisions, implemented and enforced by the Federal Trade Commission (FTC) apply to vendors of personal health records and their third-party service providers, pursuant to section 13407 of the HITECH Act.

26 See *supra* note 5.

27 See *supra* note 6.

individually identifiable health information (Protected Health Information or PHI) and a uniform format for certain electronic data transactions. PHI is information, including demographic data, that relates to the individual's past, present, or future physical or mental health or condition, the provision of health care to the individual, or the past, present, or future payment for the provision of health care to the individual, and that identifies the individual or could be used to identify the individual.[28] PHI includes many common identifiers (e.g., name, address, birth date, Social Security number). PHI maintained in electronic format is referred to as Electronic PHI or ePHI. Information that has been de-identified in accordance with HIPAA regulations[29] is not considered PHI and is not subject to HIPAA restrictions on use and disclosure.[30]

B. Entities Subject to HIPAA

Covered Entities. Covered Entities include health care providers that conduct electronic health care transactions of a kind standardized by HIPAA (which is virtually every health care provider in the United States); health insurers and health insurance plans, including employer group health plans; and health care clearinghouses.[31] Other health care organizations that do not meet the HIPAA definitions of provider, plan, or clearinghouse are not Covered Entities and not subject to HIPAA, except in those circumstances where the health care organization provides a service or performs a function for the Covered Entity as a "business associate" (e.g., a pharmacy benefit manager for the health plan).[32]

Business associates. HIPAA also regulates business associates (BAs), which are individuals and entities that perform services for a Covered Entity if the services necessitate the receipt, generation, use, disclosure, maintenance, or transmission of PHI. Individuals and entities that perform services for BAs as subcontractors (Subcontractor BAs) are also subject to HIPAA.[33] Cloud computing vendors that receive, access, store, or transmit PHI from a health care provider Covered Entity are BAs of the provider, and subcontractors of those BAs are Subcontractor BAs.[34]

C. General Prohibitions

HIPAA generally prohibits a Covered Entity, BA, or Subcontractor BA from using or disclosing PHI except as specifically permitted by HIPAA. Under the Privacy Rule, Covered Entities may generally use and disclose PHI for purposes of treatment, payment, and health care operations (as such terms are defined in HIPAA), but if the purpose is for marketing or certain types of clinical research, Covered Entities may disclose PHI only with the patient's HIPPA-compliant authorization. In other cases, PHI may be disclosed under certain limited circumstances, such as for public health purposes, in response to a subpoena or court order, for law enforcement purposes, to report certain issues to government agencies such as domestic abuse or infectious disease, or if required by law. In most

---

28 45 C.F.R. § 164.103.

29 45 C.F.R. § 164.514.

30 45 C.F.R. § 164.502(d).

31 45 C.F.R. §§ 160.103, 164.504.

32 45 C.F.R. § 164.504.

33 *Id.* § 164.504.

34 *See infra* text accompanying note 68 regarding BAs and BA Agreements.

cases, only the minimum necessary PHI may be disclosed to meet the purposes for which disclosure is made. PHI may also be disclosed to a BA if the BA provides "satisfactory assurances" that it will safeguard the PHI and comply with applicable provisions of HIPAA. The BA can provide those assurances by executing a Business Associate Agreement with the Covered Entity that complies with HIPAA.[35]

Organizational requirements. The Privacy Rule requires that Covered Entities and BAs appoint privacy and security officers, develop privacy and security policies and procedures and implement education and training programs, and develop sanctions for violation of HIPAA and organization policy.[36] The HIPAA regulations do not define exactly what the duties of a privacy or security officer should be, but rather leave it to each Covered Entity or BA to establish its own duties according to its specific requirements.

Individual rights. The Privacy Rule also requires that Covered Entities provide notice of its privacy practices to all patients or enrollees in a plan. In addition, Covered Entities, and in some cases BAs, are required to grant certain rights to individuals, including the right to access their PHI, amend the PHI in a medical record, restrict how PHI is used or disclosed in certain instances, direct and restrict how PHI is communicated to them, and obtain an accounting of disclosures of PHI by the Covered Entity.[37] The Covered Entity may require its BA to assume responsibility for all or some of these obligations.

D. Security Obligations

The Privacy Rule protects Protected Health Information (PHI) generally, whereas the Security Rule[38] applies primarily to electronic Protected Health Information (ePHI). The Security Rule is highly technical in nature and is essentially the codification of certain IT standards and best practices. The Security Rule imposes a set of standards (Standards) to protect the security of ePHI. The Standards are categorized as either "required," meaning that the Standard is mandatory, or "addressable," meaning that the Covered Entity may evaluate whether the Standard is reasonable for its particular situation. Covered Entities and BAs must implement physical, administrative, and technical safeguards to protect the confidentiality, integrity, and availability of PHI. "Confidentiality" means that the ePHI is not available or disclosed to persons not authorized to receive it; "integrity" means that the ePHI is not altered or destroyed inappropriately; and "availability" means that ePHI is accessible and usable when needed. Physical safeguards include protections such as locked offices and facilities, visitor control, workstation use and security, and data backup and storage. Administrative safeguards include risk analysis and management, information system activity review, and sanctions. Technical safeguards include access control, user identification, and authentication and encryption.

The Security Rule Standards include the following:

Risk analysis. The Security Rule requires Covered Entities and BAs to conduct a security risk analysis to identify the vulnerabilities and threats to ePHI in their organization and implement security measures to address any weaknesses noted in the systems. The risk analysis, at a minimum, should be repeated with the installation of any new IT system

---

35 45 C.F.R. § 164.504.

36 45 C.F.R. § 164.530.

37 45 C.F.R. §§ 164.520, 164.522, 164.524, 164.526, 164.528.

38 45 C.F.R. pt. 164, Subpart C.

or changes to existing systems, the addition of any new offices or facilities connected to IT, any new contractual relationships involving ePHI, including use of cloud computing, and in the event of a security incident or breach.

Encryption. HIPAA encourages the use of encryption for ePHI at rest and in motion. Encryption is a method of converting an original message of regular text into encoded text by means of an algorithm. Some confusion exists about whether encryption is required under HIPAA. The technical safeguards relating to the encryption of ePHI are defined as "addressable" (i.e., not mandatory) requirements, and the HIPAA encryption requirements for transmission security provide that covered entities *should* "implement a mechanism to encrypt PHI whenever deemed appropriate."[39]

When encrypting ePHI, care must be taken to use an encryption process " . . . in which there is a low probability of assigning meaning without use of a confidential process or key."[40] A valid data encryption process for data at rest is NIST Special Publication 800-111,[41] and for data in motion is NIST Special Publication 800-52,[42] 800-77, or other methods which are Federal Information Processing Standards (FIPS) 140-2 validated.[43] FIPS (140-2) specifies the security requirements for encryption, providing four increasing, qualitative levels intended to cover a wide range of potential applications and environments.

Security controls. As part of the technical safeguards, Covered Entities are required to implement security controls to permit access to ePHI only by authorized persons, to record and examine access and other activity in the IT systems, and to protect transmission of ePHI from unauthorized access.[44]

E. Breach Notification

A breach is defined as "the acquisition, access, use, or disclosure of [PHI] in a manner not permitted under [the Privacy Rule] which compromises the security or privacy of the [PHI]."[45] Under the Breach Notification Rule, a Covered Entity must provide notice of a breach involving "unsecured" PHI. PHI is *not* considered to be "unsecured" if it has been rendered "unusable, unreadable or indecipherable" to unauthorized individuals.[46] Electronic PHI will be considered unusable, unreadable, or indecipherable if it has been encrypted in accordance with HIPAA, as described above.[47] To be considered unusable, unreadable,

---

39 45 C.F.R. § 164.312(a)(2)(iv). *But see* action by administrative law judge on June 18, 2018, granting summary judgment to the Office of Civil Rights of the U.S. Department of Health and Human Services (OCR) against Texas MD Anderson Cancer Center for, among other things, failure to implement encryption after identifying lack of encryption as a high level of risk to ePHI security, *available at* www.hhs.gov/sites/default/files/alj-cr5111.pdf.

40 45 C.F.R. § 164.304.

41 Guide to Storage Encryption Technologies for End User Devices, NIST Special Publication 800-111 (Nov. 2007), https://nvlpubs.nist.gov/nistpubs/Legacy/SP/nistspecialpublication800-111.pdf.

42 Guidelines for the Selection, Configuration, and Use of Transport Layer Security (TLS) Implementations, NIST Special Publication 800-52, rev. 1 (Apr. 2014), https://nvlpubs.nist.gov/nistpubs/SpecialPublications/NIST.SP.800-52r1.pdf.

43 Security Requirements for Cryptographic Modules [includes Change Notices as of 12/3/2002], Federal Information Processing Standard 140-2.

44 45 C.F.R. § 164.312.

45 45 C.F.R. § 164.402.

46 *Id.* § 164.402.

47 *Id.* § 164.402.

or indecipherable, PHI in paper, film, or other hard copy media must be shredded or destroyed such that it cannot be read or reconstructed, and PHI in electronic media must be cleared, purged, or destroyed in accordance with NIST Special Publication 800-88.[48]

A security incident involving "unsecured PHI" is presumed to be a breach unless the Covered Entity or BA can demonstrate that there is a low probability that the PHI has been compromised through completion of a risk assessment considering at least the following four factors: (1) the nature and extent of the PHI involved, including the types of identifiers and the likelihood of reidentification; (2) the unauthorized person who used the PHI or to whom the disclosure was made; (3) whether the PHI was actually acquired or viewed; and (4) the extent to which the risk to the PHI has been mitigated.[49]

If the security incident is a reportable breach, the Covered Entity, or in certain circumstances the BA or Subcontractor BA, must provide notification to the affected individuals and, depending on the scope of the breach, to the U.S. Department of Health and Human Services (DHHS) and the media. Once a data breach has been confirmed, Covered Entities and any BAs or Subcontractor BAs affected by the breach are obligated to mitigate the adverse effects of the breach, including, for example, the offer of identity theft and fraud monitoring.[50]

F. Business Associates

HIPAA permits Covered Entities to disclose to entities that qualify as BAs, provided that the Covered Entity enters into a specific kind of contract, referred to as a Business Associate Agreement (BA Agreement). BA Agreements must be written, must comply with HIPAA regulations, and must, at a minimum, include the following provisions: (1) an accurate description of the services to be performed by the BA; and (2) agreement by the BA to (a) comply with applicable privacy regulations, including that use and disclosure of PHI by the BA is limited to the services covered under the BA Agreement and the minimum necessary requirements; (b) comply with the security requirements, including implementation of appropriate safeguards; (c) enter into subcontractor BA Agreements with subcontractors with whom the BA shares PHI that are at least as stringent as the BA's agreement with the Covered Entity; (d) destroy or return all PHI or, if infeasible to return or destroy, maintain the privacy and security of the retained PHI; (e) not sell PHI without authorizations; (f) assist the Covered Entity in providing individual access to, amendment of, and accountings of disclosures of PHI; (g) timely report security incidents and data breaches to the Covered Entity (or upstream BA); and (h) otherwise comply with HIPAA.[51]

G. Enforcement

The DHHS, through its Office for Civil Rights (OCR), enforces HIPAA using audit, complaint, breach investigations, and other tools at its disposal. In addition, state attorneys general are empowered to enforce HIPAA on behalf of the citizens of their state. Failure

---

48 Guidelines for Media Sanitization, NIST Special Publication 800-88, rev. 1 (Dec. 2014), https://nvlpubs.nist.gov/nistpubs/specialpublications/nist.sp.800-88r1.pdf.

49 45 C.F.R. § 164.402(2).

50 45 C.F.R. § 164.530(f).

51 45 C.F.R. § 164.504(e).

to remain HIPAA-compliant comes with steep penalties, including fines of up to $250,000 and up to 10 years in prison.[52]

H. Preemption

HIPAA generally preempts state laws unless the state law is contrary to and more stringent than HIPAA. State laws relating to HIV, mental health, and substance abuse are typically more stringent than HIPAA.

IV. Other Regulatory Requirements

The health care industry is highly regulated, and any new technology or business operation must comply with various requirements. Some of the key regulatory requirements that should be considered in the context of health care cloud computing are summarized below.

A. Fraud and Abuse Laws

Federal and state fraud and abuse laws (such as anti-kickback laws) impact arrangements between providers and others who make, receive, arrange, or recommend referrals. Beneficiary inducement laws impact arrangements between providers or third-party payors and patients. These laws generally prohibit any receipt or payment of any form of remuneration in exchange for the referral of patients or the generation of business or to induce a patient to select a particular health care provider. Where a hospital is supplying computing hardware or software or data sets to a provider or patient, for example, the arrangement must comply with the anti-kickback laws. Generally, this means that payment for the service is fixed, set in advance, and at fair-market value. Traditional methods of valuation may not make sense in the cloud computing environment. How do you value access to data or a data exchange? Where a payor or provider is giving an incentive to a patient, the incentive must comply with beneficiary laws.

B. Device Regulation

Mobile medical devices may have unique vulnerabilities to cybersecurity risk. The FDA issued guidance in late 2016 with recommendations on ways for manufacturers and providers to reduce the risk of patient harm because of these vulnerabilities.[53] Health care providers who use devices or do business with cloud computing vendors subject to the FDCA must ensure that the products and vendors they use comply with FDCA requirements.

---

52 45 C.F.R. pt. 160, Subpart D.

53 Postmarket Management of Cybersecurity in Medical Devices, Guidance for Industry and Food and Drug Administration Staff (Dec. 28, 2016), https://www.fda.gov/downloads/medicaldevices/deviceregulationandguidance/guidancedocuments/ucm482022.pdf.

V. Choosing the Right Health Care Cloud Vendor

The cloud is attractive because it is available to health care organizations of all sizes. Even smaller physician offices and clinical networks can deploy enterprise-class, HIPAA-compliant application environments with a small IT team. However, care must be taken to avoid falling into the trap of thinking that security comes automatically with moving to the cloud. Careful planning and due diligence are essential before deciding to use a cloud service and to ensure that the right framework is in place to satisfy the stringent requirements for security, confidentiality, privacy, access, tracking, auditing, and long-term preservation of personal health and financial information and other health care organization data.

Although much has been written about the importance of due diligence before deciding to use the cloud, a robust due diligence process is still missing from many cloud deployments. A combination of factors contributes to this, including a lack of personnel with a deep understanding of the cloud and a lack of time and other resources needed for due diligence.

A. Assessing the Risks

The risk assessment process is a critical part of any cloud deployment. Remember that many cloud services are built on a "cloud stack" so that each entity involved in the CSP's entire cloud supply must be examined as a part of the risk assessment and due diligence.[54] An essential part of the risk assessment process is the use of a cross-organizational team to conduct the risk assessment and due diligence. The team members typically include IT, privacy and security, legal, and operational personnel. A checklist is developed, and team members are assigned responsibilities for various aspects of the due diligence.

The principal components of the risk assessment are as follows:

1. Identify and Classify Data Assets

One of the most important steps in protecting data appropriately is to classify the data assets. The process begins with identifying the information assets or business process that will be placed into the cloud. Conduct a data inventory—the health care organization must know what data is involved in order to properly secure it. In addition to ePHI, find out what other data is involved—proprietary, personally identifiable information (PII),[55]

---

54 In the context of ePHI, each entity involved in the CSP's supply chain may be deemed a BA, so it will be necessary to determine which entities are BAs and whether their cloud services are operated in a HIPAA-compliant manner.

55   All 50 states, the District of Columbia, Guam, Puerto Rico, and the Virgin Islands have enacted legislation requiring private or governmental entities to notify individuals of security breaches of information involving personally identifiable information (e.g., name combined with SSN, driver's license, or state ID; account numbers; etc.); what constitutes a breach (e.g., unauthorized acquisition of data); requirements for notice (e.g., timing or method of notice, who must be notified); and exemptions (e.g., for encrypted information). *See* http://www.ncsl.org/research/telecommunications-and-information-technology/security-breach-notification-laws.aspx (last visited July 20, 2018).

or payment card information (PCI),[56] as such data is not regulated under HIPAA but is instead regulated under a variety of other laws and standards. Then, determine the data classification by evaluating the sensitivity, value, or regulated nature of the data that will be placed in the cloud and what controls should be in place to ensure it is properly protected. Appropriate protections are determined, in large part, by legal, financial, and operational requirements and on the criticality and risk levels of the data.

Once the data assets are classified, determine applicable regulatory, business policy, privacy, and security requirements related to the handling, processing, and storage of the data. Then ask the CSP to map out its cloud service process and explain how it addresses your health care organization's regulatory and policy requirements. This is typically done by requesting the CSP to complete a questionnaire that addresses these and other standard due diligence matters.

2. Assess Confidentiality, Integrity, and Availability of Data or Service

Important considerations in the health care due diligence process include whether the CSP provides timely and reliable access to data and cloud services; ensures data integrity, security, privacy, portability, and isolation; provides data encryption at rest and in transit, and tracks and audits data placed in the cloud service (a number of cloud services share resources among the CSP's cloud customers). Take time to understand and determine how the cloud service and cloud-based data will be accessed (i.e., password-protected web portal or mobile app).

HIPAA permits the use of cloud services by health care providers for storing and processing ePHI. Based upon OCR guidance, CSPs will typically be found to be acting as a BA of the Covered Entity health care provider based upon the fact that in many cloud service models, the CSP has access to protected ePHI. When a Covered Entity engages the services of a CSP to create, receive, maintain, or transmit ePHI on its behalf, the CSP is a BA under HIPAA. Consequently, it will be necessary for the CSP to sign a BA Agreement as a part of the cloud service procurement process.[57] Additionally, health care providers are required to conduct periodic security risk assessments, which should include an evaluation of any threats or vulnerabilities to the Covered Entity from use of the cloud and from the CSP. Health care providers may choose to repeat the risk assessment shortly after the cloud program becomes operational and periodically throughout the term of the contract with the CSP.

3. Consider Whether to Use Encryption

Covered Entities must deploy appropriate technical safeguards to preserve confidentiality of cloud-stored ePHI. Data encryption is considered an appropriate technical safeguard. If a decision not to use encryption for cloud-stored data is made, the reason for that decision must be documented, along with the alternative controls that are put in place to

---

56 Payment card information must be handled in accordance with the Payment Card Industry Data Security Standard, which is an information security standard developed by the credit card industry for organizations that handle branded credit cards from the major credit card companies.

57 U.S. Department of Health and Human Services, Guidance on HIPAA & Cloud Computing (Oct. 7, 2016), https:www.hhs.gov/hipaa/for-professionals/special-topics/cloud-computing/index.html.

provide a similar level of protection. OCR noted in its recent cloud computing guidance for HIPAA-covered entities that encryption can significantly reduce the risk of ePHI being accessed, exposed, or stolen.[58] In addition, as noted above, encryption that complies with DHHS criteria will "secure" the data such that a security incident or data breach does not require notification. Despite the protections afforded by encryption and despite concerns expressed about security, a recent survey revealed that a quarter of health care organizations do not use encryption to protect data at rest in the cloud, even though the lack of encryption potentially places sensitive data—including ePHI—at risk of exposure.[59]

Although encryption addresses confidentiality concerns, it does not ensure the availability of or safeguard the integrity of ePHI. DHHS explained in its cloud computing guidance that encryption alone is not sufficient to ensure the confidentiality, integrity, and availability of ePHI stored in the cloud.[60] Alternative controls must be put in place to ensure ePHI can always be accessed, whereas access controls must be used to maintain the integrity[61] of ePHI.

4. Determine Whether the CSP Uses a "Shared Responsibility" Cloud Model

Note that there are several major CSPs that utilize a "shared responsibility" model for privacy, security, and other regulatory compliance. When evaluating the security of a cloud solution, it is important for customers to understand and distinguish between security measures that the CSP implements and operates (security *of* the cloud) and security measures that the health care organization implements and operates related to the security of customer content and applications that make use of the cloud services (security *in* the cloud).

The "shared responsibility" concept means shifting to the health care organization much of the responsibility for security, privacy, and regulatory compliance. Essentially, the shared responsibility model requires the health care organization to determine and implement the security controls necessary to protect content, applications, system, platform, and networks in connection with use of the cloud services. The CSP, in turn, manages security of the cloud. CSPs often frame this concept as a positive feature, with explanations such as that the customer retains control of the selection and implementation of the security used to protect its own content, applications, system, platform, and networks in a manner similar to that historically used by the customer in an on-site data center. The reality is that shared responsibility can be a trap for the unwary health care organization that does not understand this model and the significant responsibilities it imposes on the customer. As discussed below,[62] the customer does not have the same control over its

---

58 *Id.*

59 *Quarter of Healthcare Organizations Do Not Encrypt Data Stored in the Cloud*, HIPAA J., Feb. 17, 2017, http:www.hipaajournal.com/quarter-of-healthcare-organizations-dont-encrypt-cloud-data-8694/.

60 Guidance on HIPAA & Cloud Computing, Department of Health and Human Services' Office for Civil Rights, https://www.hhs.gov/hipaa/for-professionals/special-topics/cloud-computing/index.html (last visited June 16, 2017).

61 Integrity of information refers to protecting information from modification by unauthorized parties. Encryption does not necessarily maintain the integrity the ePHI, such as ensuring that the information is not corrupted by malware. *Id.*

62 See Parts VI.A. and VI.B.

applications and data in the public cloud as it does in its own on-site data center. For that reason, many health care providers as a matter of policy do not use public clouds.

The implications of shared responsibility extend beyond the initial launch of the cloud service because compliance is not just a one and done task—constant monitoring and adjusting must occur as needed. The Security Rule requires access control, auditing of access to ePHI, and information system management. Health care organizations must consider how to implement auditing and logging-in with the cloud service, given that in many shared responsibility models, the health care organization, rather than the CSP, must implement those processes in a manner sufficient to meet the health care organization's HIPAA compliance requirements. Issues related to the cloud should be specifically addressed in your organization's security policies and procedures.

5. Assess Whether Your Team Is "Cloud Ready"

Before deciding whether to use a particular cloud service, health care organizations must determine whether they have trained personnel who are able to monitor compliance in the cloud service.

6. Site Visits Are Important

Plan to visit the CSP's facilities as a part of the due diligence process for those cloud services that involve sensitive or regulated data or business processes to ensure that there are appropriate physical security controls in place. Many CSPs are new to the health care market, and many are operating on a small scale and without all the security resources that a health care organization might want or expect. Determine whether the CSP has developed an appropriate Security Rule risk assessment process and has implemented reasonable measures to protect the data it collects, stores, and transmits. Specifically inquire about the CSP's physical, technical, and policy safeguards to reduce the risk and impact of a security breach. Be certain to ask the CSP whether it has experienced a data breach and, if so, how it was handled and how the CSP addressed its security deficiencies and responded to the breach.

7. Consider Interoperability and Portability

Interoperability and portability are key considerations because they can affect the cost, security, and risk involved in the use of a particular cloud service. It is essential that a health care organization be able to connect its data with other data sources.

In health care, interoperability is the ability of different information technology systems and software applications to communicate, exchange data, and use the information that has been exchanged. The goal of interoperability is for data to be shared across platforms used by the clinician, lab, hospital, pharmacy, and patient regardless of the application or CSP. Portability is about the ability to move data from one cloud service to another so that the data is usable on the other cloud service without the need to re-enter the data into the replacement cloud service. This requires a capability to retrieve your health care organization's data from one cloud service and a capability to import that data into another cloud service. Issues of interoperability and portability arise in various scenarios, including:

- customer switches between CSPs for a cloud service;
- customer uses cloud service from multiple CSPs;
- customer links one cloud service to another cloud service;
- customer links in-house business process with cloud service; and
- customer migrates business process into cloud services.

The due diligence process should include an investigation into the CSP's ability to interoperate with other cloud products and services.[63] The current cloud computing landscape consists of a diverse set of products and services that are frequently based upon proprietary architectures and technologies used by CSPs. The concern is the risk that a health care organization will be locked into a particular CSP due to the inability or difficulty and costs involved to switch to another CSP to obtain equivalent cloud services because one cloud service is not designed to interact with the other cloud service.

Consider this issue carefully (and early in the due diligence process) and include a discussion about how data could be migrated to a different CSP in a manner that allows your organization to meet its patient and other regulatory requirements. Be certain to include contractual provisions that address the format in which the CSP will return the data to the health care organization. The format or syntax of the data ideally should be the same for the two CSPs. There are times when the formats may not match, however, in which case the parties should agree up-front to map the data using commonly available tools. A health care organization takes a great risk if it does not investigate and agree to the format/syntax for the return of its data because if the semantics of the transferred data do not match between the source and target services, then data portability is likely to be more difficult or even impossible.

8. Ensure the CSP Is HIPAA Compliant

Many health care organizations are under a mistaken impression that all CSPs serving the health care market have built cloud services that are HIPAA compliant. There is no government certification available for HIPAA compliance, so be wary of such claims. The use of this phrase by a CSP often means only that the CSP has undertaken a program to comply with the Security Rule. Some of the major CSPs use operating models that align HIPAA risk management programs with FedRAMP[64] and NIST 800-53,[65] a security standard that maps to the Security Rule. NIST supports this alignment and has issued SP 800-66, *An Introductory Resource Guide for Implementing the HIPAA Security Rule*,[66] which documents how NIST 800-53 aligns to the Security Rule. Note the fact that a CSP's

63 The federal government has provided guidance on interoperability. *See* NIST Cloud Computing Standards Roadmap, NIST Special Publication 800-291, Version 2 (July 2013). There is also industry guidance on these issues. *See* Cloud Standards Customer Council, Interoperability and Portability for Cloud Computing: A Guide, Version 2.0 (2017), http://www.cloud-council.org/deliverables/CSCC-Interoperability-and-Portability-for-Cloud-Computing-A-Guide.pdf.

64 *See* FedRAMP Program Documents, *available at* https://www.fedramp.gov/documents/.

65 Security and Privacy Controls for Federal Information Systems and Organizations, NIST Special Publication 800-53 revision 4 (Apr. 2013), https://nvlpubs.nist.gov/nistpubs/specialpublications/nist.sp.800-53r4.pdf.

66 An Introductory Resource Guide for Implementing the HIPAA Security Rule, Information Security, NIST SP 800-66 (Oct. 2008), https://nvlpubs.nist.gov/nistpubs/Legacy/SP/nistspecialpublication800-66r1.pdf.

HIPAA compliance is typically product-dependent and is not usually applicable to all of the CSP's products. Verify that the cloud service your health care organization will be using complies with the Security Rule.

9. Consult HIPAA Guidance on Social Media, Mobile Technologies, and Physician Texting

The growing consumer use of social media and mobile technologies has also added to the demand for cloud services as health care organizations seek better and faster ways to reach out to existing and potential customers. Over the past several years, there were a number of instances of health care professionals accidentally disclosing the PHI of patients on social media sites and deliberately posting images and videos containing PII.[67] DHHS guidance is expected on the use of social media platforms and when prior authorization from a patient is required.[68]

In 2016, the Joint Commission[69] lifted the ban on the use of text messages for orders, then reinstated the ban, and by the end of the year partially lifted the ban, indicating that the use of a secure text messaging platform was acceptable for doctors when communicating with each other, although the use of text messages for patient orders—regardless of whether a secure, HIPAA-compliant platform was used—remained prohibited.[70] In December 2017, CMS clarified that the texting of patient orders by health care providers is not permitted because it does not comply with the applicable Medicare conditions of participation. CMS does permit texting of patient information among health care providers provided that it occurs through a secure and encrypted platform in compliance with HIPAA, conditions of participation, and/or conditions for coverage.

10. Understand the Role of Business Associates in the Cloud

Health care organizations that choose to use third-party cloud services must ensure that the CSP is aware of its responsibilities with respect to ePHI. CSPs are classed as BAs of Covered Entities if the CSP will receive, create, or have access to ePHI, and as such they are required to abide by HIPAA. The diligence process should address developing internal controls to prevent the health care organization from processing, storing, or transmitting ePHI on a cloud service without having a BA Agreement in place. This is because HIPAA requires a Covered Entity to have a BA Agreement in place when outsourcing services related to ePHI and because, without a BA Agreement, the CSP would not necessarily have an obligation to inform the health care organization of a security breach. DHHS has

---

67 HIPAA Social Media Rules (Mar. 12, 2018), https://www.hipaajournal.com/hipaa-social-media/.

68 *See* New HIPAA Guidance in 2017; *Testing, Social Media, & Case Walkthrough,* HIPAA J., Feb. 22, 2017, http://www.hipaajournal.com/new-hipaa-guidance-2017-texting-social-media-case-walk-through-8702.

69 The Joint Commission is an independent, not-for-profit organization that accredits and certifies health care organizations and programs in the United States. Joint Commission accreditation and certification is recognized nationwide as a symbol of quality that reflects an organization's commitment to meeting certain performance standards. *See* https://www.jointcommission.org/about_us/about_the_joint_commission_main.aspx.

70 45 C.F.R. § 164.530.

also explained that even if ePHI is stored in the cloud and the CSP does not hold a key to decrypt the data, the CSP is still classed as a BA.[71]

Not all BA Agreements are created equal. A number of CSPs, even leading CSPs, use BA Agreements that fail to include provisions desired or required by health care organizations. Request and review early in the due diligence process the BA Agreement for the CSP to determine whether the terms of the BA Agreement comply with HIPAA and provide adequate protection for your health care organization. Due diligence with respect to the BA Agreement should include a careful detailing of the CSP's BA Agreement responsibilities and each step the CSP takes to maintain compliance with HIPAA, including the CSP's levels of access to ePHI, terms for working with subcontractors with access to ePHI, procedures for breach notifications, and more. When working with sensitive information, precision and transparency in BA Agreements as between Covered Entities and BAs is vital to building productive and mutually beneficial relationships of trust.

In addition to the BA Agreement, the health care organization must review the CSP's cloud services agreement early in the due diligence process to determine whether a shared responsibility model is used, and whether the security, privacy, and regulatory controls are sufficient to meet your health care organization's needs.

Be alert to the fact that not all cloud services are designed with the controls required for HIPAA-protected information. The fact that a CSP signs a BA Agreement does not guarantee that the cloud service itself operates in a manner that protects ePHI as required by HIPAA. In addition, the fact that a CSP is a large, well-known provider does not necessarily mean that the CSP has established the privacy, security, and other controls needed by your health care organization for a specific cloud service. Some of the major CSPs require the customer to negotiate specifically for HIPAA protections and identify each account that contains ePHI as a HIPAA account, and may require that the customer only process, store, or transmit ePHI on the CSP's HIPAA eligible services following execution of a BA Agreement.

The explanation provided by some of the major CSPs about the scope of HIPAA-compliant services usually includes the CSP's statement that it does not access the customer's data. The CSP asserts that, as a result, it has no method of determining when ePHI is processed, stored, or transmitted with the cloud services used by any specific account. Unless the health care organization executes a BA Agreement with the CSP that specifies which accounts will process, store, or transmit ePHI, CSPs typically take the position that they would have no way of determining whether a security breach exposed "unsecured" ePHI, or whether ePHI was improperly used or accessed. Consequently, it is essential to have a BA Agreement in place with the CSP prior to using a cloud service in order to ensure timely notification in the event of a security breach that exposes ePHI.

Due diligence should include inquiry about whether the CSP uses subcontractors to provide the cloud services and whether the CSP extends security and privacy requirements to its subcontractors. It is essential to understand the cloud supply chain—who is involved in providing the cloud services, and who will have access to ePHI to ensure that all subcontractors involved have an obligation to protect ePHI.

---

71 U.S. Department of Health and Human Services, *supra* note 57, at Question 2.

B. What to Look for in BA Agreements for Cloud Services

The BA Agreement between a Covered Entity (or a BA) and a CSP is critical to enable each party to clearly understand its obligations and liabilities. As noted in this chapter, CSPs often argue that responsibility for the security of the Covered Entity's PHI lies with the Covered Entity. In particular, the CSP disclaims liability for any unauthorized access, use, or disclosure of PHI, any modification or loss of PHI, any data breach or data loss, or any service issue, even if due to malicious activity. Therefore, both the underlying service contract and the BA Agreement between the Covered Entity or BA and the CSP must be closely reviewed and carefully negotiated to ensure that appropriate and enforceable protections are in place to enable the Covered Entity to comply with HIPAA. As evidenced by recent enforcement actions, OCR is paying more attention to the efforts of Covered Entities to ensure compliance of their BAs with HIPAA.

1. Acknowledgement of BA Status and Compliance with HIPAA

CSPs may argue that they do not meet the HIPAA definition of a BA because of the type of access they may have to the Covered Entity's PHI (e.g., storage of encrypted data only with no encryption key). As noted above, OCR has clearly stated that any CSP involved with PHI on behalf of a Covered Entity is a BA. To ensure that the CSP acknowledges and agrees that it is a BA and that it is subject to HIPAA, the BA Agreement should include the HIPAA definition of a BA.[72] The BA Agreement must also clearly state that the CSP is required to comply with HIPAA and with state privacy and security laws. This means compliance not only with the Security Rule to protect the confidentiality, integrity, and availability of the data, but also with those provisions of the Privacy Rule applicable to BAs. For example, the BA is required to appoint Privacy and Security Officers, to execute BA Agreements with its subcontractors, to adhere to minimum necessary limitations, to maintain privacy and security policies, and to keep an accounting of all disclosures.[73]

2. Description of Services

The BA Agreement must include a clear definition of the services to be performed by the BA and a commitment by the BA to use the Covered Entity's PHI only for those specifically defined purposes. The description of services should clearly describe the level and type of access that the CSP may have to the Covered Entity's PHI. The Covered Entity should be cognizant of the provisions in the underlying service agreement that allow the CSP to modify the services to be performed or other terms of the agreement without the consent of the Covered Entity or with only limited notice. A health care provider may also request that the CSP identify by name or title those individuals who will need access to the provider's PHI.

3. Security Rule

The BA Agreement must require the BA to comply with the Security Rule and implement all of the Standards[74] applicable to the Covered Entity and the PHI to which the CSP has

---

72 45 C.F.R. § 160.103.

73 45 C.F.R. § 164.504(e).

74 See *supra* Part III.D.

access. In particular, the BA Agreement should require that the CSP implement physical, administrative, and technical safeguards to provide access control, prevent unauthorized access, and monitor access and system management.

When the health care organization uses a cloud, generally all of the data generated and processed resides in the space owned and operated by the CSP (or a subcontractor). The health care organization must ensure that the CSP implements the same or equivalent controls as those in place with the provider. CSPs will often reject requests to implement specific HIPAA safeguards and complete the HIPAA compliance risk analysis, arguing that they adhere to other similar security guidelines and conduct assessments under those guidelines. The BA Agreement must give the Covered Entity the right, through audit or monitoring, to confirm that the CSP's security measures are the same as or equivalent to the security measures in place at the Covered Entity, and must require the CSP to provide access to DHHS.

4. Security Incidents and Breaches

The CSP must agree to notify the Covered Entity of any security incident or breach involving the Covered Entity's PHI in a timeframe sufficient to allow the Covered Entity to investigate the incident and comply with reporting and notice obligations.

5. Termination

The Covered Entity must have the ability to terminate both the underlying service agreement and the BA Agreement if the CSP is not in compliance with HIPAA and is not able to cure the noncompliance. HIPAA requires that the BA either return all PHI to the Covered Entity or destroy it, or in the event that return or destruction is not feasible, agree to maintain the security of the PHI. CSPs will often argue that they have no obligation to retain the Covered Entity's data, particularly where the underlying contract is terminated for cause by the CSP. Alternatively, CSPs will agree to retain the PHI only for a short period of time or only in "snapshot" format. Covered Entities should ensure that the data remain available, particularly where patient medical information is involved, to ensure continuity of care. This may mean that the Covered Entity must backup and store the data locally or in another cloud.

6. Governing Law

The Covered Entity is subject to the laws of the state in which it is operating and must ensure that the CSP complies not only with HIPAA, but with any more restrictive state laws as well. The governing law for the BA Agreement should be the state of domicile of the Covered Entity.

7. Miscellaneous

HIPAA prohibits the sale of PHI without the Covered Entity's consent. The BA Agreement should include a specific prohibition on the sale of PHI. Additionally, depending on the scope of the CSPs services agreement, a Covered Entity should consider including in the BA Agreement additional non-HIPAA-required provisions, such as confidentiality provisions and indemnification for data breach.

VI. Cloud Deployment Models

It is essential for a health care organization to determine at the outset the cloud deployment model best suited for a particular business process because the type of model selected has privacy, security, portability, and interoperability implications.

A. Public Clouds

Public clouds are clouds owned and operated by CSPs and are open to the general public. Technically, there may be little or no difference between public and private cloud architectures; however, security considerations may be substantially different for services (applications, storage, and other resources) that are made available by a CSP for a public audience.[75]

B. Private Clouds

Private clouds are clouds operated and used entirely by one entity. The service may be maintained and managed by the entity itself or by third parties. The implementation may involve servers, data centers, and other cloud infrastructure maintained internally or as part of the entity's own infrastructure, or may reside off-premises. Private clouds typically have a significant physical footprint, requiring allocations of space, hardware, and environmental controls. The hardware and software involved must be replaced and updated periodically, resulting in additional capital expenditures. Health care providers in particular often use private clouds to address concerns about security and data privacy.

C. Community Clouds

Community clouds share infrastructure between several organizations from a specific community with common concerns (security, compliance, jurisdiction, etc.) and may be managed either internally or by a third party, and hosted either internally or externally. In health care, groups such as panels of providers on a network, participants in an accountable care organization, or members of a group purchasing organization could utilize a community cloud.

D. Hybrid Clouds

A hybrid cloud is a combination of two or more clouds that uses a mix of on-premises, private cloud and third-party, public cloud services, usually involving different CSPs, with coordination among the various platforms.

---

75 Peter Mell & Timothy Grance, National Institute of Standards and Technology, The NIST Definition of Cloud Computing (Special Publication 800-145) (2011), http://nvlpubs.nist.gov/nistpubs/Legacy/SP/nistspecialpublication800-145.pdf.

E. Malware and Ransomware in Health Care Clouds

Health care providers must avoid developing a false sense of security in cloud services. Health care data, whether in a public or private cloud, is a prime target of cyber thieves.[76] Health care entities are finding their systems infected with malware or held hostage by ransomware. Standard areas of attack include unpatched servers that connect the health care organization to the internet, web-based downloads, and the all-too-familiar malicious e-mail attachments or links. A July 2016 report found that the health care industry experienced ransomware attacks more than any other sector—approximately 88 percent of attacks have hit hospitals.[77]

Malware operators who exfiltrate data (i.e., make an unauthorized transfer of data) from a hospital network are typically focused on obtaining health data that can be sold to someone who will use it to commit identity theft and insurance fraud. CSPs typically do not assume responsibility for monitoring and detecting malware infections at the customer's access point ("endpoint") to the CSPs cloud service; under most cloud service arrangements, the cloud customer, rather than the CSP, must deploy and manage malware protection to its endpoints.

Ransomware operators use malicious software to encrypt health care data where it is stored and agree to unlock it only after a ransom is paid. Hospitals in California, Indiana, and Kentucky have experienced ransomware attacks on their servers. In addition to the loss of access and control over sensitive ePHI, the attacks can also compromise patient care and create serious issues for hospital business operations, including the need to transfer and divert patients to other hospitals. A hospital in Washington, D.C., was impacted so severely that it had to redirect patients to other facilities in order to maintain adequate quality of care.[78] A U.S. government interagency report indicates that, on average, there have been 4,000 daily ransomware attacks since early 2016 (a 300-percent increase over the 1,000 daily ransomware attacks reported in 2015).[79]

Health care organizations are attractive ransomware targets because many connect to the internet using a type of application server that is often not maintained with the latest

---

76 A report by credit bureau Experian found that health care organizations will be the most targeted sector, with new, sophisticated attacks emerging. "From January to June 2017, 233 breach incidents were reported to the U.S. Department of Health and Human Services (HHS), the media or state attorneys general. For the 193 attacks for which there are numbers, 3,159,236 patient records were affected." EXPERIAN, DATA BREACH INDUSTRY FORECAST 8 (2018), http://www.experian.com/assets/data-breach/white-papers/2018-experian-data-breach-industry-forecast.pdf.

77 *12 Healthcare Ransomware Attacks of 2016*, Becker's Health IT & CIO Review (Dec. 29, 2016), http://www.beckershospitalreview.com/healthcare-information-technology/12-healthcare-ransomware-attacks-of-2016.html.

78 *See Washington-Area MedStar Hospital Chain Paralyzed by Hackers' Virus Attack,* CHICAGO TRIBUNE, Mar. 29, 2016, http://www.chicagotribune.com/business/ct-medstar-hack-20160329-story.html; John Woodrow Cox, Karen Turner & Matt Zapotosky, *Virus Infects MedStar Health System's Computers, Forcing an Online Shutdown,* WASH. POST, Mar. 28, 2016, https://www.washingtonpost.com/local/virus-infects-medstar-health-systems-copmuters-hospital-officals-say/2016/03/28/480f7d66-f515-11e5-a3ce-f06b5ba21f33_story.html.

79 U.S. Dep't of Justice, How to Protect Your Networks from Ransomware (2017), https://www.justice.gov/criminal-ccips/file/872771/download.

software security patches. Hospitals with these types of servers are being exploited in increasing numbers.[80]

The significance of ransomware is demonstrated by the fact that the OCR recently issued specific guidance on ransomware (Ransomware guidance), including whether ransomware infections are considered reportable HIPAA breaches.[81] The Ransomware guidance was issued in response to differing interpretations of the applicability of HIPAA's breach rules. One interpretation is that ransomware incidents constitute a HIPAA breach based on the fact that if ePHI is encrypted through a ransomware attack, then unauthorized individuals have taken control of protected ePHI. A counterargument is that ransomware does not involve an unauthorized transfer of information from an information system to outside the network, and thus should not be considered a HIPAA breach. According to the Ransomware guidance, whether the presence of ransomware would constitute a breach under the Breach Notification Rule is a fact-specific determination.

The Ransomware guidance explains that when ePHI is encrypted as the result of a ransomware attack, a breach is presumed to have occurred because the ePHI encrypted by the ransomware was acquired (i.e., unauthorized individuals have taken possession or control of the information), and thus is a "disclosure" not permitted under the Privacy Rule. Unless the covered entity or business associate can demonstrate that there is a "low probability that the PHI has been compromised," based on the factors set forth in the Breach Notification Rule, a breach of PHI is presumed to have occurred. The Covered Entity must then comply with the applicable HIPAA breach notification provisions described above.[82]

In the event of a ransomware incident, the specific ransomware variant that infected the health care organization's network must be quickly identified and a determination quickly made as to whether it is a type that can exfiltrate data. If it is a type that is unable to exfiltrate data, then the covered entity has a basis for asserting that the ransomware did not exfiltrate data. Note that malware is different from ransomware in that malware operators use a different family of malware for data exfiltration.[83]

A thorough and accurate evaluation of the evidence acquired and analyzed as a result of security incident response activities could help entities with the risk assessment process above by revealing, for example, whether the malware propagated to other systems, potentially affecting additional sources of ePHI. Correctly identifying the malware involved can assist an entity in determining whether the malware may attempt to exfiltrate data, or whether the malware deposits hidden malicious software or exploits vulnerabilities to provide future unauthorized access, among other factors.

There is no uniform rule for determining whether a data breach has occurred when ransomware or malware is involved. According to the Ransomware guidance, each situation must be examined, even if data is encrypted, to determine whether the PHI has

---

80 *See* Matt Mellen, 2017 Cybersecurity Predictions: Ransomware and SaaS Challenges Persist in Healthcare (Dec. 5, 2016), http://researchcenter.paloaltonetworks.com/2016/12/2017-cybersecurity-predictions-ransomware-saas-chalenges-persist-healthcare/.

81 U.S. Department of Health and Human Services, Ransomware Guidance (2016) https://www.hhs.gov/sites/default/files/RansomwareFactSheet.pdf.

82 *Id.* at 6.

83 *See* Matt Mellen, How to Interpret HHS Guidance on Ransomware as a HIPAA Breach (July 25, 2016), http://researchcenter.paloaltonetworks.com/2016/07/how-to-interpret-hhs-guidance-on-ransomware-as-a-hipaa-breach/.

in fact been rendered "unreadable, unusable, and indecipherable" to unauthorized individuals.[84]

F. Risks of Accidental Oversharing of Patient Data in Cloud-Based File Sharing Apps

The current culture promotes and values sharing and collaboration of resources, information, and ideas, and the cloud has been a catalyst for sharing of ePHI among medical practitioners. Unfortunately, many of the cloud-based collaboration and sharing platforms were designed for consumer rather than business use. Many of these consumer-focused services are not suitable for use with regulated or sensitive information such as ePHI, and these cloud-based, file-sharing tools can present potentially significant security issues for health care organizations. This is because some of the key cloud file-sharing sites rely on the user to configure the security access. Some of these services are difficult to configure or lack settings that restrict access to specific named individuals, and the users end up accidentally making the data placed on the site accessible to everyone on the internet.

G. Cross-Border Data Issues

Health care providers who use cloud computing should be aware that CSPs use cloud services that transmit, access, process, and/or store data outside of the United States. Data may be moved to another location (often in a foreign country), processed in that country, and then moved back to the provider in the United States.

One key issue with cross-border cloud computing is the privacy and security of the data. Each country has its own approach to data protection, with some countries having very little or no regulation. The laws often protect only financial or proprietary data and do not extend to medical information. A related question is, which laws apply to the data? Is it U.S. law where the data is created or collected, is it the country where the data is stored (even for a short time), or is it both?[85]

VII. Conclusion

With patients acting more like consumers, healthcare organizations are adapting to meet patient expectations for convenient and timely care and confidentiality of their personal information, while providing a consistent experience across access points and care settings. Consumer expectations around engagement and self-service have spilled over from other industries into healthcare and will continue to accelerate. Healthcare organizations are expanding their use of cloud technology through hybrid solutions that combine cloud and on-premises models.[86] It is anticipated that healthcare organizations will continue

---

84 *See Ransomware Guidance, supra* note 81, at 8.

85 For discussion of the regulation of privacy in Canada, Germany, and the United Kingdom, see Chapters 9–11.

86 Chris Gervais, *From consumerism to the cloud: 5 key predictions for healthcare in 2019* Medical Economics, Jan 15, 2019, http://www.medicaleconomics.com/business/consumerism-cloud-5-key-predictions-healthcare-2019 (last visited January 31, 2019)

investing in cloud technology solutions that allow them to responsibly manage and leverage data and ensure that patient-provider interactions are made easier across different engagement channels. At the same time, however, this increased use of cloud technology has increased the vulnerability of healthcare organizations to cybersecurity threats requiring increased vigilance and protective measures.

Chapter 8

Alternative Dispute Resolution, Litigation Strategies, and Bankruptcy Considered in the Context of Cloud Agreements

By Thomas A. Capezza and Nancy L. Urizar[1]

I. Introduction

This chapter examines methods of resolving disputes arising with cloud computing agreements, focusing on the benefits of alternative dispute resolution clauses in Part II and preserving cloud contents as a litigation safeguard in Part III. Part IV discusses strategies to mitigate business interruption when a cloud provider declares bankruptcy.

II. The Benefits of Alternative Dispute Resolution Clauses

Alternative dispute resolution (ADR) is the use of processes or methods such as mediation and arbitration to resolve a dispute instead of litigation. As discussed more fully below, the benefits of including ADR clauses in cloud computing agreements include time and cost savings, maintaining confidentiality as to proprietary data and the ultimate outcome, and minimizing business disruption.

A. ADR Clauses Save Time, Money, and Business Relationships

ADR clauses have been shown to yield time and cost savings. In March 2013, the World Intellectual Property Organization (WIPO) Arbitration and Mediation Center (WIPO Center) conducted a survey to "assess the current use in technology-related disputes of Alternative Dispute Resolution . . . methods as compared to court litigation, including a qualitative evaluation of these dispute resolution options."[2] A total of 393 participants (law firms, companies, research organizations, universities, government bodies, and the self-employed) from 62 countries completed the survey; 63 of these participants, from 28 countries, complemented their written responses with a telephone interview.

---

1 Thomas A. Capezza is a director at Carter, Conboy, Case, Blackmore, Maloney & Laird, P.C., specializing in white-collar litigation, government investigations, and technology issues. Nancy L. Urizar is an associate at Goodwin Procter LLP. Research assistance by Kasey K. Hildonen and Claudia C. Cadenillas.

2 WIPO Arbitration & Mediation Cent., Results of the WIPO Arbitration and Mediation Center International Survey on Dispute Resolution in Technology Transactions 3 (2013) [hereinafter WIPO Survey Results], http://www.wipo.int/export/sites/www/amc/en/docs/survey-results.pdf; *see also* Tom A. Sides, ADR and Choice of Law Clauses in Online and Cloud Computing Agreements (Sept. 2015) [hereinafter Cloud Computing Agreements] (copy on file with authors).

Participants reported that the duration of litigation in their home jurisdiction was on average approximately three years and cost approximately $475,000. When litigating in another jurisdiction, the corresponding numbers were three and one-half years and $850,000.[3]

By contrast, participants reported that mediation[4] took an average of eight months, and 91 percent of participants reported that the costs of mediation typically did not exceed $100,000.[5] Similarly, participants indicated that arbitration[6] took a little more than one year and cost on average slightly over $400,000.[7]

Apart from mediation and arbitration, ADR proceedings based on expert determinations[8] expedited resolution of disputes in a cost-effective manner. Participants indicated on average that expert determinations took slightly more than six months; nearly three-quarters of participants indicated that the costs of expert determination would not typically exceed $50,000.[9] The efficiencies of expert determinations are all the more evident when you consider the litigation alternative—that is, the costs of retaining an expert, coupled with broader litigation costs, are higher and include persuading a judge or jury who may be unfamiliar with the subject technology. Thus, due to their technical nature, cloud-based disputes lend themselves to ADR inasmuch as experts may serve as decision makers in ADR proceedings, rather than serving as witnesses to persuade nontechnical decision makers in litigation.[10] Using ADR may also reduce "wasted management time of business executives and other participants in proceedings, lost productivity, and lost business opportunities due to the reserves required to cover the worst potential outcome of a pending dispute," which 25 percent of participants mentioned as among the costs they considered.[11]

ADR clauses also serve to minimize business disruption. Dispute-resolution procedures may be tailored to, among other things, the specific circumstances of the technology, the confidential or proprietary nature of the subject data, and the unique dynamics of the business relationship.[12] Those procedures may serve to remove litigation altogether or mandate mediation as a precondition to litigation. Thus, even where mediation is unsuccessful, it may serve to triage and thereby narrow disputed issues, improve dialogue

---

3 WIPO Survey Results, *supra* note 2, at 30.

4 Mediation, as used in this context, is an "informal procedure in which a neutral intermediary assists the parties in reaching a settlement of the dispute." *Id*. at 36.

5 *Id*. at 30.

6 Arbitration, as used in this context, is an "out-of-court procedure in which the dispute is submitted to one or more arbitrators who make a binding decision." *Id*. at 36.

7 *Id*. at 30.

8 "Expert determination," as used in this context, is a "procedure in which a matter is submitted to one or more experts who make a determination on the matter referred by the parties. The determination is binding, unless the parties have agreed otherwise." *Id*. at 36.

9 *Id*. at 32.

10 WIPO Survey Results, *supra* note 2, at 5 (reporting that specialization of the decision maker is one of the main considerations when negotiating dispute resolution clauses); *see also* Cloud Computing Agreements, *supra* note 2, at 6 (discussing the benefit of clauses requiring disputes to be determined by an area expert).

11 WIPO Survey Results, *supra* note 2, at 33.

12 *See* Cloud Computing Agreements, *supra* note 2, at 2.

between the parties, minimize business disruption, maintain business relationships, and increase the chances of settlement in litigation.[13]

B. ADR Keeps the Process Confidential by Minimizing Discovery

As a separate benefit, ADR clauses may be crafted to limit discovery and the release of proprietary data, as well as to maintain secrecy of the ultimate outcome of the dispute.[14] Court decisions have made clear that litigants have little ability to shield information from discovery, including electronic information, even when that information is in the possession of third parties. ADR clauses, therefore, present an opportunity to define the contours of document and data disclosure.

Cloud storage gained a special relevance following enactment of the Clarifying Lawful Overseas Use of Data Act, better known as the CLOUD Act.[15] In a 2016 decision, the Second Circuit addressed whether extraterritorial data is properly within the ambit of a subpoena issued under the Stored Communications Act.[16] Recently, however, legislation provided an answer with the CLOUD Act: generally, data stored outside of the United States has been deemed accessible by the U.S. government via subpoena in light of "government efforts to protect public safety and combat serious crime, including terrorism."[17]

Careful drafting of a cloud computing agreement to shepherd the parties to ADR instead of litigation may provide certain protections to a company against disclosure of confidential information by its cloud service provider in the event of a dispute. It is essential that contract provisions address exactly what data is stored, in what manner, and who will have access to it, as well as who will retain ownership of that data. Drafting standards regarding cloud storage are offered by the Legal Cloud Computing Association to address concerns such as location of data, retention policy, and ownership of data, among others.[18]

C. Uncertainties of Civil Discovery under the SCA May Be Avoided with ADR

The control that ADR clauses provide over data discovery is relevant when comparing how courts are navigating the issue of cloud-stored data with Fourth Amendment rights.

---

13 *Id.*

14 Cloud Computing Agreements, *supra* note 2, at 5 (highlighting that ADR serves the purpose of maintaining confidentiality).

15 Pub. L. No. 115-141, div. V, 132 Stat. 348, 1213 (2018).

16 *In re* Warrant to Search a Certain E-Mail Account Controlled & Maintained by Microsoft Corp., 829 F. 3d 197 (2d Cir. 2016). Prior to enactment of the CLOUD Act, the U.S. Supreme Court granted certiorari to determine "whether, when the Government has obtained a warrant under [the Stored Communications Act], a U.S. provider of e-mail services must disclose to the Government electronic communications within its control even if the provider stores the communications abroad." United States v. Microsoft Corp., 138 S. Ct. 1186, 1187 (2018). Due to the enactment of the CLOUD Act, the court dismissed the case in a per curiam decision stating that that "no live dispute remains. . . . This case, therefore, has become moot." *Id.* at 1188.

17 CLOUD Act, Pub. L. No. 115-141, div. V, § 102(1), 132 Stat. 1213 (2018).

18 *See LCCA Security Standards*, Legal Cloud Computing Association, http://www. legalcloudcomputingassociation.org/standards (last visited July 24, 2018) (proposing standards such as "Data Retention Policy" and "Ownership of Data," seeking to be "responsive to the needs of the legal profession").

The applicable legislation to this issue is the Stored Communications Act (SCA).[19] Adopted in 1986 as part of the Electronic Communications Privacy Act,[20] the SCA sought to address relatively new communications technology (such as e-mail)[21] by regulating voluntary and involuntary disclosure of communications held by third-party service providers in an "electronic communication service" or "remote computing service."[22]

Subject to certain exceptions, the SCA generally prohibits service providers from knowingly divulging to any person or entity the "contents" of a communication while in electronic storage by that service or while carried or maintained on that service.[23] Courts have labored with the distinction the SCA draws between electronic communication service (ECS) providers and remote computing service (RCS) providers, having established different standards of disclosure in litigation for each. An ECS provider is defined as "any service which provides to users thereof the ability to send or receive wire or electronic communications."[24] An RCS provider, by contrast, is defined as one offering, "provision to the public of computer storage or processing services by means of an electronic communications system."[25]

The significance of the distinction between ECS and RCS lies in the different criteria necessary to establish an exception to the general rule prohibiting disclosure by a third-party provider under the SCA—that is, an ECS provider is prohibited from divulging "the contents of a communication while in electronic storage by that service,"[26] *essentially prohibiting all content disclosures in civil litigation,* although the definition of "content" itself is debatable.

By contrast, an RCS provider cannot divulge the content of any electronic communication that is carried or maintained, "solely for the purpose *of providing storage or computer processing services.*" However, the SCA protection will not apply if the provider has access for purposes "other than storage or computer processing."[27] This language is illustrated in situations where a cloud user consents to receiving targeted advertisements when signing up to use a free cloud service. "By sharing their data with the cloud provider, users make possible the advertising services that pay for the costs associated with providing the cloud service . . . ."[28] Based on this practice, some argue that a cloud provider

---

19 18 U.S.C. §§ 2701–2712 (2012).

20 Ilana R. Kattan, Note, *Cloudy Privacy Protections: Why the Stored Communications Act Fails to Protect the Privacy of Communications Stored in the Cloud,* 13 VAND. J. ENT. & TECH. L. 617, 619 (2011).

21 *Id.* at 627.

22 18 U.S.C. § 2701 *et seq.*

23 18 U.S.C. § 2702(a)(1)–(2).

24 18 U.S.C. § 2510(15).

25 18 U.S.C. § 2711(2). "Electronic communications system" is defined as "any wire, radio, electromagnetic, photooptical or photoelectronic facilities for the transmission of wire or electronic communications, and any computer facilities or related electronic equipment for the electronic storage of such communications." 18 U.S.C. § 2510(14).

26 18 U.S.C. § 2702(a)(1); Crispin v. Christian Audigier, Inc., 717 F. Supp. 2d 965, 973 (C.D. Cal. 2010). "Electronic storage" is "(A) any temporary, intermediate storage of a wire or electronic communication incidental to the electronic transmission thereof; and (B) any storage of such communication by an electronic communication service for purposes of backup protection of such communication." 18 U.S.C. § 2510(17).

27 18 U.S.C. § 2702(a)(2)(B) (emphasis added).

28 William Jeremy Robison, Note, *Free at What Cost?: Cloud Computing Privacy Under the Stored Communications Act,* 98 GEO. L.J. 1195, 1214 (2010).

(which provides an RCS) is permitted by contract to access its users' content in order to create user-specific advertising.[29]

If an RCS provider is permitted access to user information for advertising purposes, such information would not be protected by the SCA, allowing the provider to divulge the contents to the government in response to a subpoena.[30] This is an important distinction between ECS and RCS providers in terms of discovery in litigation: if the cloud provider is found to be an RCS provider, the customer data it holds may be outside the scope of SCA protections.[31]

The distinction between ECS and RCS providers has evaded courts across the circuits, preventing them from consistently applying the principles of, among other areas, discovery and document production. This is particularly problematic when a given provider begins its service to a client as an ECS provider, but later through the retention of materials becomes an RCS provider. Thus, critics have clamored for legislative amendment that would eradicate this distinction and the disparate treatment.

This brief examination of just one complex issue that arises in litigation involving cloud-stored data and the potential for disclosure of confidential information speaks volumes to the importance of considered drafting of such agreements. When negotiating and drafting cloud-computing agreements in general, and ADR clauses in particular, the parties must determine whether communications are covered by the SCA and what type of service provider maintains the communication. "In mediation, there is generally no discovery of participants or witnesses. Further, a confidentiality clause can be drafted to require the arbitration or mediation itself to be confidential in order to avoid negative publicity for corporations."[32]

A more difficult question currently the focus of the courts, however, is what protections are afforded when a party to an action subpoenas communications directly from the third-party provider. As noted by numerous courts and commentators, section 2702 of the SCA lacks any language that explicitly authorizes a service provider to divulge the contents of a communication pursuant to a subpoena or court order.[33] Taking into consideration the above-discussed complexities as to what information is considered protected under the SCA, as well as the case law in this area, companies should be aware that simply storing their information with a third-party provider will not necessarily shield that information from discovery. A third-party provider can likely share the metadata without

---

29 *See* Alexander Tsesis, *The Right to Erasure: Privacy, Data Brokers, and the Indefinite Retention of Data,* 49 WAKE FOREST L. REV. 433, 455 n.89 (2014) (citing Troutman Sanders LLP, *The Stored Communications Act and Document Subpoenas to Cloud Computing Providers,* INFO. INTERSECTION (Apr. 11, 2013)).

30 *Id.; see also* 18 U.S.C. § 2702(a)(2)(B).

31 Additionally, the provider of an RCS may divulge the contents of a communication with the "lawful consent" of the subscriber to the service, whereas the provider of an ECS may divulge such a communication only with the "lawful consent of the originator or an addressee or intended recipient of such communication." 18 U.S.C. § 2702(b)(3). For instance, one of Dropbox's main utilities is storage of information, which categorizes this service as RCS. However, if a user chooses to share a Dropbox link to another person, this communication now becomes ECS. Eric R. Hinz, Note, *A Distinctionless Distinction: Why The RCS/ECS Distinction in the Stored Communications Act Does Not Work,* 88 NOTRE DAME L. REV. 489, 515 (2012).

32 *See* Cloud Computing Agreements, *supra* note 2, at 5.

33 *See, e.g., In re* Subpoena Duces Tecum to AOL, LLC, 550 F. Supp. 2d 606, 611 (E.D. Va. 2008) ("[T]he statutory language of the [SCA] does not include an exception for the disclosure of electronic communications pursuant to civil discovery subpoenas.").

violating the SCA, and furthermore, as illustrated below, information considered in the control of a party to an action will generally be found discoverable under Fed. R. Civ. P. 26(b)(1), regardless of whether it is stored on a third-party server.

In *Flagg v. City of Detroit*,[34] a notable and oft-cited case, the plaintiff served defendants (the city and its employees) with two subpoenas. Plaintiff sought discovery of information that supported his allegations of an inadequate investigation of his mother's murder.[35] The defendants argued that the SCA "*wholly precludes* the production in civil litigation of electronic communications stored by a *non-party service provider.*"[36] SkyTel, Inc. was the nonparty service provider contracted to provide text-messaging services to the city and its employees. The services ended in 2004, but SkyTel remained in possession of the text messages.[37] The court analyzed SkyTel's role as a *nonparty* provider and concluded that the archive was maintained as "computer storage," which defines the SkyTel service as an RCS and thus outside of the scope of the SCA protections and open to discovery requests.[38] Given that the court found the city was still in legal control of the text messages, however, the court concluded that the straightforward solution in this case was for the plaintiff to prepare and serve a Rule 34 request to compel the city (instead of SkyTel under an SCA motion) to provide the information.[39]

This case illustrates that courts have not yet decided whether the SCA prohibits a non-party service provider (e.g., cloud providers) from divulging contents stored for the customer. A well-written ADR clause can help one avoid such uncertainty and subsequently a FRCP 34 motion in litigation by safeguarding the confidentiality of the materials involved. The complexities of the SCA, evolving cloud technology, lagging legislation, and the court rulings in this uncertain arena make the point that ADR clauses in cloud computing agreements are a viable, if not necessary, option to ensure preservation of confidential and proprietary data.

Cases attempting to interpret the SCA expose the risks to civil litigants of broad discovery rulings.[40] In those cases, courts have endeavored to balance the growing trend toward cloud-stored data with rights conferred by the SCA in the context of discovery during civil litigation.[41] Due to significant progress, courts have struggled with the application of discovery production principles to cloud-computing systems.[42] As seen above, ADR offers a way to regain control over these discovery principles.

---

34 Flagg v. City of Detroit, 252 F.R.D. 346 (E.D. Mich. 2008).

35 *Id.* at 351.

36 *Id.* at 347 (emphasis added).

37 *See id.* at 363.

38 It should be noted that these facts led the court to determine that SkyTel had ceased to be an active provider of text messaging services, although it continued to maintain a database of text messages sent. The district court found that it had become an RCS provider because it served in the capacity of a "virtual filing cabinet" for the city. *Id.* at 347–48, 361.

39 *Id.* at 366.

40 *See* Negro v. Superior Court, 179 Cal. Rptr. 3d 215 (Cal. Ct. App. 2014).

41 *See* Eric Johnson, Note, *Lost in the Cloud*, 69 Stan. L. Rev. 867, 900 (2017).

42 The SCA does not merely absolve a service provider from responding to a request for covered communications, it also affirmatively prohibits disclosure and authorizes a civil action against the provider for unauthorized disclosure. In some cases, a party who acquires protected communications through a subpoena could even be exposed to sanctions and liability in a civil suit if the party acquires protected communications through an improper subpoena. *See* Theofel v. Farey-Jones, 359 F.3d 1066, 1074–75 (9th Cir. 2004) (reversing a dismissal of an SCA claim). Recognizing the strength of the protections under the SCA, courts in some cases have granted a party's motion to quash subpoenas to nonparty service providers. *Id.* at 1071–72.

D. ADR Allows a Choice-of-Law Clause

Further, ADR clauses in cloud computing agreements should include a choice-of-law provision; such clause is referred to as the "seat of arbitration."[43] The law that governs the agreement as a whole does not necessarily govern mediation and arbitration; therefore, the seat of arbitration, or governing law, must be specified. Forum selection, jurisdiction, and governing law clauses are essential for cloud computing agreements in that these agreements deal with products, services, and users that often span multiple jurisdictions. Choice-of-law clauses will lead to increased certainty and enforceability, and avoid costly and lengthy litigation with uncertain outcomes.[44]

E. Limitations on ADR

There are limits to ADR clauses, however. When drafting ADR clauses, parties must be mindful of local laws that may not be waived by ADR agreements. These include, but are not limited to, laws designed to protect local business and consumers, such as obligatory warranties, import and customs, dealer protection, criminal laws, as well as bankruptcy and insolvency.[45] For example, in *America Online, Inc. v. Superior Court*,[46] a California appellate court voided forum selection and choice-of-law clauses that would have moved the case to Virginia and applied Virginia law. The California court reasoned that the clauses violated California public policy inasmuch as California consumers would have been denied protections under the California Consumers Legal Remedies Act.

Valid forum-selection clauses, however, will generally be upheld by U.S. courts unless the agreed-upon forum is inappropriate or contrary to public policy; only under extraordinary circumstances will such a provision be overridden.[47] *AT&T Mobility LLC v. Concepcion* is an example of a court finding that federal law preempts a state rule that declared an arbitration clause to be against public policy.[48] In *AT&T*, the plaintiffs purchased mobile services that advertised an offer of free phones; yet, they were still charged $30.22 in sales taxes.[49] A complaint was filed and later turned into a putative class action alleging that AT&T engaged in false advertising and fraud.[50] AT&T moved to compel arbitration under the terms of the service contract, which did not allow class-wide arbitration.[51] The Supreme Court cited section two of the Federal Arbitration Act (FAA), which states arbitration clauses are generally "valid, irrevocable, and enforceable, *save upon such grounds as exist at law or in equity for the revocation of any contract*."[52] The court refers to the

---

43 Cloud Computing Agreements, *supra* note 2, at 3.

44 E. Casey Lide, Note & Comment, *ADR and Cyberspace: The Role of Alternative Dispute Resolution in Online Commerce, Intellectual Property and Defamation*, 12 Ohio St. J. on Disp. Resol. 193, 200 (1996) ("Parties can develop arbitration agreements which stipulate their choice of law, eliminating potential delays which may result from a dispute over jurisdiction.").

45 *See* Cloud Computing Agreements, *supra* note 2, at 9.

46 Am. Online, Inc. v. Superior Court, 90 Cal. App. 4th 1 (Cal. Ct. App. 2001).

47 Atlantic Marine Const. Co. v. U.S. Dist. Court, 571 U.S. 49, 62–66 (2013); Cloud Computing Agreements, *supra* note 2, at 10.

48 AT&T Mobility LLC v. Concepcion, 563 U.S. 333 (2011).

49 *Id*. at 337.

50 *Id*.

51 *Id*.

52 *Id*. at 339 (citing 9 U.S.C. § 2) (emphasis added).

italicized language as "the saving clause," and concluded that class arbitration is inconsistent with the FAA.[53]

In sum, considering the many benefits of ADR clauses and the complexities they address, cloud computing agreements should contain express ADR language.

III. Preserving Cloud Contents as a Litigation Safeguard

In those instances where ADR is not pursued or is unsuccessful, and the parties find themselves in litigation, there are a number of strategies of which a litigant should be mindful. The strategies presented below allow individuals to comply with their responsibilities as a litigant and avoid sanctions for inadequate care of evidence.

As has already been established, litigants have a duty to comply with information requests, including government and private-party subpoenas and discovery rules for anticipated, pending, or active litigation.[54] Moreover, these responsibilities are complicated by multijurisdictional and extraterritorial data storage and transfer. Again, whether a warrant issued pursuant to the SCA[55] may compel an e-mail service provider to disclose e-mails held on servers outside the United States has been debated by federal courts of different circuits with varying results and concluded with the enactment of the CLOUD Act.

A. Brief History of Cloud Storage Litigation

As mentioned above, in *In re Warrant to Search a Certain E-Mail Account Controlled & Maintained by Microsoft Corp.*,[56] initially the Second Circuit significantly narrowed the application of discovery principles relative to electronically stored information. The court denied[57] the government's application to enforce warrants to obtain e-mail information stored outside of the country by Microsoft. The court reasoned that American courts do not have such authority because it is presumed that the SCA's reach is limited to the borders of the United States.[58] As such, the government conceded that the SCA does not contemplate extraterritorial application.[59]

---

53 The actual question in the case was whether FAA section two preempted California's *Discover Bank* rule, which classifies *most* collective arbitration waivers in consumer contracts as unconscionable. The court held that the *Discover Bank* rule was preempted because class arbitration is poorly suited to tend to the higher stakes of litigation. *See id.*

54 *See* Fed. R. Civ. P. 37.

55 18 U.S.C. § 2703.

56 829 F.3d 197 (2d Cir. 2016).

57 The Court of Appeals decision in this case is even more impactful on the application of discovery principles in cases involving electronically stored information (ESI). Indeed, unlike the parties in *Flagg*, the party demanding the information in *Microsoft* was the U.S. government, which has generally been given greater access under the SCA and under legal precedent. *Id.*

> The concurrence pointed out that the decision to limit the scope of the warrant resulted from an outdated law, not a choice by Congress to hamstring investigations of foreign conduct that might violate American laws. He pointed out that "there is no evidence that Congress has *ever* weighed the costs and benefits of authorizing court orders."

> *Id.*

58 *Id.* at 210 (citing Morrison v. Nat'l Austl. Bank Ltd., 561 U.S. 247 (2010) and RJR Nabisco, Inc. v. European Cmty., 136 S. Ct. 2090 (2016)).

59 *Id.* at 210–16.

Two courts distinguished this reasoning. In *In re Info. Associated with One Yahoo Email Address That Is Stored at Premises Controlled by Yahoo*,[60] the government made an application for a warrant pursuant to 18 U.S.C. § 2703 to compel Yahoo to disclose e-mail records, specifically, "all responsive information—including data stored outside the United States—pertaining to the identified account that is in the possession, custody, or control of Yahoo." Likewise, a second case, *In re Information Assoc. with [Redacted]@gmail.com*, rejected a motion to quash subpoenaed records from Google stored internationally.[61] The court reasoned that Google's representatives in California could access, compile, and disclose to the government the subject records and information with the push of a button and without ever leaving their desks in the United States.[62]

As previously stated, the issues raised in the *Microsoft* case were ultimately resolved by the CLOUD Act, making electronic information generally accessible to the U.S. government on the basis of public welfare and terrorism. Upon interpretation of this act in civil litigation, potential litigants must consider disclosure obligations when evaluating the terms of a prospective cloud computing agreement. In other words, when considering cloud storage, a customer must be aware of how one can preserve the information in order to be ready for litigation, including multijurisdictional and extraterritorial data storage and transfer.[63]

B. Strategies for Preserving Information Stored in the Cloud

Pursuant to FRCP Rule 34(a) a party may request during litigation the production of documents and various other categories of items that are "in the responding party's possession, custody, or *control*."[64] The items that may be sought under the rule include "electronically stored information"—both electronic communications and archived copies of such communications that are preserved in electronic form.[65] Thus, putting aside the multijurisdictional and extraterritorial issues, disclosure responsibilities are complicated by the delegation of "control," which "complicat[es] the decision a business makes about storing critical or sensitive data in the cloud."[66]

Regarding what constitutes "control," the Sixth Circuit and other courts have held that documents are deemed to be within the "control" of a party if the party "has the legal right

---

60 No. 17-M-1234, 2017 U.S. Dist. LEXIS 24591 (E.D. Wis. Feb. 21, 2017).

61 *In re* Information Assoc. with [Redacted]@gmail.com, 2017 U.S. Dist. LEXIS 92601, *36 (D.D.C. 2017).

62 *Id.*

63 Cindy Pham, Note, *E-Discovery in the Cloud Era: What's a Litigant To Do?*, 5 HASTINGS SCI. & TECH. L.J. 139, 180 (2013) ("[An] attorney should work closely with the company's IT staff to understand what kind of cloud infrastructure the company uses . . . , what is stored in the cloud, what the terms of the service agreement are, and what data retrieval options and tools are available.").

64 FED. R. CIV. P. 34(a)(1) (emphasis added); *see also* Cooper Indus., Inc. v. British Aerospace, Inc., 102 F.R.D. 918, 919 (S.D.N.Y. 1984) ("Documents need not be in the possession of a party to be discoverable, they need only be in its custody or control.").

65 FED. R. CIV. P. 34(a)(1)(A); *see* FED. R. CIV. P. 34, Advisory Committee Note to 2006 Amendment; Zubulake v. UBS Warburg LLC, 217 F.R.D. 309, 317 & nn. 36–38 (S.D.N.Y. 2003).

66 Andrew M. Hinkes & Gavin C. Gaukroger, *Cloud Computing: New Discovery Challenges Await*, FED. LAW., Feb. 2011, at 48, 49.

to obtain the documents on demand."[67] In light of the rule's language, "[a] party responding to a Rule 34 production request 'cannot furnish only that information within his immediate knowledge or possession; he is under an affirmative duty to seek that information reasonably available to him from his employees, agents, or others subject to his control.'"[68] The requisite "legal right to obtain" documents has been found in contractual provisions that confer a right of access to the requested materials.[69]

For purposes of potential litigation, parties also must consider the retention practices of a given cloud provider.[70] A cloud customer that has decided to engage a cloud provider should do so mindful of its duty to maintain records, regardless of the contract or the service provider's ability to supply the records. Customers should therefore contemplate agreements for the return or transfer of their data. Indeed, electronic evidence in litigation may be treated like any other evidence, and litigants may be penalized for failing to turn over such information. Although it is not expected for a party to save "every shred of paper" upon recognizing litigation, a litigant still has the "duty to preserve what it knows, or reasonably should know, is relevant in the action."[71] In an effort to comply with a duty to preserve evidence, a party will be free to preserve electronic evidence in any format it chooses, including inaccessible formats if those are considered material for discovery.[72]

Finally, as in any litigation involving electronic evidence, data authentication is potentially an issue in cloud computing disputes.[73] As with other cloud computing issues, the core authentication concern for electronic evidence stored in the cloud is the company's loss of direct control over the information. In short, the terms of the cloud computing contract and data management as it relates to the cloud computing service must be consistent with authentication requirements. Although there is no extensive guidance on authentication of cloud-stored information, courts have warned that there is no difference in data authentication requirements as between electronically stored information and information recorded on paper. If anything, one must be aware that electronic data might be held to a higher standard because information can be easily manipulated.[74] Success in authenticating data generally does not depend on "legal or factual arguments, but rather

---

67 *In re* Bankers Trust Co., 61 F.3d 465, 469 (6th Cir. 1995); *see also* Mercy Catholic Med. Ctr. v. Thompson, 380 F.3d 142, 160 (3d Cir. 2004); Searock v. Stripling, 736 F.2d 650, 653 (11th Cir. 1984).

68 Gray v. Faulkner, 148 F.R.D. 220, 223 (N.D. Ind. 1992) (internal quotation marks and citation omitted); *see* Flagg v. City of Detroit, 252 F.R.D. 346, 353 (E.D. Mich. 2008).

69 *See, e.g.*, Anderson v. Cryovac, Inc., 862 F.2d 910, 928–29 (1st Cir. 1988); Golden Trade, S.r.L. v. Lee Apparel Co., 143 F.R.D. 514, 525 (S.D.N.Y. 1992).

70 Pham, *supra* note 63, at 181–82 (an attorney working with a client who contracted with a cloud provider should attempt to learn "where the data is physically located and what the cloud provider's archival and retention capabilities are"); *see also* Hinkes & Gaukroger, *supra* note 66, at 51.

71 Quinby v. WestLB AG, 245 F.R.D. 94, 103 (S.D.N.Y. 2006).

72 *Id*. at 103–04; Zubulake v. UBS Warburg LLC, 220 F.R.D. 212, 218 (S.D.N.Y. 2003).

73 Steven W. Teppler, *Testable Reliability: A Modernized Approach to ESI Admissibility*, 12 Ave Maria L. Rev. 213, 217 (2014) ("The inherently mutable nature of computer-generated data creates new issues that have a significant and detrimental effect on reliability, authentication, and ultimately on the issue of admissibility."); *see also* Pham, *supra* note 63, at 160 ("[S]ince the Federal Rules do not require that a third-party cloud provider preserve evidence without a duty to do so, once the information is located, preserving potentially relevant ESI may be difficult, if not impossible.").

74 Griffin v. State, 419 Md. 343, 351 (2011) ("A number of social networking websites, such as MySpace, enable members to create online profiles . . . *Anyone can create a MySpace profile at no cost . . . .*") (citations and quotation marks omitted; emphasis added).

the amount of time and resources a litigant devotes to the problem."[75] Thus, an attorney using cloud services must be mindful of the "basics" of data authentication and its admissibility. Is the information stored relevant to potential litigation? Different authenticating factors will apply to different types of information.[76] A good practice is to be mindful of the usual form of proof when working with a cloud clause to ensure a practitioner or other interested party is not impaired or unable to authenticate data.[77]

IV. Strategies for Mitigating Business Interruption When a Cloud Provider Declares Bankruptcy

When choosing a cloud provider, a customer should consider how its business will be affected if the cloud provider files for bankruptcy protection or, in the worst-case scenario, goes out of business. This is particularly important if the cloud provider will be providing data storage or processing services or access to critical software applications because a customer's business operations could be significantly impaired if it were to lose access to crucial data or software applications.

Cloud providers typically file for bankruptcy protection under either Chapter 7 (liquidation)[78] or Chapter 11 (reorganization)[79] of the Bankruptcy Code.[80] Under Chapter 7, the debtor's nonexempt assets are liquidated, and the proceeds are used to pay the creditors, whereas under Chapter 11, the debtor may elect to either: (1) restructure its financial obligations so that it may emerge from bankruptcy and continue to operate its business under a court-approved plan of reorganization; or (2) liquidate its assets. Whether the bankruptcy petition is filed pursuant to Chapter 7 or Chapter 11, a customer must have a backup plan for the worst-case scenario: that it no longer has access to any data stored in the cloud provider's environment or to critical software applications.

A. The Bankruptcy Estate

Chapter 7 and Chapter 11 bankruptcy cases begin with the filing of a bankruptcy petition with the bankruptcy court by either the debtor or the creditors of the debtor who meet certain requirements. The bankruptcy is considered voluntary if the petition is filed by the debtor and involuntary if filed by the creditors. In both Chapters 7 and 11 cases, the filing of the bankruptcy petition triggers the creation of the bankruptcy estate. The bankruptcy estate consists of all property in which the debtor had an interest at the time of the filing of the petition.

---

75 Jeffrey Bellin & Andrew Guthrie Ferguson, *Trial by Google: Judicial Notice in the Information Age*, 108 Nw. U. L. Rev. 1137, 1157 (2014).

76 Hon. Paul W. Grimm et al., *Authenticating Digital Evidence*, 69 Baylor L. Rev. 1, 11 (2017) ("[T]he importance of any factor will be case-dependent. And there is no intent to imply that all of the factors listed must be met before the proffered digital evidence can be found authentic.").

77 The Federal Rules of Evidence provides that information about a process or system can be authenticated by "describing a process or system and showing that it produces an accurate result." Fed. R. Evid. 901(b)(9).

78 11 U.S.C. §§ 701–784.

79 *Id.* §§ 1101–1174.

80 *Id.* §§ 101–1532.

In Chapter 7 bankruptcy cases, the bankruptcy estate is administered by a trustee whose primary role is to liquidate the debtor's assets and distribute the proceeds to the nonsecured creditors. In Chapter 11 bankruptcy cases, unless a trustee is appointed, the debtor becomes the "debtor-in-possession" and remains in control of the bankruptcy estate while the business undergoes reorganization or liquidates its assets.

If a customer's data is to be stored in the cloud provider's environment, it is critical that the cloud services contract clearly state that the customer will remain the owner of any confidential or proprietary data provided by the customer to the cloud provider so that the customer's confidential or proprietary data is not considered part of the bankruptcy estate. In addition, to ensure that any confidential or proprietary data generated by the cloud provider while performing the services is owned by the customer and not the bankruptcy estate, the cloud provider contract should include a present assignment of the cloud provider's rights in that confidential or proprietary data to the customer.

If the cloud provider contract includes software development services, a customer should also confirm that the cloud provider contract includes a provision assigning ownership to the customer of any software developed by the cloud provider.

B. The Automatic Stay

The filing of the bankruptcy petition under either Chapter 7 or Chapter 11 also triggers the automatic stay (an injunction that prohibits creditors from attempting to collect debts that arose before the filing of the bankruptcy petition). The automatic stay prohibits the commencement or continuation of any action or proceeding against the debtor, including collection activities, foreclosures, repossessions of property, and lawsuits.[81]

The primary purpose of the automatic stay is to give the debtor a "breathing spell" from creditors so that it can focus on formulating a reorganization plan or liquidate its assets while continuing to operate the business without interference from the creditors. Under Chapter 7, the trustee may be authorized for a limited period of time to operate the business if the operation "is in the best interest of the estate and consistent with the orderly liquidation of the estate."[82] Under Chapter 11, the debtor as the debtor-in-possession may continue to operate the business while it prepares the plan of reorganization.[83]

Although a business may continue to operate following the filing of the bankruptcy petition under either Chapter 7 or Chapter 11, this does not guarantee that the debtor or trustee, as applicable, will continue to operate the business, even if all actions or proceedings have been stayed. Customers should keep in mind that the debtor may not be in a financial position to continue to operate the business and that the trustee may not have the necessary experience to run the business. A customer should also keep in mind that even if the business continues after the filing of the petition, the period of time during which the debtor or trustee, as applicable, continues to operate the business might not be long enough for the customer to migrate its data and systems to a new cloud provider. To protect itself from this situation, a customer may want to include a provision in the applicable contract requiring the cloud provider to store a backup copy of the data with a third-party provider and perform regular updates to that data.

---

81 *Id.* § 362(a). Certain types of actions are excluded from the automatic stay. *Id.* § 362(b).
82 *Id.* § 721.
83 *Id.* §§ 1107–1108.

C. Executory Contracts

One of the benefits of both Chapter 7 and Chapter 11 bankruptcy is that the trustee or debtor-in-possession may, with some exceptions, assume or reject executory contracts to which it is a party. An executory contract is one in which the parties to the contract have material obligations yet to be performed at the time of the filing of the bankruptcy petition.[84] Executory contracts typically include both software license agreements and cloud provider contracts.

If the trustee or debtor-in-possession assumes the executory contract, then it will be required to continue performing its obligations under the contract. For a customer of a cloud provider contract that is assumed, this is good news because the customer will continue to have access to the services provided by the cloud provider under the contract and its data.

On the other hand, if the trustee or debtor-in-possession rejects the executory contract, then it will not be required to perform any of its obligations under the contract. The rejection will be treated as a material breach of the contract by the debtor, and the customer will obtain an unsecured claim for money damages. For a customer, rejection of its cloud provider contract means that it will no longer have access to the services.

The Bankruptcy Code gives licensees of intellectual property certain protections when the trustee or debtor-in-possession rejects its licensing agreement. Under section 365(n) of the Bankruptcy Code,[85] a licensee may elect to retain its rights to the licensed intellectual property (including to any embodiments of the intellectual property, such as the source code of the software and any documentation). If the licensee elects to retain its rights to the licensed intellectual property, it must continue to pay any licensing fees. The licensor will not be required to perform any of its obligations under the contract, however, including any of its maintenance obligations.[86] For the licensee, this means that the licensor will not have to make available any updates, upgrades, or bug fixes to the licensed software. This could be problematic unless the licensee has the necessary resources to maintain the software (such as by modifying the source code or developing additional code) while it looks for another solution to meet its needs.

Whether section 365(n) applies to cloud provider contracts will depend on whether the bankruptcy court decides that the trustee or debtor-in-possession is a licensor of a right to intellectual property. Given that cloud vendor agreements do not typically include grants of copyright licenses because the customer is not receiving a copy of the software, it is not clear whether the bankruptcy court will find that section 365(n) applies to the cloud provider agreement. Although not binding on the bankruptcy court, customers could increase the likelihood that the bankruptcy court will find that section 365(n) applies to their contract if the cloud provider agreement is drafted so that it conforms to the language and the requirements of section 365(n) (i.e., drafting the cloud provider contract as a license to intellectual property). The addition of such language will depend on the type of services provided by the cloud provider (e.g., SaaS, PaaS, or IaaS) because, in some instances, such license grant will not be consistent with the rights granted to the customer.

---

84 *See In re* Kemeta, LLC, 470 B.R. 304, 322–25 (Bankr. D. Del. 2012).
85 11 U.S.C. § 365(n).
86 *Id.* § 365(n)(2)(C)(ii).

If the bankruptcy court finds that section 365(n) applies, the customer will have the right to elect to continue to use any software applications that are hosted by the cloud provider and to obtain a copy of the object code, source code, and documentation.[87] However, because the cloud provider will not be required to continue to host the software application or meet any of its service-level commitments, the customer must either host the software internally or find a third-party vendor to host the applications and provide the service levels.[88] This may give the customer a temporary solution while it identifies an alternative solution.

D. Strategies for Mitigating Business Interruption

What can the customer do to prevent business interruption if its cloud provider files for bankruptcy protection, or worse, goes out of business?

If the cloud provider' services are critical to the operation of the business, then the customer should probably prepare for the worst. The customer should focus on developing a reliable, practical, and cost-effective solution that will allow the customer to continue to access the services and its data in the event its cloud provider goes out of business. This may include developing a short-term solution that will allow the customer to continue having access to the hosted software applications and its data while it identifies an alternative solution to meet its business requirements.

Depending on the importance of the data to the customer, the customer may want to include provisions in the cloud provider agreement requiring the cloud provider to store a backup copy of the data with a third-party provider and perform regular updates to that data. If the customer has the resources to bring the data in-house, the customer may include provisions in the cloud services agreement requiring the cloud vendor to deliver periodic copies of all data to the customer. In either case, the cloud provider should be required to deliver the data in the right format so that it can be easily accessed and used by the customer and any third-party provider.

If the hosted software applications are critical to the operation of the business, and the customer has the necessary resources to deploy the software application in-house, the customer should consider setting up a third-party escrow agreement with a third-party agent. Pursuant to the escrow agreement, the cloud provider would be required to place the source code of the software application, relevant documentation (including user manuals), and a list of any third-party software necessary to run the software into escrow. The cloud provider would also be required to provide periodic updates to the escrowed materials to ensure that escrowed materials reflect the latest versions of each of the escrowed materials. The escrowed materials would be released to the customer upon the filing of the bankruptcy petition. The cloud provider contract should also include a present license to use the source code and documentation, effective as of the release of the escrowed materials. The license grant should be drafted as a present grant (including the language "hereby grants") so that the customer may rely on section 365(n) in the event the cloud provider rejects the cloud vendor contract.

Choosing a cloud provider is an important decision, particularly if the cloud provider will be storing the customer's data or hosting mission-critical applications. A customer

---

87 *Id.* § 365(n)(4)(A)(ii).
88 Part IV.D, below, suggests a strategy for accomplishing this.

must be proactive in implementing a backup plan that will allow it mitigate the negative effects to its business if its cloud provider goes out of business.

V. Conclusion

Alternative Dispute Resolution ("ADR") is the use of processes or methods for decision-making, such as mediation and arbitration, to resolve a dispute instead of litigation. As supported by a study by the WIPO Center, the benefits of including ADR clauses in cloud-computing agreements include time and cost savings. ADR clauses also help maintain confidentiality as to proprietary data and the ultimate outcome of a case, as well as minimize business disruption. Indeed, dispute-resolution procedures may be tailored to, among other things, the specific circumstances of the technology, the confidential or proprietary nature of the subject data, and the unique dynamics of the business relationship.

A well-written ADR clause can also help an entity avoid the uncertainties of evolving legislation, such as the CLOUD Act and the SCA, and the ongoing interpretation of same. New legislation, however well-intended, remains relatively open to interpretation. This leaves one's personal and sensitive information potentially unprotected. Moreover, for purposes of potential litigation, parties also must consider the retention practices of a given cloud provider, the authentication of data, as well as the return or transfer of data.

In sum, considering the many benefits of ADR clauses as noted above, cloud computing agreements should contain express ADR language.

Chapter 9

Cloud Computing in Canada

By Lisa R. Lifshitz and Myron Mallia-Dare[1]

I. Introduction

Doing business in Canada often seems deceptively easy for Americans. After all, Canadians speak and write in the same language (albeit with some unusual accents and odd spellings), share common cultural references, eat similar foods, and cheer for the same sports teams. For the most part, Canada's legal system springs from the same English traditions as the United States. U.S. cell phones will function in Canada (although the roaming charges will be hellish), and even most toll-free "U.S. only" numbers generally work here. Although it's true that Canadian money is more colorful, few Canadian establishments will turn away U.S. greenbacks, and a considerable number of Canadian companies currently opt to transact in U.S. dollars on a daily basis.

Despite the facile similarities, however, there actually are pronounced differences between the two nations, including variations in laws and regulations, and U.S. organizations that intend to do business in Canada often ignore these differences, sometimes to their peril. In the early days of cloud computing, for example, U.S. cloud vendors refused to recognize the distinct requirements of Canadian law, steadfastly and blithely requiring prospective Canadian customers to sign up to their standard-form cloud agreements with no effort to accommodate for specific end-user legal requirements. Although this practice endures with smaller U.S. vendors, larger and more sophisticated American technology companies, including Microsoft Corporation, IBM, and Salesforce.com, recognized that they were losing clients, particularly those from the financial, health care, and government sectors, who simply could not sign up to standard U.S. form agreements that did not meet Canadian regulatory and legal requirements. In time, therefore, Canadian subsidiaries of American corporations found themselves creating "Canada specific," localized versions of their technology contracts that endeavoured to better meet Canadian regulatory requirements in order to compete with Canadian cloud vendors. Other U.S. vendors that continue to do business in Canada have declined to create more Canadian-specific forms, but grudgingly acknowledge that some changes may be required to their standard form documents in order to "get the deal" done and do business with Canadian clients. The battles continue today.

This chapter provides a non-exhaustive overview of the laws and regulations applicable to cloud computing in Canada and is intended to be of particular relevance to cloud vendors that wish to do business in Canada. Accordingly, it pays special attention to those areas of Canadian law that are relevant to cloud computing but that differ from existing American requirements. Please note that this chapter is not intended to provide a complete and comprehensive overview or analysis of all issues or matters relevant to cloud

---

1 Lisa R. Lifshitz is a partner in the Business Law Group and chair of the Technology, Privacy and Data Management and Emerging Technology Groups at Torkin Manes LLP. Myron Mallia-Dare is an associate in the Business Law Group at Torkin Manes LLP.

computing in Canada and is merely intended to provide general guidance. For this reason, we suggest seeking the advice of expert legal counsel in Canada who can assist in navigating the shoals in Canadian law applicable to cloud computing.

By way of background, Canada is a federal state in which certain powers are allocated to the federal government, and others to the ten provincial governments and three territorial governments. Under the Constitution Act,[2] power is divided between the federal and provincial/territorial governments, with each government being supreme in its area of jurisdiction. Yet, in some areas of business, including cloud computing, both federal and provincial laws may apply. Canada is unique in that two separate and distinct legal systems coexist. English common law is applied in the three territories and nine of the ten provinces, but civil law is applied in the Province of Québec, including to contracts that are made there and technically to any contract involving a consumer located in Québec.

II. Privacy and Security

A. Canadian Data Protection Laws

The collection, use, and disclosure of personal information in Canada is governed by a patchwork of federal and provincial laws. Which law applies to an organization will depend upon where it is located and the industry in which that organization is engaged. Canada's privacy laws, both provincial and federal, are drafted to be technology neutral and, as such, will apply to the use, storage, or disclosure of personal information via a cloud service model.

In the majority of Canada's provinces and territories, the use of personal information for "commercial" purposes in the private sector is governed by the federal Personal Information Protection and Electronic Documents Act (PIPEDA).[3] PIPEDA governs the use of "personal information" in those provinces and territories that have not enacted "substantially similar" legislation. "Personal information" is broadly defined to include "information about an identifiable individual."[4]

Currently, only the provinces of British Columbia,[5] Alberta,[6] and Québec[7] have enacted legislation that has been declared to be "substantially similar" to PIPEDA[8] (termed herein as personal information protection acts, or PIPAs). Private-sector organizations

---

2 The Constitution Act, 1867, 30 & 31 Vict., c. 3 (Eng.).

3 Personal Information Protection and Electronic Documents Act, 2000 S.C., ch. 5 [hereinafter PIPEDA].

4 *Id.* § 2.

5 Personal Information Protection Act, 2003 S.B.C., ch. 63.

6 Personal Information Protection Act, 2003 S.A., ch. P-6.5 [hereinafter Alberta PIPA].

7 An Act Respecting the Protection of Personal Information in the Private Sector, R.S.Q., ch. P-39.1 [hereinafter Québec PIPA]. On September 13, 2013, the Manitoba Personal Information Protection and Identity Theft Prevention Act (the Act)—the first broadly applicable private-sector privacy statute to be enacted in Canada since 2004—received Royal Assent, but the Act is still awaiting proclamation and is not yet in force.

8 *See* Organizations in the Province of British Columbia Exemption Order, SOR/2004-220; Organizations in the Province of Alberta Exemption Order, SOR/2004-219; and Organizations in the Province of Québec Exemption Order, SOR/2003-374. In addition to the foregoing, several provinces have enacted sector-specific legislation, such as regarding health information, that have been declared to be "substantially similar," but discussion of these is beyond the scope of this chapter. *See, e.g.,* Ontario's Personal Health Information Protection Act, 2004 S.O., ch. 3, Sched. A., which will be discussed later in this chapter.

carrying on business solely within these jurisdictions are required to comply with the applicable provincial law, rather than PIPEDA. Overall, the legal requirements under these provincial privacy laws are largely equivalent to those created under PIPEDA; indeed, a substantially similar provincial law must exist before an order exempting organizations from the application of PIPEDA may be made.[9]

The legislative situation is more complicated for organizations such as cloud vendors that conduct business across provincial boundaries. Within an exempt province, an organization's use of personal information will be governed by applicable provincial legislation. However, PIPEDA will apply to organizations located in exempt provinces when they collect, use, or disclose personal information across provincial boundaries or internationally.[10] As cloud computing by definition involves the use of remotely located computing resources, it will almost invariably involve the use of extra-provincial or international computing resources, thus triggering PIPEDA compliance. Depending upon the facts, where a Canadian organization transfers personal information into a cloud computing environment, it may also be required to consider its obligations under three other distinct provincial privacy laws in addition to international privacy legislation.

Canadian privacy legislation, including PIPEDA, reflects the following 10 principles derived from the OECD Guidelines: (1) accountability, (2) identifying purposes, (3) consent, (4) limiting collection, (5) limiting use, disclosure, and retention, (6) accuracy, (7) safeguards, (8) openness, (9) individual access, and (10) challenging compliance. These principles are the foundation of privacy laws in Canada.

B. Cross-Border Transfers and Data Protection

Organizations, including cloud vendors, that collect, use, or disclose personal information are generally required to provide security for that information appropriate for its sensitivity. In creating safeguards for personal information, some legislation obligates organizations to implement physical, organizational, and technological measures to ensure adequate safety of any personal information received.[11] Physical data-protection mechanisms may include restricting access to secure locations. Organizational data-protection measures will include ensuring that only certain personnel have access, or the access keys, to personal information. Lastly, and particularly important in cloud computing, technological controls will include data encryption, passwords, and access keys. The extent to which each of these protection methods is required will vary with the sensitivity of the information in question; more sensitive information will require greater protection and vice versa.

In addition to protecting personal information in their control, as a general rule, organizations are required to limit their use, disclosure, and retention of personal information. Principle 4.1.3 of PIPEDA specifically requires organizations that outsource business functions involving the transfer of personal information to a third party to retain responsibility for the personal information and ensure that once transferred, it retains a comparable level of

---

9 PIPEDA, *supra* note 4, § 26(2)(b).

10 The Office of the Privacy Commissioner of Canada, *Questions and Answers regarding the application of PIPEDA, Alberta and British Columbia's Personal Information Protection Acts* (5 Nov. 2004), https://www.priv.gc.ca/en/privacy-topics/privacy-laws-in-canada/the-personal-information-protection-and-electronic-documents-act-pipeda/legislation-related-to-pipeda/02_05_d_26/.

11 PIPEDA, *supra* note 4, Sch. 1, Principle 7.

protection in the hands of the third party.[12] As such, any Canadian company that is choosing to outsource its data to a cloud provider must nonetheless ensure that any personal information transferred to such cloud provider is dealt with in a manner that meets the organization's own local legal obligations. This typically requires the cloud provider to be contractually bound to secure the information in an adequate manner, considering the sensitivity of the information, as well as specifying in considerable detail the data protection mechanisms and any data breach notification requirements that apply to the outsourcing organization.

PIPEDA requires that the customer engaging the cloud provider comply with the requirements to obtain consent to the collection, use, and disclosure of personal information, secure the data accordingly, ensure the accountability for the information, and be transparent in its practices.[13] As discussed in the Introduction, it is not uncommon for Canadian organizations to inform and advise a non-Canadian cloud provider of the obligations required under PIPEDA on behalf of the organization.

Further, if the U.S.-based cloud provider has a real and substantial connection to Canada and collects, uses, or discloses the personal information of Canadians in the course of a commercial activity, the Office of the Privacy Commissioner (OPC) expects that the cloud provider will protect personal information in accordance with PIPEDA, irrespective of where it is domiciled.[14] If the cloud provider collects, uses, or discloses the personal information of Canadians in the course of commercial activity and does not comply with PIPEDA, the Federal Court of Canada has held that the OPC has jurisdiction to investigate complaints in respect of such activities.[15]

The OPC, in connection with the Office of the Information and Privacy Commissioners of Alberta and British Columbia, has released a useful set of guidelines for small- and medium-sized enterprises that wish to use or already use the cloud.[16] The OPC correctly states in the Cloud Guidelines that cloud computing is a type of outsourcing. The OPC reiterated that if an organization chooses to outsource personal data for processing or other services to a cloud service provider, it remains accountable for protecting its customers' personal information, and it must be transparent about its information management and

---

12 PIPEDA, *supra* note 4, Sch. 1, Principle 4.1.3.

13 The Office of the Privacy Commissioner of Canada, *Frequently asked questions about cloud computing*, https://www.priv.gc.ca/en/privacy-topics/technology-and-privacy/online-privacy/cloud-computing/02_05_d_51_cc_faq/.

14 The Office of the Privacy Commissioner of Canada, *Cloud computing and privacy*, https://www.priv.gc.ca/en/privacy-topics/technology-and-privacy/online-privacy/cloud-computing/02_05_d_51_cc/ [Cloud Computing and Privacy]; The Office of the Privacy Commissioner of Canada, *Report on the 2010 Office of the Privacy Commissioner of Canada's Consultations on Online Tracking, Profiling and Targeting, and Cloud Computing*, http://publications.gc.ca/site/eng/9.694473/publication.html [OPC Report]. *See also* A.T. v. Globe24h.com, [2017] F.C. 114, where the Federal Court of Canada held that PIPEDA will apply to a foreign-based organization where there is evidence of a real and substantial connection between the foreign resident's activities and Canada.

15 *See* Lawson v. Accusearch Inc., [2007] F.C. 125, where the Federal Court of Canada held that the OPC has jurisdiction to investigate complaints relating to the trans-border flow of personal information. The test in *Lawson* was confirmed in PIPEDA Report of Findings #2014-015 from September 3, 2014, where the OPC concluded that PIPEDA did apply to Adobe's Canadian consumers impacted by a data breach. *See* https://www.priv.gc.ca/cf-dc/2014/2014_015_0903_e.asp.

16 Officer of the Information and Privacy Commissioner of Alberta, Office of the Information and Privacy Commissioner of British Columbia and the Office of the Privacy Commissioner of Canada, *Cloud Computing for Small and Medium-sized Enterprises: Privacy Responsibilities and Considerations* (14 June 2012), http://www.priv.gc.ca/information/pub/gd_cc_201206_e.asp [hereinafter Cloud Guidelines].

privacy practices even when the services to be provided are free.[17] The OPC highlights the following items for small- and medium-sized enterprises (SMEs) to consider if they are contemplating using the cloud (or if they are already in the cloud), but they would be applicable to any organization considering using the cloud:

1) the risks and benefits of moving to the cloud, including what will be stored and why, and the sensitivity of the personal information;

2) the terms of the contract with the cloud provider;

3) whether the cloud is secure (the OPC further recommends that organizations considering this question (i) limit access to the information and restrict further uses by the provider; (ii) ensure that the provider has in place appropriate authentication/access controls; (iii) manage encryption; (iv) ensure that there are procedures in place in the event of a personal information breach or security incident; (v) ensure that there are procedures in place in the event of an outage to ensure business continuity and prevent data loss; (vi) ensure periodic audits are performed; and (vii) have an exit strategy);

4) whether the organization has the individual's consent to outsource the information;

5) limitations on the cloud provider's ability to use the personal information;

6) the expectations of the individuals whose personal information will be stored in the cloud;

7) whether the organization has a thorough understanding of the laws of the jurisdiction in which the personal information and other data will be stored; and

8) which party is in control.[18]

The OPC confirmed that many standard cloud computing agreements are not sufficient to allow SMEs to meet their privacy obligations under Canadian privacy laws. The OPC pointed to specific clauses within such agreements that were especially problematic from the perspective of compliance. Such clauses included terms that allowed the cloud provider to unilaterally change the terms and conditions of the agreement, limit its liability for the information, and/or subcontract to various other providers.

To comply with their obligations under Canadian privacy laws, SMEs must use contractual or other means to ensure that the cloud provider appropriately protects any personal information, and that such information is handled in a manner that meets the organization's own legal obligations. SMEs using cloud computing services must proactively maintain control over personal information that is sent to a provider, and take steps to prevent and limit secondary uses of personal information. In addition, Canadian organizations must ensure that any personal information transferred to a cloud provider is secure and protected in compliance with applicable privacy laws.

C. Mandatory Data Breach Notification Requirements

On June 18, 2015, Canada passed the Digital Privacy Act,[19] also known as Bill S-4, to amend PIPEDA. Bill S-4 included, among other amendments, sections about mandatory data-breach notification and record-keeping requirements.[20] Although Bill S-4 received

---

17 *Id.*

18 *Id.*

19 Digital Privacy Act, 2015 S.C., ch. 32 (Can.).

20 PIPEDA, *supra* note 4, Division 1.1.

royal assent in June 2015, the sections pertaining to breaches of security safeguards came into force November 1, 2018.[21] These sections require an organization to both report to the Privacy Commissioner and notify the affected individuals of any breach of security safeguards involving personal information under its control, if it is reasonable in the circumstances to believe that the breach creates a "real risk of significant harm" to an individual. PIPEDA defines "significant harm" as including, among other harms, humiliation, damage to reputation or relationships, and identity theft. A "real risk" requires consideration of the sensitivity of the information, the probability of misuse, and any other prescribed factor.

If the impacted organization determines that the breach creates a real risk of significant harm, then the organization must provide a report in the prescribed form to the Privacy Commissioner as soon as feasible after it is determined that a breach occurred.[22] PIPEDA also requires that organizations provide sufficiently detailed information when notifying individuals about the breach, and such notice must occur "as soon as feasible" after the organization confirms that the breach has occurred.[23] The Data Breach Regulations generally require that the notice to individuals be given directly to the individual. Direct notification must be given to the affected individual in person, by telephone, mail, e-mail, or any other form of communication that a reasonable person would consider appropriate in the circumstances. Indirect notification must be given by an organization if: (1) direct notification would likely cause further harm to the affected individual; (2) direct notification would likely cause undue hardship for the organization; or (3) the organization does not have contact information for the affected individual. In all cases, such indirect notification must be given by public communication or similar measure that could reasonably be expected to reach the affected individuals.

PIPEDA additionally requires organizations that notify individuals of breaches to notify any other third-party organizations, government institutions, or part of a government institution of a potentially harmful data breach if the organization making the notification concludes that such notification may reduce the risk of harm that could result from the

---

21 Order in Council 2018-0369, Government of Canada, http://orders-in-council.canada.ca/attachment.php?attach=36009&lang=en.

22 *See* Breach of Security Safeguards Regulations, SOR/2018-64 (2018-03-27) (hereinafter Data Breach Regulations). Any notification to the Privacy Commissioner must include: (1) a description of the circumstances of the breach and, if known, the cause; (2) the day on which, or the period during which, the breach occurred or, if neither is known, the approximate period; (3) a description of the personal information that is the subject of the breach to the extent that the information is known; (4) the number of individuals affected by the breach or, if unknown, the approximate number; (5) a description of the steps that the organization has taken to reduce the risk of harm to affected individuals that could result from the breach or to mitigate that harm; (6) a description of the steps that the organization has taken or intends to take to notify affected individuals of the breach in accordance with subsection 10.1(3) of the Act; and (7) the name and contact information of a person who can answer, on behalf of the organization, the Commissioner's questions about the breach.

23 Under the Data Breach Regulations, the notification to individuals must include: (1) a description of the circumstances of the breach; (2) the day on which, or period during which, the breach occurred or, if neither is known, the approximate period; (3) a description of the personal information that is the subject of the breach to the extent that the information is known; (4) a description of the steps that the organization has taken to reduce the risk of harm that could result from the breach; (5) a description of the steps that affected individuals could take to reduce the risk of harm that could result from the breach or to mitigate that harm; and (6) contact information that the affected individual can use to obtain further information about the breach.

breach or mitigate the potential harm. PIPEDA also requires that organizations maintain a record of every breach of security safeguards involving personal information under its control for a minimum of 24 months after the day on which the organization determines that a breach has occurred. Organizations must be prepared to provide access to, or a copy of, the record if requested by the Privacy Commissioner, and the records must be sufficiently detailed to enable the Privacy Commissioner to verify compliance with PIPEDA.

Organizations that are found to have violated the mandatory reporting requirements for breaches of security safeguards or the requirement to maintain records of any breach could be found guilty of a summary offence and fined up to CAD $10,000 or, in more serious cases, may be found guilty of an indictable offence and fined up to CAD $100,000 per violation.

Similar to PIPEDA, Alberta's PIPA has mandatory security breach reporting requirements that apply to all private-sector organizations within the province.[24]

The recent amendments to PIPEDA regarding mandatory data-breach notification will likely have a significant impact on Canadian entities that wish to do business with U.S. cloud vendors. All U.S. cloud vendors should now be prepared to flow the obligations discussed above in their vendor contracts with Canadians to ensure that such Canadian clients can meet their regulatory breach notification requirements, particularly the timing of notification, and avoid financial penalties.

For example, any contract made with a U.S. cloud vendor should explicitly contain provisions requiring such vendor to notify Canadian customers "as soon as feasible" of any actual or alleged breaches of personal information under their custody and control, immediately take all necessary measures to investigate and mitigate such breaches, and prevent further breaches. Given that it can be a matter of discussion as to whether the cloud vendor or the customer would make the actual notification to the appropriate regulatory authority in the event of a data breach, it is suggested that this point be clarified in the actual cloud vendor agreement. The cloud contract should also specify whether the cloud vendor is prepared to comply with Canadian privacy law in these matters, or set forth in detail the vendor's privacy obligations under these laws, perhaps in a separate addendum, including the information required under the Data Breach Regulations, so that the Canadian customer can make the required notification as necessary following a data breach. The cloud agreement should also confirm that the U.S. cloud vendor is willing to cooperate with, and assist in, any investigation by the customer or any regulatory authority (at the cloud vendor's own cost) to determine the reasons for a security/privacy breach and whether the vendor has taken adequate steps to contain the breach, assess and mitigate the harm, and prevent its future occurrence. Canadian customers will expect the cloud vendor to investigate all data breaches and report the results of the investigation to the customer as soon as feasible after the vendor has determined the breach has occurred. Canadian customers may also want their U.S. cloud vendors to ensure by contract that all of the vendor's subcontractors, contractors, and employees are required to: (1) immediately advise the cloud vendor of any data breaches in respect of personal information in the custody of such subcontractors, contractors, and employees; and (2) promptly investigate and remediate such data breaches, and advise the cloud vendor of such investigation and remediation. The Canadian customer will likely expect that all costs associated with

---

24 Alberta PIPA, *supra* note 6, § 34.1.

any investigation and any remedial steps taken by the U.S. cloud vendor, its subcontractors, or contractor are the responsibility of the primary U.S. cloud vendor. Lastly, the cloud agreement should also require the cloud vendor to keep and maintain a record of every data breach involving personal information under its control in accordance with the Data Breach Regulations.

In light of the incoming data-breach notification requirements, it will not be unusual for Canadian organizations to revisit their existing cloud computing agreements with American vendors to allow them to monitor and report data breaches in compliance with PIPEDA and Alberta's PIPA, and to ensure that any relevant agreements with third parties allow for compliance. U.S.-based cloud providers should also revisit their internal policies and procedures to ensure that they are able to meet the breach reporting requirements, and to support their client's notice obligations in accordance with these breach notification obligations and the additional related record-keeping requirements.

III. Cloud Computing in the Health Care Sector

Cloud computing in health care has become more prevalent in recent times. This surge in use has been due to ability of cloud computing to handle large amounts of data and facilitate sharing of information and collaboration across various health care providers. The majority of the provinces and territories in Canada have passed legislation relating to information collected, used, or disclosed by organizations operating within the health care sector. If a province or territory has enacted privacy laws that are deemed to be substantially similar to those of PIPEDA, such province's provincial and territorial privacy laws regulate the collection, use, and disclosure of health information, including the processing of information by cloud service providers, within that province or territory. If a province or territory has not enacted health privacy laws, or privacy laws that are not deemed to be substantially similar to PIPEDA, then PIPEDA may also apply to health information in those provinces or territories.

In Ontario, the Personal Health Information Protection Act[25] (PHIPA) governs the ability of "health information custodians" to collect, store, utilize, and disclose information with respect to an individual's Personal Health Information (PHI). PHIPA broadly defines "PHI" as:

> identifying information about an individual in oral or recorded form," and includes information that (a) relates to the physical or mental health of the individual, including information that consists of the health history of the individual's family, (b) relates to the providing of health care to the individual, including the identification of a person as a provider of health care to the individual, (c) is a plan of service within the meaning of *the Home Care and Community Services Act*, 1994 for the individual, (d) relates to payments or eligibility for health care, or eligibility for coverage for health care, in respect of the individual, (e) relates to the donation by the individual of any body part or bodily substance of the individual or is derived from the testing or examination of any such body part or bodily substance, (f) is the individual's health number, or (g) identifies an

---

25 Personal Health Information Protection Act, 2004 S.O., C3, Sched. A [hereinafter PHIPA].

individual's substitute decision-maker. "Identifying information" means information that identifies an individual or for which it is reasonably foreseeable in the circumstances that it could be utilized, either alone or with other information, to identify an individual.[26]

PHIPA also imposes obligations on entities that provide services to health information custodians such as "health information network providers" or those persons that act on behalf of a health information custodian with respect to PHI—that is, "agents." A health information custodian is defined as either an organization or person described under PHIPA that, due to their obligations or rights under PHIPA, are granted custody or control of personal health information.[27] Examples of custodians include long-term care service providers, health care practitioners, community care access corporations, hospitals, and pharmacies.

In the context of cloud computing, service providers that store or process personal health information on behalf of the health information custodian fall within PHIPA's definition of "agents." An agent of a health custodian may only collect, use, disclose, retain, or dispose of PHI if: (1) the health information custodian permits the agent to do so; (2) it is necessary for purposes of carrying out its duties or obligations to the health information custodian; (3) doing so is not contrary to any laws; and (4) doing so complies with any restrictions the health information custodian imposes on the agent.[28] Agents who provide services that enable two or more custodians to share PHI by electronic means are defined as health information network providers and have additional obligations under PHIPA.

Health information network providers are required to notify health custodians of unauthorized access to PHI records[29] and provide custodians with reports, where practical, detailing the access and use of the PHI.[30] PHIPA also requires that health information network providers and health custodians enter into written agreements outlining: (1) the services to be provided; (2) the administrative, technical, and physical safeguards employed; and (3) a requirement that the health information network provider will comply with PHIPA.[31]

PHIPA requires health information custodians to take reasonable steps to safeguard PHI and ensure that the PHI in their custody or control is protected against theft, loss, and unauthorized use or disclosure.[32] Further, the custodian must protect against unauthorized copying, modification, and disposal of the PHI.[33]

PHIPA also contains mandatory breach notification obligations. In the event that an individual's PHI is stolen, lost, or accessed by unauthorized persons, the health information custodians must notify the affected individual, the Information and Privacy Commissioner of Ontario, and in certain circumstances the relevant regulatory colleges.[34]

---

26 *Id.* § 4(1).
27 *Id.* § 3(1).
28 *Id.* § 17(2).
29 PHIPA O. Reg. 329/04: GENERAL, § 6(3)1.
30 *Id.* § 6(3)4.
31 *Id.* § 6(3)7.
32 PHIPA, *supra* note 25, § 12.1.
33 *Id.*
34 *Id.* § 12(2).

Individuals and organizations who are found to have contravened PHIPA may face significant fines. For example, parties who wilfully collect, use, or disclose PHI in contravention of PHIPA are punishable by a fine of up to CAD $100,000 for individuals and CAD $500,000 for organizations.[35] The health privacy legislation in other Canadian provinces imposes similar penalties against parties that are found to have contravened their obligations under the applicable health privacy laws. In Saskatchewan, organizations can face fines of up to CAD $500,000, and individuals can be fined up to CAD $50,000 as well as face imprisonment of up to one year.[36] Both Manitoba[37] and Alberta[38] impose penalties of up to CAD $50,000 for knowingly breaching their respective health privacy laws. Alberta's legislation imposes more significant fines against individuals and organizations that knowingly disclose health information pursuant to a subpoena, warrant, or order issued or made by a court, person, or body having no jurisdiction in Alberta that compels production of information, or pursuant to a rule of court that is not binding in Alberta. In this instance, organizations can face fines of up to CAD $500,000, and individuals can be fined up to CAD$10,000.[39]

As indicated above, certain U.S.-based cloud vendors have expressed reluctance to modify their standard agreements to accommodate the additional requirements imposed by Canadian personal health privacy statutes such as PHIPA. In addition to the suggested requirements set out in Part II, *supra*, such contracts typically include robust confidentiality provisions about how such personal information can be used by the cloud vendor (including clear prohibitions against any secondary use), the exact administrative, technical, and physical safeguards employed by the vendor to protect such information, and how the vendor will ensure that the PHI in its custody or control is protected against theft, loss, and unauthorized use or disclosure in addition to the proper destruction/disposal of such information once the cloud agreement is terminated. It is highly unlikely today that any Canadian health information custodian in possession of sensitive health information would consider entering into a cloud contract that involves such data in the absence of a commitment to fully comply with such legal requirements.

IV. Financial Services

Governmental or quasi-governmental bodies in Canada, such as the Office of the Superintendent of Financial Institutions Canada (OSFI), provide guidance with respect to record-keeping requirements, including the protection and distribution of such records, for financial institutions. OSFI regulates and supervises federally regulated financial institutions (FRFIs) including banks, federally incorporated trust and loan companies, life insurance companies, fraternal benefit societies and property and casualty insurance companies. OSFI also regulates pension plans and foreign bank representative offices.

OSFI acknowledged in 2012 the potential risks that arise when FRFIs outsource certain functions and developed Guideline B-10, Outsourcing of Business Activities,

---

35 *Id.* § 17.2.

36 The Health Information Protection Act, SS 1999, c H-0.021, § 64(2).

37 The Personal Health Information Act, CCSM c P33.5, § 64(1).

38 Health Information Act, RSA 2000, c H-5, § 107(6).

39 *Id.* § 107(7).

Functions and Processes (B-10),[40] which specifies the requirements for how FRFIs may engage third parties for the purposes of outsourcing, including cloud computing.[41] Prior to outsourcing any business functions, FRFIs are required to determine whether the outsourcing agreement is "material" by considering various factors, such as the impact of the arrangement on their finances and operations, the ability to have internal controls if the service provider were to fail, the cost of the outsourcing arrangement, the difficulty and cost of finding an alternate service provider or conducting the activity in-house, and the potential that multiple outsourcing arrangements provided by the same service provider can have an important influence on the organization. For arrangements that are deemed "material," the FRFI must implement a risk-management program that meets specified requirements. In these cases, OSFI requires the organizations to undertake a due diligence process to determine how to manage the risks associated with the outsourcing process. The process must include an assessment of the service provider, including its operational practices, financial stability, and for foreign service providers, the legal requirements of the jurisdiction in which they are located and any political, social, or economic conditions affecting it. The decision to proceed with the outsourcing service must be documented in a written contract.

OSFI requires that FRFIs maintain their own accountability for outsourced services; accordingly, any contract, including those with cloud vendors, must address the scope of the service provided, the frequency and form of reports from the service provider to the organization, the contingency procedures/business continuity plans in place in case the system breaks down, the audit rights of the FRFI, the rules and any limitations on subcontracting, and the confidentiality and security requirements specified by the FRFI.[42] B-10 recommends that the security and confidentiality policies adopted by the service provider be equal to those of the FRFI and should meet a reasonable standard in the circumstances.[43]

With respect to personal information, FRFIs must also comply with PIPEDA. This includes the obligation that the FRFI use contractual or other means to protect personal information and to ensure that a third-party provider provides a comparable level of protection for such personal information while it is stored or processed on behalf of the FRFI.[44]

Under B-10, the FRFI must have the ability either to monitor the outsourced services to verify that they are provided in accordance with the FRFI's requirements, or to cause an independent auditor to evaluate the services provided on its behalf. The FRFI should also have the right to review the service provider's internal control environment as it relates to the services provided.[45]

In January 2019 OSFI issued an "Advisory on Technology and Cyber Security Incident Reporting" confirming the obligation of FRFIs to report high or critical severity technology or cybersecurity incidents to OSFI. For the purposes of the Advisory, a technology or cyber incident is defined to have the potential to, or has been assessed to,

---

40 Office of the Superintendent of Financial Institutions, Outsourcing of Business Activities, Functions and Processes, No. B-10, http://www.osfi-bsif.gc.ca/Eng/Docs/b10.pdf [hereinafter OFSI].

41 Office of the Superintendent of Financial Institutions (2012), New technology-based outsourcing arrangements, http://www.osfi-bsif.gc.ca/Eng/Docs/cldcmp.pdf.

42 OFSI, *supra* note 40, § 7.2.1.

43 *Id.* § 7.2.1(j).

44 PIPEDA, *supra* note 3, Sch. 1, Principle 4.1.3.

45 *Supra* note 40, § 7.2.1(h).

"materially impact the normal operations of a FRFI, including confidentiality, integrity, or availability of its systems and information." The Advisory will take effect on March 31, 2019, and applies to all FRFIs.[46]

The Advisory notes that FRFIs should define incident materiality in their incident management framework (when in doubt about incident materiality, FRFIs are advised to "consult their OSFI Lead Supervisor")[47].

A reportable incident may have any of the following characteristics: (i) significant operational impact to key/critical information systems or data; (ii) material impact to FRFI operational or customer data, including confidentiality, integrity or availability of such data; (iii) significant operational impact to internal users that is material to customers or business operations; (iv) significant levels of system / service disruptions; (v) extended disruptions to critical business systems / operations; (vi) the number of external customers impacted is significant or growing; (vii) negative reputational impact is imminent (e.g., public/media disclosure); (viii) a material impact to critical deadlines/obligations in financial market settlement or payment systems (e.g., Financial Market Infrastructure); (ix) significant impact to a third party deemed material to the FRFI; (x) material consequences to other FRFIs or the Canadian financial system; or (xi) a FRFI incident has been reported to the Office of the Privacy Commissioner or local/foreign regulatory authorities.[48]

The Advisory sets out aggressive reporting requirements for FRFIs. A FRFI must notify its Lead Supervisor as promptly as possible, but no later than **72 hours** after determining a Technology or Cyber Security Incident meets the incident characteristics in the Advisory. This is in contrast to the mandatory data breach requirements set out in PIPEDA, which requires organizations to notify the OPC, individuals and third-party organizations of breaches of security safeguards "as soon as feasible" after it has been determined that the breach creates a real risk of significant harm to an individual.

In additional to the foregoing notification requirements, FRFIs are also expected to notify OFSI's Technology Risk Division via email at TRD@osfi-bsif.gc.ca. When reporting a Technology or Cyber Security Incident to OSFI, a FRFI must do so in writing (electronically or by paper). If specific details are unavailable at the time of the initial report, the FRFI must indicate "information not yet available" and the FRFI is expected to provide best known estimates and all other details available at the time.

The Advisory sets out certain reporting criteria that the FRFI must meet. The FRFI's initial report to OFSI should include the following details: (i) the date and time the incident was assessed to be material; (ii) the date and time/period the incident took place; (iii) the incident severity; (iv) the incident type (e.g. DDoS, malware, data breach, extortion); (v) the incident description, which includes: (a) known direct/indirect impacts (quantifiable and non-quantifiable) including privacy and financial; (b) known impact to one or more business segment(s), business unit, line of business or regions, including any third party involved; (c) whether incident originated at a third party, or has impact on third party services, and (d) the number of clients impacted; (vi) the primary method used to identify the incident; (vii) the current status of incident; (viii) the date for internal

---

46   Available online at http://www.osfi-bsif.gc.ca/Eng/fi-if/rg-ro/gdn-ort/adv-prv/Pages/TCSIR.aspx [hereinafter the Advisory].

47   *Supra* note 47 at 2.

48   *Supra* note 47 at 2.

incident escalation to senior management or Board of Directors; (ix) the mitigation actions taken or planned; (x) known or suspected root cause; and (xi) name and contact information for the FRFI incident executive lead and liaison with OSFI.[49]

FRFIs are required to provide regular updates (e.g., daily) as new information becomes available, and until all material details about the incident have been provided. Depending on the severity, impact and velocity of the incident, the Lead Supervisor may also request that a FRFI change the method and frequency of subsequent updates. OSFI further expects FRFIs to provide situation updates, including any short term and long term remediation actions and plans, until the incident is contained/resolved. Lastly, following incident containment, recovery and closure, the FRFI should report to OSFI on its post incident review and "lessons learned."[50] The Advisory concludes with a non-exhaustive but useful table that provides some examples of reportable incidents.

Along with the requirements outlined in B-10, PIPEDA and the Advisory, financial institutions must also comply with various other pieces of federal and provincial legislation that establish obligations with respect to information about its customers.[51] As such, any cloud providers wishing to offer services to financial institutions must be aware of the additional obligations placed on these institutions and tailor their services and cloud agreements to comply with such obligations. It is notable that several U.S.-based cloud vendors doing business in Canada have created specific forms of cloud addendum that offer additional protection made solely available to financial institutions to accommodate these requirements, and therefore allow such financial institutions to comply with their legal requirements.

V. Canada's Anti-Spam Legislation

A. Legislative Overview

Any vendor of cloud services in Canada must be aware of Canada's Anti-spam Legislation (CASL),[52] which came into effect July 1, 2014, and is one of the world's most onerous anti-spam statutes. CASL regulates unsolicited commercial electronic messages (CEMs) sent by commercial enterprises to individuals as well as the unsolicited installation of software. Due to the significant monetary penalties and criminal charges for noncompliance under CASL, individuals and organizations, including those offering cloud services, must take steps to confirm that they are not sending CEMs in contravention of its requirements.

U.S. cloud vendors that intend to do business in Canada can be caught by CASL in various ways. In the absence of (1) an existing business relationship with a prospective

---

49 *Supra* note 47 at 2-3.

50 *Supra* note 47 at 3.

51 *See* Bank Act, 1991 S.C., ch. 46, § 157(2)(e), whereby directors of a bank shall establish procedures to provide disclosure of information to customers of the bank that is required to be disclosed by the Bank Act and for dealing with complaints as required by subsection 455(1) of the Bank Act.

52 An Act to promote the efficiency and adaptability of the Canadian economy by regulating certain activities that discourage reliance on electronic means of carrying out commercial activities, and to amend the Canadian Radio-television and Telecommunications Commission Act, the Competition Act, the Personal Information Protection and Electronic Documents Act and the Telecommunications Act, 2010 S.C., ch. 23 [hereinafter CASL].

e-mail recipient, (2) express consent from such intended recipient, or (3) being otherwise able to point to one of the limited exemptions under CASL, any U.S.-based cloud provider that intends to send CEMs to prospective Canadian recipients as part of its marketing efforts (i.e., to promote or advertise its services) will be caught by the legislation. Accordingly, any such cloud vendors will be obliged to communicate with prospective Canadian clients in a manner that complies with the requirements of CASL, including obtaining the appropriate consent from individuals and recording and tracking such consent, and ensuring that the CEM includes all of the information required under CASL.

Additionally, U.S. providers may unwittingly run afoul of CASL if their Canadian cloud customers employ such U.S.-based cloud providers to send out CEMs on their behalf, but do not have sufficient authorization under CASL to do so. Accordingly, U.S. cloud providers who are engaged to send CEMs on behalf of a third party to Canadians should also take steps to ensure that such third party complies with CASL. This can be achieved by confirming that such third party has received the appropriate consents to send CEMs to all individuals. Similarly, cloud providers who engage third parties to send CEMs on such cloud provider's behalf are also obligated to ensure such third party's compliance with CASL. In both instances described above, cloud providers may wish to contractually require the relevant third party to indemnify the cloud provider from any fines or penalties arising out of such third party's failure to comply with CASL.

Additionally, any U.S.-based cloud provider must ensure that it only sends CEMs for business purposes and not otherwise misuse the e-mail addresses that it collects while providing cloud services, for example by selling them to third parties for additional profit.

CASL prohibits the sending of CEMs without prior consent, and permits them to be sent only if certain formal requirements are met. CASL also prohibits the installation of software on the computers of recipients/owners without prior consent.

CASL defines CEMs as electronic messages that encourage participation in "commercial activities," irrespective of any expectation of profit.[53] CASL broadly defines what is meant by "commercial activities" to include not merely offers of purchase or sale, but also the advertising of offers, investments, and the promotion of persons who participate in such commercial activities. Content that promotes commercial activity, the inclusion of hyperlinks to a person's website, or business-related contact information are all factors in determining whether it is "reasonable" to find that an electronic message is a CEM under CASL.[54]

B. Consent

Consent can be either expressly given by the recipient[55] or, in limited circumstances, implied.[56] For express consent, CASL requires individuals that are the recipients of CEMs to actively and expressly "opt in" to receive such CEMs. A cloud vendor must have consent prior to sending a CEM. Under CASL, an electronic message requesting consent to send CEMs is itself a CEM; thus, organizations are prohibited from sending these CEMs with-

---

53 CASL, *supra* note 47, § 1.
54 *Id.* § 1(2).
55 *Id.* § 10(1).
56 *Id.* § 6.

out first obtaining consent to do so.[57] The recipient must take proactive action to indicate his or her express consent (through an opt-in mechanism, such as signing up via a web site). If a cloud vendor does seek to obtain express consent, it is required to outline the purpose for which the consent is sought, "clearly and simply" identify itself, and if sending the message on another's behalf, identify that other person.[58] The identification obligations for the "request for consent" additionally require the following:

1) the name by which the person seeking consent carries on business;[59]

2) if the sender is seeking consent on another's behalf:
   a. the name by which that person carries on business; and
   b. a statement indicating which person is seeking consent (i.e., the sender or the other named party);[60]

3) the mailing address, either a telephone number or voice messaging system, e-mail address, or web address of the person seeking consent.[61]

In addition, the contact information must be valid for the period covered by the consent.[62]

According to CASL, the purpose of incorporating these requirements in the original request for consent is to enable the recipient of the message to readily contact the sender.[63] This obligation to provide contact information, together with the requirement that the request for consent include a statement informing the recipient that he or she can withdraw consent,[64] ensures that the recipient is apprised of his or her right not only to "opt-in" to the CEMs, but also to "opt-out" at any time.

CASL contains only a limited list of specific circumstances and strict timelines within which a sender such as a cloud vendor can claim to have the implied consent to send CEMs. Under CASL, consent can be implied only where:[65]

1) there is an "existing business relationship" or "nonbusiness relationship" between the sender and recipient as defined under CASL;

2) the recipient's electronic address is conspicuously published, and the recipient has not indicated that he or she does not wish to receive unsolicited CEMs at that address (the Implied Consent Guidance Document also noted that if that statement is not present, the message must relate to the recipient's business role, functions, or duties in an official or business capacity); or

3) the recipient has disclosed to the sender his or her electronic address to which the CEM was sent, without having indicated a desire not to receive unsolicited CEMs, and the messages are relevant to the person's business role, functions, or duties.

---

57 *See* Canadian Radio-television and Telecommunications Commission, *From Canada's Anti-Spam Legislation (CASL) Guidance on Implied Consent* (Sept. 4, 2015), https://crtc.gc.ca/eng/com500/guide.htm.

58 CASL, *supra* note 47, § 10. *See also* FAQs: About the Law, Canada's Anti-Spam Legislation (Jan. 20, 2013), http://fightspam.gc.ca/eic/site/030.nsf/eng/h_00050.html.

59 Electronic Commerce Protection Regulations, SOR/2012-36, § 4(a) [hereinafter CRTC Regulations].

60 *Id.* § 4(b)–(c).

61 *Id.* § 4(d).

62 CASL, *supra* note 47, § 11(4).

63 *Id.* § 6(2)(b).

64 CRTC Regulations, *supra* note 54, § 4(e).

65 CASL, *supra* note 47, § 10(9).

It should be noted that the following types of CEMs are exempt from the consent requirements of CASL, although the form requirements remain:

1) replies to requests by the recipient of the CEM for quotes or estimates for the supply of goods, property, or services;[66]
2) messages that facilitate, complete, or confirm commercial transactions in which the recipient is involved;[67]
3) messages that provide warranty, product recall, safety or security information regarding products or services the recipient uses or has purchased;[68]
4) messages that provide factual information about products or services purchased by the recipient as part of an ongoing subscription or membership, or information about that subscription or account;[69]
5) messages pertaining directly to employment or benefit plans in which the recipient is involved;[70] and
6) messages delivering products, goods, services, or updates to which the recipient is entitled under the terms of a transaction previously entered.[71]

C. Formal Requirements and Withdrawing Consent

CASL sets out specific formal requirements for any CEMs. All CEMs must include the prescribed information regarding the sender and incorporate an "unsubscribe mechanism" to protect a recipient's right to control the messages it receives, notwithstanding the recipient's prior consent.[72] This mechanism must allow the recipient to, at no cost, "unsubscribe" from future CEMs by using either the same electronic means used to send the message, or any other practicable electronic means.[73] To further simplify the process, CASL requires that the sender, such as a cloud vendor, provide an electronic address or link to which the indication may be easily sent.[74] This unsubscribe mechanism, like the sender's contact information, must be valid for at least *60 days* after the day on which the message was sent to ensure recipients have sufficient opportunity to readily terminate their subscription.[75]

Once either the "unsubscribe" or the "withdrawal of consent" mechanism is triggered, the sender has 10 business days to give effect to the recipient's intention. Failure to do so constitutes a violation of CASL, exposing the sender to substantial penalties, and as will be discussed below, CASL jurisprudence to date indicates that the CRTC takes these formal requirements seriously.[76]

---

66 *Id.* § 6(6)(a).
67 *Id.* § 6(6)(b).
68 *Id.* § 6(6)(c).
69 *Id.* § 6(6)(d).
70 *Id.* § 6(6)(e).
71 CASL, *supra* note 47, § 6(6)(f).
72 *Id.* § 6(2)(c).
73 *Id.* § 11(1)(a).
74 *Id.* § 11(1)(b).
75 *Id.* §§ 6(3), 11(2).
76 *Id.* § 11(3).

D. Extra-Jurisdictional CEMs

It should be noted that the ambit of CASL extends to messages sent from, or accessed by, computer systems located in Canada, giving CASL extra-territorial application. CASL does not apply to CEMs that are simply routed through Canada.[77] In other words, U.S.-based cloud vendors that currently do business in Canada or otherwise target Canadians are currently covered by CASL and are required to comply with the extensive (and onerous) requirements listed above.

Faced with concerns that some businesses in Canada would be obliged to comply with both CASL and the laws of foreign jurisdictions,[78] an exclusion was incorporated into Industry Canada's Regulations (IC Regulations) explicitly exempting CEMs sent from Canada that a sender "reasonably believes" will be accessed in one of the prescribed foreign states (e.g., the United States and Spain).[79] As a caveat to the use of the extra-jurisdictional CEM exemption, the IC Regulations require that the CEMs sent from Canada must comply with the local laws of that prescribed foreign state.[80] These particular IC Regulations were created to reduce the burden on businesses sending CEMs to recipients in prescribed foreign states by recognizing the existence of legislation in those states that regulate the conduct prohibited by CASL.[81] Unfortunately, all businesses that operate in Canada, including U.S. subsidiaries or foreign-owned companies, will have to undertake this analysis to determine whether CASL requirements apply to their messages.

E. Penalties

CASL includes monetary penalties and criminal sanctions for noncompliance:

1) maximum administrative penalties of CAD$1,000,000 and CAD$10,000,000 ordered against individuals and other "persons," respectively, who fail to comply with CASL;[82] and

2) criminal sanctions may also apply—CASL amends the Competition Act,[83] making prohibited conduct also reviewable under the Competition Act.

Furthermore, officers, directors, or agents who acquiesce or participate in the violation of CASL will be held personally liable for such violations, whether an action is commenced against the organization on whose behalf the CEM was sent or not.[84]

CASL also contains provisions allowing for a private right of action against any allegedly noncompliant party for an amount equal to the actual loss or damage suffered by the applicant/recipient of noncompliant CEMs plus additional statutory damages. Although the private-right-of-action provisions were scheduled to come into force on July

---

77 Industry Canada's Regulatory Impact Analysis Statement, at 3, http://fightspam.gc.ca/eic/site/030.nsf/eng/00271.html, which was issued along with the IC Regulations, [hereinafter RIAS].
78 *Id.* at 8.
79 Electronic Commerce Protection Regulations, SOR/2013-221 at § 3(f) and Schedule (¶ 3(f)).
80 *Id.*
81 RIAS, *supra* note 72, at 8.
82 CASL, *supra* note 47, § 20(4).
83 Competition Act, RSC 85, ch. C-34.
84 *Id.* § 31.

1, 2017, the government suspended the implementation of certain provisions indefinitely in response to concerns raised by organizations across all sectors.

Although the monetary penalties that can be levied against a cloud provider for failure to comply with CASL are certainly not as onerous those that may result from its failure to comply with the Europe's GDPR, CASL nonetheless has "teeth," particularly from a Canadian perspective, and the CRTC has not hesitated to sanction companies that they perceive to be in breach.[85]

Individuals and organizations that engage in the sending of CEMs, and service providers who send CEMs on their behalf, should take steps to audit their practices and confirm that they are sending CEMs in compliance with CASL. This includes reviewing consent procedures and practices and developing template CEMs that meet CASL's prescribed form requirements. Senders of CEMs should also audit their current mailing lists to confirm that all they have the appropriate consent from recipients.

VI. Government Procurement

Various federal,[86] provincial,[87] and municipal[88] legislation in Canada governs the collection, use, disclosure, storage, and disposal of personal information by government bodies and institutions. This legislation also applies to information that service providers, such as cloud providers, store on behalf of government bodies and institutions. Under the Constitution Act,[89] provincial legislation will apply both to the private sector and to municipal institutions, universities, schools, and hospitals.

In the majority of Canadian provinces, there is no general prohibition on the transfer of data outside of Canada by public bodies; thus, public bodies are free to use the services of foreign service providers, including cloud providers. British Columbia and Nova Scotia are exceptions to this rule, and public bodies in those provinces are restricted from

---

85 *See, e.g.,* Lisa R. Lifshitz, *CASL Lessons Learned*, Canadian Law. Online, July 20, 2015, *available at* https://www.canadianlawyermag.com/author/lisa-r-lifshitz/casl-lessons-learned-2958/; Lisa R. Lifshitz, *How to Send E-mails to Canadians Safely*, Bus. L. Today, Apr. 2016, https://www.americanbar.org/publications/blt/2016/04/04_lifshitz.html. A complete list of CRTC citations, penalties, undertakings, and violations, including those relating to CASL, can be found at https://crtc.gc.ca/eng/DNCL/dnclce.htm.
86 Privacy Act, 1985 R.S.C., ch. P-21.
87 *See, e.g.,* Freedom of Information and Privacy Protection Act, 2000 R.S.A., ch. F-25 (Alberta), Freedom of Information and Protection of Privacy Act, 1996 R.S.B.C., ch. 165 [hereinafter BC FOIPPA]; Freedom of Information and Protection of Privacy Act, CCSM ch. F175 (Manitoba); Personal Health Information Privacy and Access Act, 2009 S.N.B., ch. P-7.05 (NB); Access to Information and Protection of Privacy Act, 2002 S.N.L., ch. A-1.1 (Newfoundland); Freedom of Information and Protection of Privacy Act, 1993 S.N.S., ch. 5 [hereinafter Nova Scotia FIPPA]; Freedom of Information and Protection of Privacy Act, 1990 R.S.O., ch. F-31 (Ontario); Freedom of Information and Protection of Privacy Act, 1988 R.S.P.E.I., ch. F-15.01 (Prince Edward Island); An Act respecting Access to documents held by public bodies and the Protection of personal information, CQLR ch. A-2.1 (Québec); Freedom of Information and Protection of Privacy Act, 1990–91 S.S., ch. F-22.01 (Saskatchewan); Access to Information and Protection of Privacy Act, 2002 R.S.Y., ch. 1 (Yukon); Access to Information and Protection of Privacy Act, 1994 S.N.W.T., ch. 20 (Northwest Territories); Access to Information and Protection of Privacy Act, 1994 S.N.W.T. (Nu), ch. 20 (Nunavut).
88 *See, e.g.,* Municipal Freedom of Information and Protection of Privacy Act, 1990 R.S.O., ch. M.56 (Ontario).
89 The Constitution Act, *supra* note 2, § 92.

transferring data outside of Canada, which often causes difficulty for U.S.-based providers that wish to sell cloud-based services to government clients in those provinces. Providers should note that, even in the absence of explicit restrictions on foreign transfer, it is not atypical to see public bodies contractually require that personal information held on its behalf be stored and accessed only in Canada, for example for political or "patriotic" reasons.

Subject to limited exceptions, British Columbia's Freedom of Information and Protection of Privacy Act (FOIPPA) requires that a public body ensure that personal information in its custody or under its control is stored[90] and accessed[91] in Canada, unless that public body has received consent for the storage or disclosure of such information outside of Canada. To rely on the consent exemption, public bodies must have received consent from all relevant individuals prior to storing the personal information outside of Canada. Depending on the types of information stored, gaining consent from all relevant individuals is often unworkable; thus, it is usually not practical to rely upon consent as a means to allow for the use of a cloud provider whose servers are located outside of Canada.

Similarly, Nova Scotia's Personal Information International Disclosure Protection Act[92] (PIDPA) requires public bodies to ensure that personal information under its custody and control, or the custody and control of a service provider engaged on its behalf, is stored and accessed only in Canada.[93] As with BC's FOIPPA, PIDPA allows for the storage of personal information outside of Canada if consent has been provided by all relevant individuals. In addition, PIDPA allows for the storage of personal information outside of Canada if such storage is necessary and authorized by the head of a public body or the responsible officer of a municipality.[94]

For public bodies in Québec, Québec's Act Respecting Access to Documents Held by Public Bodies and the Protection of Personal Information creates a direct obligation on public bodies to ensure that any public information stored outside of Québec receive the same protections as such personal information would receive under Québec's Act prior to disclosure.[95] Therefore, cloud providers wishing to market to public bodies in Québec must confirm that they are able to store and access data in accordance with the Québec Act.

Public bodies throughout Canada have an obligation to protect personal information under their custody or control and confirm that any personal information is afforded the appropriate protection through security safeguards. These public-sector privacy laws establish the standards for the collection, use, security, and disclosure of personal information by public bodies and, in turn, cloud providers wishing to offer services to such public bodies. Yet, the requirements and obligations with respect to the collection, use, and disclosure of personal information by a public body will depend on what public-sector privacy legislation applies. When entering into an agreement with a public body to

---

90 BC FOIPPA, § 30.1.

91 *Id.* § 33.1.

92 2006 S.N.S., ch. 3 [hereinafter Nova Scotia PIDPA].

93 *Id.* § 5.

94 Nova Scotia PIDPA, *supra* note 87, § 5(1)(c). Please note that the head of the public body must report and provide reasons to the minister justifying his or her decision for allowing personal information to be stored outside of Canada.

95 An Act respecting Access to documents held by public bodies and the Protection of personal information, CQLR c A-2.1, § 70.1.

provide services, cloud providers are typically required to contractually agree to comply with "applicable privacy laws." As a result, U.S. cloud providers should review any applicable legislation to confirm that they are able to meet the legislative requirements of the public body—including, as mentioned above, municipalities, universities, and hospitals.

VII. Additional Considerations for Cloud Vendors in Canada

The following discussion will briefly touch upon some additional considerations that prospective U.S.-based cloud vendors should consider when seeking to do business in Canada.

A. Québec's Language Requirements

Québec is governed by a civil code and not common law. As a result, its legal system differs from all other Canadian provinces and creates certain obligations applicable to cloud providers that are exclusive to Québec and should be addressed by cloud providers looking to do business in this province. Québec's Charter of the French Language (the Québec Charter) requires that all consumer products or services be made available in French and that French is the language of work, instruction, and communication.[96] As such, cloud providers wishing to offer services in Québec are required to ensure that all standard form contracts that have been predetermined by one party, or that contain printed standard clauses, and all related documents, be written in French.[97] The parties may also mutually agree to additionally draft the above outlined contracts/documents in another language. In addition, catalogues, brochures, folders, commercial directories, and any similar publications must also be made available in French.[98] It should be noted that the websites are deemed to be a "similar publication" and thus may be required to be made available in French. Presently, the Office québécois de la langue française (Quebec Board of the French Language), the public institution responsible for linguistic officialization and enforcement of the Québec Charter, has indicated that only organizations that have a place of business or address in Québec would be required to have a French website.[99] Yet, this interpretation may change in the future.

For cloud providers wishing to provide supplementary software to their customers in Québec, the Québec Charter requires that all computer software, including game software and operating systems, whether installed or uninstalled, must be available in French unless no French version exists.[100] The Québec Charter does allow for software to be available in languages other than French, provided that the French version can be obtained on terms that are no less favourable, except regarding price which may be changed to reflect

---

96 Charter of the French language, CQLR c C-11 [hereinafter Québec Charter].

97 *Id.* § 55.

98 *Id.* § 52.

99 Office de la Langue Francaise's Information and Communication Technologies in French (Feb. 2010), https://www.oqlf.gouv.qc.ca/ressources/bibliotheque/depliants/20100212_depliant6fva.pdf.

100 Québec Charter, *supra* note 91, § 52.1.

higher production or distribution costs, and that it has technical characteristics that are at least equivalent.[101]

B. Consumer Protection Laws

In Canada, each province has enacted its own consumer protection legislation that governs transactions between organizations and consumers located in that province. For example, in Ontario the Consumer Protection Act[102] (Ontario CPA) applies to all consumer transactions (subject to some exceptions) in which the consumer (a natural person) is located in Ontario at the time the transaction takes place. The Ontario CPA sets out specific obligations on the part of the supplier for "consumer agreements formed by text-based internet communications" in which the consumer's total payment obligation is greater than CAD$50.00.[103] For example, if the CAD$50.00 threshold is met, then the supplier must provide the prescribed information to the customer prior to entering into the agreement.[104] In addition, the supplier must provide a consumer with a written copy of the internet agreement within 15 days after the consumer enters into the agreement. The written copy of the internet agreement must include the prescribed information as outlined in the Ontario CPA.[105]

Québec has some of the strongest consumer protections laws in Canada. These laws are applicable to agreements for cloud services and may even apply to cloud services that are made available free of charge.[106] Under Québec's Civil Code, Québec courts have jurisdiction to hear an action involving a consumer contract if the consumer is a resident of Québec, even if the consumer has waived such jurisdiction by way of a choice-of-venue clause.[107] Québec's Consumer Protection Act requires that all consumer agreements are to be governed by the federal laws of Canada and the provincial laws of Québec, and that any choice-of-law clause to the contrary is prohibited.[108] In addition, an organization is prohibited from excluding liability for its own acts or the acts of its representatives.[109] The Québec CPA requires that any clause in a consumer contract that is not applicable in the province of Québec must be immediately followed by a prominently presented statement to this effect.[110]

Mandatory arbitration clauses are prohibited under consumer protection laws in certain Canadian provinces such as Québec,[111] Ontario,[112] and Alberta.[113] For example, in Ontario, any term in a consumer agreement or related agreement that requires disputes

---

101 *Id.*
102 Consumer Protection Act, 2002 S.O., ch. 30, Sched A [hereinafter Ontario CPA].
103 *Id.* § 37.
104 *Id.* § 38(1).
105 *Id.* § 39(1).
106 *See* Demers c. Yahoo! Inc., 2017 QCCS 4154, whereby the court rejected Yahoo's position that there cannot be a consumer contract for free services because a consumer contract cannot be formed without consideration.
107 Civil Code of Québec, ch. C.C.Q.-1991, § 3149.
108 Consumer Protection Act, C.Q.L.R. ch. P-40.1, § 19.
109 *Id.* § 10.
110 *Id.* § 19.1.
111 *Id.* § 11.1.
112 Ontario CPA, *supra* note 97, § 7(2).
113 Consumer Protection Act, 2000 R.S.A., ch. C-26.3, § 16(1).

arising from such agreement be submitted to arbitration is invalid. Consumers in Ontario will therefore have the right to commence an action relating to such agreement in the applicable Ontario court.

It is fair to say that existing "standard form," U.S.-based cloud agreements would likely fail to address some or all of these requirements under Canadian consumer protection laws. Thus, prospective cloud vendor organizations wishing to do business in Canadian provinces should become aware of these particular laws and determine what steps they are willing to take to comply with the unique requirements of each province in which they wish to do business.

C. Jury Trials

Lastly, it is worth noting that jury trials for civil cases are uncommon in Canada. Unlike in the United States, litigants do not have a constitutional right to request a jury trial for civil matters. Although in most Canadian provinces a party may have the right to request a jury trial, courts have the right and discretion to strike such a request and have the matter proceed before a judge.[114] In addition, certain provinces require that claims for certain matters proceed only by bench trial.[115]

In Québec, jury trials are not available to litigants in civil trials and are limited only to criminal trials. In addition, it is generally understood throughout Canada that complex cases with unusual legal or factual disputes are not suited for jury trials; thus, such matters will proceed only before a judge. In the end, this fact likely benefits the U.S.-based cloud provider because judges are unlikely to award large monetary penalties or punitive damages, and Canadian damage awards are notoriously parsimonious compared to their U.S. counterparts.[116]

VIII. Conclusion

As this brief overview of some of the relevant legal differences between Canada and the United States illustrates, U.S.-based cloud vendors that wish to do business in Canada should be mindful of the need to consider the application of foreign sources of law that will require a more flexible approach. Such vendors should also recognize and anticipate that their standard form agreements will likely require additional customization and localization in order for Canadian end-customers to be able to do business with them.

---

114 *See* Ontario's Rules of Civil Procedure, 1990 R.R.O., Reg 194, r 47.02(2).

115 *See* Ontario's Courts of Justice Act, 1990 R.S.O., ch. C43, § 108(2), which prohibits jury trials for claims for certain kinds of relief such as for specific performance of a contract.

116 By way of illustrating the legal/cultural differences between Canada and United States, in case of *Jones v. Tsige*, 2012 O.N.C.A. 32, which established the existence of a tort of invasion of privacy, the court found that damages for intrusion upon seclusion in cases where the plaintiff has suffered no pecuniary loss should be "modest but sufficient to make the wrong that has been done" and fixed the range at up to C$20,000 (which likely did not even cover the legal fees to try the case). For an analysis of the *Jones v. Tsige* case, *see A New Tort is Born! Ontario Recognizes its First Privacy Tort,* Bus. L. Today, Mar. 2012, https://www.americanbar.org/publications/blt/2012/03/keeping_current.html.

Chapter 10
Cloud Computing in Germany

By Katharina Garbers-von Boehm and Sylle Schreyer-Bestmann[1]

I. Introduction

As a vehicle for providing need-based, flexible, information technology (IT) services through networks (usually the internet), cloud computing gives rise to questions on various levels in the German and European Union (EU) legal spheres. In addition to data protection issues (see Part III, *infra*), these questions primarily concern classification of contracts under contract law and the consequences under the law governing post-purchase warranties and liability, as well as compliance with general terms and conditions and intellectual property issues (see Parts II and IV, *infra*).

The legal regime in Germany governing cloud computing is rather complex because there are contractual relationships between various legal subjects, and the contracts usually combine different components of service. Moreover, the virtual structure of cloud services allows parties from different countries with various legal traditions to be involved.

The focus here is on public clouds through which a provider makes IT services available to a number of cloud customers. Private clouds, which provide IT services within a company or an institution, are not as complex from a legal point of view because all of the parties involved belong to the same controlling organization.

II. Civil Law Issues

After discussing the most relevant questions regarding the contractual classification of cloud computing contracts (Part II.A), the typical components appearing in contracts governing cloud computing services under German law will be described (Part II.B). Given that cloud computing contracts are in many cases transnational, questions relating to the forum for adjudication and the applicable law will also be considered (Part II.C), as well as the different regimes regarding liability (Part II.D), termination and insolvency (Part II.E.), data ownership and intellectual property (Part II.F), and, last but not least, data access (Part II.G).

A. Classification under German Contract Law

The German Civil Code (*Bürgerliches Gesetzbuch*) classifies contractual relationships under several headings: work, rent, service, etc. The classification of cloud computing contracts has not been conclusively established. The German Civil Code dates from the year 1900 and has not been amended to expressly provide for such modern types of IT

---

1   Dr. Katharina Garbers-von-Boehm, LL.M., is partner at Büsing Müffelmann & Theye (Berlin) (Berlin); Sylle Schreyer-Bestmann, LL.M. (King's College London), is counsel at CMS Hasche Sigle (Berlin).

contracts. Court rulings have categorized certain types of contracts in this area as typical contracts, i.e., contracts that are specified by the German Civil Code. If it is not possible to categorize them as such typical contracts, then they are atypical contracts, or contracts "sui generis." In this case, the legal provisions of the German Civil Code are not automatically applicable to the contract; only the provisions that suit the nature of the contract at hand apply.

The classification depends on the specific contractual content and services to be rendered in each case. Cloud computing contracts govern the relationship between the cloud customer and the cloud service provider. In order to classify the contracts, it is necessary to consider the manner in which cloud computing functions, its various applications, and the different forms it may take.

To determine which statutory regime from the civil code applies to a specific cloud computing contract (be it SaaS, PaaS, or IaaS),[2] one must consider each element of the contract (use of hardware, use of a software application, provision of a platform to execute applications, storage, etc.) and classify it as either a service contract (*Dienstvertrag*), a contract for works and services (*Werkvertrag*), a contract for safekeeping (*Verwahrung*), or a lease (*Mietvertrag*), taking into account the different technical services included in the contract. When doing so, the legal or economic focus of the contract is the decisive factor for determining how the contract is classified. Unlike the situation in numerous other European countries where cloud computing contracts fall under services law, in Germany a standard cloud contract is usually classified as a lease agreement. However, the classification varies depending on the specific structure and content of the cloud contract.

1. Service Contracts, Contracts for Works and Services, Contracts for Safekeeping, and Leases

Section 611 of the German Civil Code regulates a contract in which a service, but not a particular verifiable result, is owed. Given that a cloud customer generally expects to receive the promised service (such as storage space), and it will usually not suffice if the provider merely endeavors to provide the service, such contracts are not normally classified as service contracts.[3] Nevertheless, individual contractual components may fall under the law governing service contracts.

If a specific result is owed under a contract for works and services, section 631 of German Civil Code applies. The typical service under such contracts is producing and creating an individual work, e.g., the creation of software with certain features or the construction of a building. The cloud service provider does indeed owe a specific result: provision of a technical solution. However, such solutions normally are not individually negotiated and customized. Rather, the cloud service provider can also provide the service to another customer when the initial customer no longer requires the service. Therefore, cloud computing solutions as a whole are not usually classified as contracts for works and services, but certain additional services tailored to a cloud customer may be so classified.

---

2   See Chapter 1.

3   According to rulings of the Federal Court of Justice, this is different from a contract providing access, which is considered a service contract and primarily involves provision of the service of transporting data into and out of the internet.

It is also possible to classify cloud computing as a safekeeping contract governed by section 688 of the German Civil Code. Safekeeping entails the provision of space for an object as well as proper care of the object that is kept. However, the proper care for data stored by the cloud service provider and ensuring the necessary security are not usually considered to fall within this classification.

In the prevailing view, cloud computing contracts are mostly classified as lease contracts governed by section 535 of the German Civil Code. There is no jurisprudence regarding cloud computing contracts in the narrower sense, but an ASP contract[4] was qualified as a lease in a 2006 decision by the Federal Court of Justice.[5] Most scholars who have addressed the issue conclude that this decision is applicable to cloud computing contracts because such contracts concern the provision of a movable or an immovable object for use by a user:

- Software and computing capacity are deemed to have the characteristics of a "thing" within the meaning of the applicable legal statute, section 90 of the German Civil Code, and thus can be rented.[6] Cloud computing combines software, storage, work platforms, and computing services in the contractual obligations, making them available for use by the cloud customer. It is irrelevant that possession is not involved because provision for use is sufficient in the context of a lease.
- At the same time, the cloud customer need not have sole power of disposition over the IT service that forms the subject of the contract, as provision of common usage is sufficient under the law governing leases.
- Another argument for classifying cloud computing contracts as leases is the fact that the cloud customer does not normally incur costs for maintenance, updating, security, or other maintenance services. Rather, these services are among the obligations of the service provider, which may thus be analogized to the landlord of a rented apartment.

If the focus of the contract is a service that can be classified as a lease, it will be so classified even if it includes secondary services belonging to other categories. If the other services cannot be considered as secondary obligations of a lease relationship, however, then the contract must be classified separately in this respect, resulting in the classification of each part of the contract in a different contractual category as described below.

It is also possible for the contract to be classified as a contract for works and services in its entirety. This is the case if the cloud service provider not only provides storage capacity, but assumes responsibility for an entire process in addition to providing software. It can also be classified as a service contract if the contract mainly involves providing support services. If there are various elements and it is not possible to classify one of them as the focus of the contract, then the cloud contract is considered a mixed contract. In this case, the legal consequences are regulated individually for each particular component of the contract.

---

4   An application service provider (ASP) is a business providing computer-based services to customers over a network.

5   Federal Court of Justice BGH, decision dated Nov. 15, 2006, XII ZR 120/04, NJW 2007, 2394.

6   *Id.*

2. Warranties for Defects and Other Grounds for Liability of the Cloud Provider

The legal regime applying to warranties for defects depends on the type of cloud computing contract, i.e., which legal regime is applicable to the contract as a whole, or certain elements of the contract according to the classification described in Part II.A.1 above.

- The strictest liability for cloud service providers applies if the cloud computing contract is classified as a lease. The cloud service provider, as lessor, is required, for example, to maintain the leased object (cloud service) in accordance with the contractual condition. If this warranted characteristic of the cloud is not maintained— for example, if the customer cannot access the cloud service—then the customer is released from the obligation to pay. The cloud service provider is also liable as lessor for the customer's damage based on defects existing at the start of the contract term regardless of the lessor's responsibility for those defects,[7] as well as for defects arising later during the lease if they are the fault of the lessor. Such claims against the cloud service provider will usually fail when it comes to the burden of proof because the cloud customer will usually not be able to specify and prove the damage and its cause. At the same time, the cloud service provider has a high level of flexibility when structuring remuneration under the lease provisions, making it possible to include restrictions on the scope of use.
- Completely different regimes apply to warranties for defects if the contract is classified as a service contract (more favorable to the cloud provider) or a contract for works and services (more favorable to the customer).
- However, liability in connection with cloud computing contracts can, independently of the contractual regime, result as well in tort claims and general duties to prevent hazards and ensure safety.
- Compensation claims can arise out of special laws such as the Product Liability Act.

3. General Terms and Conditions

Given that cloud computing services are characterized to a large extent through standardization, the services are usually offered under German law on the basis of standard terms of service (*Allgemeine Geschäftsbedingungen, AGB*).

To be effective, such standard terms must be validly incorporated into the content of the contract in accordance with section 305 *et seq.* of the German Civil Code. The rules on how to validly include such terms depends on whether the contracting party is a consumer or an enterprise.

The requirements for consumer contracts are more stringent with a correspondingly strict review of the content of the terms and conditions—clauses that deviate significantly from statutory law (usually lease law, see Part II.A.1, *supra*) are not valid. Thus, the classification of the contract is an important factor when assessing the validity of terms of service.

Depending on where the main focus of the cloud computing contract is placed, the applicable statutory obligations can be waived only within narrow limits or not at all. For

---

7   Section 536a(1) of the German Civil Code.

instance, in the case of a lease, the duty of maintaining the property and the right to terminate a contract for good cause cannot be waived, and a blanket exclusion of reductions of payment cannot be stipulated within general terms and conditions.

B. Typical Contractual Components

Given that none of the types of contracts provided for under statutory law fits cloud computing perfectly, and it remains unclear which legal regime applies in the case of regulatory gaps in the contract, precisely worded contracts are in the interest of both parties. The focus of the content should be the identification of the performance obligations, the specification of the legal consequences of contractual breaches, and the agreements on data protection, data security, and confidentiality. The contract should be clearly worded and comprehensible, and allow amendments in case it becomes necessary to adapt it to changed circumstances.

1. Specification of Services

It is not possible to make a general statement on what is required in the description of services because there is no such thing as a general cloud computing contract. To achieve legal certainty, eliminate liability risks, and prevent conflicts, it is advisable to word the specification of services as precisely as possible. At a minimum, it should specify the services owed and include a technical description as well as a specification of the associated infrastructure, the manner of data transmission, the cooperation duties of the cloud customer, the availability of the service, performance criteria, and the change request procedure.

2. Service Level Agreement

The service level agreement (SLA) is closely linked to the specification of services and forms an integral part of the cloud computing contract. Depending on their structure, SLAs can determine how the contract is categorized. SLAs usually include a specification and method of measuring the quality and quantity of service owed, response time for restoring service outages, and rules on monitoring performance and penalties in case of underperformance. The precise structure depends on what type of cloud service is provided.

3. Emergencies

To minimize the cloud customer's risk in case of an operational interruption, it is advisable to include an emergency management plan in the contract. This should include the assessment criteria for an emergency as well as the procedure in the event of an emergency and the resulting responsibilities on both sides. Reaction times, restarting times, and alternative solutions should also be specified. In most cases, emergency management is regulated through standardized clauses stipulated by the cloud service provider.

4. Remuneration

When stipulating the remuneration in the contract, it is necessary to achieve a balance between the customer's interest in a high degree of flexibility and the provider's interest in investment security. Cloud services are usually priced according to usage, whereby a minimum turnover or a basic rate is commonly used to safeguard the provider's interests. The cloud service provider generally charges a basic fee to cover his costs and a variable payment on top. The parties involved are free to come to an agreement on the details of the remuneration. The remuneration will depend on the services provided and can be measured by data volume, the number of transactions, duration of use, or through an all-inclusive rate.[8]

In addition to the level of remuneration, the contract should contain clauses on the duration of the contract, on penalties in the event of default, and on price adjustment because cloud computing contracts are generally of long duration.

5. Other Important Points

In addition to the aforementioned, other essential components of the contractual agreement should address licenses, data protection (see Part III, *infra*), compliance with specialized statutory regimes (see Part IV, *infra*), confidentiality, data security, protection against misuse, and termination of the contract.

To protect business and operational secrets, sensitive data, trade secrets, and other information disclosed in the context of cloud computing, it may be advisable, particularly from the customer's perspective, to provide for a contractual penalty to ensure compliance with the confidentiality obligations.[9]

C. Jurisdiction and Applicable Law for Cross-Border Matters

In many cases, cloud computing contracts are transnational, for example if the branches or registered offices of the cloud customer and the cloud service provider are located in different countries. Even if the parties to the contract are located in the same country, however, the contract may have an international element if a foreign jurisdiction is specified in a choice-of-law clause.

1. Place of Jurisdiction

The place of jurisdiction must be distinguished from applicable law because they do not always go hand in hand. The issue of the place of jurisdiction is primarily dependent on the type of claims and the party asserting them. In addition to lawsuits between cloud customers and providers, other disputes may also arise in connection with cloud use.

For proceedings within the EU, either the Brussels Ia Regulation[10] or national law may apply, depending on the situation. For contracts with a U.S. connection (e.g., with a U.S.-based cloud service provider), national law on jurisdiction applies unless otherwise

---

8   *See* Meents in: Borges/Meents, Cloud Computing, 2016, section 4, margin no. 176 ff.
9   *See id.* at margin no. 197.
10 Its predecessor, the Brussels I Regulation (Council Regulation (EC) No. 44/2001 of December 22, 2000, on jurisdiction and the recognition and enforcement of judgments in civil and commercial matters) [hereinafter Brussels I] applies to all proceedings that were initiated before January 10, 2015; the Brussels Ia Regulation (Regulation (EU) No. 1215/2012 of the European Parliament and of the Council of 12 December 2012 on jurisdiction and the recognition and enforcement of judgments in civil and commercial matters) [hereinafter Brussels Ia] applies to all proceedings initiated thereafter.

agreed in the contract. In Germany, this is set out in section 12 *et seq.* of the German Code of Civil Procedure (*Zivilprozessordnung*). In this context, section 23 of the Code is of primary relevance. Under this provision, for proprietary claims[11] brought against a person who is not domiciled in Germany, the court where the assets of the person or the object that form the subject of the claim is domiciled has jurisdiction. For a German court to have jurisdiction, there must be a sufficient focus of the matter in Germany. This can be the case if, for example, a U.S.-based cloud service provider has assets or other receivables in Germany or otherwise does business in Germany.[12]

Whether the Brussels Ia Regulation applies depends on whether the defendant is domiciled in a member state of the EU or whether the lawsuit concerns a company or individual from outside the EU. If the defendant is domiciled in the EU, the member state where he or she is domiciled is the place of general jurisdiction,[13] but the parties are free to agree on a different place of jurisdiction.[14] Under the Brussels Ia Regulation, however, the place of jurisdiction of the consumer (i.e., the usual location of the consumer) takes precedence over such a contractual provision in consumer contracts.[15]

2. Applicable Law

The general rules on conflict of laws are decisive for determining applicable law, such as the provisions of the Rome I Regulation,[16] which have been standardized throughout Europe and concern contractual obligations in connection with different countries. In addition, regarding international trade, the United Nations Convention on Contracts for the International Sale of Goods (CISG)[17] applies. However, the CISG is not relevant for cloud computing contracts if they are based on lease law (see Part II.A.1, *supra*). Rome I generally applies to contractual obligations under civil law and commercial law,[18] which involves the laws of different countries. The law that governs a contract can be chosen by the parties pursuant to Article 3 of Rome I. This is usually set forth in the contract's general terms and conditions. Special regulations may apply in the case of consumer contracts.[19]

As a consequence of the so called *ordre public* limit or public policy exception, a legal norm of another country does not apply if the application of such norm is not compatible with material principles of German law. Restrictions in the choice of law also apply to domestic matters. For example, if a cloud customer and a cloud service provider are domiciled in the same country, but make their contract subject to the law of another country, Article 3(3) of Rome I provides that where all other elements relevant to the situation at

---

11 In the context of German civil procedure law, the term "proprietary claim" refers to all claims that fall neither under the rights of individuals (e.g., personality rights) nor family law.

12 *See* Thole in Borges/Meents, Cloud Computing, 2016, section 15, margin no. 36.

13 Brussels Ia, *supra* note 10, art. 4(1); Brussels I, *supra* note 10, art. 2(1). This general jurisdiction may be overridden, however, by exclusive jurisdiction and special competencies.

14 Brussels Ia, *supra* note 10, art. 25; Brussels I, *supra* note 10, art. 23.

15 Brussels Ia, *supra* note 10, art. 18(2).

16 Regulation (EC) No 593/2008 of the European Parliament and of the Council of 17 June 2008 on the law applicable to contractual obligations [hereinafter Rome I].

17 United Nations Convention on Contracts for the International Sale of Goods (Vienna, 1980).

18 Certain areas of law, such as corporate law, are excluded from the scope of application under article 1(2) of Rome I.

19 Rome I, *supra* note 16, art. 6.

the time of the choice are located in a country other than the country whose law has been chosen, the law of such country is applicable, and not the chosen law.

Cloud computing contracts usually contain a choice-of-law clause. If the parties to the contract did not validly agree on a choice of law, then pursuant to Article 4(1) of Rome I, the applicable law is to be determined on the grounds of an objective link. The classification is based on the type of contract. Article 4(1) specifies the applicable law for a number of different types of contracts. If the type of contract is not listed there, the applicable law is based on Article 4(2), which states that "the contract shall be governed by the law of the country where the party required to effect the characteristic performance of the contract has his habitual residence."

Depending on the specific content, a cloud computing contract could fall under one of several types of contracts (see Part II.A.1, *supra*), and, accordingly, a different rule would apply. However, the classification as both a service contract and a lease result in applicability of the law where the provider's headquarters are located.[20] Please note that the classification of the contract has implications for the applicability of national laws on certain types of contracts, such as warranties in lease law, which do not apply to service contracts (see Part II.A.2, *supra*). If the cloud customer is a consumer, applicable law is the law of the country where the consumer has his or her usual place of residence.[21]

D. Liability and Cloud Computing

Provisions concerning liability are of particular significance for cloud computing contracts. The problems that arise may be technical in nature and can entail potentially damaging results, for example if the cloud cannot be accessed or if data is lost.

As a rule, standard contractual clauses form the basis for liability issues and are often stipulated in the provider's general terms and conditions. In this context, the limits of substantive law must be observed (see Part II.A.3, *supra*). Cloud service providers (particularly in the United States) usually try to exclude liability for indirect damage and consequential damage. Clauses stipulating a maximum liability amount are also of particular significance.

Under German law, the validity of standardized liability exclusions and maximum liability amounts is based on section 305 *et seq.* of the German Civil Code, the basic tenets of which apply to both business-to-consumer and business-to-business transactions. Under this provision, an exclusion or limitation of liability is not valid for injury to life, limb, or health.[22] This could be of significance for cloud contracts if they are used in the medical field or to run technical systems.[23] In other respects (except in the case of consumer contracts), it is possible to limit liability: liability disclaimers are permissible even for harms resulting from gross negligence. However, this does not apply to injuries to life, limb, or health.

---

20 *See* Rome I, *supra* note 16, art. 4(1)(b) as read with art. 19 for the contract for provision of services and art. 4(2) for leases.

21 *See id.* art. 6(1).

22 German Civil Code § 309(7).

23 *See* Boehm, Franziska: Challenges with cloud computing contracts: Classification, liability and ownership of data, ZEuP 2016, 358 (373).

Exclusions of liability for damage resulting from a breach of a main contractual obligation are not valid either. Although it is not possible to devise a general definition of "main contractual obligation," the interests of the customer in the careful handling of his or her data and the ability to access the cloud at any time are likely to belong to this category. Accordingly, a complete exclusion of liability for damage to or loss of data and the accessibility of data will most likely be considered invalid. It remains to be seen how courts will rule on this issue.

In this context it is worth considering including in the cloud services contract a provision establishing the extent to which the cloud customer is liable to the provider if he or she fails to comply with safety standards. The risk that damage will occur is indeed limited, but considering the fact that cloud structures are used by multiple parties, it is advisable to be prepared for such an eventuality.

E. Termination of the Contract and Insolvency

A cloud computing contract must include provisions governing how and when it may be terminated, as well as the effect of termination. This is necessary to ensure that it is possible for the cloud customer to change providers at the end of the contract or be in a position to manage his or her data alone, and to ensure that access to data is not lost.

The contract should also address issues arising out of insolvency of one of the contractual parties. If the customer is facing insolvency, it is important that he or she can still access his or her data and does not lose data if the provider terminates the contract. If the provider can no longer perform services due to insolvency, the customer should be able to change providers while the provider is still able to render the services.

F. Data Ownership and Intellectual Property

1. Ownership Rights in Data

As a rule, the cloud service provider provides only storage space for the customer's data. From the customer's perspective, this should not entail any changes to the legal position of the data—that is, the data should be treated as if it were on the customer's own storage medium. However, cloud service providers (particularly non-Europeans) often use clauses that regulate the rights to uploaded data. In this context it is important to note that the cloud service provider may be subject to legal limitations, particularly when one considers the disputed issue of categorizing and allocating data under EU and German civil law. In summary, it can be said that data ownership clauses do not usually establish a transfer of ownership in terms of property law because there is no absolute right to data according to German law. The law of obligations usually applies to transfer of data. Cloud computing contracts should therefore be formulated in terms that regulate a transfer of "rights" in materials protected by copyright and not a transfer of "data ownership"[24] if such a transfer of rights is desired. For material that is not copyright protected, confidentiality clauses can be used if the material is confidential. Other than that, an obligation not to pass on data can be stipulated only in the relationship between the parties and cannot be invoked vis-

---

24 *See id.* at 386.

à-vis third parties. Whether such clauses are valid is another issue and must be assessed under German law governing general terms and conditions.

2. Copyright

Copyright issues are also of relevance in cloud computing. The software used by the cloud service provider is a work protected under copyright law. In addition, the customer data stored in the cloud may be protected by copyright.

Furthermore, either the customer or the cloud service provider may be a user of third-party copyrights. The cloud service provider should take precautions against the possibility that the customer may infringe the copyrights of a third party, such as by providing for contractual guarantees in which the user guarantees not to use any infringing material (software or other content).

3. Patent Law Protection for Software in Only Exceptional Cases

The issue of protecting software in connection with cloud computing is relevant under patent law. Whereas U.S. patent law protects business methods to a certain extent,[25] such protection does not exist under European and German patent law due to a lack of "technical nature."[26] Therefore, software is generally not patentable under European law due to its lack of technical nature. However, given that this is a widely discussed issue, further development in the law can be expected. Although software can be protected by a patent under certain conditions (e.g., a sufficient degree of technical content), these conditions are typically not met in cloud computing.

G. Data Access

Given that one of the main interests of the cloud customer is uninterrupted access to his or her data, the contract should address data access. It is possible to establish post-contractual rights to gain access to or receive data under German civil law.[27] There is, however, no explicit legal claim to gain access to or receive the data stored. It is therefore advisable to specify the service provider's obligation and the procedure for surrendering data (such as conversion into a certain format and other technical details), in particular where access after termination of the contract is concerned.

III. Data Protection

A. Introduction

Data protection is one of the key issues surrounding the use of cloud services and requires close attention when structuring the contractual relationship between customers

---

25 In *Bilski v. Kappos,* 561 U.S. 593 (2010), the Supreme Court of the United States confirmed that, although abstract ideas cannot be patented, business methods are not inherently unpatentable.

26 Pursuant to section 1(3) no.3, (4)4 German Patent Act and art. 52(2)(c), European Patent Convention, "schemes, rules and methods for . . . doing business" shall not be regarded as inventions.

27 *See, e.g.,* GERMAN CIVIL CODE § 667.

and cloud service providers. The discussion below addresses the current legal situation in Germany. The primary piece of legislation is the General Data Protection Regulation[28] (GDPR). The GDPR is directly applicable in all EU member states and replaces both the EU Data Protection Directive[29] and the German Federal Data Protection Act (*Bundesdatenschutzgesetz*, FDPA). The GDPR became effective as of May 25, 2018, and cloud computing providers were required to comply by that date. A new FDPA also came into effect in May 2018, but its importance is limited to issues for which the GDPR provides flexibility for EU member states (e.g., for data processing of personal data of employees by their employers).

There are always data protection risks if a cloud customer has personal data processed by a cloud service provider. Given that the term "personal data"[30] is broadly interpreted, data protection is always an issue as a practical matter. Exceptions are made only in those cases in which a customer transfers anonymous data to the cloud service provider.

Under the GDPR, affiliated companies are not given preferential treatment with regard to transferring personal data among themselves. The comments below therefore also apply to use of cloud services that one company provides to an affiliated company.

If a cloud customer does not comply with data protection regulations, this may result in liability mainly on the part of the customer, but also on the part of the cloud provider. The data subject may be entitled to damages. The supervisory authorities may impose fines or issue orders. The supervisory authorities have various investigative powers, e.g., to order the controller or the processor to provide any information it requires for the performance of its tasks, to carry out investigations in the form of data protection audits, to notify the controller or processor of alleged infringements of the GDPR, to obtain access to all personal data and further information, and to obtain access to the premises of the controller or processor.[31] They further have corrective powers, e.g., to issue warnings, to order the controller or processor to bring processing operations into compliance with the provisions of the GDPR, and to impose a temporary or definitive limitation, including a ban on processing.[32] Administrative fines may be imposed in addition to or instead of these measures, depending on the circumstances of each individual case.[33] Administrative fines for noncompliance are up to €20 million or, in the case of a business enterprise, up to four percent of the total worldwide annual turnover of the preceding financial year, whichever is higher. [34]

---

28 Regulation (EU) 2016/679 of the European Parliament and of the Council of 27 April 2016 on the protection of natural persons with regard to the processing of personal data and the free movement of such data, and repealing Directive 95/46/EC [hereinafter GDPR].

29 Directive 95/46/EC of the European Parliament and the Council of 24 October 1995 on the protection of individuals with regard to the processing of personal data and on the free movement of such data.

30 GDPR, *supra* note 28, art. 4(1).

31 *Id.* art. 58(1).

32 *Id.* art. 58(2).

33 *Id.* art. 58(2)(i).

34 *Id.* art. 83.

B. Applicability of the GDPR

1. Material Scope of Application

The GDPR applies where "personal data" is concerned. Personal data means any information relating to an identified or identifiable natural person, known as the "data subject."[35] This includes information directly related to a person (e.g., address, e-mail address that uses the holder's name, marital status, professional activities) and information that can be linked to a person (e.g., identification number, insurance number, telephone number). The information may relate to the data subject's identity or characteristics (e.g., name, address, date of birth, profession, personal characteristics, physical characteristics, and biometric data such as photographs or fingerprints). It may also relate to factual circumstances concerning the data subject, in particular in relation to another person or thing. This also includes cell phone data or GPS location data attributable to a data subject.[36]

Only data on *natural persons* is protected under data protection law. Data on *legal entities* (e.g., limited liability companies, stock corporations) is not within the scope of data protection law. However, personal data of natural persons working within a legal entity, for instance their e-mail address or phone number at work, falls within the scope of data protection law.

If a particular piece of information clearly relates to a particular person, then the person is "identified" and the information constitutes "personal data." If a piece of information is not alone sufficient to identify a person, but becomes sufficient when combined with other information, then it relates to an "identifiable" person and, again, constitutes "personal data." The issue of when a person is deemed identified is highly disputed. According to the so-called relative approach, it depends on whether the data controller is able to attribute information (e.g., IP address, cookie) to a certain individual. This includes the data controller's knowledge and the knowledge of third parties that the controller can obtain with a reasonable amount of effort. Some information may be considered personal data for one data controller, but not for another.

Under the previously applicable FDPA, German data protection authorities (DPA) rejected this distinction and preferred to take an "absolute approach." Under the absolute approach, if a data controller's possession of certain data allows the data controller to identify a person when combined with other data, then the data is considered "personal data," regardless of whether that other data is accessible to the data controller (e.g., IP addresses, cookies, identification numbers). This understanding of the DPA meant that end-to-end encrypted data was treated as personal data if the cloud customer was in possession of the decryption key.[37] Personal data generally remains personal even when encrypted. Therefore, the only case where data protection law does not apply is where the data controller has proof that it is actually not possible to attribute data to a certain person. Then the data is anonymous and data protection law does not apply.[38]

---

35 *Id.*

36 Paal/Pauly, General Data Protection Regulation, Art. 4, margin no. 15.

37 Cloud Computing Guideline issued by the working groups technology and media at the conference of data protection officers of the federal and state authorities and the working group international data traffic of the Düsseldorf group, Version 2.0, Oct. 9, 2014, at 12 (hereinafter CC Guideline).

38 GDPR, *supra* note 28, Recital 26 ("The principles of data protection should . . . not apply to anonymous information . . . .").

The GDPR itself does not specify whether it follows the relative or the absolute approach. The European Court of Justice (ECJ) rendered a decision in a case referred by the German Federal Court of Justice involving the 1995 Data Protection Directive on whether a dynamic IP address is to be considered personal data. The court appears to follow the relative approach. In other words, it depends on whether the data controller has the (legal) means to establish the identity of the data subject. However, the court did not resolve the issue, so it remains to be seen how future cases will be decided.[39]

2. Territorial Scope of Data Protection Law

The territorial scope of application of the European data protection law is defined in Article 3 of the GDPR. Various circumstances may render the GDPR applicable to the given case.

a. Establishment of a Controller or a Processor in the European Union

The regulation applies to the processing of personal data "in the context of the activities of an establishment of a controller or a processor in the Union."[40] Whether the processing itself takes place in the Union is not relevant.[41]

The term "establishment" refers to "the effective and real exercise of activity through stable arrangements. The legal form of such arrangements, whether through a branch or a subsidiary with a legal personality, is not the determining factor in that respect."[42]

This means that an "establishment" for purposes of the regulation does not have to be an establishment in terms of corporate law. A local office is sufficient for the GDPR to be applicable. During the validity of the Data Protection Directive, the ECJ applied "a flexible definition of the concept of 'establishment,' which departs from a formalistic approach whereby undertakings are established solely in the place where they are registered."[43] This definition is likely still applicable under the GDPR.

The ECJ has ruled that the following factors are to be considered in determining whether a company has an "establishment" in a certain Member State:

- The fact that the activity of the controller in respect of the data processing, "in the context of which that processing takes place, consists of the running of property dealing websites concerning properties situated in the territory of that Member State and written in that Member State's language and that it is, as a consequence, mainly or entirely directed at that Member State."[44]
- The fact "that that controller has a representative in that Member State, who is responsible for recovering the debts resulting from that activity and for representing the controller in the administrative and judicial proceedings relating to the processing of the data concerned."[45]

---

39 ECJ decision of Oct. 19, 2016, Case C-582/14 (Breyer/Germany).
40 GDPR, *supra* note 28, art. 3(1).
41 *Id.*
42 *Id.*, Recital 22.
43 ECJ decision of Oct. 1, 2015, Case C-230/14 (Weltimmo v. Nemzeti Adatvédelmi és Információszabadság Hatóság), ¶ 29.
44 *Id.* ¶ 41.
45 *Id.*

- "[T]he presence of only one representative can, in some circumstances, suffice to constitute a stable arrangement [and therefore an establishment] if that representative acts with a sufficient degree of stability through the presence of the necessary equipment for provision of the specific services concerned in the Member State in question."[46]

- "[T]he concept of 'establishment' . . . extends to any real and effective activity—even a minimal one—exercised through stable arrangements."[47]

- "[P]rocessing of personal data is carried out in the context of the activities of an establishment of the controller on the territory of a Member State . . . when the operator of a search engine sets up in a Member State a branch or subsidiary which is intended to promote and sell advertising space offered by that engine and which orientates its activity towards the inhabitants of that Member State."[48]

- "[W]hile the fact that the undertaking responsible for the data processing does not have a branch or subsidiary in a Member State does not preclude it from having an establishment there . . . , such an establishment cannot exist merely because the undertaking's website is accessible there."[49]

On the other hand, "the issue of the nationality of the persons concerned by such data processing is irrelevant."[50]

This ground of jurisdiction requires the processing of personal data in question to be carried out not "by" the establishment concerned itself, but only "in the context of the activities" of the establishment. Even if the establishment has a distinct legal personality and the processing is carried out by the parent company without any intervention on the part of the establishment, the processing is carried out "in the context of the activities" of that establishment if the latter is intended to promote and sell, in that Member State, advertising space offered by the parent company which serves to make the service offered by that company profitable.[51]

b. Controllers and Processors Not Established in the EU

Under certain circumstances, the GDPR applies to controllers and processors established outside the EU, e.g., in the United States. This is the case where the processing activities are related to (i) the offering of goods or services to data subjects in the EU, or (ii) the monitoring of the data subject's behavior to the extent the behavior takes place within the EU.[52] At present it is unclear how close the relationship between the company "offering goods or services" or "monitoring the behavior" and the European market must be for the GDPR to apply, in particular for cloud service providers; clarifying court decisions are yet to come. The relevant recitals of the GDPR and criteria proposed by legal scholars may serve as an orientation until further notice.

---

46 *Id.* ¶ 30.

47 *Id.* ¶ 31.

48 ECJ decision of May 13, 2014, Case C-131/12 (Google Spain SL and Google Inc. v. Agencia Española de Protección de Datos [AEPD] and Mario Costeja Conzález), ¶ 60.

49 ECJ decision of July 28, 2016, Case C-191/15 (Verein für Konsumenteninformation v. Amazon EU Sàrl), ¶ 76.

50 ECJ decision of Oct. 1, 2015, *supra* note 43, at ¶ 41.

51 ECJ decision of May 13, 2014, *supra* note 48, at ¶ 55.

52 GDPR, *supra* note 28, at art. 3(2).

(i) Offering of Goods or Services

As far as the offering of goods or services is concerned, the crucial point is whether the service in question is directed at customers in the EU. The following are indicators that a service is so directed: the language(s) in which the service is offered, the currencies that the service provider accepts (or for which the provider offers a conversion utility that converts the customer's preferred currency into the currency that is accepted by the provider), and the terms and conditions (especially fees and delivery time) for shipping to the EU.[53] However, "the mere accessibility of the controller's, processor's or an intermediary's website in the Union, of an email address or of other contact details, or the use of a language generally used in the third country where the controller is established, is insufficient to ascertain such intention."[54] If a U.S.-based cloud service provider offers its services in only English, and this service merely happens to be accessible in the EU, the GDPR should not be applicable.[55] If, however, the service is adapted in any way to the specific needs of EU customers, the service provider should ensure compliance with the GDPR.

(ii) Monitoring the Behavior of the Data Subject

A company is monitoring the behavior of the data subject for purposes of the GDPR if the data subject is "tracked on the internet including potential subsequent use of personal data processing techniques which consist of profiling a natural person, particularly in order to take decisions concerning her or him or for analysing or predicting her or his personal preferences, behaviours and attitudes."[56] A prime example of such monitoring is the tracking of a user's search queries on platforms like Amazon or Google in order to personalize future advertising for the customer. Such tracking (via cookies, pixel tags, social plug-ins, web beacons, or other technologies) is within the scope of the GDPR if the behavior that is monitored (not the monitoring) takes place in the EU. Whether the acquired personal data is intended for personalized advertising, political, scientific, or other purposes is not relevant.[57] This ground of applicability of the GDPR could, for example, apply to cloud service providers domiciled in the United States if the cloud service provider offers its EU customers the opportunity to participate in a study concerning the usability of the cloud service and if the study involves the monitoring of the customers' behavior.

C. Processing Carried Out on Behalf of a Data Controller

As the number of companies that outsource staff management and data storage increases, so does the need for regulations that ensure the protection of the personal data entrusted to cloud service providers. The scenario described below addresses transferring data to a cloud service provider in a case where the technical infrastructure is located in the EU or EEA. Subsequently, the additional requirements applicable to service providers located elsewhere will be addressed.

Most cases of data processing by a cloud computing service provider can be regulated in the form of data processing on behalf of a controller. The cloud customer is the

---

53 Gierschmann/Schlender/Stentzel/Veil, General Data Protection Regulation, Art. 3 margin no. 23.
54 GDPR, *supra* note 28, at Recital 23.
55 Gola, DS-GVO/Piltz, Art. 3 margin no. 28.
56 GDPR, *supra* note 28, at Recital 24.
57 Paal/Pauly/Ernst, General Data Protection Regulation (2018), Art. 3 margin no. 20.

"controller" of the personal data transmitted to the cloud service provider as the "processor." The legal responsibility for complying with the GDPR in connection with collecting, processing, and using personal data remains with the controller, i.e., the cloud customer. The cloud customer instructs the cloud service provider to render technical services, whereupon the provider as processor of the personal data must comply with those instructions. The cloud customer is therefore fully responsible for the data processing carried out by the cloud service provider.

The advantage of data processing on behalf of a controller is that personal data can be provided to the cloud service provider without the consent of the data subjects and merely on the basis of a contract concluded between cloud customer and provider. This is because passing data from the data controller to the data processor is not deemed data transmission. In contrast to data processing on behalf of a controller, a transmission of data is a form of "processing" of data that may only occur on a basis that is legally permissible or with the consent of the data subject. The relevant data protection regulations for data processing on behalf of a controller are set out in Article 28 of the GDPR.

The conditions that must be met for cloud computing services to qualify as data processing on behalf of a controller are as follows:

Duty to comply with instructions. The obligation of the cloud service provider to comply with the instructions of the cloud customer is an essential feature of data processing on behalf of a controller.[58] The cloud customer must retain the authority to make final decisions on the type, scope, and purpose of data collection, processing, and use of its personal data, and the cloud service provider may only render cloud services on the basis of the customer's instructions. If the cloud service provider deviates from the controller's instructions, it is liable for all resulting damages.[59]

A written agreement that includes specified content. The cloud customer and the cloud service provider must enter into an agreement regulating the data processing services. The agreement—which can be either a contract or another legal act under Union or Member State law[60]—must be in writing, including in electronic form,[61] and must include specified provisions.[62]

The following issues must be addressed in the contract:[63]

- The subject matter and the duration of the processing;
- The nature and the purpose of the processing, the type of personal data, and categories of data subjects;
- The obligations and rights of the controller;
- The obligations and rights of the cloud service provider specified under Article 28(3)(a)–(h) GDPR, including the obligations to process the personal data only on documented instructions from the controller and to implement appropriate technical and organizational measures to ensure a level of security appropriate

---

58 GDPR, *supra* note 28, at art. 29.
59 *Id.* art. 82(2).
60 *Id.* art. 28(3).
61 *Id.* art. 28(9).
62 *Id.* art 28(3).
63 *Id.* art. 28(3).

to the risk of the data processing (e.g., the pseudonymization and encryption of personal data).[64]

- The obligations of the cloud service provider to assist the controller by appropriate technical and organizational measures, insofar as this is possible, for the fulfilment of the controller's obligations to respond to requests for exercising the data subject's rights laid down in Chapter III of the GDPR and to assist the controller in ensuring compliance with its obligations pursuant to Articles 32 to 36;
- The obligation of the cloud service provider to ensure that persons authorized to process the personal data have committed themselves to confidentiality or are under an appropriate statutory obligation of confidentiality;
- The cloud service provider's duty to make available to the controller all information necessary to demonstrate compliance with the obligations under Article 28 and to allow for and contribute to audits, including inspection, conducted by the controller or another auditor mandated by the controller;
- The provider's right to issue subcontracts to other processors;
- The provider's obligation to immediately inform the controller if, in its opinion, an instruction infringes the GDPR or other Union or Member State data protection provisions;
- The provider's obligations to delete and return of stored data.

Use of subcontractors. Cloud service providers often use subcontractors to render technical services. It is important to assure that the relationship between the cloud service provider and the subcontractor is also structured as data processing on behalf of a controller. Article 28(2) of the GDPR provides that a processor "shall not engage another processor without prior specific or general written authorisation of the controller."[65] Although Article 28(2) does not mention the electronic form, some European legal scholars assume that the electronic form should be equally sufficient for such authorisation.[66] Until this legal opinion has been confirmed by the Court of Justice of the European Union, the controller's authorization should always be in writing, i.e., signed by the controller personally. The data protection obligations that are set out in the agreement between the controller and the processor should be imposed on the subcontractor. Where the subcontractor fails to fulfill its data protection obligations, the initial cloud service provider remains fully liable to the controller.[67] The authorization may be general or specific. If the parties choose the first option, the processor must inform the controller of any intended changes concerning the addition or replacement of other processors, and the controller has the right to object to such changes.[68]

Monitoring the cloud service provider. The controller is under a statutory obligation to use only processors "providing sufficient guarantees to implement appropriate technical and organisational measures in such a manner that processing will meet the requirements of [the GDPR] and ensure the protection of the rights of the data subject."[69] From commencement of data processing by the cloud service provider and regularly thereafter,

---

64 Additional "technical and organizational measures" are listed in *id.* art. 32(1).
65 *Id.* art. 28(2).
66 *See* Gierschmann/Schlender/Stentzel/Veil, Art. 28, margin no. 38.
67 GDPR, *supra* note 28, at art. 28(4).
68 *Id.* art. 28(2).
69 *Id.* art. 28(1).

the data controller is required to monitor and ensure compliance with the statutory standards and contractually agreed technical security standards. For this purpose, the cloud service provider must allow for and contribute to audits, including inspections, conducted by the controller or another mandated auditor.[70] The results of such monitoring must be documented. Failure to fulfill this obligation may result in fines up to €10 million or, in the case of an undertaking, up to two percent of the total worldwide annual turnover of the preceding financial year, whichever is higher.[71] It is often not possible for the cloud customer to monitor on site at the service provider's computer center. A practical alternative is for the cloud service provider to adhere to an approved code of conduct as referred to in Article 40 or an approved certification mechanism as referred to in Article 42. Such codes of conduct or certification mechanisms may, however, serve only as an indication that the cloud service provider meets the requirements of Article 28(1); they do not relieve the controller of its obligation to monitor the processor if the circumstances of the case indicate that the cloud service provider does not meet those requirements.

Further requirements to be met by the cloud service provider under the GDPR. The GDPR entails an increase in the level of responsibility borne by the cloud service provider in complying with data protection obligations. Failure to comply may subject the provider to an administrative fine or require payment of compensation to the data subject.

- The cloud service provider has expanded reporting and documentation obligations. Under Article 30(2) of the GDPR, the cloud service provider must keep a record of all the categories of processing activities it carries out on behalf of a customer. This is different from the former legal situation under the FDPA where the obligation to keep records of procedures is borne solely by the cloud customer as controller.

- The cloud service provider is obligated under Article 33(2) of the GDPR to notify the cloud customer of any personal data breach. These obligations to notify and maintain documentation will require additional time and costs on the part of the cloud service provider.

- Pursuant to Article 27(1) of the GDPR, a cloud service provider domiciled outside the EU must designate in writing a representative in the EU. The representative serves as a point of contact for the DPA and the data subject, in addition to the cloud service provider. Cloud service providers domiciled in the United States must appoint such representatives if they offer their services to EU customers.

D. International Data Transfer

One important feature of cloud computing services is that data processing and storage are carried out without a focus on geographical boundaries. Rather, the data can be stored anywhere in the world where the cloud provider operates its computing centers. This is not congruent with data protection requirements, which are based on the location of the computing center where data is processed or stored.

---

70 *Id.* art. 28(3)(h).
71 *Id.* art. 83(4).

1. Within the EU

If data is processed in a member state of the EU,[72] there are no additional requirements on data processing in a cloud apart from the requirements set out under Part III.C., *supra* (namely, a valid agreement on data processing on behalf of a controller and the mandating of a EU-representative).

2. "Third Countries"

The case differs if the cloud service provider is domiciled (or has its principal infrastructure) outside of the EU, such as in the United States. This also applies to commissioned data processing if the cloud service provider is located in the EU but engages subcontractors based outside the EU. In such cases, the GDPR requires additional measures to ensure an adequate level of data protection.[73]

"Adequate" does not mean "identical to the protection under the GDPR," but "must be understood as requiring the third country in fact to ensure . . . a level of protection of fundamental rights and freedoms that is essentially equivalent to that guaranteed within the European Union."[74] The requirement may be met by, among other things, a decision of the Commission "that the third country, a territory or one or more specified sectors within that third country . . . ensures an adequate level of protection"[75] or the provision of "appropriate safeguards" by the controller or processor.[76] Another possibility is obtaining the consent of the data subjects,[77] but this is usually rather impractical due to the large number of data subjects.

The appropriate safeguards referenced above may be provided by:

- standard data protection clauses adopted by the Commission;[78]
- binding corporate rules (BCRs) between group enterprises that have been approved by the competent supervisory authority;[79] or
- ad-hoc contracts between controller and processor that ensure an adequate level of data protection, if authorized by the supervisory authority.[80]

---

72 The GDPR is not directly applicable in European countries that are not EU Member States. This applies to Iceland, Norway, Liechtenstein, and Switzerland. These countries have not yet ratified the GDPR and are therefore treated as "third countries" in terms of data protection law. However, the so-called EFTA council (the free trade council of Iceland, Norway, Liechtenstein, and Switzerland) is currently debating the ratification of the GDPR; the latest developments of the negotiating process are published regularly at http://www.efta.int/eea-lex/32016R0679.

73 GDPR, *supra* note 28, at arts. 44–49.

74 ECJ decision of Oct. 6, 2015, Case C-362/14 (Maximillian Schrems v Data Protection Commissioner).

75 GDPR, *supra* note 28, at art. 45(1). This is known as an "adequacy decision."

76 *Id.* art. 46(1).

77 *Id.* art. 49(1)(a).

78 *Id.* art. 46(2)(c).

79 *Id.* art. 47. BCRs are defined as "personal data protection policies which are adhered to by a controller or processor established on the territory of a Member State for transfers or a set of transfers of personal data to a controller or processor in one or more third countries within a group of undertakings, or group of enterprises engaged in a joint economic activity." *Id.* art. 4(2). The mandatory content of BCRs is set out in *id.* art. 47(2).

80 *Id.* art. 46(3)(a).

Both binding corporate rules and ad-hoc contracts must be assessed individually by the DPA, however, and are thus quite difficult to implement. Therefore, the discussion below addresses the alternatives used most frequently in practice: standard contractual clauses and adequacy decisions by the European Commission.

a. Standard Contractual Clauses

Standard contractual clauses (SCCs) are a set of contractual provisions governing the handling of personal data that have been approved by the European Commission as a means to ensure an adequate level of protection.[81] An SCC must be used in its approved form. Certain specifications of the data processing must be set out in the schedules.

Subcontractors outside of the EU can also be included in the SCCs. Even if only one subcontractor is located outside of the EU, and the cloud service provider is located in the EU, the cloud customer must agree on the SCCs directly with the subcontractor. It is possible for the cloud service provider to act on behalf of the subcontractor in this respect.

b. Adequacy Decision of the European Commission—Safe Harbor and U.S. Privacy Shield

The controller and the cloud service provider need not take action to ensure an adequate level of protection if an adequacy decision of the European Commission has been issued for the country or region where the latter is domiciled. The effect of an adequacy decision is that personal data can flow from the EU to a third country without any further safeguard necessary.[82]

In the view of the European Commission, the data protection level in the United States is not equivalent to the level in the EU. In the past, it was deemed an adequate level of data protection if a U.S. company to which data was going to be transferred certified itself in accordance with the so-called safe harbor principles. However, on October 6, 2015, the European Court of Justice ruled that the decision by the European Commission that facilitated the transfer of data with U.S. companies was invalid.[83] In particular, the court decided that personal data is not sufficiently protected from access by government agencies, particularly the National Security Agency. The decision rendered the exchange of data with the United States on the basis of safe harbor invalid and put the United States on the same level as other "third countries" such as Russia and China.

On July 12, 2016, the safe harbor's successor came into force: the EU-U.S. Privacy Shield.[84] Through a new system of self-certification of enterprises established in the United States, the Privacy Shield fills the gap that was left when Safe Harbor was declared

---

81 *Id.* art. 46(1), (2)(c).

82 *See Adequacy of the Protection of Personal Data in Non-EU Countries*, European Commission, https://ec.europa.eu/info/law/law-topic/data-protection/data-transfers-outside-eu/adequacy-protection-personal-data-non-eu-countries_en. The Commission has recognized Andorra, Argentina, Canada (commercial organizations), Faroe Islands, Guernsey, Israel, Isle of Man, Jersey, New Zealand, Switzerland, Uruguay, and the United States (limited to the Privacy Shield framework) as providing adequate protection. *Id.*

83 ECJ decision of Oct. 6, 2015, Case C-362/14 (Maximillian Schrems v Data Protection Commissioner), http://eur-lex.europa.eu/legal-content/EN/TXT/?qid=1484231241699&uri=CELEX:62014CA0362.

84 *See EU-US Privacy Shield*, European Commission, https://ec.europa.eu/info/law/law-topic/data-protection/data-transfers-outside-eu/eu-us-privacy-shield_en (referencing Commission Implementing decision of July 12, 2016).

invalid. The Privacy Shield program is administered by the International Trade Administration within the U.S. Department of Commerce. To join the Privacy Shield framework, the U.S.-based organization is required to self-certify to the Department of Commerce and publicly commit to comply with the framework's requirements. The commitment will become enforceable under U.S. law.[85] Privacy Shield has been heavily criticized, and an Irish organization called Digital Rights filed a complaint against it; however, the complaint was rejected by the General Court of the European Union on grounds of inadmissibility.[86] Thus, it remains unclear whether the Privacy Shield will withstand a review by the European Court of Justice.[87]

The SCCs approved under the 1995 Data Protection Directive will remain valid until amended, replaced, or repealed by the Commission.

IV. Data Protection Requirements and Other Statutory Compliance Requirements for Specially Regulated Sectors

In addition to data protection law, the cloud customer must comply with a number of statutory requirements addressing other matters. Further, any binding internal policies at its company may have to be taken into consideration.

Special provisions that are applicable to certain professional groups are outlined briefly below. In particular, there are professional groups to which section 203 of the German Criminal Code (*Strafgesetzbuch*) applies because these groups are subject to the professional obligation of confidentiality (such as doctors, lawyers, tax consultants, auditors, and members of private insurance companies for health, accident, and life insurance). For these professional groups the disclosure of professional secrets constitutes a criminal offence. The term "professional secret" is interpreted broadly (e.g., the fact that a doctor treats a specific patient or the fact that a customer has taken a life insurance policy are "professional secrets"). In November 2017, section 203 of the Criminal Code was amended. Section 203 (3) German Criminal Code now stipulates an exception to the prohibition of disclosure of professional secrets: professional secrets may be disclosed to third persons, e.g. cloud service providers, who are involved in the professional activities of the person entrusted with confidential information, insofar as this disclosure is *necessary* for the service rendered by this third person. In other words, the disclosure of the professional secrets to a third person must be strictly limited to the extent necessary for the proper performance of services. The exception to the prohibition of disclosure also applies to

---

85 Further information and a list of organizations that have joined Privacy Shield are available at https://www.privacyshield.gov.

86 Order of the General Court of Nov. 22, 2017, Case T-670/16 (Digital Rights Ireland Ltd./European Commission).

87 The General Court and the European Court of Justice are the two major courts of the European Union. Although the General Court hears applications for annulment from individuals, companies, and national governments, the European Court of Justice hears applications from national courts for preliminary rulings, annulment, and appeals. The Court of Justice of the European Union (CJEU) is not a third court, but the umbrella term for the General Court and the European Court of Justice.

such third persons rendering the service if they in turn make use of other persons (i.e., sub-contractors).

In order to compensate for a reduction in the protection of secrets under criminal law, these "other participating persons" (i.e., the cloud service provider and its sub-contractor) are themselves included in the criminal liability, section 203 (4) German Criminal Code if they disclose a professional secret to third persons without authorisation.

The professional secrecy bearers have to obligate the other participating person, e.g., the cloud service provider, to secrecy. In the case of omission otherwise a punishability threatens them, if this participating person reveals unauthorized a professional secret, section 203 (4) German Criminal Code. An analogous regulation can also be found for the participating persons (e.g., cloud service providers) who make use of sub-contractors and do not oblige them to secrecy in the event that the sub-contractor discloses a secret without authorisation, section 203 (4) German Criminal Code.

In order to avoid a risk of prosecution, professional secrecy bearers must therefore ensure that external service providers are obliged to maintain secrecy. Likewise the external services providers must ensure that any sub-contractor involved in rendering services to professional secrecy holders are obliged to maintain secrecy.

Accordingly, every service provider/sub-contractor to whom confidential information is disclosed must be subject to a non-disclosure agreement.

A. Healthcare

In the healthcare sector, vast amounts of health-related data are collected and processed as "special categories of personal data" within the meaning of article 9 of the GDPR. Given that the nature of this data is sensitive, the legal requirements and security standards are particularly restrictive. In addition to the special provisions in article 9(2) GDRP, different legal requirements apply to hospitals depending on whether they are run publicly or privately, or by a church-affiliated organization. The federal states also have their own laws regulating data protection and hospitals. The provisions of the Social Code (*Sozialgesetzbuch*, SGB) also apply,[88] as does the German Criminal Code.[89] There are also special provisions governing use of data for research purposes and evaluation of statistics by public bodies, in addition to special regulations for certain areas such as the Genetic Diagnostics Act and the German Principles of Data Access and Verifiability of Digital Documentation for tax-related healthcare data.

There are special problems associated with transmission of health-related data to third countries such as the United States. In addition to the requirements for a "third country transfer" stipulated in Articles 44–49 of the GDPR,[90] the requirements for the processing of "special categories of personal data" (Art. 9 GDPR) must be met.

B. Banks and Insurance Companies

Cloud computing for regulated companies in the financial and insurance sectors must also meet special standards. The regulations vary depending on the type of company.

---

88 SGB I, SGB V, SGB X.
89 Section 203; see *supra* Part IV.
90 See *supra* Part III.D.2.

Applicable regulations include the German Banking Act, the Insurance Regulatory Act, and the Securities Trading Act. There are also internal policies whereby the minimum regulatory requirements for risk management must be observed as the administrative rules applicable to banks and insurance companies.

1. Banks

Employees of banks generally are not within the professional groups covered by section 203 of the German Criminal Code. In the prevailing view, however, the case differs for savings banks and state banks if they are organized as public law institutions—section 203(2) does apply to employees of such entities.[91] However, given that banking secrecy is protected by the German constitution, special conditions apply when data is processed by banks. Banks are obliged to observe confidentiality with respect to all customer-related facts and valuations. Banks may only pass on information about customers if required under statutory regulations, if the customer has consented, or if an authorization for bank information has been provided (this usually concerns standardized, general pieces of information between credit institutions in the context of normal bank transactions and is regulated in the general terms and conditions).

Cloud computing raises no special issues so long as the customer data covered by banking secrecy rules does not leave the "sphere of control" of the bank, for example if an internal cloud is used. There are no legal provisions specifically concerning banks in the GDPR; the relevant provisions are those of the German Banking Act. The prevailing view is that section 25b of the German Banking Act allows relocating data and thus the possibility that knowledge of customer data may be gained by third parties outside of the bank.[92]

Relocation of data may be permissible without obtaining explicit consent from the bank customers. However, this is only the case if it is ensured that the business is conducted in an orderly manner, data is handled confidentially, and there is a statement of commitment to this effect ("extended banking secrecy").[93] As the content and scope of the banks' confidentiality obligation toward their customers is determined by the contractual arrangements between them, in the individual case the relevant contract will determine whether it is permissible to relocate data by way of cloud computing; however, as a general rule it can be assumed that the bank's customer would not object to necessary outsourcing.[94]

Furthermore, in accordance with section 25b of the German Banking Act, the cloud provider must be obligated to maintain banking secrecy and ensure that the conditions for commissioned data processing are met.[95] Moreover, the requirement that the business is properly organized in connection with cloud computing, particularly if activities and processes are outsourced to another company, must be observed in accordance with section 25b.[96]

---

91 *Cf.* Lenckner, Schönke/Schröder, StGB (German Criminal Code), 2014, sec. 203, margin no. 44.
92 Borges/Meents, l.c., at 436.
93 Borges/Meents/Eckhold § 24 margin no. 70.
94 Schimansky/Bunte/Lwowski/Krepold, Bankrechts-Handbuch, § 39, margin no. 29.
95 See *supra* Part III.C.
96 Thalhofer: Grenzenlos: Compliance bei Cloud Computing, CCZ 2011, 222.

2. Insurance Companies

Insofar as "special categories of personal data" (such as health-related data) are involved, the above rules[97] also apply to insurance companies. The data is also subject to the requirements of section 203 of the German Criminal Code in certain areas of insurance, such as health insurance, accident insurance, and life insurance.

In addition, the requirements of section 32 of the Insurance Regulatory Act apply to the insurance sector. These provisions entail specific requirements for outsourcing services within the scope of application. For instance, in addition to properly executing the outsourced activities, management must also have the ability to control and monitor, and the regulatory authorities must have reasonable rights to inspect and monitor.

IV. Conclusion

A. Civil Law Issues

There is not specific statutory regime for cloud computing. Contracts relating to cloud services are contracts sui generis. In order to minimize legal uncertainties regarding the statutory regime applying to cloud computing contracts under German law, describe the applicable rules in the contract. For example, it is not possible to call a contract a "service agreement" in order to benefit from the liability regime of a service agreement if, under the circumstances, the contract in fact constitutes a lease agreement. Therefore, one should not rely on the title of the contract and the statutory rules, but explicitly provide contractual rules for all conceivable scenarios within the borders of mandatory law.

Under German law, it is possible for some elements of a contract to be governed by one statutory regime, and other elements by another regime. This may lead to legal uncertainty regarding the applicable rules, e.g., as far as liability is concerned. Therefore, we recommend providing for explicit clauses for all scenarios, even if this might seem redundant in the first place.

Given that the warranty rules are not clear due to the various types of contracts and individual circumstances, it is of utmost importance to ensure that the contract expressly stipulates the details in this area. However, note that express warranty terms in the contract can override what is provided for by law only to the extent no mandatory law is set aside by such terms—in any event, as far as general terms and conditions are concerned.

German law concerning general terms and conditions is comparatively strict with respect to consumer contracts. Mandatory consumer protection laws remain in effect even where foreign law applies.

Due to the technical complexity of cloud services, the technical departments involved must work closely together when drafting the specification of services.

The contract should specify penalties for failure to meet the SLA that are sufficient to motivate the service provider but are not disproportionate, e.g., in relation to the value of the contract. Excessive penalties may be held invalid.

Assuring confidentiality and data security requires a combination of legal restrictions and technological protections.

---

97 See *supra* Part IV.A.

German law imposes significant restrictions on the validity of contractual exclusions of liability. Given that there is a high level of consumer protection under EU legislation, this applies even more so if a consumer is a party to the cloud contract.

B. Data Protection

It is advisable to align the data processing steps in the area of cloud computing with the requirements of data protection law because the term of "personal data" is interpreted very broadly.

Most cases can be regulated in the form of data processing on behalf of a controller (i.e., the customer). It is necessary that customer and the service provider enter into an agreement which regulates in detail the data processing service and must contain various specific provisions stipulated in the GDPR. It is thus advisable for cloud service providers to use standard contracts that meet such requirements. The technical security measures that the cloud service provider must implement must be described in detail in a schedule to the agreement.

If the cloud service provider is domiciled (or has its principal infrastructure) outside of the EU, the GDPR requires additional measures to ensure an adequate level of data protection. In such cases the providers should propose the EU Standard Contractual Clauses ("SCCs") to their customers in order to establish an adequate level of data protection. These SCCs can be incorporated into the set of agreements on cloud computing services. The text of the SCCs should not be changed and therefore either a schedule should be used or a supplementary agreement should be entered into. If the cloud service provider is located in the EU but engages a subcontractor based outside the EU, then the cloud customer must enter into SCCs directly with the subcontractor. If the cloud service provider is domiciled in the U.S., at present it is sufficient if the cloud service provider is certified in accordance with the regulations of the Privacy Shield. However, it is important to keep abreast of current developments on Privacy Shield. If the Privacy Shield framework is invalidated due to a review by the CJEU, it will be necessary to employ SCCs to ensure an appropriate level of data privacy.

In addition to data protection law, cloud customers may have to comply with a number of statutory requirements addressing other matters. In particular if the cloud customer is a member of a certain professional group which is subject to professional confidentialy obligations sanctioned by section 203 German Criminal Code, the agreement with the service provider and likewise the agreement between the service provider and its sub-processor must also contain a non-disclosure agreement.

Finally, considering the requirements illustrated here, it is important to verify what data will be placed in the cloud before cloud services are used. Different types of data may require different levels of data protection depending on how sensitive they are.

Chapter 11

Negotiating Cloud Agreements Internationally: European Union Considerations

By David Flint[1]

I. Introduction

This chapter begins with a discussion in the Part that follows of the status of cloud service providers under the General Data Protection Regulation[2] (GDPR); Part III discusses general considerations relating to data protection under the GDPR; Part IV discusses the applicability of the GDPR to cloud service providers located outside Europe; Part V discusses the obligations of processors under the GDPR; Part VII discusses the interaction of the right to be forgotten with the GDPR; Part VII discusses data protection officers; Part VIII discusses international data transfers, with a focus on issues arising under the EU/US Privacy Shield; Part IX discusses cloud computing issues in the context of financial services; and Part X discusses contracting issues.

II. Status of Cloud Service Providers under the GDPR

The processes and procedures that a controller must consider are set out primarily in Articles 5–11 of the GDPR and will depend on the nature of the cloud computing model the business has chosen: (1) a private cloud, where the customer is the only user of the service, albeit the infrastructure may be managed by a third-party cloud service provider under an outsourcing contract; (2) a community cloud, where a group of cloud customers share the same service, typically because they have common regulatory or security issues; (3) a public cloud, where the infrastructure is managed by the cloud service provider and the resources are made available to the public generally over the internet (this encompasses providers such as iCloud, Microsoft Azure, Google Web Services, Carbonite, and Amazon Web Services); or (4) a hybrid cloud, which is a combination of the other models depending on the data and services required.

The other differentiator relates to the types of service the cloud service provider is offering in its cloud: (1) Infrastructure as a Service (IaaS), where the customer merely purchases access to raw computing power; (2) Platform as a Service (PaaS), where customers can write their own applications to run within the offered platform, which in turn may be hosted on a cloud IaaS; (3) Software as a Service (SaaS), where the provider offers access to a complete software application the user accesses through a web browser, reducing the need for the user to install software on his or her own machine and allowing for a wider

---

1 Solicitor, Scotland. E-mail: df@davidflint.com.

2 Regulation on the protection of natural persons with regard to the processing of personal data and on the free movement of such data, and repealing Directive 95/46/EC (General Data Protection Regulation) O.J. L119, 4/5/2016, at 1–88.

range of devices to be supported and for all users to be on a consistent software experience irrespective of their device or operating system.

These service models can be layered on top of each other, and each can be provided by a different party. For instance, the SaaS cloud provider may offer its programs to users from a server hosted on an IaaS cloud owned and operated by a different cloud service provider. The use of layered services means that at any time there could be a number of controllers and a number of processors acting together to deliver content or services involving the processing of personal data.

Under the GDPR, it is a controller who has primary responsibility for ensuring that the data protection principles (Articles 5–11 of the GDPR) are observed both by itself and by any processor. It is therefore important to determine whether the cloud service provider is acting as a processor or is also a controller in its own right. In its *Guidance on the Use of Cloud Computing*,[3] the UK Information Commissioner noted that this determination of roles should not be difficult in the case of a private cloud or a community cloud (subject to issues of data sharing), but in the case of a public cloud it will be difficult for a controller to have any meaningful control over the way the cloud service provider operates. Thus, the UK Information Commissioner notes that, "the cloud customer does not transfer data protection obligations to the cloud provider simply by choosing to use its services in order to process his personal data."[4]

The mere fact that the personal data stored by the controller is stored in the cloud may itself give rise to a number of new categories of personal data, and in some of these cases the cloud service provider may in fact be the controller as well as the processor. Within the jurisprudence of cases brought under rules implementing the now-replaced Data Protection Directive, metadata created by logs on access, usage, and transaction history of individual users may well be "personal data" and therefore subject to the application of the GDPR. For example, it would be expected that the cloud service provider would maintain logs of what files were accessed when and from what IP address. IP addresses have been held to constitute personal data;[5] therefore, the cloud service provider would seem to be the controller in respect of (at least) the IP address it collected and logged.

The UK Data Protection Act 2018[6] (mirroring Articles 5 and 28 of the GDPR) requires the controller to have a written contract with the processor setting forth that the processor is to process the personal data only on documented instructions from the controller and ensuring that the processor will comply with security obligations equivalent to those imposed on the controller itself.

With the use of hybrid clouds and public clouds offered by global providers, it becomes almost impossible for individual users to determine whether the provider is complying with those obligations. The UK Information Commissioner suggests that use of an industry-recognized standard or certification may assist the controller;[7] however, as indicated above, the cloud service provider may also be a controller with its own primary obligations.

---

3 UK Information Commissioner's Office, Guidance on the Use of Cloud Computing (2012), https://ico.org.uk/media/fororganisations/documents/1540/cloud_computing_guidance_for_organisations.pdf.

4 *Id.* ¶ 32.

5 Judgment of the Court of Justice of the European Union of 19 October 2016 in Case 582/14, Patrick Breyer v. Germany, http://curia.europa.eu/juris/document/document.jsf?text=&docid=184668&pageIndex=0&doclang=en. *See also* GDPR Recital 26.

6 Section 59(5) and (6), http://www.legislation.gov.uk/ukpga/2018/12/pdfs/ukpga_20180012_en.pdf.

7 UK Information Commissioner's Office, *supra* note 3, at ¶ 62.

III. Data Protection and the GDPR

A company whose personal data is in the hands of a cloud service provider is a controller of the data and is responsible for ensuring that the cloud service provider complies with the requirements of the GDPR. In reality, however, a controller using a cloud service really has no effective control over the activities of the cloud service provider (in its capacity as a processor); despite any contractual attempts to the contrary, there is no real degree of control over the cloud provider whose terms and conditions will exclude all responsibility and liability for almost all activity. A recent investigation carried out by the author disclosed that of some 20+ cloud service providers, the extent of liability accepted was restricted to a quantum of less than $500 in most cases, with the more extensive acceptance of liability generally not exceeding the annual value of the contract. Most contracts excluded all liability for everything, including loss of data. Given that maintenance of the customer's data is the essence of the cloud-computing contract, the effect is to give little or no remedy against the cloud service provider.

Under the GDPR, the data subject who has suffered "material or nonmaterial damage" as a result of the infringement of the GDPR is entitled to claim compensation against the processor as well as the controller for any damage suffered. For the cloud service provider, this may be a particularly unattractive scenario because it may well have greater resources than the controller and significantly less opportunity to limit its exposure by way of contract. Additionally, processors are liable to the fining regime of article 83 of the GDPR (potentially 4 percent of worldwide turnover, or €20m, whichever is higher).

The cloud service provider as processor is required to develop and enforce internal procedures and processes to protect personal data. Recital 81 of the GDPR imposes a heightened obligation on controllers to validate the processor they may have selected:

> To ensure compliance with the requirements of this Regulation in respect of the processing to be carried out by the processor on behalf of the controller, when entrusting a processor with processing activities, the controller should use only processors providing sufficient guarantees, in particular in terms of expert knowledge, reliability and resources, to implement technical and organisational measures which will meet the requirements of this Regulation, including for the security of processing. . . .

Recital 83 further requires that "the controller or processor should evaluate the risks inherent in the processing and implement measures to mitigate those risks, such as encryption." This is to be done "taking into account the state of the art and the costs of implementation in relation to the risks and the nature of the personal data to be protected."

Recitals 81 and 83, taken together, suggest that the cloud service provider is required to take an interest in the nature of the data provided to it by the controller. This may give rise to a number of additional issues for the cloud service provider, not the least of which is that it may be required to put into place more individualized offerings for its clients, and that controllers must carry out personalised risk assessments for their clients.

The accountability principle of the GDPR[8] means that a cloud service provider is required to maintain full documentation setting out the activities it is undertaking and the

---

8 GDPR art. 5(2).

nature of the data on which the processing occurs. Such documentation is required to be produced to a supervisory authority when requested.

Article 28 sets out new restrictions on the business freedom of the cloud service provider as processor in relation to subcontracting (which would include the provision of backup and mirroring services). In addition to the expected provisions in relation to ensuring that such subcontract processors meet the data protection principles, Article 28 provides that,

> [t]he processor shall not engage another processor without prior specific or general written authorisation of the controller. In the case of general written authorisation, the processor shall inform the controller of any intended changes concerning the addition or replacement of other processors, thereby giving the controller the opportunity to object to such changes.[9]

The controller must thus be advised of the identity of all subcontractors so that it can object to their use. Article 28 additionally makes a processor responsible for the conduct of its subcontractors:

> Where a processor engages another processor for carrying out specific processing activities on behalf of the controller, the same data protection obligations as set out in the contract or other legal act between the controller and the processor as referred to in paragraph [28(3)] shall be imposed on that other processor by way of a contract or other legal act under Union or Member State law, in particular providing sufficient guarantees to implement appropriate technical and organisational measures in such a manner that the processing will meet the requirements of this Regulation. Where that other processor fails to fulfil its data protection obligations, the initial processor shall remain fully liable to the controller for the performance of that other processor's obligations.[10]

This means that where the cloud service provider uses a subcontractor, it is required to ensure that the terms and conditions of that subcontract relationship exactly mirror its contract with the controller.

How this new control of processors and their subcontractors will operate is unclear. If the controller has its personal data processed by, say, a payroll company whose software is on servers operated by Amazon Web Services or Azure (which are therefore acting as subcontractors of the payroll company), is the controller required to approve the use of AWS or Azure as an infrastructure platform? The cloud does not fit neatly into the established data-protection pigeonholes of the European data-protection regime. What if the payroll company instructs its customers on how to process their data using the company's software, which is on the Azure platform? Must customers really consent to the use by the payroll company of the Azure platform?

Articles 28(3)(c), (f), and (h) and Article 30 require controllers processors to take security measures appropriate to the processing and its risks. Although it is likely that controllers will know the nature and purposes of the intended processing and can secure the data by encrypting it before upload, or by ensuring proper backups internally or to another cloud data center, the cloud service provider will not be able to tailor its security

---

9 *Id.* art. 28(2).
10 *Id.* art. 28(4).

measures for the individualized requirements of its hundreds or thousands of customers. How the cloud service providers can comply with the requirements of article 30 and avoid fines of 4 percent of turnover, or €20m, is unclear.

The inevitable consequence of the GDPR must be significantly longer cloud computing contracts with greater customer disclosure, warranties, representations, and possibly a greater involvement of the cloud service provider in the stored data. The cloud service provider will, for the first time, be required to consider what data is being stored using their service.

The wording of the GDPR is not ideally suited for cloud computing; if cloud service providers are "processors," then those who provide them with infrastructure must be "sub-processors" and be bound by the provisions of the regulation. This must be addressed in contracts now because there are many contracts that predate the GDPR's entry into force. If these contracts are not changed, the allocation of risk, responsibility, and liability will not be addressed properly.

One possible way forward is to make use of codes of conduct and certification. Article 40 of the GDPR encourages the adoption of codes of conduct as a way to promote compliance. Such a code could include provisions addressing "fair and transparent processing," "the collection of personal data," "the pseudonymisation of personal data," "the information provided to the public and to data subjects," and other matters. It is also possible to demonstrate compliance by participation in a certification or seal program approved by the supervisory authorities.[11]

On September 27, 2016, a Code of Conduct for Cloud Infrastructure Service Providers was issued by the Cloud Infrastructure Services Providers in Europe (CISPE),[12] following a dialogue with the EU Article 29 Working Party[13] for its approval. This dialogue commenced prior to 2014, and two opinions[14] have been issued by the Article 29 Working Party on Cloud Computing, the most recent in 2015. In February 2017, CISPE announced additional progress in the adoption of the Code of Conduct, noting its determination that over 30 cloud services were already in compliance.[15]

The UK Information Commissioner has suggested that encryption of data may be a suitable way to ensure that personal data can only be accessed by those lawfully entitled to do so.[16] This would apply to data "in transit" between the controller/user and the cloud service provider, but would also encompass data "at rest" in the possession of the cloud service provider. Encryption of data raises a number of issues beyond the scope of this chapter, but from the perspective of European data protection law, the robustness of the

---

11 *Id.* art. 41.

12 Press Release, Cloud Infrastructure Providers Unveil Ground-Breaking Data Protection Code of Conduct, https://cispe.cloud/wp-content/uploads/pdf/CISPE-PRESS-RELEASE-27092016.pdf.

13 This Working Party was set up under Article 29 of Directive 95/46/EC. It is an independent European advisory body on data protection and privacy. Its tasks are described in Article 30 of Directive 95/46/EC and Article 15 of Directive 2002/58/EC. *See* http://ec.europa.eu/justice/data-protection/index_en.htm.

14 Opinion 05/2012 on Cloud Computing, http://ec.europa.eu/justice/data-protection/article-29/documentation/opinion-recommendation/files/2012/wp196_en.pdf; Opinion 02/2015 on C-SIG Code of Conduct on Cloud Computing, http://ec.europa.eu/justice/data-protection/article-29/documentation/opinion-recommendation/files/2015/wp232_en.pdf.

15 https://cispe.cloud/wp-content/uploads/2017/02/CISPE-PR-EN-FINAL-20171602.pdf.

16 https://ico.org.uk/for-organisations/guide-to-the-general-data-protection-regulation-gdpr/security/?q=DPIA. See Article 32(1)(a) and Recital 83 GDPR.

encryption used and the security of the encryption keys become paramount. It is unlikely that a scenario in which the data held by the cloud service provider were held in an unencrypted form, or in which the keys were held by someone other than the controller (or in a manner which meant that only he or she could access them) would meet the requirements of the GDPR.

IV. Application of GDPR to a Cloud Service Provider Located Outside the EEA

The GDPR recognizes that cloud service providers may be located, or may have facilities located, outside the European Economic Area (EEA).[17] Post Brexit, that will include facilities located in the United Kingdom (including Gibraltar). Notwithstanding that the cloud service provider (or the facility) is outside the EEA, it may still have obligations under the GDPR as a processor. A cloud service provider based outside the EEA is subject to the GDPR if it either (1) offers goods and services to EU data subjects; or (2) monitors the behavior of EEA data subjects.[18] Merely having a website accessible in the EEA is not per se sufficient to lead to GDPR applicability, but offering to sell goods or services in the EEA from that website would be; factors such as language used would be relevant.

V. Obligations of Processors under the GDPR

Processors under the GDPR have a responsibility for compliance in addition to controllers, and a number of additional obligations and challenges:

- only processors that guarantee compliance with the GDPR can be appointed by the controller;[19]
- processors must keep records of their processing activities performed on behalf of the controller;[20]
- processors must cooperate with data protection authorities in the performance of their tasks;[21]
- processors must notify any data breach to the controller without undue delay;[22]
- to the extent that the GDPR requires the appointment of a data protection officer, that requirement applies to processors;[23]

- data subjects can bring claims directly against a processor[24] where it has not complied with obligations imposed on processors by the GDPR, or acted outside or contrary to the lawful instructions of the controller.

---

17 The European Economic Area consists of the EU plus Norway, Liechtenstein, and Iceland.
18 GDPR art. 3(2).
19 *Id.* art. 28 & Recital 81.
20 *Id.* art.30(2) & Recital 82.
21 *Id.* art.31.
22 *Id.* art.33(2).
23 *Id.* art.37.
24 *Id.* art.82(1)–(2) & Recital 146.

VI. Right to Be Forgotten

One of the more well-known changes to be set out in detail by the GDPR is the "right to be forgotten"—the ability for data subjects to request the deletion of personal information concerning them,[25] codifying the court decisions under the directive. However, according to an article by *SkyHighNetworks*,[26] the average organization uses 738 cloud services, so dealing with deletion requests will pose quite a challenge. The request to delete data applies not only to data held directly by the controller, but also all copies that may be stored by third-party cloud service providers. All 738 of those parties will be processors, and under the GDPR will have financial and tortious liability for any failings.

The problem is exacerbated by the fact that many cloud service providers retain data indefinitely or for an indefinite period, or do not deal with data retention at all in their terms and conditions; the fact that many (particularly in the United States) retain the right to "share data" with another third party makes it even more difficult to ensure that all personal data has been destroyed.

VII. Data Protection Officers

A controller or processor must appoint a data protection officer (DPO)[27] if local laws require it to do so[28] or if its data processing activities involve:

- "regular and systematic monitoring of data subjects on a large scale";[29] or

- processing special-category personal data on a large scale.[30]

The qualifications and functions of the DPO are set out in articles 38 and 39 of the GDPR, but in general terms, the DPO's function is to monitor compliance with the GDPR, liaise with data protection authorities, and carry out privacy impact assessments (before any new processing occurs). The DPO is the point of contact in an organization for data subjects. The DPO may be an officer or employee of the controller or the processor, but he or she must carry out his or her functions independently of those entities. The DPO must be given adequate resources to carry out his or her duties, and the DPO's employment cannot be terminated as a result of the performance of his or her duties as DPO.

A cloud service provider, as a processor, based outside the EEA will still be required to meet the requirements of the GDPR to carry out impact assessments and appoint representatives[31] and possibly DPOs if they are to avoid the penalty provisions of the GDPR.

---

25 *Id.* art.17.

26 https://www.skyhighnetworks.com/cloud-security-blog/only-1-in-100-cloud-providers-meet-proposed-eu-data-protection-requirements/.

27 GDPR art. 37.

28 *See, e.g.,* Section 69 of the UK Data Protection Act 2018, which requires a DPO to be appointed where the processing is for law enforcement.

29 GDPR art. 37(1)(b).

30 *Id.* art. 37(1)(c) (referencing Article 9, "personal data revealing racial or ethnic origin, political opinions, religious or philosophical beliefs, or trade union membership, and the processing of genetic data, biometric data for the purpose of uniquely identifying a natural person, data concerning health or data concerning a natural person's sex life or sexual orientation," and Article 10, "personal data relating to criminal convictions and offences or related security measures").

31 *Id.* art. 27.

VIII. International Data Transfers and the GDPR

One feature of the cloud is that cloud service providers can have data centers located in multiple jurisdictions. This may be a sensible approach for several reasons, including for data accessibility and backup and for compliance with national legislation requiring domestication of data storage. In considering the use of a cloud service in relation to any personal data of a natural person, transfers of data to a third country (including a data center situated in a third country, whether as a mirror site or a backup location or otherwise) can be made only in accordance with the principles set out in Recitals 101–116 and Articles 44–49 of the GDPR.

In particular, transfers of data to a country that is outside the EEA are permitted on the basis of an adequacy decision,[32] binding corporate rules,[33] or subject to appropriate safeguards.[34] It is not acceptable to make the transfer based only on the controller's own assessment of the adequacy of the protection afforded.

A. Adequacy Decisions and Privacy Shield

As of late 2018, the EC had made adequacy determinations for the following countries: Andorra, Argentina, Canada (commercial organizations), Faroe Islands, Guernsey, Israel, Isle of Man, Jersey, New Zealand, Switzerland, and Uruguay. As to the United States, the EC has determined that a system called Privacy Shield[35] provides adequate protection.

Privacy Shield is a self-certification scheme for which organizations may sign up when processing personal data from the EU.[36] The scheme was formally adopted on July 12, 2016. However, before the EU would agree to Privacy Shield, there were conditions that the United States had to meet. These conditions were met by enactment of the Judicial Redress Act,[37] followed by additional negotiations with the EU that resulted in what is known as the "Umbrella Agreement."[38] The Umbrella Agreement ensures that personal data transferred for law enforcement purposes between the European Union and the United States are adequately protected and are aligned to previous international agreements

---

32 *Id.* art. 45.

33 *Id.* art. 47.

34 *Id.* art. 46.

35 Privacy Shield Framework, Privacyshield.gov, https://www.privacyshield.gov/EU-US-Framework.

36 In order to enter the Privacy Shield, an organization must (1) be subject to the investigatory and enforcement powers of the Federal Trade Commission (FTC), the Department of Transportation (DoT), or another statutory body that will effectively ensure compliance with the Principles (other U.S. statutory bodies recognized by the EU may be included as an annex in the future); (2) publicly declare its commitment to comply with the Principles; (3) publicly disclose its privacy policies in line with these Principles; and (4) fully implement them. EU-U.S. Privacy Shield Framework Principles Issued by the U.S. Department of Commerce, https://www.privacyshield.gov/Privacy-Shield-Principles-Full-Text. This means that many organizations are not eligible for the Privacy Shield because they are not within the jurisdiction of the FTC or DoT.

37 5 U.S.C. § 552a.

38 *See* Council Decision (EU) 2016/2220 of 2 December 2016, (OJ L 336/1-2); Agreement between the United States of America and the European Union on the protection of personal information relating to the prevention, investigation, detection, and prosecution of criminal offences (OJ L 336/3–13); Joint EU-U.S. statement following the EU-U.S. Justice and Home Affairs Ministerial meeting of 5 December 2016, https://www.consilium.europa.eu/en/press/press-releases/2016/12/05/eu-us-ministerial-mtg-on-jha/.

involving both countries. The Umbrella Agreement ensures that EU individuals can seek judicial review if their personal data is disclosed unlawfully by a U.S. enforcement agency. The Umbrella Agreement also allows for judicial review when EU individuals are not allowed access to their personal data or not allowed to amend personal data held by a U.S. enforcement agency. This mirrors the rights that U.S. citizens already have within the EU.

The Judicial Redress Act was brought into force to extend the protections that are allowed under the Privacy Act 1974. The extended protections relate to the rights of citizens from designated EU countries. This act has been well received, with numerous technology companies and the U.S. Chamber of Commerce endorsing the enactment. However, there are exceptions to who can utilize the rights under this act. At present, the act applies to the EU but excludes Denmark and the United Kingdom. Accordingly, there must be an argument that Privacy Shield is insufficient to protect nationals of those countries because they cannot bring suit in the United States in the same manner as a U.S. citizen. To date, this is not an argument that seems to have been advanced.

The status of Privacy Shield has been called into question by the U.S. Congress's 2018 enactment of the CLOUD Act.[39] The CLOUD Act gives power to the executive branch to enter into executive agreements with foreign governments to agree on data-sharing arrangements with little congressional oversight and bypassing the protections that would be required by using a Mutual Legal Assistance Treaty.

The CLOUD Act raises serious issues for the European data protection regime and for U.S. cloud service providers offering services to EEA data subjects. Taking the facts of the Microsoft Ireland case[40] as an example, if an e-mail relating to a U.S. national's account held in Ireland is seized by the U.S. Department of Justice (DOJ) under the powers in the CLOUD Act, it is possible (probable) that mixed in will be personal data about data subjects in the EEA.

It is unclear how that ties in with the protections afforded by the GDPR. One must wonder how the CLOUD Act can be seen as compatible with the Privacy Shield. Here is personal data about persons in the EEA seized by the U.S. DOJ with no judicial process in the EEA member state, no privacy statement, no consent, and no safeguards.

For those negotiating cloud agreements that involve the storing of personal data of EEA data subjects, it is unclear how it will ever be possible to contract in a wholly GDPR-compliant manner with a cloud service provider with a U.S. operation (irrespective of where their data center may be located), given the wide reach of the CLOUD Act. Warranties and indemnities are unlikely to suffice, given the requirement to comply with a DOJ subpoena domestically.

Another challenge to the viability of Privacy Shield arises from the European Parliament's passage of a nonbinding resolution[41] asking the European Commission (the Commission), the EU's executive body, to suspend the Privacy Shield framework "unless the U.S. is fully compliant" by September 1, 2018. Although the Commission is not bound by this resolution, they certainly must take it into account.

The parliament's resolution cites a number of reasons for asking the Commission to suspend the Privacy Shield pending U.S. compliance, including the reauthorization and

---

39 Pub. L. No. 115-141, div. V, 132 Stat. 348, 1213 (2018).

40 *In re* Warrant to Search a Certain E-Mail Account Controlled & Maintained by Microsoft Corp., 829 F. 3d 197, 201 (2d Cir. 2016).

41 Resolution no. 2018/2645(RSP).

amendment of section 702 of the Foreign Intelligence Surveillance Act, which allows U.S. intelligence agencies to collect information on non-U.S. persons located outside of the United States, and the CLOUD Act, which allows U.S. law enforcement agencies to access personal data stored abroad.

The resolution also cites the improper use of 2.7 million EU citizens' Facebook data by Cambridge Analytica, and the failure of the United States to appoint a sufficiently independent ombudsperson as required by the Privacy Shield. According to the parliament, the Privacy Shield "does not provide the adequate level of protection."

B. Binding Corporate Rules[42]

Binding corporate rules are internal rules for data transfers within multinational companies. Binding corporate rules are like a code of conduct. They allow multinational companies to transfer personal data internationally within the same corporate group to countries that do not provide an adequate level of protection.[43] The drawback of using binding corporate rules is that they tend to take a long time to negotiate and draft and are therefore expensive for organizations implementing them.

C. Appropriate Safeguards

The third principal method of complying with the GDPR's rules on international transfer of data is to employ appropriate safeguards in the form of contractual clauses that control handling of the data. The validity of the model contract clauses employed by Facebook is currently the subject of litigation before the Court of Justice of the European Union.[44]

IX. Cloud Computing in the Context of Financial Services

The European Banking Authority (EBA) is presently consulting on a set of Guidelines on Outsourcing (the Guidelines), addressing outsourcing arrangements used by financial institutions.[45] The EBA notes the trend within the financial services industry, like many others, toward engaging third-party service providers to reduce costs and improve flexibility and efficiency. In recent years, this trend has accelerated further through the emergence of financial technology or "FinTech." Owing to the significant technological changes that have taken place within the financial services industry, the relationship between institutions and outsourcers is increasingly important and requires heightened regulatory attention. At the same time, the EBA wishes to establish a "more harmonized framework" for

---

42 *See* GDPR article 4(20) ("'binding corporate rules' means personal data protection policies which are adhered to by a controller or processor established on the territory of a Member State for transfers or a set of transfers of personal data to a controller or processor in one or more third countries within a group of undertakings, or group of enterprises engaged in a joint economic activity"); *Id.* art. 47.

43 *See* https://ec.europa.eu/info/law/law-topic/data-protection/data-transfers-outside-eu/binding-corporate-rules_en.

44 https://eur-lex.europa.eu/legal-content/EN/ALL/?uri=CELEX%3A62018CN0311.

45 https://www.eba.europa.eu/-/eba-consults-on-guidelines-on-outsourcing.

the outsourcing arrangements of financial institutions. The broadened scope of the draft Guidelines addressees reflects these changes.

The draft Guidelines provide a clear definition of outsourcing and specify the criteria to assess whether an outsourced activity, service, process, or function (or part of it) is critical or important. In particular, the revised Guidelines cover credit institutions and investment firms subject to the Capital Requirements Directive (CRD),[46] but also payment institutions subject to the revised Payment Services Directive (PSD2)[47] and electronic money institutions subject to the e-money Directive.[48] The Consultation Paper on the Guidelines[49] provides a detailed overview not only of the new Guidelines, but also for the present regime for financial services companies.

With effect from the entry into force of the new Guidelines (expected to be June 30, 2019), the existing Committee of European Banking Supervisors (CEBS) Guidelines[50] and the EBA's recommendations[51] will cease to apply. Businesses will have a transitional period (expected to be until December 31, 2020) to change their existing outsourcing arrangements to comply with the new Guidelines.

Section 4 of the draft Guidelines contains 13 specific guidelines on outsourcing. As well as helpfully reminding institutions what should be included in contracts for outsourcing arrangements (probably equally applicable to outsourcing in other sectors), key issues addressed within the Guidelines include: proportionality of governance arrangements; responsibility of the management team of an institution; need for a written outsourcing policy; conflicts of interest; business continuity planning; internal audits; documentation requirements; due diligence when selecting an outsourcing provider; risk assessment; security of data and systems; access, information, and audit rights; termination of an outsourcing arrangement; and oversight.

The draft Guidelines provide much food for thought in terms of what is expected of institutions when engaging in outsourcing, especially the outsourcing of critical and important functions. Although the draft Guidelines have been issued within the ambit of the financial services industry, the points made are equally valid in relation to any other outsourcing to the cloud exercise.

X. Contractual Issues

With the commoditization of cloud services, it is difficult for individual users (whether consumer or business) to influence the terms on which such services are provided. Given that many of these services are provided on the basis of laws other than those of Europe, regard should be had for these likely differences; the issues that arise under GDPR have been mentioned above but are nonetheless relevant here.

---

46 Directive 2013/36/EU.
47 Directive (EU) 2015/2366 (PSD2).
48 Directive 2009/110/EC.
49 https://www.eba.europa.eu/documents/10180/2260326/Consultation+Paper+on+draft+Guidelines+on+outsourcing+arrangements+%28EBA-CP-2018-11%29.pdf.
50 https://www.eba.europa.eu/documents/10180/104404/GL02OutsourcingGuidelines.pdf.pdf.
51 https://www.eba.europa.eu/documents/10180/2170125/Recommendations+on+Cloud+Outsourcing+%28EBA-Rec-2017-03%29_EN.pdf.

It is likely that the period in which claims are to be brought against the cloud service provider will be significantly shorter than the normal period for claims under national law.

This will lead to a contractual disconnect between the period under which the enterprise may have liability to its clients, customers, and others and the period in which recourse can be had against the cloud service provider.

It may be possible for the cloud service provider to amend its terms of service unilaterally by posting changes on its websites; unless the enterprise had managed to negotiate specific terms with the cloud service provider, it may be in the unenviable position of being bound by the new provisions with no ability to flow those changes downstream.

Warranties on performance, availability, and uptime are unlikely to meet the exact needs of the business, and that may be an issue with standard form contracts, which often contain provisions specifying locations outside Europe for judicial forum and choice of law. In a B2B contract, courts are unlikely to enforce jurisdiction where such a provision is agreed upon, given that there exist in most jurisdictions legislation dealing with what are considered to be "unfair contract terms." In a B2C contract, the position may be less clear, but individual consumers will generally not have the financial clout to challenge such a provision.

When contracting with U.S. cloud service providers, the provisions of the CLOUD Act, mentioned above, must be considered. Indeed, the question of what access law enforcement and regulatory authorities have and the permissibility or otherwise of encrypted data is something that must be reviewed on a country-by-country basis.

Liability caps, acceptable use provisions, and provisions on data destruction all must be considered to ensure symmetry between the cloud service contract and the requirements of national laws, which may require data retention for a longer period or have a different view on acceptable use. Where the use meets national laws but not the law of the cloud service provider (or vice versa), there must be some mechanism for ensuring data recovery at the least.

Overall, the data protection issues mentioned above will permeate every aspect of the cloud service relationship and will touch, directly or indirectly, on most of these contractual concerns.

XI. Conclusion

When negotiating Cloud Agreements internationally it should not be forgotten that it will not only be United States law which will impact on the contractual provisions but also the substantive, regulatory and procedural rules of other jurisdictions in which the counterparties or their clients may be located. There are many rules which cannot be waived or avoided in other jurisdictions, including rules on data localisation or the sovereign cloud which may require data in relation to those within a particular country (or some of that data) to be retained in that country. For that reason, in an international context, local advice should always be sought to ensure that the Cloud Agreement is compliant with local rules.

In this chapter, the European data protection rules of the GDPR have been mentioned in detail but there are other rules, both general and sectoral, which may have a role to play. Additionally, this is a fluid, fast moving area of jurisprudence and any standard agreements which are used will require to be reviewed regularly to ensure that the agreement complies with all the relevant rules and laws of all the impacted jurisdictions.

Chapter 12

Negotiating the Exit—Ensuring Successful Transition

By Cheryl M. Burtzel[1]

I. Introduction

Most cloud services agreements are undertaken with the best of intentions. The procuring company believes that it has found the best cloud vendor for its needs, allowing the company to control costs, protect its data, and scale and manage its IT functions efficiently and effectively. The cloud vendor would like to see the engagement continue for a long time, building its customer base, revenue, and service offerings, but what happens if the customer's needs change, and the cloud vendor cannot fulfill these needs under the existing services agreement? What if the cloud vendor's performance does not meet standards established in the agreement or otherwise? Things change, and then what happens?

One of the most important considerations when selecting a cloud provider concerns how your data will be managed or handled when you exit the services of one cloud provider and move to either another provider or back to your own environment. Ensuring that the data stored or created using a cloud provider's platform is available and portable when the services end is critical to the success of any cloud services deal, as is carefully reviewing and negotiating termination and transition-out provisions—particularly for the procuring company or entity.

This chapter addresses termination and other transition issues that parties to a cloud services arrangement should consider and address in their agreements.[2] Ideally, terms governing transition of the cloud services relationship should be negotiated and finalized prior to the commencement of services delivery. Delaying these discussions to a later time can leave your data and computing needs at risk. Although the initial stages of any relationship can seem like a honeymoon period, a customer beginning a cloud vendor relationship should think strategically about the ending of the relationship before signing an agreement. Any agreement involving control over a customer's sensitive data should address some minimum requirements for return of that data and processes surrounding termination.

---

1 Cheryl McManus Burtzel is a partner at Duggins Wren Mann & Romero LLP, an Austin, Texas law firm. She can be reached at cburtzel@dwmrlaw.com. Biographical information can be found at http://www.dwmrlaw.com/attorney/cheryl-m-burtzel/ or at https://www.linkedin.com/in/cheryl-burtzel-techlaw/.

2 Please note that specific jurisdictions and, in the United States, specific industries or regulatory frameworks in those industries (such as healthcare or financial services), may have additional requirements for managing and protecting data that impact cloud and other data services arrangements.

II. Termination Clauses; Timing

Termination provisions for cloud services vary from cloud vendor to cloud vendor and from customer category to customer category. Not surprisingly, termination and other provisions for consumers and smaller entities utilizing cloud services often will be materially different from those offered to large enterprise or institutional customers.

In earlier cloud services deals for enterprise or large customer transactions,[3] the contract term was established for periods of potentially five calendar years or longer—with extensions for equal duration unless the customer provided specific notice to the cloud vendor well in advance of the anniversary of the effective date of the contract.[4] Termination clauses in these outsourcing transactions provided early-termination penalties or fees, essentially resulting in claims that the customer pays the cloud vendor the balance of fees due for the remainder of the agreed term of the contract. Under such provisions, if the customer decided to terminate the agreement in year two of a five-year term, for example, the customer could be responsible for paying a termination fee assessed for the balance of the contract payments even though the cloud vendor would no longer be delivering services.[5]

---

3 Cloud services have become available due to the dramatic changes and evolution of the technology industry. Without the innovations in technology that first occurred in the 1960s, such as the development of the Advanced Research Projects Agency Network (ARPANet), some argue that the cloud would not have developed. Subsequent developments include virtualization and symmetric multiprocessing in the 1970s, web hosting in the mid-1990s, and virtual private servers as well as grid/utility computing, which arose in the late 1990s, along with the standardization of the internet. Information technology and related infrastructure further evolved into what is known as the cloud in today's marketplace, and the innovations will continue. Among the many articles discussing the history of the cloud, *see* the following three insightful articles: (1) Regalado, *Who Coined 'Cloud Computing'?*, MIT TECH. REV. (Oct. 31, 2011), *available at* https://www.technologyreview.com/s/425970/who-coined-cloud-computing/; (2) Mohamed, *A History of Cloud Computing*, COMPUTER WEEKLY, Mar. 2009, *available at* www.computerweekly.com/feature/a-history-of-cloud-computing; and (3) *30 Years of Accumulation: A Timeline of Cloud Computing*, GOVERNMENT COMPUTER NEWS (May 30, 2013), *available at* https://gcn.com/articles/2013/05/30/gcn30-timeline-cloud.aspx/.

4 Large enterprise customers were engaging in data services and outsourcing transactions long before cloud services and distributed computing became ubiquitous. These transactions frequently were initiated in the financial services industry, among others, and were the subject of lengthy, heavily negotiated contracts and statements of work. For example, in many industries, what used to be mainframe processing and time-sharing or outsourcing deals are now cloud services deals driven through distributed computing, data centers, and the internet, with a subscription for services from a provider rather than a long-term outsourcing contract. Many outsourcing deals required a cloud vendor to procure additional mainframe computers or other storage—an expensive proposition. In order to recover their investment, these cloud vendors often built the financial models for an outsourcing deal based on a commitment from the customer to pay the outsourcing fees for a specific time period. The contract then generally included a termination-fee provision that was triggered upon an early contract termination. The termination-fee provisions were designed to recover the investment expended by the cloud vendor to procure necessary technology and other sunk costs generated in order to support the contracted period. Termination fees generally were due and payable at time of termination.

5 These termination penalties or fees generally were assessed in cases where the customer decided to terminate for convenience reasons. In addition, the penalty or fee often was triggered even when the customer claimed that a material breach had occurred because whether a breach had occurred often would be disputed.

Contract terms for current cloud services deals often are shorter in duration than in the past. For example, some cloud services providers allow customers to terminate the services arrangement at any time upon notice to the service provider, provided that any already-incurred fees or expenses are paid. Large enterprise or institutional customers also are seeing shorter contract terms proposed in many instances.

Although the move to shorter contract terms is a positive development for many cloud services customers, termination clauses raise several issues that should be examined as part of your evaluation of a cloud vendor's cloud services offering. These issues include:

1) no "data hostage" clauses
2) data turnback and destruction
3) transition support and services
4) use and ownership of data developed during delivery of services

The remainder of this chapter will highlight these four areas of concern and provide strategies for handling each issue.[6] The chapter concludes with a discussion and analysis of three separate termination clauses.

A. No "Data Hostage" Clauses

Cloud services agreements (as well as other outsourcing or data storage or services agreements) often contain termination clauses that condition the cloud vendor's return of data upon payment of cloud vendor fees and other obligations. Some customers view these clauses as data hostage clauses.

In the cloud services arena, these clauses frequently provide that the cloud vendor may terminate the agreement at any time payment is not timely received, and that no access to services or your data will be provided. Some clauses even go to the extreme of providing that the customer's data will be deleted immediately or within a short time period upon the customer's failure to timely pay for services. Cloud providers vary considerably in their handling of this issue in the termination of cloud arrangements. Careful review of termination clauses and other provisions is required to determine what model is used in the specific cloud services arrangement proposed.

Typical strategies for mitigating the impact of a data hostage clause include the negotiation of terms requiring that the cloud vendor provide access to your data pending resolution of a dispute upon payment or any other dispute that arises under the contract. In addition, establishment of an expedited informal dispute resolution process for any terminations under the contract may be achievable.

Furthermore, a customer should establish good data management practices for its operations in any environment independent of whether the customer utilizes cloud services. Regularly backing up data stored in the cloud or elsewhere is important, as is documentation of your data management practices and procedures. Periodically auditing or otherwise verifying that your entity's data management practices have not changed, or

---

6 Very few of these agreements have been the subject of litigation to date. Many disputes surrounding cloud or data storage agreements are resolved informally, either in the early stages of litigation or before going to court. As such, there is minimal judicial guidance on cloud agreements generally and termination rights clauses specifically. Query whether data hostage clauses are enforceable, particularly in smaller company transactions or in consumer-related cloud arrangements where the customer has little, if any, leverage to negotiate revised terms.

determining that they need revision, is important as well. Finally, conducting information security assessments and stress testing your systems and practices to help assure that your entity meets the data security and protection requirements to which it is bound, by contract or under applicable regulatory and statutory regimes, is critical for enterprise compliance needs.

B. Data Turnback and Data Destruction

Understanding the process and timeline for the return of your data at the end of a cloud services relationship is important. Data portability[7] is a significant concern for most cloud services customers. Your agreement with a cloud services provider should address the following issues at minimum:

1) In what format will the data be returned to you?
2) What cost, if any, will apply to exporting your data at the end of the agreement?
3) What timelines apply to the return of your data?

The format of the data as stored on the cloud service is important for the future use of the data in another provider's environment or in your own IT environment. The data should be provided to you, or at least be made accessible to you, in a commonly used format that is accessible and useful to you regardless of the platform. Unless you have specified the format in which the data will be returned, it is likely that a cloud provider will supply your data in a proprietary or otherwise inaccessible format. If data is presented in a format you cannot use, you may incur additional costs in order to convert the data to a usable format as well as additional licensing or other costs in order to achieve the needed conversion.

Converting data from one format to another can be an expensive proposition. Costs for such an effort can vary widely. Among other things, a person seeking to convert data from one format to another must assess:

1) the format in which the data is presented;
2) the size of each data store to be converted;
3) the platform architecture of the data as presented;
4) the platform architecture of the desired data model;
5) the availability of the computing resources and inter-platform connectivity;
6) the design changes in the data models;
7) the age of the data and the frequency of updates;
8) the quality or state of the data;
9) the privacy and sensitivity of the content in the data to be converted;
10) the availability of the appropriate tool for conversion;
11) the availability of personnel with the skills needed to reformat the data; and
12) the importance of the data in question to your operations.

---

7 As used in this chapter, the term "data portability" refers to the customer's ability to use the customer's data in any environment and not just in the cloud vendor's environment. In other words, data portability implies that the data is made available to the customer in formats that are not proprietary or otherwise limited to use only in the service provider's environment. The term "data portability" also has become important given the requirements of article 20 of the European Union's General Data Protection Regulation (GDPR) as well as other regimes and requirements. Note, however, that the article 20 requirements are broader.

Data conversion often is possible only if the target format (i.e., *your* format) supports the same data features and constructs of the source data (in this case, the data you receive back from your cloud vendor). The conversion effort can be particularly difficult if the data is stored in a complex or proprietary data format. Further, in some cases, the customer may need to re-enter some data to help assure it is accurately converted.

Each of the issues listed above also may affect the time needed to export the data, regardless of format, from the cloud vendor's system and uploading to another cloud vendor's environment or to your organization's environment. Consequently, when reviewing the time available for data transfer at the end of your relationship with a cloud provider, ensure that the cloud vendor retains the data for a period sufficient to achieve a successful transfer to your new cloud vendor or to your own environment. Many cloud services agreements are silent on transition periods or affirmatively state that data will be deleted immediately upon termination. Neither option is satisfactory for a customer that wants its data returned or would like the data transferred to a new service provider. During planning for cloud vendor engagement, a customer should think through how the data will be returned. Preferably, as part of the planning for engagement of a cloud services provider, the customer should clearly understand its options for data transfer and develop strategies to manage risks associated with retention and return of its data.[8]

When reviewing a cloud services agreement, the customer also should ensure that data is maintained by the cloud provider or by your organization with the format and integrity needed to address your organization's data retention and destruction obligations. The customer should ensure that the data's characteristics and integrity do not change when transferring, storing, or archiving data. Your organization may also have data retention requirements established by regulations governing the industry sector in which it operates.[9] In the United States, the regulatory requirements depend upon your organization's industry sector and a variety of other factors. U.S. privacy laws currently focus upon the use and requirements for the type of data collected. For example, the Health Insurance Portability and Accountability Act (HIPAA)[10] and the Health Information Technology for Economic and Clinical Health Act (HITECH)[11] are laws governing the collection and use of individuals' health information by health care providers, insurance companies, and others who may have access to or use an individual's personal health information.

The Gramm-Leach-Bliley Act, related statutes, and their implementing regulations establish some of the requirements governing use and collection of financial

---

8 These strategies could include maintaining backup repositories for data a customer stores in the cloud as well as negotiation of transition responsibilities with the cloud vendor.

9 A few examples include the following: (1) the Sarbanes-Oxley Act, as amended, 15 U.S.C. §§ 7201 *et seq.*; (2) the Health Insurance Portability and Accountability Act, as amended, 42 U.S.C. §§ 17901 *et seq.*; (3) the Health Information Technology for Economic and Clinical Health Act, as amended, 42 U.S.C. § 17902 *et seq.*; (4) the Gramm-Leach-Bliley Act, as amended, 15 U.S.C. §§ 6801 *et seq.*; (e) the Federal Power Act, as amended, 16 U.S.C. § 825(a); the Natural Gas Act, as amended, 15 U.S.C. § 717 *et seq.*; and many others.

10 The Health the Insurance Portability and Accountability Act, as amended, 42 U.S.C. §§ 17901 *et seq.*

11 The Health Information Technology for Economic and Clinical Health Act, as amended, 42 U.S.C. § 17902 *et seq.* HIPAA and HITECH govern what U.S. "covered entities" are required to do to protect the health information regarding individuals, including the flowdown of confidentiality requirements to persons and entities they retain to assist the covered entities in the operation of their services or facilities.

information,[12] as does the Fair Credit Reporting Act,[13] among others. In addition, given that a number of the data-related or privacy statutes do not pre-empt state law, many U.S. state governments have instituted additional requirements regarding the use and collection of data. One example of state action affecting the retention and use of data in the cloud in the United States is the proliferation of data breach notification statutes. All 50 U.S. states have adopted requirements for data breach notification. Although there are similarities between these 50 enactments, there also are significant differences in those statutes. For example, the statutes differ on: (1) when a person must be notified of a breach affecting their information; (2) how notification must be delivered; (3) who must be notified (the affected individual and/or law enforcement, state consumer protection authorities, state attorneys general, and others); (4) what triggers a breach; and so forth.[14]

In addition to statutory and regulatory requirements, the contracts or other commitments your organization has undertaken with your customers, business partners, and suppliers are likely to have some terms addressing the confidentiality and retention of data provided, stored, or developed during the relationship. If you decide to utilize cloud services for your organization's data processing or storage needs, it will be important that existing and future third-party agreements and commitments made to others are understood and are met. Organizations providing products or services to government agencies using government funds (either as a contractor or a grant recipient), or as a subcontractor to another private sector company that is a government supplier or grantee, will have data retention and records requirements applying to their performance under such contracts. Further, many companies procuring products or services for their own use may be required to comply with certain government regulatory requirements due to your customer's obligations in its government contract. In either case, your organization is likely to have audit and records- and data-retention obligations that should be considered when engaging a cloud vendor.[15]

Records and data retention needs also arise whenever your organization is involved in litigation, investigations, or audits. Given that many records and the data associated with your operations or customers now are online, access to metadata as part of discovery requests or investigative demands has been the subject of considerable litigation in the United States. Metadata, simply, is data describing other data. Metadata often is used for web pages via a metatag describing the content, where the data was generated (on what device), in what format, who created the data and when, who modified the data and when, and who can access or update the data.[16] All of this information may be useful

---

12 The Gramm-Leach-Bliley Act, as amended, 15 U.S.C. §§ 6801 *et seq.*

13 The Fair Credit Reporting Act, as amended, 15 U.S.C. §§ 1681 *et seq.*, was enacted to promote the accuracy, fairness, and privacy of consumer information held in the files of consumer reporting agencies. It establishes requirements regarding the permissible uses of consumer credit reports, background checks, and related issues.

14 As of this writing, no federal law requires a uniform approach to breach notification, nor does such a law pre-empt state law creativity in this arena. State laws will be enforced as applicable and will be read to mandate additional requirements. Although there have been attempts to enact federal legislation pre-empting state laws in this arena, none of this legislation has been enacted to date.

15 *See, e.g.,* 10 U.S.C. § 2313, as amended, and 48 C.F.R. pt. 4, subpart 4.7 (Contractor Records Retention).

16 For example, the metadata for digital images now often includes information regarding the date and time of capture, a file name, the device settings when the image was captured (f-stop, exposure, and the like), and the geolocation of the capture.

or important to discovery for litigation, an investigation, or an audit. Failing to preserve the metadata for data stored in the cloud or elsewhere can adversely impact your organization's position or credibility when discovery or an audit or investigation is occurring. Your organization therefore should assure that it has a records and data retention program and policy, and that you take appropriate measures to comply with your policy. You also should have procedures and a process for preserving or retaining data and metadata whenever an audit, investigation, or litigation ensues.[17] Furthermore, when deciding to engage a cloud vendor for your data services needs, understanding the actual processing of your data and the cloud vendor's approach to data retention (including retention of metadata) and storage is important. A few issues to understand when contracting with the cloud vendor are:

1) What happens to your data when it is uploaded to the cloud vendor's cloud? Or when your data is transferred back to your entity or to another environment?

2) Is the metadata preserved as created, stored and transferred? Or will the processing and handling of your data in the cloud vendor's environment "remove" the metadata or write over the metadata?

3) What process will be followed to initiate a litigation hold or to otherwise make certain the data is available for access and review by your team when handling a claim, audit or investigation?

These and other issues are some of the questions to assess as you enter into and implement the cloud services relationship. The answers to these questions may require your organization to take additional action to preserve data apart from the cloud environment. If you cannot reach satisfactory terms with the cloud vendor on these issues, but still must move ahead due to your infrastructure needs, will any of your internal processes or procedures require changes in order to meet your compliance and operational needs? Which compliance requirements will be supported by the cloud environment, and what changes in your practices will be needed? A clear understanding of the impact of the cloud environment on your existing operations is required; otherwise, your operations and compliance requirements may not be met.

Termination assistance obligations and data return or destruction requirements are additional recommended provisions for your cloud services agreement. Termination assistance clauses should always be included in a cloud services agreement in order to help assure the smooth transition of your data and operations back to your data center or to another service provider. In most cases, your organization will need a reasonable timeframe to effect the transition, including the download or transfer of your data from the cloud vendor's environment. Your agreement also should specify that the data remain available during, at a minimum, the agreed-upon transition period. The transition also may require technical or other assistance from the cloud vendor, as well as cooperation with your internal team and/or your new cloud services provider. Your contract should describe the:

---

17 For an introductory discussion of these issues, *see* Philip J. Favro, *A New Frontier in Electronic Discovery: Preserving and Obtaining Metadata*, 13 B.U. J. Sci. &Tech. L. 1 (2007). This article is only one of the many law review articles and practice notes available discussing this important issue. In addition, several decisions regarding discovery disputes and other controversies involving access to metadata have been decided by courts, usually in the pretrial and discovery process.

1) costs associated with these services;
2) level of assistance and expertise required (such as access to qualified technical staff);
3) timeframe for assistance, including the length of the assistance period and availability requirements;
4) materials to be provided from your current cloud environment;
5) format for the data/data portability; and
6) the additional cost for transition services (if any).

Typical termination assistance clauses may require payment of additional fees so be sure to understand when and how additional fees will apply. These clauses also frequently include requirements for good-faith completion of the transition services, reasonable cooperation in completing the transition (both with your internal team and with any replacement cloud vendor), and continuing obligations to maintain your access to the data for the transition period. Without these assurances and terms, your organization's ability to function well likely will be impaired. Ensuring that your organization will have access to needed characteristics of the data when uploaded, created, stored, and returned is critical.

Many organizations require the cloud vendor to provide a transition services plan early in the relationship between the parties. Some organizations ask to see a plan during the procurement process, and others require development of such a plan early in the implementation of the services. At a minimum, the transition plan should be a required component of your termination clause. Some cloud vendors may attempt to convince your team that transition issues are difficult to define, especially given the fluid and ever-developing nature of technology and business models in this arena. Although this claim often is true, the cloud vendor should have considerable experience in managing and implementing cloud engagements, and should therefore have at least some expertise in managing a transition and in providing the necessary services to effect an orderly transition back to your own environment or to another cloud vendor. If your cloud vendor selection process does not examine this element of the services from a cloud vendor, it should; otherwise, your organization's operations may be adversely impacted.

Finally, the customer should understand what happens to its data when its termination assistance period and transition has completed. The cloud provider should be required to return or destroy the data that you have uploaded to its cloud upon completion of its termination obligations so that the data your organization needs to protect or control is not compromised. A cloud provider may push back on requests for destruction of data at termination and may require payment of additional fees in order to do so. Your organization should have a clear understanding of the way data is stored and managed in the cloud vendor's cloud environment. You also should understand how the cloud vendor will use data created while in the cloud and what control or rights the cloud vendor claims over data developed in the course of providing services.

C. Use and Ownership of Data—Including Data Developed During Delivery of Services

When an entity stores data in the cloud, it no doubt must revise the data or use it to produce new data. Although updated data potentially could be deemed a derivative work of the original data uploaded by the customer, who owns the data generated due to use of the cloud environment?

To date, there is no universally recognized standard addressing the ownership of data uploaded in the cloud. Consequently, any entity or person choosing to upload data to a cloud service should carefully review and understand the specific terms and conditions for the service. What do those terms say about your data? How can the cloud provider use your data and/or access data stored in its cloud for the cloud vendor's own purposes?

Accordingly, any organization considering a cloud services relationship should carefully review and understand what the cloud provider's agreement states regarding ownership of data, what the cloud services provider can do with your data while it is in the cloud vendor's cloud environment, and where the data will be physically stored. In addition, some agreements have included clauses that allow the cloud vendor to use data that is "anonymized" for trend analysis and marketing purposes. Your organization should assess whether your industry's requirements would permit such uses. Among other things, understanding the characteristics of the "anonymized" data when used by the cloud provider, and whether such use is permissible under the regulatory requirements for your industry, is critical.

III. Crafting Appropriate Transition Clauses

To illustrate the concepts discussed in this chapter, Part III will analyze three sample contract clauses on termination of the cloud relationship. These clauses are taken from actual, publicly available terms and conditions appearing on the webpages of cloud services providers of various sizes. Names identifying the particular cloud services provider have been removed, and some editing of the clause has occurred to focus the language on termination rights and issues. Each sample is followed by commentary on the issues raised by the clause.

Sample 1

Term. The term of this Agreement will commence on the Effective Date and will remain in effect until terminated under this Section. Any notice of termination of this Agreement by either party to the other must include a Termination Date that complies with the notice periods below.

Termination for Convenience. You may terminate this Agreement for any reason by providing us notice and closing your account for all Services. We may terminate this Agreement for any reason by providing you at least 30 days' advance notice.

Termination for Cause. (i) Either party may terminate this Agreement for cause if the other party is in material breach of this Agreement and the material breach remains uncured for a period of 30 days from receipt of notice by the other party. No later than the Termination Date, you will close your account. (ii) We may also terminate this Agreement immediately upon notice to you (A) for cause if we have the right to suspend as otherwise provided in these terms, (B) if our relationship with a third-party partner who provides software or other technology we use to provide the Service Offerings expires, terminates or requires us to change the way we provide the software or other technology as part of the Services, or (C) in order to comply with the law or requests of governmental entities.

Sample 1 does not establish a firm termination date or contract term for the cloud services. The agreement is "evergreen"—that is, it will remain in effect until terminated.

Both the customer and the cloud vendor may terminate the cloud services for convenience upon a minimum of 30-days advance written notice. Both parties also may terminate for material breach 30 days following notice of breach.

The Termination for Cause provision establishes a cure period of 30 days following receipt of notice from the nonbreaching party. Note, however, subpart (ii) of this provision provides immediate termination by the cloud vendor upon notice to the customer if other provisions allow a suspension of the service; if third-party products or services used by the cloud vendor's service expire, terminate, or require changes to the way the cloud vendor provides its cloud service; or to comply with law or requests of governmental entities. Each of these elements of "for-cause" termination by the cloud vendor requires further explanation and discussion.

First, a customer should clearly understand when and for what reason the cloud vendor may "suspend" the service. If your organization requires 24-7 access to data stored in the cloud, what alternatives or backups are available to allow you to function during a suspension? Have you backed up your data for use in these circumstances?

Second, subpart (ii)(B) signals that the cloud vendor is reliant upon third parties to provide at least some of the functionality for the service. Although all information technology and related services rely to varying degrees on third-party product or services, it is important to understand to what degree your particular cloud vendor is relying on another party to perform the services you are requesting. If, for example, the cloud vendor you are considering is so heavily reliant on another provider to perform the services, then perhaps you should re-examine the justification for the relationship. This author has been involved in resolution of cloud provider nonperformance issues where the cloud providers have collected fees for cloud services in advance from the customer while hosting the customer's data on a site provided by another cloud vendor. When the original cloud providers failed to pay the subcontractor, the subcontractor then shut down the cloud vendor's site for nonpayment, placing the customer in a very difficult position.

Third, the "comply with the law or requests of governmental entities" requirement also should be addressed in more detail, particularly if your organization is operating under specific industry requirements (as in the energy, utilities, healthcare, or financials services arenas). Typically, a customer should consider requiring release only in response to a subpoena or court order. In addition, the customer should consider requiring some notice of the request and an ability to contest the release of certain information when appropriate.

Note also that the clause does not address data turnback or assistance to be provided at the end of the relationship. There also is no data retention or retrieval period specified. No termination assistance and no process for retrieval of your data at the end of the contract is addressed, nor is destruction of your data.

Sample 2

1.   *Term. This Agreement is valid for the duration of the applicable Services Period specified in the Order Form which this Agreement accompanies, including any renewals thereof. After expiration of the initial Services Period, the Services shall automatically renew for consecutive one (1) year terms unless either party provides the other party with written notice of its intention not to renew no later than thirty (30) days prior to the end of the then current term.*

2.   *Termination and Suspension.*

(a)   *Services provided under this Agreement shall be provided for the Services Period defined in Customer's Order Form, unless earlier suspended or terminated in accordance with this Agreement or the Order Form. Upon expiration or termination of the Services Period, Customer will no longer be allowed to access or use the Services.*

(b)   *Notwithstanding the foregoing, at any time within sixty (60) days after the termination or expiration of the Services Period, Customer may request Cloud Vendor in writing to return Customer Data that may be stored on or otherwise existing in the Services at the time of the request. Upon Cloud Vendor's receipt of such request, Cloud Vendor shall within a reasonable time return a copy of the Customer Data stored on the Services at the time of the request to Customer in Cloud Vendor's standard format or such other format as Cloud Vendor may reasonably choose. At the end of such sixty (60) day period, and except as may be required by law, Cloud Vendor may delete or otherwise render inaccessible any of the Customer Data that remains in the Services. Customer agrees that Cloud Vendor shall have no additional obligation to continue to hold, export or return Customer Data and that Cloud Vendor will have no liability whatsoever for deletion of Customer Data pursuant to these terms.*

(c)   *Cloud Vendor may immediately suspend or terminate on a temporary basis Customer's access to or use of the Services if Customer violates any provision of this Agreement or the Order Form, or if (in Cloud Vendor's reasonable judgment) the Services or any component thereof are about to suffer a threat to security or functionality. Cloud Vendor will use reasonable efforts to provide advance notice to Customer of such suspension or termination. If any cause for the temporary suspension/termination is not cured by Customer to Cloud Vendor's satisfaction within thirty (30) days after Cloud Vendor's written notice thereof, then Cloud Vendor may, in addition to any other rights and remedies that Cloud Vendor may have, terminate the Services permanently without liability or refund to Customer of any kind.*

(d)   *Either party may terminate this Agreement and/or any applicable Services in the event the other party breaches any of the terms of this Agreement and fails to cure such breach within thirty (30) days after receiving written notice thereof. In the event of a breach by Customer, Customer's use of the Services may be suspended during the applicable cure period.*

(e)   *Provisions that survive termination or expiration of this Agreement are those relating to limitation of liability, disclaimers, indemnity, payment and others which by their nature are intended to survive.*

Sample 2 relies on an order form that specifies the applicable services period. Order forms often include additional terms that may impact the rights and obligations under the cloud agreement and as such should be reviewed closely. The term of the agreement is also "evergreen," for additional one-year periods, unless a party provides notice 30 days in advance of the end of the applicable period. Managing contract periods and renewals applicable to an agreement are important elements of the overall management of the relationship for your cloud services agreement. First, the contract period often locks in a particular pricing model for that term. Second, renewal of a contract can be simplified with an evergreen term because neither your organization nor the cloud vendor must provide a notice or other communication to continue the contract relationship, and as such your organization would be less likely to experience a gap in services delivery while a contract extension or amendment is completed. Further, the notice period for a contract renewal— whether the contract is evergreen or is renewed by an action or contract amendment for a specified period—provides the parties an opportunity to review the contract relationship and decide whether to continue to work together. The customer's assessment of the cloud vendor relationship should be ongoing, however, because a simple notice period of 30 days is unlikely to provide a sufficient time to conduct a reasonable procurement process for a replacement cloud vendor, nor is 30 days enough time to plan a transition (whether back to the customer's internal site or to another cloud vendor).

The Termination and Suspension provision states in subpart (a) that the customer will not be able to access or use the services upon expiration or termination of the services under the cloud agreement. This language would be a concern without subpart (b). Subpart (b) establishes a 60-day period following termination or expiration of the services period for the customer to request the cloud vendor to return customer data "that may be stored on or otherwise existing in the Services at the time of the Request." Presumably, "Customer Data" is defined elsewhere in the agreement. Note that the provision goes on to provide that the cloud vendor will provide a copy of the customer data "within a reasonable time" following the customer's request. The provision also specifies that that customer data will be provided "in the Cloud Vendor's standard format or such other format as Cloud Vendor may reasonably choose." Thus, if a different format is required or preferred by the customer, the customer should negotiate or otherwise request the specific format for data return.

Subpart (b) also provides that the cloud vendor will delete "or otherwise render inaccessible" the customer's data that remains in the service at the end of the 60-day period "except as required by law." The customer should inquire about the particular laws that may require maintenance or retention of a copy of the customer's data on or in the cloud vendor's service. It also may be important to understand the cloud vendor's data retention policies, and how and when the data you store in the cloud may become unavailable. Overall, ensuring your data is available is paramount to your operations. As such, one approach for the customer is to assure that your organization does not enter into an agreement that allows a cloud vendor to destroy its data unless a reasonable period has been established for data transition back to the customer or to another cloud vendor, or perhaps the passage of a more lengthy period of time passes before the cloud vendor is allowed to destroy your data. Given that having access to its data is a critical need for most organizations, a crisp focus on data turnback should include a requirement that your cloud vendors not destroy your data without a reasonable period of availability and transition (including notices to your organization and other steps before the data is actually destroyed).

Subpart (c) describes the circumstances that may result in immediate termination or suspension of the customer's access to or use of the services: (1) if the customer violates any provision of the agreement or order form or (2) if, in the cloud vendor's reasonable judgment, the services or any component of the services are about to suffer a threat to security or functionality." In response to the former, the customer should consider negotiating in a limitation on the provision and including a cure period. For example, the customer may seek to specify that a *material* breach of its obligations be the grounds for termination or suspension, and not just any violation however minor. In response to item (2), consider amending the provision to require the cloud vendor to expeditiously resolve the security or functionality issue, requiring notice to the customer of the security or functionality concern, and allowing the customer an out from the agreement if the cloud vendor fails to restore service within a reasonable period. Your focus on these issues will depend largely upon the nature of the data you have stored in the service as well as the data's criticality to your operations.

Note also that the clause allows a breach termination by the nonbreaching party if the breaching party fails to cure a breach within 30 days after receiving notice. The first concern with this clause is the requirement that the cure be made to the cloud vendor's satisfaction. Seeking a standard of commercially reasonable cure would be advised, rather than the cloud vendor's satisfaction. Second, 30 days may not be sufficient time to effect a cure, depending upon the breach. The customer should consider seeking a longer term or an ability to extend the cure period upon a showing of reasonable efforts to effect a cure. Finally, another way to address this provision is to negotiate levels of severity of the breach, including appropriate periods depending upon the impact of the breach to the other party's operations or ability to function. In any case, the goal is to provide your organization with some flexibility and a reasonable means to address a difficult situation without adversely affecting your operations and your data.

Sample 3

(a) *This Agreement shall commence on the Effective Date and shall continue in force for [x] years or until it is terminated in accordance with the Agreement.*

(b) *Without prejudice to its other rights pursuant to law and this Agreement, if a Party is in material breach of one of its obligations under this Agreement, the other Party will have the right to terminate the Agreement by sending the other Party written notification via registered mail of any such breach, with the express invitation to remedy such breach within 30 (thirty) days of the date of receipt of the same notice. If such Party fails to remedy the material breach within such term, the Agreement shall be terminated.*

(c) *To the extent permitted by the applicable law, either Party may by written notice to the other Party immediately terminate this Agreement where the other Party ceases to carry on business, is unable to pay its debts when they fall due, is declared bankrupt, or an order is made or a resolution passed for the winding up of that other Party or the appointment of an administrator, receiver, liquidator or manager of that other Party.*

(d) *Either Party may terminate without cause the Agreement upon [x] ([x]) days [sic] written notice to the other Party sent via registered mail.*

Sample 3 establishes a term as a period of a year or years. The clause does not provide a renewal process, so the customer may wish to add one.

Subpart (b) provides a termination for material breach, with an opportunity to cure within 30 days of receipt of the breach notice. The comments made in the analysis for Sample 2 also would be useful here.

Subpart (c) provides that immediate termination may occur in the event of a bankruptcy or other financial distress of a party. Both provisions are mutual—that is, either party can terminate on these for-cause grounds.

The fourth paragraph allows either party to terminate the agreement for convenience upon [x] days of receipt of a written notice.

What is missing from Sample 3? As presently drafted, there is no discussion of (1) an obligation to return customer data (in any format); (2) a process for return of customer data; (3) the cloud vendor's obligation to destroy or otherwise render inaccessible customer data; and (4) making customer data available upon termination for customer retrieval.

Each of these issues requires careful consideration of the need to preserve your access to data and the processes for management of the contract and the transition of your data upon termination.

It bears repeating that the three samples included above were taken from actual cloud services terms posted on a cloud vendor's website. In fact, two of the cloud vendors' sites allowed a customer to simply click through the site and procure the services immediately based solely on the terms displayed on the cloud vendor site.

IV. Conclusion

A particular cloud services agreement may or may not address the various issues raised in this chapter and elsewhere. The express terms of the cloud services agreement will govern your rights and obligations, as well as those of the cloud provider, regarding your data and what you can expect upon termination of the relationship, or any other part of the relationship with the cloud vendor. Without your focus on the regulatory issues, data turnback, and other needs impacted by the terms of a cloud services agreement, your organization's operational needs and continued operation may be at risk. The bottom line is that if a particular issue is important to you, make sure to negotiate the particular written terms you need with your cloud vendor in order to achieve your objective. If you are unable to do so, you should develop operational practices or procedures to help address the risk presented by a particular contract term. As mentioned throughout this book, there are few, if any, standards that currently apply to cloud services arrangements. If a particular standard or term is important to your organization, it is critical to ensure that that the issue is favorably handled in your written agreement with the cloud vendor, or that your organization has addressed the risk in other ways.

Chapter 13

Effective Cloud Negotiations—Tips and Best Practices

By Ted Claypoole with research assistance by Taylor Ey[1]

I. Introduction

Cloud contracts can be difficult to negotiate. A cloud provider's rigid pricing structure and low risk tolerance can lead to a "take it or leave it" attitude that frustrates prospective customers. Conversely, a cloud customer's hesitance to release day-to-day control of important data can lead to near-hysterical positions on information security, server location, and even exclusive use of equipment. Inexperienced cloud customers may not understand the nature of the services they are seeking, and inexperienced cloud providers have not had time to appropriately price levels of risk. Each side must trust the other in important respects.

A thoughtful, well-prepared lawyer serving as navigator can be vital for clients navigating these choppy waters. This chapter is primarily written from the position of the cloud customer, although it contains a number of items that can be helpful to cloud providers in negotiation. Although cloud providers and their extensive sales teams prepare cloud agreements every day, the customer may never have seen a cloud agreement before. Therefore, the provider generally knows what it wants and what it can do, whereas the cloud customer may not have considered all aspects of risk and cost in the cloud agreement. The lawyer may act as a voice of judgment, guiding the cloud customer through seas treacherous with risks unfamiliar to the client.

II. Talk to Your Client

A customer looking for a cloud vendor should have reasons for needing this service. Explore those reasons and encourage the cloud customer to explore its own needs before the contract discussions commence.

Is your client choosing a cloud vendor to replace a current cloud contract? If so, why the need for a change, and what problems are driving the client from the current provider? Is the client unhappy with performance? If so, then you know that negotiating strong service levels and building into the next contract a short fuse for a cost-free exit will be an important priority. Is the client unhappy with surprise price increases? Then cost predictability may be an important factor in the next cloud agreement. Did the vendor drop your client's service at any point? Then adequate back-up provisions and contingency planning will be a priority going forward. In any case, a lawyer should know what the client found objectionable about the situation it is replacing to identify client priorities for the next deal.

---

1 Ted Claypoole is a partner, and Taylor Ey is an associate, at Womble Bond Dickinson.

Is the client currently managing its data internally? Then you may need to negotiate a trial period for the client to confirm a seamless transition from company servers to the cloud. Your client may also be interested in meeting the actual humans at the cloud vendor who will be responsible for managing the cloud customer's data and negotiating for the right to replace those people or at least approve anyone who may be controlling the cloud customer's data in the future.

Although a cloud arrangement is generally considered an infrastructure or operational matter within the customer's business, a lawyer negotiating for this engagement will still want to ensure that the desires of multiple stakeholders are considered when negotiating the contract. For example, usually the cloud services will be for housing a specific set of data that is managed by either a line of business within the customer's company, or an operational entity like the human resources or marketing department. This data controller is the first, and often most important, stakeholder in the cloud contract. The money to pay for the cloud services will usually be coming out of the data owner's budget, so the data owner will likely have priorities on a multitude of cost issues, including total payments, certainty of cost, and price of scaling up the operation. The data owner will want input on the service levels agreed to by the vendor and probably the terms of extraction at the end of the agreement.

Your client will have risk management teams with a stake in the agreement, whether that responsibility lies in the legal department, audit, or a compliance group. These stakeholders will also care about service levels and what compensation and/or exit provisions the cloud customer will receive if those service levels are not met. They will also be interested in indemnities, insurance, termination rights, warranties, and any type of limitation on liability. The risk management professionals often are the negotiating lawyer's primary contact within the client organization, so the risk management issues may receive outsized attention. Although their concerns are important, a careful lawyer should take into consideration the concerns of other stakeholders as well.

The cybersecurity department is another risk-oriented player, and it will probably have specific concerns around hosting, protection, use, and return of data, as well as contingency planning, disaster recovery, and force majeure provisions. Many large companies have sophisticated data security teams that will provide their own contract exhibits describing the types and levels of security expected from a cloud vendor. The privacy officer is often a separate interested stakeholder who is less concerned about how the data is held within a database, and more concerned about the access that the cloud vendor will have to the data and what, if anything, the cloud vendor will be allowed to do with the data.

The client company's finance department will be most concerned with the cost of the services and perhaps in measuring those costs over the life of the contract. The financial group may want to compare the costs of the new venture with the costs of the internal hosting and processing the new venture will replace, so the ability to receive certain metrics from the cloud provider may be important to the finance team. Usually, if the data owners and the risk managers can keep the finance team happy, then the contract is more likely to be considered successful within the client's organization.

Also determine whether any important executives within the company have a special interest in this set of data or in the success of the cloud vendor agreement. Sometimes it doesn't matter if the rest of the stakeholders are comfortable with a deal if the company's president or chief technology officer is not satisfied. A lawyer should ask the client relationship manager whether any executives have taken an interest in this deal, and if so, talk with the executive's office or representative to collect this view of the company's priorities.

Once the lawyer has reviewed the client's current circumstances, its immediate needs, and the priorities of the important stakeholders, then the lawyer can examine the client's traditional negotiating strategies. Does the client have its own client-centric cloud agreement or favorable contractual clauses that it insists on forcing a vendor to sign? Does the client have regulatory requirements that make certain provisions non-negotiable? Does the client regularly send its data to the cloud, but only with certain assurances? The success of a negotiation can depend on whether the cloud customer client meets its predetermined institutional requirements. Even if the client has never executed a cloud contract before, it may have internal policies and procedures that must be met. A good lawyer precedes a negotiation by asking the right questions.

III. Prioritize Needs

After all the stakeholders have spoken, the lawyer for a cloud customer should build a list of the client's priorities. What are the must-have items? Are there any deal-breaker issues that would cause the client to walk away from the deal despite the effort sunk into negotiations? How much risk is the cloud customer willing to accept, and would a change in the vendor's price affect the client's risk tolerance? The lawyer can rank the client's priorities into tiers so that some terms may be traded for advantages in more important terms for the client.

What data and business processes will the client be placing in the cloud if the contract is executed? Are these processes vital to the client's day-to-day operations? How long could the client's business survive without the data and processes managed under this cloud agreement? A month? A week? A day? By raising these practical matters, a lawyer can fight past a cloud customer's short-term thinking and identify its true priorities. If the client's business could only last one day without the information managed under this cloud agreement, then contingency planning and immediately accessible backup are priorities to be attained, even at great cost.

Is the data managed under the cloud contract sensitive enough that the client is concerned a competitor might buy the cloud provider to receive a competitive advantage? If so, then the cloud provider should be willing to terminate the agreement without harm to the cloud customer if the cloud provider is purchased or controlled by any company on the customer's short list of competitors. In addition, all cloud contracts should contain restrictions on what the cloud provider can do with the information that it hosts and manages so that even upon the acquisition of the cloud provider by a competitor of the cloud customer, the cloud customer could sue if its data were used in any manner contrary to the contract.

Unless and until its lawyer asks the right questions and maps the client's priorities, the cloud customer is not prepared to begin negotiations. The exercise of finding and listing the most important client priorities helps both client and lawyer expend their efforts in the right places, push for a better deal, and ultimately feel happier with the deal when the contract is executed.

IV. Perform the Vendor Research (Begin with an RFP)

Many cloud providers develop mature contract management systems granting no flexibility to negotiate the risk or price terms. In particular, because cloud providers are offering one resource—access to their servers—to many different customers, the providers cannot or will not allow intricate customizations to their customers. However, this is not true for all companies offering cloud services, so do not limit your client to considering only a single provider.

Some cloud providers will respond to a company Request for Proposals (RFP) on cloud service. If your client is willing to take this route, then it is most likely to find a contract that best fits its needs. By beginning with an RFP, the cloud customer makes the effort before a contract is negotiated to think through the customer's priorities, price sensitivities, and risk tolerance. This exercise not only increases the likelihood of a better choice of vendor and a better deal from the vendor, but also a customer who is happier with the result because management is more certain that it received what it needed. Creating an RFP is more work than simply negotiating a single deal with a single provider, but it turns the tables so that the customer controls the process, rather than, as in most negotiations, enabling the vendor to use its superior knowledge of risks and rewards in the cloud to dictate terms to customers.

Even if a customer is unwilling to begin the process of creating an RFP and sending it out to dozens of prospective cloud providers, the cloud customer should still explore all of the possible vendors that could meet its needs. These reviews are crucial. The more a customer relies on one prospective vendor, the more that vendor can set the terms of agreement. By considering alternatives to the largest and best-known providers, a cloud customer may discover dozens of small- and mid-sized cloud providers that are more likely to customize their approaches to an engagement than the top-five big cloud providers ever would.

Furthermore, the market now supports boutique cloud products that may perfectly match the needs of companies in regulated industries like health care, energy, or financial services. Serious research into the relevant cloud providers can be the best step toward a successful cloud venture. Do not allow a cloud customer to consider only Amazon Web Services (AWS) and Google Cloud on the grounds that time is too short to examine other options. Without the crucial first step of researching and choosing the best cloud vendor for the job, a customer is likely doomed to pay too much and accept too much risk in the contract.

V. Know the Options

Your client may be aware of the types of cloud services that vendors offer and what features and protections can be purchased, but it would nevertheless help all parties involved if you have studied the options and the risks involved. Many of the largest cloud providers offer standard packages that are differentiated by how much the cloud customer is willing to pay.

For example, for the lowest-cost package, a cloud vendor is generally unwilling to negotiate any of the significant terms in its standard agreement or service level agreement. If the cloud customer is willing to pay a substantially higher price, however, then the options open for more attractive terms and for stricter service levels. Demanding the lowest possible prices plus the highest possible protections and risk-shifting is likely to lead only to frustration, especially when the provider has developed its system to match customer cost to provider risk. Researching these issues before the negotiation can save time and money.

VI. Focus on the Real Security Risks

For nearly every small- to medium-sized client company, placing data with AWS, Microsoft Azure, or IBM Cloud provides much better protections from hacking attacks than the client's own data center, which may consist of three servers in a basement. The big cloud providers spend many millions of dollars on data security each year, hire many of the best information-protection professionals available, and work closely with governments across the world to anticipate and counter threats large and small. Most companies cannot come close to achieving this level of protection using on-premises storage. Thus, contrary to what many lawyers and their clients believe, wresting real data-security promises from the large providers may not be difficult, and extra contractual language on levels of data security may not be substantially more protective of client information sent into these clouds. Fighting for every inch in this space can be a waste of everyone's time.

Conversely, a cloud customer may devote insufficient attention to other problems that may arise when important business data leaves the customer's hands, such as the risk that a cloud service provider may cease business, or the risk that the cloud provider holds the customer's data hostage at the end of a contract term. The cloud provider's fiscal health is a more important issue than many customers believe. For decades, the adage "Nobody was ever fired for buying IBM" assumed that the solidity and dominance of the larger technology organizations serve as a protection against any sort of failure. Although the current solid financial status of a Google, Amazon, Microsoft, or IBM may be foundations not worth questioning, many cloud providers do not boast such robust balance sheets. In addition, technology companies may merge or become acquired, moving a cloud customer's business into an entirely different structure. Lawyers for cloud customers should at least raise the issue of business security because a failure of the cloud provider could shut down a cloud customer's business.

More likely to cause trouble would be the end-of-term requirements built into a cloud contract. The cloud customer's lawyer should insist not only on the safe return of the customer's cloud-resident data, but that the data is returned in a short timeframe, in a format usable by the cloud customer, and all at a reasonable cost. Remember that, generally speaking, when the cloud customer terminates a cloud agreement, the customer is not only repudiating the services of the cloud provider, but is likely planning to patronize one of the provider's rivals. Therefore, at the end of a cloud contract, the provider has no natural reason to accommodate the wishes of a terminating customer, and experience has demonstrated that many such providers chafe at requests for accommodation. The primary time in the relationship when a cloud provider wants to meet the customer's wishes as much as possible is prior to initial commitment, before the provider is holding the customer's crown jewels on its servers. Thus, a good attorney for a cloud customer will force the cloud provider to address the cloud customer's termination needs in the initial contract. Otherwise, the cloud customer is left to the questionable mercies of the jilted provider upon termination for recovery of its important business data.

In addition, some cloud customers may perceive a security risk from the possibility of a government gaining access to the cloud customer's data without notice. Clearly, this risk is unlikely to occur if the customer holds such sensitive data itself. However, when the data passes to a third party, then the data may be vulnerable to access, review, and analysis by a government actor that serves a "silent subpoena" on the cloud provider, forbidding the provider to give notice to its customer. This risk may not be negotiated away in many circumstances, so if the customer holds or creates data that it must shield from a government where the customer is resident, the customer may want to avoid placing that particular data in the cloud. Some cloud providers have tried a "passive solution" to address an order to allow government access to a cloud customer's data without providing notice to the cloud customer. These companies keep a banner up on their websites that states that the provider has *not* been served with such an access notice and gag order. When served with such a notice, the company plans to remove the website banner, and any customer who checks can assume that the government has served a gag-ordered access request. Although not perfect, and possibly not legal, this strategy can give the cloud customer some comfort.

In short, a narrow focus on hacking defenses misses the point of cloud risks to customer data. Several data risks exist in the cloud agreement, and the lawyer should be attuned to all of them.

VII. Technical Issues for Cloud Providers

A prospective cloud customer should check technical interoperability issues before beginning contract negotiations. Will the cloud service provider be able to host, manage, or operate the customer's applications within the service provider's cloud? Any number of technical issues can arise that would make a particular cloud service offering an impractical option for a particular customer. Where systems are mismatched, often the technical issues are caused by faults in the customer's system, rather than the cloud provider's system, so each prospective cloud customer should deeply review its platforms and operating systems to confirm that they will access and work with the cloud system. In addition, each application intended for the cloud should be tested to confirm that it can properly operate in a cloud environment. As time passes, more and more systems and applications are cloud-ready, but many customers still have legacy systems with eccentric configurations and even older hardware or software unable to work properly outside of its original environment. Involving the technology team early in the process is important.

Although cloud providers tend to be understandably protective of access to their systems, they will generally be happy to provide their own technicians to meet with the technical team from any prospective customer. The technologists should be able to tell their business management that a software and cloud solution is appropriate for the job well before a contract negotiation begins. However, in some circumstances, a prospective cloud customer's lawyer may need to check and confirm that the particular cloud solution at hand will provide the anticipated benefits for both parties; otherwise, the entire negotiation exercise will fail.

Sometimes interoperation issues arise because the cloud customer plans to use multiple vendors to manage an entire set of business processes. These issues can become more complex and may entail the lawyer negotiating a test run or at least an interoperability check for all of the parties before the final contract negotiations can begin. Occasionally, the cloud provider will plan to use subcontractors to provide some or all of the services the customer anticipates needing, requiring the cloud customer to determine whether a subcontracted management of its data is a good idea, which may require including additional obligations into the agreement that bind both contractor and subcontractor. In any case, the lawyers should be aware of technical and business complexities in the proposed arrangement, and should determine whether such issues can be managed before the final deal is discussed.

VIII. Managing Client Expectations While Meeting Your Ethical Obligations

Your client has a right to zealous representation. Your client also has a right to the full measure of your expertise and judgment. If you do not understand the nature and the risks to your client of contracting for cloud services, then misdirected zealousness is all that you can provide your client. How can a lawyer negotiate a business deal for installation of software or for a cloud service that will take over entire operations of the client's business without understanding, at least at a basic level, how that technology will create value and risk for the client? Cloud services involve all of the operational complexities and business risks described in this book, and a lawyer would not only be remiss, but would likely violate the rules of legal ethics, if the lawyer managed a litigation or negotiation without understanding these complexities and risks.

Rule 1.1 of the ABA's *Model Rules of Professional Conduct* reads: "A lawyer shall provide competent representation to a client. Competent representation requires the legal knowledge, skill, thoroughness and preparation reasonably necessary for the representation."[2] This rule has been interpreted to include a lawyer's situational awareness during client representation, including relevant business and even technical matters that are important to a client's legal needs. The comments to the rule tie its requirements to a basic knowledge of changing technology, stating: "To maintain the requisite knowledge and skill, a lawyer should keep abreast of changes in the law and its practice, including the benefits and risks associated with relevant technology. . . ."[3] Recognizing the rapid pace of technological change, state bar regulators have been emphasizing technological competence for lawyers. Twenty-seven states have adopted a rule analogous to the ABA's Rule 1.1.[4]

U.S. state bar ethics opinions are beginning to address attorney responsibility for knowing and understanding the technology associated with cloud computing. The ABA has compiled a growing collection of cloud ethics opinions, and interested attorneys should check this site for the latest cases.[5] Most of these cases involve lawyers

---

2 MODEL RULES OF PROF'L CONDUCT R. 1.1.

3 *Id*. cmt. 8.

4 DEL. LAWYERS' RULES OF PROF'L CONDUCT R. 1.1 cmt. 8 (2013); PA. RULES OF PROF'L CONDUCT R. 1.1 cmt. 8 (2013); N.M. RULES OF PROF'L CONDUCT R. 16-101 cmt. 9 (2013); CONN. RULES OF PROF'L CONDUCT R. 1.1 cmt. (2014); KAN. RULES OF PROF'L CONDUCT R. 1.1 cmt. 8 (2014); ARK. RULES OF PROF'L CONDUCT R. 1.1 cmt. 8 (2014); IDAHO RULES OF PROF'L CONDUCT R. 1.1 cmt. 8 (2014); N.C. RULES OF PROF'L CONDUCT R. 1.1 cmt 8 (2014); WYO. RULES OF PROF'L CONDUCT R. 1.1 cmt. 6 (2014); ARIZ. RULES OF PROF'L CONDUCT R. 1.1 cmt. 6 (2015); W. VA. RULES OF PROF'L CONDUCT R. 1.1 cmt. 8 (2015); MINN. RULES OF PROF'L CONDUCT R. 1.1 cmt. 8 (2015); N.Y. RULES OF PROF'L CONDUCT R. 1.1 cmt. 8 (2015); OHIO RULES OF PROF'L CONDUCT R. 1.1 cmt. 8 (2015); UTAH RULES OF PROF'L CONDUCT R. 1.1 cmt. 8 (2015); MASS. RULES OF PROF'L CONDUCT R. 1.1 cmt. 8 (2015); IOWA RULES OF PROF'L CONDUCT R. 32:1:1 (2015); ILL. RULES OF PROF'L CONDUCT R. 1.1 cmt. 8 (2016); N.H. RULES OF PROF'L CONDUCT R. 1.1 cmt. 8 (2016); VA. RULES OF PROF'L CONDUCT R. 1.1 cmt. 6 (2016); N.D. RULES OF PROF'L CONDUCT R. 1.1 cmt. 5 (2016); COLO. RULES OF PROF'L CONDUCT R. 1.1 cmt. 8 (2016); OKLA. RULES OF PROF'L CONDUCT R. 1.1 cmt. 6 (2016); WASH. RULES OF PROF'L CONDUCT R. 1.1 cmt. 8 (2016); FLA. RULES OF PROF'L CONDUCT R. 4-1.1 cmt. (2017); WIS. RULES OF PROF'L CONDUCT R. 20:1.1 cmt. 8 (2017); TENN. RULES OF PROF'L CONDUCT R. 1.1 cmt. 8 (2017).

5 American Bar Association, *Cloud Ethics Opinions Around the U.S.*, AM. BAR ASS'N, https://www.americanbar.org/groups/departments_offices/legal_technology_resources/resources/charts_fyis/cloud-ethics-chart.html (last visited May 2, 2018).

negotiating with cloud providers for cloud platforms that the lawyers intend to use, not lawyers negotiating cloud agreements on behalf of clients. However, the findings are instructive. For example, the State Bar of Arizona, in an opinion on maintaining client files in cloud storage, stated that it is:

> important that lawyers recognize their own competence limitations regarding computer security measures and take the necessary time and energy to become competent or alternatively consult available experts in the field. The competence requirements of [Ethics Rule] 1.1 apply not only to a lawyer's legal skills, but also generally to "those matters reasonably necessary for the representation."[6]

In any cloud agreement, it is reasonably necessary to understand how the remote nature of data storage and loss of a cloud customer's direct control over its own operations threaten confidentiality of information and the ongoing business processes. Without this understanding, a lawyer is not properly supporting cloud clients.

A 2012 New Hampshire opinion described 10 concerns for attorneys to consider before using a cloud service, including reputation of the service provider, security of stored data, ownership of data, confidentiality obligations with respect to the shared data, and data retention after an agreement is terminated.[7] The New Hampshire opinion acknowledges that "[t]here is no hard and fast rule as to what a lawyer must do with respect to each client when using cloud computing. The facts and circumstances of each case, including the type and sensitivity of client information, will dictate what reasonable protective measures a lawyer must take when using cloud computing."[8] This is also a sensible way to look at a lawyer's obligation to understand cloud contracts on behalf of cloud customers. Understanding the circumstances, including the nature of technological and business risk, is necessary to meet core ethical obligations.

A year later, the Ohio Bar issued an ethics opinion that describes how Rule 1.1's demand for technology competency requires attorneys to understand cloud storage vendor practices, including service level agreements, confidentiality safeguards, data storage locations, and possible international law issues.[9] The Ohio Bar's discussion of service level agreements is particularly relevant to lawyer's understanding risks in the cloud. Concerns raised by this opinion include:

---

6 State Bar of Ariz., Ethics Op. 09-04 (2009), http://www.azbar.org/Ethics/EthicsOpinions/ ViewEthicsOpinion?id=704.

7 N.H. Bar Ass'n, Ethics Comm. Advisory Op. 2012–13/4 (2012), https://www.nhbar.org/ethics/opinion-2012-13-04. For example, one of the 10 issues is described as follows:

> Do the terms of service state that the provider merely holds a license to the stored data, as for example Google's do? Some providers routinely inform those accessing their service that it is the provider—not the user—that "owns" the data. If the provider owns the stored data, the lawyer may run afoul of Rule 1.15, which requires that the client's property "be identified as property of the client." To comply with Rule 1.15, the provider may not "own" the data stored in the cloud

> *Id.*

8 *Id.*

9 Ohio State Bar Ass'n, OSBA Informal Advisory Op. 2013–03 (2013), https://www.ohiobar.org/For-Public/LegalTools/Documents/OSBAInfAdvOp2013-03.pdf. The Ohio State Bar also quoted the Pennsylvania Bar's relevant official comment: "The 'cloud' is 'merely "a fancy way of saying stuff's not on your [own] computer."'" (quoting Pa. Bar Ass'n Comm. on Legal Ethics and Prof'l Responsibility, Formal Op. 2011-200 (2011)).

- Does the agreement create a legally enforceable obligation on the vendor's part to safeguard the confidentiality of the data?
- How may the vendor respond to government or judicial attempts to obtain disclosure of your client data?
- What is the vendor's policy regarding returning your client data at the termination of its relationship with your firm?
- What plans and procedures does the vendor have in case of natural disaster, electric power interruption, or other catastrophic events?[10]

These issues highlight the depth of knowledge that a lawyer in Ohio and elsewhere must have to properly negotiate for productive use of cloud services.

The ABA's Commission on Ethics 20/20 proposed that the ABA House of Delegates adopt minor changes to existing rules, rather than specific regulation aimed at specific new technologies.[11] Given the pace of technological change affecting business and legal contracts, this strategy seems well suited to allow states to regulate lawyers without constantly pushing to catch up with regulations directed at newly relevant technologies. However, the strategy makes it unlikely that states will speak directly to the obligation of knowing cloud computing, instead of obligations to keep up with the client's important technology as a general matter.

IX. Passing Legal Requirements to the Cloud Provider

Many cloud customers have legal obligations that attach to the management and storage of data and business processes.[12] If they outsource some or all of the responsibility for protecting these data and business processes, then the contract covering the transaction must apply the customer's legal obligations to the outsource provider. As cloud providers accept responsibility for hosting, processing, and managing regulated data, the providers must also accept responsibility for protecting regulated data as the law requires.

---

10 *Id.* at 4.

11 *See* ABA Commission on Ethics 20/20, Introduction and Overview 2 (Aug. 2012), https://www.americanbar.org/content/dam/aba/administrative/ethics_2020/20120508_ethics_20_20_final_hod_introduction_and_overview_report.authcheckdam.pdf.

12 For example, the Health Insurance Portability and Accountability Act (HIPAA) and Gramm-Leach-Bliley Act (GLBA) both impose such requirements. For HIPAA, *see* U.S. Dep't of Health & Human Servs., Office for Civil Rights, *Guidance on HIPAA & Cloud Computing*, HHS.GOV, https://www.hhs.gov/hipaa/for-professionals/special-topics/cloud-computing/index.html (last updated June 16, 2017). Regulations promulgated pursuant to HIPAA, known as the Privacy Rule and Security Rule, specify a variety of requirements that are relevant to cloud computing. *See* 45 C.F.R. § 164.502(e) (a covered entity must obtain certain written assurances from its business associates before disclosing protected health information (PHI) to the business associate); 45 C.F.R. § 164.306 (describing general rules on security standards for electronic protected health information (ePHI)); 45 C.F.R. § 164.308(b) (a covered entity must obtain certain written assurance from its business associates before disclosing ePHI to the business associate); 45 C.F.R. § 164.314 (regulating the content of contracts between covered entities and business associates with respect to security for ePHI).

For GLBA, *see* 16 C.F.R. § 314.4 (detailing requirements for regulated financial institutions in overseeing their service providers, including contractual safeguards related to security, confidentiality, and integrity of financial information).

This is especially important for any lawyer representing a cloud customer. First, if the cloud provider does not agree to meet the required legal obligations, the cloud customer is arguably automatically failing to comply with required regulations. Data security regulators generally require *both* that the original data controller remain liable for lapses in data protection, *and* that vendors processing the data be bound to meet the same data protection standards. Second, even if the relevant regulators are more forgiving, the cloud customer is still committed to meeting standards to which the cloud vendor will not commit, leaving the cloud customer with liability for overseeing the handling of data over which it has no control. Finally, from a practical standpoint, a regulatory obligation is a rigid negotiation hammer that the cloud customer's lawyer can use to beat on the cloud provider in contract discussions. The regulatory obligation is not a preference of the cloud customer, but rather an imposed requirement, and its terms must be accepted by all parties.

Meeting legal obligations for data security may entail building and maintaining the appropriate protections around the regulated data, but it may also involve actions that a cloud provider must take upon learning that the regulated data has been compromised. Some states provide a time limit following a data exposure to provide notice to data subjects that information regarding them has been compromised. If the exposure or hack happens through a cloud platform, then the cloud provider must commit to meeting germane notice requirements or at least providing relevant information to its cloud customer in time so that the customer may meet the deadline for notifications. Lawyers for the cloud customer should know all of the relevant laws relating to the data expected to reside in the cloud and impose specific responsibility for meeting those laws—whether preparing security or following a data breach—to the cloud provider holding the data.[13]

---

13 All 50 states have security breach notification laws that require an entity holding personal data in computerized form to notify affected consumers once it becomes aware of a breach of the security of the system holding the data. Many of the state laws require that the notification be made "in the most expedient time possible and without unreasonable delay." *See, e.g.,* CAL. CIV. CODE § 1798.82(a). Some laws specify a particular number of days after learning of the breach within which the notice must be given. *See, e.g.,* CONN. GEN. STAT. ANN. § 36a-701b(b)(1) (requiring notice to affected Connecticut residents within 90 days after discovery of a breach); FLA. STAT. ANN. § 501.171(4) (requiring notice to affected Florida residents within 30 days of the determination of a breach); IOWA CODE § 715C.1-2 (requiring notice to the Iowa Director of Consumer Protection within five business days of notice to consumers if greater than 500 Iowa residents are affected, where notice to such consumers must be made "in the most expeditious manner possible and without unreasonable delay"); LA. ADMIN. CODE tit. 16, pt. III, § 701 (requiring notice to the Consumer Protection Section of the Attorney General's office within 10 days of notice to affected Louisiana residents if at least one Louisiana resident must be notified, which must happen "in the most expedient time possible and without unreasonable delay"); ME. REV. STAT. ANN. tit. 10, § 1348(3) (requiring notice to affected Maine residents within seven business days after law enforcement determines notice will not impede its investigation); MD. CODE ANN., COM. LAW § 14-3504(b)(3) (requiring notice to affected Maryland residents within 45 days after determination of a breach); N.M. STAT. ANN. § 57-12C-6(A), -10 (requiring notice to affected New Mexico residents within 45 days after discovery of a breach, and notice to the New Mexico attorney general and consumer reporting agencies within 45 days if greater than 1,000 New Mexico residents are affected); OHIO REV. CODE § 1349.19(B)(2) (requiring notice to affected Ohio residents within 45 days after determination of a breach); 11 R.I. GEN. LAWS § 11-49.3-4(a)(2) (requiring notice to affected Rhode Island residents within 45 days after determination of a breach); TENN. CODE ANN. § 47-18-2107(b) (requiring notice to affected Tennessee residents within 45 days after determination of a breach); VT. STAT. ANN. tit. 9, § 2435(b)(1), (b)(3)(B) (i) (requiring notice to affected Vermont residents within 45 days of determination of a breach, and notice to the Vermont attorney general within 14 days after determination of a breach if notice is required for Vermont residents); WASH. REV. CODE § 19.255.010(16) (requiring notice to affected Washington residents within 45 days after discovery of a breach, and notice to the Washington attorney general within 45 days after discovery of a breach if greater than 500 Washington residents are affected and must be notified); WIS. STAT. § 134.98(3) (a) (requiring notice to affected Wisconsin residents within 45 days of learning of a discovery of a breach).

Legally mandated security protections can lead to a negotiation battle over who pays the costs of meeting the regulatory obligation. If a cloud provider is hacked, the law does not state whether the provider or the customer will pay for required remediation. This must be provided for in the contract, and a cloud customer's lawyer can fight for costs to be covered if the provider's mistake leads to regulatory costs. Be aware that many cloud providers will resist agreeing to pay these costs even if they agree to meet the regulatory standards.

Recognition of the need to meet data protection obligations has led to the creation of HIPAA-compliant cloud services for hospitals and doctors' offices and financial regulatory-compliant cloud services for banks and credit unions. In addition, several cloud service providers claim to comply with the Payment Card Industry Data Security Standards, which are contractual requirements that a merchant must meet if the merchant plans to accept credit and debit cards as payment.[14] In addition, some cloud providers offer the option of using servers in Canada or the European Union (EU) in order to keep data collected from those jurisdictions within the same jurisdiction and not trigger the onward transfer requirements of laws in the EU and Canada. Thus, if your cloud client encounters resistance to meeting required regulatory protections, then seek out a cloud provider that already advertises compliance with the relevant requirements.

X. Software Offered as a Cloud Service

As cloud services grow more prevalent, cloud vendors build software and other business solutions into their offerings so that the software your client uses no longer is served onto the client's computers, but instead is operated out of the cloud and simply accessed by your client from any number of devices. This business model is known through the technology industry as Software as a Service, or simply SaaS. Serving software in this manner is becoming so popular that you may see many specific variants of the model, such as Application as a Service, Infrastructure as a Service, or Platform as a Service. However, know that each is essentially a version of the same concept. SaaS and its variants place their software products into the cloud and rather than allowing customers to operate the software on client systems, they charge, often in by-the-drink usage models, for customers to access the software, upload the customer's data into the software, and then view or otherwise access the processed results of the software's activity.

For the customer's lawyer, the SaaS business/technical model creates extra layers of risk, often masked by the way that vendor contracts are written. The SaaS customer must be concerned with both aspects of the service being offered: (1) accessibility and performance of the cloud, and (2) performance and utility of the software itself. In other words, the software may work exactly the way your client wants, but if your client cannot access the software because the internet or cloud service is too slow or operating poorly, then the client will not gain value from the deal. Similarly, if the client has easy access to software that does not perform its proper functions, then the client will not gain value from the deal.

---

14 *See generally* PCI Security Standards Council, Third-Party Security Assurance Special Interest Group, Information Supplement: Third-Party Assurance (2014), https://www.pcisecuritystandards.org/documents/PCI_DSS_V3.0_Third_Party_Security_Assurance.pdf.

Thus, a lawyer for the SaaS customer must insist on service levels that speak to the general speed and accessibility of the cloud platform, and that describe how the software will perform once it is accessed by the SaaS customer. A SaaS contract is essentially two contracts in one, and the SaaS customer is poorly served if it cannot quickly, cheaply, and easily drop the service if either the cloud aspect or the software aspect is not working correctly. The customer's attorney should tie a termination-for-cause provision to failure to provide satisfactory service on either of these elements independently of each other.

Generally, a vendor will want a 30-day cure period before a SaaS customer's termination-for-cause right can be exercised. This should never be allowed to remain in the contract. Once a vendor has violated its service levels, a cloud customer should be allowed to immediately terminate the contract. It makes no sense to give the vendor more chances for continued violations by allowing a cure period for this type of contract breach. For example, if the SaaS vendor promises that its customer can access the service 99.99 percent of business hours in the U.S. Eastern time zone, and the vendor fails to provide such access for a number of months agreed between the parties, then such a failure should trigger the customer's right to terminate immediately. Giving the vendor an additional 30 days to fix the problems may work in other contract contexts, but not in the case of service levels. Tying a vendor's right to cure to the service level promises may provide the vendor with an unfair right to continue to provide poor service throughout the entire term of the agreement without triggering a customer's ability to extract itself from a deal that is clearly not working correctly. In SaaS agreements, the customer's right to terminate for cause must be tied to all of the important aspects of vendor performance (different termination rights for different types of failures), and must stand on its own without allowing the vendor to cure its service level violations.

That said, if the customer is not allowing a vendor to cure service level violations, then the customer must be realistic about what qualifies as a service level problem. If the SaaS customer is insisting on access to services 99.999 percent of the hours in a week, which equals about six seconds total down time in any one week, then it would likely be considered unreasonable for the customer to have a right to terminate for cause if the vendor fails to meet its obligation for just one week. Thus, it might be more reasonable for the SaaS customer to seek a right to terminate for cause if the vendor fails to provide complete access to the operational software for 99.5 percent per month (under four hours down time per month) for two consecutive months, or any three months in a 12-month rolling period. This way, the vendor has a chance to overcome one bad incident, but the customer has the opportunity to exit the contract cleanly if access problems continue. Both sides are treated fairly, and the vendor has no need for a right to cure that amounts to a perpetual right to fail and fail again. The same should be true if access to the software is perfect, but the software itself does not perform to specifications.

Another difficult topic to negotiate in SaaS contracts is the treatment of customer data and the information derived from that data. Unlike traditional software licensing models, in SaaS deals, the SaaS vendor holds and processes the SaaS customer's information. Depending on the nature of the SaaS operation, this customer information may be crucial data for the operation of the customer's business. Data security, contingency planning, and disaster recovery are therefore crucial because the SaaS customer cannot afford to lose the data, but has no direct control over how it is managed and protected. The SaaS customer's lawyer must be certain to elicit promises from the vendor to protect the information, including via backup copies on servers in different locations, so the vendor can bring back the customer's data no matter what disaster befalls the vendor's original data centers. As you will read elsewhere in this book, specific security obligations are also important, as is access to reports from the vendor's internal and external security auditors.

In addition, the vendor must commit to returning data to the customer upon termination. When it comes to data, the SaaS contract is different from many standard cloud contracts. In some cloud arrangements, the vendor simply provides a set of servers and some basic software infrastructure for the cloud customer to operate independently. The customer can run the application software of its choice using these resources. When the information is returned, it arrives in the same chunks that the customer was using online. However, in a SaaS model, the vendor is providing both the servers and the operational functionality to the customer, and the customer can insert its own data, but can otherwise only operate within the rules of the SaaS software. Therefore, the customer's data may not be recognizable outside the context of the SaaS program. It is therefore imperative to require the SaaS contractor to return the SaaS customer's data in a format and context that the customer understands so that the customer's business is not interrupted. This type of customer protection must be built into the SaaS contract from the beginning, with a clear understanding by all parties of what will be delivered at termination, and how the customer can transform or immediately use the data when the relationship ends.

In addition, the SaaS customer's lawyer must be prepared to limit the SaaS provider's access to and use of not only the customer's data, but also the metadata and derivative data that the SaaS provider is producing when processing the data. Generally speaking, a SaaS customer would not be expecting to share the utility of its processed information with the SaaS vendor. The vendor is being paid to process the data for the customer, and benefiting from the customer's internal information itself is not part of the deal. In addition, the SaaS customer may be processing data from individual consumers or employees, or some other data that is protected under law, and the SaaS vendor should have no legal right to do anything more than process this protected information on behalf of the customer and then return the data and its processed results to the customer. Thus, the vendor should be limited in what it can do with the customer's information provided under a SaaS contract.

The processed transactions themselves create their own information, however, and a vendor can often extract value from the transactional information gleaned from a customer's use of SaaS processing. For example, if the SaaS vendor is processing invoices and payments made by its customers to their suppliers, then the SaaS vendor could quickly determine which of the suppliers would give discounts for immediate payment, or which suppliers would allow 90 days between invoice and payment without adding penalties to the next invoice. This information could be valuable and, especially if based on the processing of millions of payments from thousands of SaaS customers, the SaaS vendor could sell its gleaned knowledge in the public marketspace. Doing so might create problems between the SaaS customers and their suppliers, however, who would consider their payment and invoicing policies to be trade secrets. Thus, the lawyer for a SaaS customer should work to limit the SaaS vendor's use of information derived from the SaaS customer's data, just as the customer limits the vendor's use of customer's data itself. The SaaS vendor should not be allowed to use metadata surrounding SaaS customer data, or any of the various derivative works that it could make from the customer's data. It would be reasonable to limit the SaaS vendor's right to analyze and use such derivative data only for the internal purposes of testing and improving the SaaS product, but not to package and sell to third parties.

SaaS contracts should be considered a cloud agreement with a software license attached. The vendor should not be allowed to avoid providing useful services simply because its form agreement crams the two elements of the services together.

XI. Contentious Issues in Cloud Contracts

Much of this book is dedicated to exploring the most difficult issues facing cloud customers when negotiating with cloud providers, but several of those provisions can be addressed with the practice tips that are the subject of this chapter. To that end, this chapter will conclude by recommending negotiating positions and responses to some of the thorniest and most contentious provisions in cloud contracting.

A. Service Levels

At its core, the cloud contract is a promise by the customer to pay an agreed sum in return for a promise by the vendor to provide services. Every cloud contract is specific on how much the customer will pay and the rules surrounding such payments. Few cloud contracts are equally specific about measuring and delivering the vendor's services and the alternatives and consequences when the vendor does not deliver services in the manner prescribed.

Therefore, the two most significant actions the cloud customer's lawyer can take are to carefully define and provide a method for measuring the services to be provided, and to prepare a cost-free release for the client when those services fall below the promised levels. The lawyer must understand that defining and measuring service levels are very difficult in any negotiation. First, measuring services is itself a difficult task. The parties must choose and agree upon metrics that can describe accurately whether the services have succeeded in meeting the customer's needs. Thus, the customer must think deeply about what it needs from this contract and under what circumstances the customer would judge that services were no longer operating in an anticipated manner.

Second, describing and measuring technical services takes more technical knowledge than most lawyers bring into the negotiation. The customer's lawyer should interview the cloud customer's technology team and business team to map out the metrics that each group wants to use to measure successful provision of services. Unless the lawyer has deep experience in managing and litigating cloud contracts, it is unlikely that the lawyer alone will be able to provide an adequate contractual basis for measuring service levels. Technical help is required.

Third, the technology team, business team, and lawyer must next define what will constitute success and failure on the basis of the selected metrics. It is not enough to know what aspects of the services you are measuring. The lawyer, with help from the client, must determine what number represents the minimum level of service allowable under the contract. When will a hiccup in service constitute a service level failure? Is 99.9 percent uptime enough? And is that measured by the week or month? These determinations can be used to justify a vendor's failure to provide an entire workday of service, but still remain comfortably within service levels. The customer's lawyer should also know which measured levels of failure will trigger a penalty to the vendor, and which levels will trigger a cost-free termination right by the customer. Different failure measurements should be used to trigger different customer rights.

Next, the cloud vendor will usually fight hard to avoid both being meaningfully measured at all and being measured as tightly as the customer desires. Given that so few cloud customers understand the importance and workings of service levels, most cloud providers can muddy the waters by offering inadequate measurements of meaningless metrics. The cloud customer should go into the negotiation with an understanding of the important metrics, or the customer is likely to be lost in the muddle—intentionally or otherwise—of service mumbo jumbo written into the contract by the cloud provider. Most standard vendor-provided service level agreements are designed to limit the vendor's liability rather than to provide real service level measurement. They tend to choose meaningless metrics and provide the cloud customer with "service credits" for failing to meet those metrics. Of course, once the vendor provides service credits—minor relief from a portion of next month's scheduled payment—then the vendor adds contract provisions providing that these service credits are the only liability the vendor must suffer for poor service. The upshot of these provisions is that in many cases, the vendor could simply stop providing services at all (its only true duty under the contract), and the customer can neither sue for damages nor terminate the agreement without penalty, locking the customer into an unfair and destructive business relationship, with the customer's only solace being the 10-percent discount on the customer's next monthly payment to a failing vendor. For these reasons, the cloud provider's service level agreement should never be accepted without serious questions and changes.

Then there is the messy way that cloud services are delivered. The cloud customer wants to measure accessibility and performance (including time needed to complete tasks and effectiveness and certainty of task completion), but many of these metrics depend not only on the service offered by the cloud provider, but also on the efficiency of the internet itself and of the customer's systems. Given these measurement problems, vendors are often correct when they claim that some of the service being measured is beyond their control. A good cloud customer's attorney can find a way to hold the vendor to meaningful service levels while allowing the vendor to slide on service problems beyond the vendor's control.

A cloud customer's lawyer should also build into the contract a right to terminate without penalty if the vendor fails to provide a certain level of services. Many vendor-provided agreements will not include such a provision at all, which means that even if the cloud provider stopped offering the service altogether, or failed to make its own services work in a meaningful way, the cloud customer would need to pay a penalty to the failed vendor to escape the contract and to receive its data back in a usable format. If the cloud customer is not receiving the service it was expecting, then the cloud vendor should let the customer leave the business relationship. As discussed above, in nearly every case, a right to cure the vendor's mistakes should not be applied to service level promises. The service levels should stand on their own and be exempted from any provider right to cure; otherwise, the vendor effectively has the right to fail forever and never be held accountable.

B. Negotiating Security

Given that cloud vendors provide services to dozens, hundreds, or thousands of customers similar to your client, they are understandably shy about allowing any one of those customers to dictate overall security measures or to audit the cloud vendor in any way that would expose the data of cloud customers to each other. This can make them unwilling to take risks in their contracting, and, as noted above, often a cloud customer must pay more than standard fare to buy vendor accommodation on security items.

The good news is that data security is an important item for nearly all cloud customers, so a good number of the better-managed cloud providers have anticipated this need and will volunteer to provide strong protections and the results of professional audits. Also noted above is the fact that some cloud providers use their willingness to meet regulatory standards as a sales differentiator so that they can attract companies in regulated industries. In these cases, the cloud customer should accept the value of these promises and still push for any specific data security items needed in the cloud relationship. Where a cloud provider offers a standard operational audit recognized by the industry, it is often wasted effort to push for additional and supplemental audits, even if the secondary audit standards are favored by the cloud client. If the vendor is already allowing one type of audit, the customer's efforts are better spent pulling different and more relevant security concessions from the vendor.

In any case, the cloud customer should demand reasonable and industry-standard security standards in the physical, technical, and administrative arenas. Technical security promises are the easiest to secure, although some cloud customers are unfortunately fixated on the physical separation of their data into dedicated servers when the wonders of virtualization truly make physical separation a distinction without a difference. Many cloud providers will discuss physical security, but most refuse to reveal the real-world protections to their customers, but if the business process being placed into the cloud is important enough, the cloud customer should be pushing for a tour of the facilities to confirm the vendor's promises. On the other hand, administrative safeguards are easier to prove when a cloud client requests to see the policies and operational reports from the cloud vendor's facilities. The cloud customer's best and sometimes only opportunity to review all levels of security may come during contract negotiations.

C. Administrative Issues

A lawyer should ask a cloud customer client how important geography is, and why it matters to the client. Differences in international laws can be a powerful reason to demand that certain information be kept in the United States, Canada, or the EU, and certainly there are important reasons to keep data away from Russia or China. In addition, a client may have substantial reasons to demand geographically separated back-up facilities and redundancies, but some jurisdictional restrictions that cloud customers request may be without reasonable basis, so a lawyer should push cloud customers for deeper reasoning beyond, "What is your preference?" Not all cloud providers can or will meet geographical requests.

Access to data for litigation purposes is a growing administrative request of cloud providers. Regulatory or litigation requirements may force the cloud customer to separate certain information out from the main body of data, may require that certain data be held longer and be made searchable, and may require that data in use be tagged for how it was managed. Attorneys for cloud customers should build into the cloud agreements the requirement of cloud providers to meet and properly act upon judicial or regulatory demands to save and produce certain information. Keep in mind that the legal demands may go well beyond the data held in the cloud, to the metadata surrounding the initial information, the access and movement logs about the information, and even testimony from employees of the cloud provider about how the information was treated. In the United States, the CLOUD Act of 2018 allows federal law enforcement agencies to demand access to the data held by U.S.-based cloud providers even if that data is held outside the United States.[15] If a cloud customer does not have a litigation cooperation provision built into its cloud agreement, then it may be caught between the demands of courts and regulators and the resistance of its own vendors.

D. Legal Liability Protections

For cloud customers, one of the hardest positions to shake loose is the cloud vendor's attachment to contractual terms that absolve it of liability, even for its own mistakes, missteps, and misdeeds. It is perfectly reasonable for a cloud customer to expect vendor indemnification for willful misconduct, violation of law, and infringement of intellectual property rights by the cloud provider. If a cloud provider is not willing to go even this far in accepting liability for its own failures and malicious actions, the prospective cloud customer may be best served by dropping that vendor from consideration. A vendor's hard line on protecting itself from its own irresponsibility does not bode well for long-term treatment of the customer or its business processes. It is also reasonable for the cloud customer to request and receive indemnification for third-party actions that result from a vendor's gross negligence or recklessness. A full indemnification, defense, and hold-harmless clause triggered by the cloud provider's negligence may be a bridge too far for the vendor, but this doesn't mean that the prospective customer shouldn't ask for this contract provision on the theory that a cloud provider should stand behind its own actions.

A more complicated set of discussions ensues when the cloud customer demands indemnification, defense, and hold-harmless provisions triggered by a data breach on the vendor's systems and servers. It may simplify this issue to ask whether the cloud provider has cybersecurity insurance. If the customer can tie a liability commitment to the vendor's insurance policy, then it may be easier for the vendor to allow movement from pre-set positions on hacking liability. This is one area where reminding the vendor that it should stand behind its own actions does not often work because the vendor knows that it may be successfully hacked no matter how strong its security is, and because, in all probability, a successful hack of the vendor that affects your client will have affected 100 other clients of the cloud provider as well. Wholesale data management leads to wholesale liability if the vendor is successfully attacked. Giving in to a cloud customer on this matter could lead to an avalanche of claims arising from a single incident.

The other side of this contractual coin is the liability limitation provision. Cloud customers should be certain that they have exempted hard-won indemnification promises from the inevitable limitations on liability that the cloud provider will want to impose. The confidentiality and limited-use-of-data provisions should also be so exempted to establish the importance to the cloud customer of avoiding misuse of its data. This includes both the limitations on types of damages and any cap on damages. It makes sense to also argue that results of a data breach should be similarly exempted from such limitations on liability.

When it comes to a total cap on liability, most vendors will propose a limitation defined by a formula, usually tied to the amount a customer paid over not more than a one-

---

15 Clarifying Lawful Overseas Use of Data Act (CLOUD Act), Pub. L. No. 115–141, div. V, 132 Stat. 348, 1213. The CLOUD Act amends, *inter alia*, the Stored Communications Act, 18 U.S.C. § 2701 *et seq.* The principal new provisions are §§ 2713 and 2703(h).

year period. The cloud customer should try to break out of this formula-based thinking, which is designed to mask the low ceiling of a vendor's liability within an intricate formula. A customer should always work out the actual likely liability cap provided by the formula because the number is likely to be significantly low. In fact, often the liability cap provided by such a formula is so low that a vendor does not need to meet its obligations under the contract because the cost for a cloud customer to enforce those obligations is much more than could ever be collected under the formula. Therefore, a customer should always push for a liability cap that is a clear number everyone understands, and a number high enough to make enforcement lawsuits worthwhile. Liability caps are triggered only in a worst-case scenario and generally have no relationship to the amount it costs to bring the customer services; therefore, the cloud customer should demand that any liability cap be expressed in easy-to-understand dollar terms so that both parties and the judge ruling on the contract later will know the size of the cap. There should also be enough money under the cap to ensure that the cloud provider has an incentive to meet its obligations.

XII. Conclusion

Lawyers have both an ethical obligation and good practical reasons to learn enough about cloud technology to properly represent themselves and their clients in cloud contract negotiations. Knowing the cloud is simply an extension of knowing your client's business, knowing the risks facing your client, and understanding the relevant aspects of the world in which your client conducts business. Talking to the client, understanding the client's priorities, and managing client expectations are not peculiar to cloud deals. They are a core part of solid legal practice.

Chapter 14

Above, Beyond, and Around the ABA's 2012 Model Rules of Professional Conduct: Growing On- and Off-shore and Low-tech Challenges for U.S. Lawyers and Law Firms Using Cloud Computing

By Sarah Jane Hughes[1]

I. Introduction

Over the past several years, we have seen a significant increase in the number of high-profile hacking and ransomware incidents involving lawyers' and law firms' communications with clients and clients' property stored in electronic forms. In 2017 alone, hackers infiltrated international law firms such as DLA Piper in an incident that disrupted internal and external communications and froze access to stored files over an extended period.[2] In 2016, hackers from China invaded the merger-and-acquisition files of two major international law firms based in New York City.[3]

The adage that holds "if it can happen, it will happen" now applies to cyber attacks on lawyers and law firms, just as on other professionals and enterprises. Such incidents increasingly occur at law firms that have significant cross-border representations and that use internet- and cloud-based services to communicate with its employees and clients, and to store files used in representing clients around the world.

In 2011, Roland L. Trope and I published an article that described the types of cloud-computing, social media, and other internet-enabled tools that lawyers and law firms were using to communicate with clients, among members of the same firms or other firms working on the same deals, and with others, and the types and terms of service of cloud-computing options then available to them.[4] We relied on the then-effective provisions of the American Bar Association's Model Rules of Professional Conduct (MRPC or Rules)—those prior to the 2012 MRPC Amendments that enhanced technical competence and other Rules described below—as the lens through which to evaluate the ethical duties lawyers and law firms had to clients, and to make recommendations to lawyers and law firms on how to adjust certain business practices to meet the such ethical duties. We

---

1 Sarah Jane Hughes is a faculty member at Indiana University's Maurer School of Law.

2 *See* Nicole Perlmuth, *Cyberattack's Fallout Lingers As Nations Mull Self-Defense,* N.Y. Times, July 7, 2017, at B1 (reporting that DLA Piper did not have all of its systems back "to normal" more than a week after the cyber attack occurred).

3 *See* Press Release, Sec. & Exch. Comm'n, Chinese Traders Charged with Trading on Hacked Nonpublic Information Stolen from Two Law Firms (Dec. 27, 2016), https://www.sec.gov/news/pressrelease/ 2016-280.html (noting that enforcement action was the SEC's first action charging hacking into a law firm's computer network).

4 Sarah Jane Hughes & Roland L. Trope, *Red Skies in the Morning—Professional Ethics at the Dawn of Cloud Computing,* 38 Wm. Mitchell L. Rev. 111 (2011).

also commented on the issues presented by increasing reliance on cloud computing and how to manage the ethical responsibilities that it implicated.

In August 2012, the ABA updated its MRPC and related comments, speaking to some of the issues our article had identified. The Rules continue to describe ethical requirements in broad terms.

The ABA has devoted considerable resources to helping U.S. lawyers meet their MRPC responsibilities. For example, in 2013 the ABA published *The ABA Cybersecurity Handbook*,[5] updating it in late 2017.[6] Also in 2017, the ABA published the *Guide to Cybersecurity Due Diligence in M&A Transactions*,[7] which law firms considering mergers with other firms should review before committing to any merger, and which every lawyer advising clients who are considering mergers or acquisitions of business enterprises should study. The number of publications from the ABA related to cyber security and lawyers continues unabated.

With so much attention devoted to the ABA's 2012 amendments to the MRPC, and with such excellent ABA books and other publications looking at how the Rules are being implemented, one might ask why this book devotes a chapter to lawyers' professional responsibilities and the cloud.

The answer is that lawyers and law firms who are using cloud computing and storage for information about pending transactions, litigation, and clients must look at the ever-changing scope of the responsibilities imposed by the MRPC, but not explained in detail. Effectively, the Rules are like vases that are filled with contents from a variety of sources.

Thus, for lawyers and law firms to meet their basic MRPC duties to clients, they must think "above, beyond, and around" the text of the MRPC to additional types of risks to which they and their clients' digital assets are exposed in using cloud storage and file-sharing. The fear is that lawyers and law firms will place too much reliance on the purely technological aspects of cyber security and fail to pay proper attention to "low-tech" concerns that affect the competence, diligence, communications, confidentiality, and safeguarding of clients' property in degrees just as damaging to clients and lawyers or law firms.

Part II introduces topics considered part of these "above, beyond, and around" categories of concerns. The examples relate to low-tech concerns as opposed to high-tech concerns.

Part III briefly reviews the four Rules most pertinent to lawyers' and law firms' use of technologies including cloud computing. These Rules set basic standards, but they do not prescribe how lawyers and law firms should comply. Indeed, lawyers and law firms are required to look outside the Rules to appreciate, implement, and monitor their compliance with the Rules. This is necessary both to appreciate the scope of the Rules and to meet externally imposed duties that relate to these Rules that stem from both technology and nontechnology sources.

---

5 Am. Bar Ass'n, The ABA Cybersecurity Handbook: A Resource for Attorneys, Law Firms, and Business Professionals (Jill D. Rhodes & Vincent I. Polley eds., 2013).

6 Am. Bar Ass'n., The ABA Cybersecurity Handbook: A Resource for Attorneys, Law Firms, and Business Professionals (Jill D. Rhodes & Robert S. Litt eds., 2017).

7 Am. Bar Ass'n, Guide to Cybersecurity Due Diligence in M&A Transactions (Thomas J. Smedinghoff & Roland L. Trope eds., 2017).

Part IV looks at non-U.S. laws governing access by government authorities to documents or data received or held abroad in lawyers' or law firms' hands. The data stored outside the United States—whether by design or due to the storage practices cloud providers employ—is exposed to different risks in specific investigations or government surveillance activities. These issues require specialty knowledge and planning to satisfy the MRPC principles. This part also describes litigation between Microsoft and other cloud providers and the United States government over secrecy orders of indefinite duration that courts may issue under 18 U.S.C. §2705(b)—that is, whether, when a warrant is directed to a third party, the senders or originators of the data are entitled to notice that the warrant has been issued. These issues, which Microsoft raised in a warrant challenge, would trigger other duties to select, plan, communicate, and secure data under the MRPC.

Part V looks at the duties imposed not by the legal profession, but by clients or clients' regulators. These sources of duties include the New York State *Cybersecurity Requirements*,[8] and the Association of Corporate Counsel's 2017 *Model Information Protection and Security Controls for Outside Counsel Possessing Company Confidential Information.*[9] The U.S. Customs and Border Protection's publication of its new "electronic devices" border search policies in early 2018[10]—and the ABA's new advisory that responds to them[11]—present more examples of externally imposed standards that affect lawyers' and law firms' responsibilities under the MRPC.

These high-tech and low-tech externally sourced duties are examples of the "above, beyond, and around" sources that lawyers and law firms should consider as they monitor and improve their compliance with the Model Rules. The low-tech issues are less likely to receive suitable attention if the information-technology professionals managing cybersecurity issues and cross-border practice issues are not lawyers or are not supervised by knowledgeable lawyers, no matter how talented the IT professionals.

The conclusion offers a few new recommendations for readers' consideration on cloud computing and lawyers' ethical duties.

II. "Above, Beyond, and Around" Issues Affecting Competence, Diligence, Confidentiality, Communications, and Safeguarding Clients' Property

"Above, beyond, and around" risks do not emanate from technology itself. Rather, they flow from how technology works and from the ways lawyers and law firms use cloud

---

8 N.Y. State, Dep't of Fin. Servs., Cybersecurity Requirements for Financial Services Companies, N.Y. COMP. CODES R. & REGS. tit. 23, pt. 500 [hereinafter NYS DFS Cybersecurity Regulation].

9 ASS'N OF CORP. COUNSEL, MODEL INFORMATION PROTECTION AND SECURITY CONTROLS FOR OUTSIDE COUNSEL POSSESSING COMPANY CONFIDENTIAL INFORMATION (2017), http://advocacy.acc.com/2017/03/model-information-protection-and-security-controls-for-outside-counsel-possessing-company-confidential-information/ [hereinafter ACC Model Controls].

10 U.S. Customs & Border Protection, CBP Directive No. 3340-049A: Border Search of Electronic Devices (Jan. 4, 2018), https://www.cbp.gov/document/directives/cbp-directive-no-3340-049a-border-search-electronic-devices [hereinafter CBP Directive No. 3340-049A].

11 Am. Bar Ass'n, ABA Center for Professional Responsibility, Electronic Device Advisory for Mid-Year Meeting Attendees (Jan. 10, 2018), https://www.americanbar.org/content/dam/aba/events/meetings_travel/scerp-electronic-device-advisory-djcbsg-1-10-18.authcheckdam.pdf [hereinafter Electronic Device Advisory 2018].

technologies. Lawyers and law firms also need to implement, monitor, and retailor their practices to meet externally imposed cyber and other requirements that go above, beyond, and around the MRPC in certain sector-specific practices such as financial institution and defense contracting, in merger-and-acquisition transactions, in intellectual property or technology-transfer deals, and in cross-border work particularly, including internal investigations.

These "above, beyond, and around" prospects are not confined to risks posed by hackers, as threatening as those risks and actors are. These additional risks arise because of the presence of some or all the following factors:

- the convergence of new regulations and widely applicable standards, causing the cybersecurity demands on lawyers and law firms to rise dramatically, and new civil or criminal vulnerabilities for data security events;
- the increasing degree of collaboration on transactions among multiple offices of the same firm as opposed to the former practice of keeping clients' files in hard copy at one location;
- more than one firm being involved in negotiating transactions, or the transactions involving cross-border actions or actors with the likely use of more than one cloud storage system by the participants in the transaction;
- the built-in redundancy of data stored in clouds;
- the prospect, if not probability, that some of the data is stored outside the borders of the United States or of the situs of the law firm's office handling the transaction, and that data could be stored in multiple jurisdictions;
- government surveillance, here and abroad, in the name of national security or trade policy;
- inspections at border crossings and airports of electronic devices under programs such as that recently affirmed by the U.S. Customs and Border Protection agency;
- the private and public sectors' appetites for data collection and "Big Data" generally;
- the growing cross-border trade in trade secrets and the like by state-sponsored actors as well as private enterprises;
- differing national standards pertaining to attorney-client privilege and due process rights of clients governing access to their intangible assets such as trade secrets, merger-and-acquisition plans, internal investigation reports, compliance plans, and the like[12] that may be in the hands of their lawyers or in their own stored files;
- increasingly short timelines and stiff fines, particularly in the European Union's General Data Protection Regulation (GDPR), for notifying affected persons that their data has been compromised;[13] and

- the truism that the weakest link in any project or data transmission or storage system is likely to cause damage that lawyers and law firms will find extremely difficult to predict or prevent.

---

12 *See* Jack Ewing & Bill Vlasic, *German Authorities Raid U.S. Law Firm Leading Volkswagen's Emissions Inquiry,* N.Y. Times, Mar. 16, 2017, https://www.nytimes.com/2017/03/16/business/volkswagen-diesel-emissions-investigation-germany.html.
13 For a discussion of the applicability of the GDPR to cloud computing, see Chapter 10.

Laws and practices related to these "above, beyond, and around" risks provide content to the MRPC described in the next part of this chapter that lawyers and law firms must understand, adapt to, and monitor for their own compliance purposes and to competently advise clients.

III. The 2012 Amendments to the MRPC Related to Technology Competence, Diligence, Communications, Confidentiality of Information, Safekeeping Property, and Responsibilities of Partners or Supervisory Lawyers

In 2012, the ABA amended the Model Rules of Professional Conduct[14] and the comments to some Rules, and expanded the duties of lawyers and law firms to obtain technical competence and to consider technology in the management of their work and their dealings with, and on behalf of, clients. The amendments focused on the following Model Rules: Rule 1.1 (Competence), Rule 1.3 (Diligence), Rule 1.4 (Communications), Rule 1.6 (Confidentiality of Information), Rule 1.15 (Safekeeping Property), and Rule 5.1 (Responsibilities of a Partner or Supervisory Lawyer). These Rules and their related comments frame ethical duties of lawyers and law firms and have been the subject of many articles and presentations at ABA meetings and in other forums since 2012. They may seem like old hat to readers; however, the amendments signal that these are more dynamic rules that serve as the constants around which the special risks described in later parts of this chapter rotate, even if they no longer supply the specifics of the duties they impose on lawyers and law firms.

The special risks that this chapter describes arise in new forms as technology makes possible cross-border communications, file-sharing and storage, and other collaborations on projects and transactions, and introduces workplace efficiencies that potentially contribute to the risks addressed in this chapter. The five MRPC mentioned below are in their own sequential order with no intention to impose any priority to their relationships to the rest of this chapter. They should be viewed as a reminder of why the less-cyber-specific "above, around, and beyond" issues presented in this chapter also need lawyers' attention.

A. Rule 1.1 Competence

Rule 1.1 reads as follows:

> A lawyer shall provide competent representation to a client. Competent representation requires the legal knowledge, skill, thoroughness and preparation reasonably necessary for the representation.

---

14 MODEL RULES OF PROF'L CONDUCT (2012), https://www.americanbar.org/groups/professional_responsibility/publications/model_rules_of_professional_conduct/model_rules_of_professional_conduct_table_of_contents.html.

Although the ABA did not amend Rule 1.1 in 2012, it did amend Comment 8 (Maintaining Competence). Comment 8 currently reads:

[8] To maintain the requisite knowledge and skill, a lawyer should keep abreast of changes in the law and its practice, including the benefits and risks associated with relevant technology, engage in continuing study and education and comply with all continuing legal education requirements to which the lawyer is subject.

With the amendment of Comment 8, this duty now encompasses a duty of technology competence in at least the 31 states whose state supreme courts or other rule-setting bodies have adopted the amended comment to Rule 1.1.[15] Commentators have described the amendment of Comment 8 to include the duty of technical competence as a "sea change" in lawyers' ethical responsibilities.[16] Rule 1.1's new scope encompasses the types of specialized knowledge and anticipation of the first three "above, beyond, and around" challenges mentioned above. The Association of Corporate Counsel's *Model Controls* described in Part VI further expand the scope of MRPC 1.1.

B. Rule 1.3 Diligence

Rule 1.3 reads as follows:

A lawyer shall act with reasonable diligence and promptness in representing a client.

Comments to Rule 1.3 do not directly speak to the lawyer's inability to act with reasonable diligence and promptness in the event of a loss of access to data or communications facilities holding information needed to respond to court- or transaction-imposed deadlines. Indeed, none of the comments to this rule directly or indirectly address obstacles to diligent representation that arise from a loss of data or of access to communications facilities such as e-mail that lawyers, law firms, and their clients take for granted. However, the lawyer's duty of diligence requires that he or she maintain timely access to files and specific communications (letters, e-mails, and facsimile exchanges), and that the lawyer can use these files and communications in ongoing representations of his or her clients.

Thinking about Rule 1.3's requirements, we can examine the risks that arose from the June 27, 2017 cyber attack that affected DLA Piper's offices worldwide.[17] This attack, initially thought to be a Petya-style ransomware attack, proved in short order to be pure malware—with no ransom method to retrieve data or systems that had been affected.[18] DLA Piper lost access to its e-mail and other systems, and the event continued to interrupt DLA Piper's access to pre-event e-mails and some files through at least July 6, 2017.[19]

---

15 *See* Robert J. Ambrogi, *Tech Competence*, LawSites, https://www.lawsitesblog.com/tech-competence/ (last visited July 19, 2018) (providing a list of adopting states and the effective dates of the adoptions and evaluating actions by other states that are less than formal adoptions of new Comment 8).

16 *Id.*

17 *See* Perlmuth, *supra* note 2, at B1, B5.

18 *See* Phil Muncaster, *Maersk Admits NotPetya Might Cost It $300m,* Info Security Mag., Aug. 18, 2017, https://www.infosecurity-magazine.com/news/maersk-admits-notpetya-might-cost (reporting, among other things, that the perpetrators provided no decryption keys to unwind damage; Maersk lost its Master Record Book to virus and incident may cost Maersk $300 million).

19 *See* Perlmuth, *supra* note 2, at B5.

However, recent reports reveal that DLA Piper employed diligence in preparing for and recovering from a cyber attack.

Another example comes from the VW-Jones Day incident in which German authorities seized documents and data under review at Jones Day's Munich office, which is discussed in Part IV.

C. Rule 1.4 Communications

Rule 1.4 reads as follows:

(a) A lawyer shall:

(1) promptly inform the client of any decision or circumstance with respect to which the client's informed consent, as defined in Rule 1.0(e), is required by these Rules;

(2) reasonably consult with the client about the means by which the client's objectives are to be accomplished;

(3) keep the client reasonably informed about the status of the matter;

(4) promptly comply with reasonable requests for information; and

(5) consult with the client about any relevant limitation on the lawyer's conduct when the lawyer knows that the client expects assistance not permitted by the Rules of Professional Conduct or other law.

(b) A lawyer shall explain a matter to the extent reasonably necessary to permit the client to make informed decisions regarding the representation.

Lawyer-client communications duties covered by Rule 1.4 include communications related to cloud computing if cloud-computing usage requires the client's informed consent, affects the means by which a client's objectives will be accomplished, and may affect—whether positively or negatively—the status of a matter handled by the lawyer or how the lawyer is able to comply with requests for information. Thus, lawyers must understand how cloud computing affects their clients and their ability to perform work that clients assign to them. For example, DLA Piper was unable to communicate with clients during the period immediately following the cyber attack, and was unable to retrieve some electronic files and e-mails that might be requested by clients themselves or by clients' adversaries or regulators. In Jones Day's case, prosecutors seized records from Jones Day's custody, rendering those records unavailable to Jones Day's lawyers and other staff members for analysis or for return to VW, the client. In both cases, high-tech and low-tech concerns, including usage of clouds, affected lawyers' ability to perform. In addition, in both cases, communications among lawyers, law firms, and clients were interrupted by the use of clouds for data storage and transmission.

D. Rule 1.6 Confidentiality of Information

Rule 1.6 reads as follows:

(a) A lawyer shall not reveal information relating to the representation of a client unless the client gives informed consent, the disclosure is impliedly authorized in order to carry out the representation or the disclosure is permitted by paragraph (b).

(b) A lawyer may reveal information relating to the representation of a client to the extent the lawyer reasonably believes necessary:

...

(c) A lawyer shall make reasonable efforts to prevent the inadvertent or unauthorized disclosure of, or unauthorized access to, information relating to the representation of a client.

Comments to Rule 1.6 further explain the extent to which the Rule places responsibility on lawyers and law firms not to reveal the representation or its substance. For example, Comment [2] provides:

[2] A fundamental principle in the client-lawyer relationship is that, in the absence of the client's informed consent, the lawyer must not reveal information relating to the representation. ...

Comments [3] and [4] add to this burden:

[3] The principle of client-lawyer confidentiality is given effect by related bodies of law: the attorney-client privilege, the work product doctrine and the rule of confidentiality established in professional ethics. The attorney-client privilege and work product doctrine apply in judicial and other proceedings in which a lawyer may be called as a witness or otherwise required to produce evidence concerning a client. The rule of client-lawyer confidentiality applies in situations other than those where evidence is sought from the lawyer through compulsion of law. The confidentiality rule, for example, applies not only to matters communicated in confidence by the client but also to all information relating to the representation, whatever its source. A lawyer may not disclose such information except as authorized or required by the Rules of Professional Conduct or other law. ...

[4] Paragraph (a) prohibits a lawyer from revealing information relating to the representation of a client. This prohibition also applies to disclosures by a lawyer that do not in themselves reveal protected information but could reasonably lead to the discovery of such information by a third person. ...

Comment 12 to Rule 1.6 permits disclosures when "other law" supersedes Rule 1.6's requirements, and the lawyer discusses the disclosures required by other law with the client. If the other law requires disclosure, the lawyer must comply. Communications by lawyers about the risks of being required to make disclosures by other law are part of the "low-tech" aspects of a well-functioning approach to data security and cloud computing.

E. Rule 1.15 Safekeeping Property

Rule 1.15 reads as follows:

(a) A lawyer shall hold property of clients or third persons that is in a lawyer's possession in connection with a representation separate from the lawyer's own property. ... Other property shall be identified as such and appropriately safeguarded. Complete records of . . . such ... property shall be kept by the lawyer and shall be preserved for a period of [five years] after termination of the representation. . . .

Comments to Rule 1.15 include Comment [1]'s mandate: "A lawyer should hold property of others with the care required of a professional fiduciary. Securities should be kept in a safe deposit box, except when some other form of safekeeping is warranted by special circumstances."

To lawyers today, the focus of Comment [1] on safe deposit boxes seems rather old-fashioned. Lawyers do still need safe deposit boxes, however, and must go further to translate this mandate into new forms, including contemporary standards of safeguarding data by means appropriate to cloud computing and electronic storage and transmission. These new forms of data and storage environments may no longer strike us as involving "special circumstances," as the Comment suggests, because lawyers and law firms have been using electronic tools for many years.

Means to safeguard data have been in place for nearly 25 years, beginning from when e-commerce and widening use of the internet began. Moreover, standards for safeguarding data have been in place since the enactment of last major updates of federal pro-privacy laws in the Gramm-Leach-Bliley Financial Services Modernization Act of 1999[20] (GLBA) and the Fair and Accurate Credit Transactions Act of 2003 (FACTA).[21] These two statutes impose different duties on lawyers and law firms, both directly and indirectly. Additionally, federal agency policy statements and enforcement actions have spelled out federal agencies' expectations of what their own regulated entities should do to protect data—and those expectations flow down to lawyers and law firms that represent regulated entities. Finally, the Health Insurance Portability and Accountability Act of 1996 (HIPAA) also imposes strict conditions on safeguarding of health-care information.[22]

These statutes and regulations impose standards on safekeeping of electronic information that are achieved by a trio of administrative controls on access, physical security, and other technical measures. This trio of routes or measures—administrative, physical, and technical—was articulated in response to Congress's direction to providers of financial services, both depository and nondepository, in Title V of GLBA. Federal agencies with rule-writing responsibilities under that title, including the Federal Trade Commission, Securities & Exchange Commission, and Board of Governors of the Federal Reserve System, employed all three types of measures in their "safeguarding" regulations.[23] Safe disposal of information containing consumers' nonpublic personal information is also regulated through FACTA and federal regulations that implement it.[24]

---

20 15 U.S.C. §§ 6801–6809.

21 FACTA added section 628 to the Fair Credit Reporting Act, which is codified at 15 U.S.C. § 1681w, and requires that the federal banking agencies, the National Credit Union Administration, and the Federal Trade Commission promulgate consistent regulations for the safe disposal of information from consumers' credit transactions records and reports.

22 Pub. L. 104-191, §§ 261–264. For more details on the HIPAA requirements, *see* U.S. Dep't of Health and Human Services, Standards for Privacy of Individually Identifiable Health Information, 45 C.F.R. pt. 160, 164 (2000).

23 *See, e.g.,* Federal Trade Commission, Standards for Safeguarding Customer Information, 16 C.F.R. pt. 314.

24 Federal Trade Commission, Disposal of Consumer Report Information and Records Rule, 16 C.F.R. pt. 682.

The balance of the comments to Rule 1.15 pertain to clients' funds and those with lawful claims against them, including lawyers themselves. Rule 1.15 is important even if its focus on funding and physical property including certificated securities seems somewhat out of place in this chapter.

In late 2016, the U.S. Attorney for the Southern District of New York arrested a Macau resident and unsealed indictments against that person and two additional persons for hacking into U.S. law firms to gain information of merger and acquisition transactions and to engage in trading with that information.[25] The Securities and Exchange Commission also filed civil complaints against the same persons, seeking disgorgement of gains and injunctive relief.[26] For varied reasons, intangibles such as those related to mergers or acquisitions, or presumably patent applications, are increasingly likely targets of hackers. In the case of e-files or documents related to internal or external investigations, such intangibles may also be seized by law enforcement officials or even adversaries while in the possession of the law firm or lawyer, depending on the precise laws of the relevant jurisdiction over who may seize them.

Although Rule 1.15 applies to intangible holdings, such as documents related to mergers and acquisitions, its comments are not as instructive about safeguarding intangibles as they are about tangible property or funds. Nevertheless, protecting intangible property hinges on the same trio of protection approaches—administrative, physical, and technical security—that, in the United States and elsewhere, are the standards required of enterprises and individuals that hold personally identifiable information. Thus, as intangible property becomes increasingly valuable and is held by lawyers and law firms, the custodians must consider how they store that type of client property, how they grant access to the locations where it is stored, and what other technical security features are employed to safeguard it. The alternative—to revert to paper, locked storage, and deal rooms with limited access, without cloud computing—would impose costs on deals, compliance, investigations, and lawyers themselves in terms of how they communicate and even where they work during deals.

F. Rule 5.1: Responsibilities of Partners, Managers, and Supervisory Lawyers

Rule 5.1(a) provides:

> A partner in a law firm, and a lawyer who individually or together with other lawyers possesses comparable managerial authority in a law firm, shall make reasonable efforts to ensure that the firm has in effect measures giving reasonable assurance that all lawyers in the firm conform to the Rules of Professional Conduct.

Accordingly, the partners and managers of law firms are responsible for compliance with the MRPC, including ensuring that their use of cloud computing is accompanied by clients' informed consent, and is protected by appropriate administrative, physical, and technical measures.

---

25 *See* Ron Cheng, *China-Based Hacking Case Against U.S. M&A Firms Illustrates Cyber Security and Enforcement Issues*, FORBES, Jan. 11, 2017, https://wwwforbes.com/sites/roncheng/2017/01/11/china-based-hacking-case-against-u-s-ma-firms-illustrates-cyber-security-and-enforcement-issues/. The hacking allegedly covered the period from April 2014 to late 2015 and netted the hackers gains of more than $4 million. *Id.*

26 *Id.*

The next parts of this chapter look at these MRPC and several recent events, and the challenges they pose to lawyers' and law firms' use of cloud computing from perspectives different from those that have so far attracted the most attention in print.

IV. Non-U.S. Laws May Govern Access by Governments to Documents or Data Received or Held Abroad in Lawyers' or Law Firms' Hands

Although not limited to materials stored in the cloud or even on electronic devices, the first of the "above, beyond, and around" challenges to compliance with the MRPC described in this chapter comes from "low-tech" sources—differing non-U.S. laws on attorney-client privilege. One recent example involved the seizure on March 15, 2017, by prosecutors in Munich, Germany materials belonging to Volkswagen from the Munich offices of Jones Day.[27] The prosecutors obtained a warrant for the documents from a local court. Jones Day at first asserted that the records were governed by attorney-client privilege and that the prosecutors could not seize them. The prosecutors persisted, however, maintaining that German law on those subjects was significantly less protective than other nations' laws. VW filed a complaint with a Munich court to prevent prosecutors from using the seized materials, and Germany's Federal Constitutional Court, the Bundesverfassungsgericht (BVerfG), issued an interim order on July 26, 2017, barring prosecutors' use of the documentation pending a final decision by the BVerfG.[28] On July 6, 2018, the BVerfG rendered final determinations on various constitutional challenges to the prosecutors' securing and seizing of documents in the possession of Jones Day's Munich office.[29] The core holdings by the court included that:

- prosecutors' securing of documents "neither constitutes a violation of the *Volkswagen AG's* right to informational self-determination nor of its right to a fair trial, and that there is no recognized legal interest in bringing an action concerning the search";
- Jones Day is not a holder of fundamental rights and lacks standing to lodge a constitutional complaint; and
- lawyers working for Jones Day do not have standing to lodge a constitutional complaint.[30]

---

27 *See* Ewing & Vlasic, *supra* note 12.

28 *German Court Blocks Prosecutors from Using VW Law Firm Seizures*, REUTERS.COM, July 26, 2017, 3:49 p.m., https://uk.reuters.com/article/germany-emissions-court/update-1-german-court-blocks-prosecutors-from-using-VW-law-firm-seizures-idUKL5N1KH809. For additional detail on the interim order, *see* Peter Bert, *Case of the Week: Federal Constitutional Court Issues Interim Order in Jones Day/ Volkswagen Case*, DISP. RESOL. IN GERMANY, July 26, 2017, http://www.disputeresolutiongermany. com/2017/07/case-of-the-week-federal-consitutional-court-issues-interim-order-in-jones-dayvolkswagen-case/.

29 Bundesverfassungsgericht, Press Release, Constitutional Complaints Relating to the Search of a Law Firm in Connection with the 'Diesel Emissions Scandal' Unsuccessful (July 6, 2018), https://www. bundesverfassungsgericht.de/ShareDocs/Pressemitteilungen/EN/2018/bvg18-057.html (English version).

30 *Id.* at 1.

Thus, it appears that there are no constitutional barriers in Germany to prosecutors' use of data and documents related to the VW case that were seized from Jones Day.

The seizure and subsequent whirlwind of actions aimed at protecting the seized documents by German prosecutors demonstrated that U.S. lawyers and law firms should not assume that the same standards, including protections for confidential material and attorney-client privilege, will attach if the documents involved are stored in their own offices or devices outside the borders of the United States. This would appear to be the case whether the documents are stored in or out of the cloud. For example, in the VW-Jones Day seizure, one commentator observed that, although VW called the seizure "a clear violation of legal principles," "the status of privilege in Germany is actually anything but clear."[31] The same commentator points out three additional issues—all of the "low-tech" variety—that will complicate use of clouds and conduct of investigations abroad. First, that privilege may not be in existence in the non-U.S. location.[32] Second, in Germany at least, the outcome may depend on the nature of the engagement entered into—not the prior criminal versus all-other-forms issue, but rather how local law decides what is a formal engagement versus some other status.[33] Third, it is now clear that a law firm or its lawyers are not able to initiate a constitutional complaint in Germany to protect documents they have received from clients.

Other commentators writing after the BVerfG's July 2017 order generally have identified similar themes for consideration. DLA Piper lawyers based in Germany articulated principles they submit are already settled matters in Germany and highlight issues for lawyers and law firms:

- Defense correspondence and defense documents and any work products of an internal investigation conducted by outside counsel (e.g., protocols of witness interviews, summary of results of review of documents, and legal assessments) are privileged under German law and may not be seized.
- The results of an internal investigation conducted by in-house counsel or auditors is not protected; accordingly, the German authorities may seize these documents.
- If the internal investigation serves other purposes than the defense of the corporation (e.g., the preparation of claims against or the defense against claims of third parties, assessment of claims against (former) board members, or to inform regulators abroad), a general attorney-client privilege may not apply to such documents.[34]

The DLA Piper team also offered four "preliminary conclusions" about the ability of German prosecutors to reach work products produced in internal investigations that may affect decisions about how and where to perform work and store documents:

- Engagement letters should state the extent to which the investigation is conducted for defense purposes.

---

31 Chris Johnson, *US Firms Face Ambiguities of Attorney-Client Privilege Law Abroad,* Am. Law., Sept. 1, 2017, https://www.law.com/americanlawyer/almID/1202797117880/.

32 *Id.* (observing that in Germany, until recently, unless one was a criminal defense counsel, no privilege arose, and that later protection for client correspondence broadened to include independent lawyers, regardless of the type of legal matter under consideration).

33 *Id.* (observing that Germany's highest court, the BVerfG, would be considering that question in its ultimate decision on the merits of the challenge).

34 *See Decision of the German Constitutional Court on Attorney-Client Privilege in Internal Investigations To Be Expected* (Sept. 2017), https://www.dlapiper.com/~/media/files/insights/publications/2017/09/client_alert_legal_privilege_germany.pdf.

- Those defense documents should be marked as such and be stored in custody of the law firm.
- Documents and work products for other purposes, such as for remedial actions, civil litigation, or disclosure to foreign authorities, should be separated from purely defense documents.
- Engagement letters also should spell out other purposes for which the documents are in the lawyer's or law firm's hands in order to claim attorney-client privilege.[35]

Although the final decision from the German court replaces the "preliminary conclusions" that DLA Piper offered its readers, the substance of the firm's recommendations can serve as a reminder of issues to consider when U.S.-based law firms are engaging in representation of clients abroad where legal cultures, rules about standing, and the like may differ from those with which U.S. lawyers are more familiar.

Thus, the seizure and subsequent legal maneuvers in the VW-Jones Day matter point to the continuing relevance of some traditional notions, such as standing, nature of the engagement, scope of any protection or privilege, and even citizenship. These are certainly "low-tech" considerations for U.S. lawyers.

Would these questions arise if the data had been in a third-party cloud accessed by the lawyers? Would the outside lawyers have to be the direct clients of the cloud provider? Would these issues arise if the lawyers were using documents in a secure facility at the offices of the clients? Would those facilities have to be restricted to only outside lawyers? Does this dispute suggest that the equivalent of the "third-party doctrine" announced by the U.S. Supreme Court also may apply elsewhere? These questions are so far unanswered in many jurisdictions other than the United States and Germany, but the resolution of these disputes in favor of prosecutors will now guide lawyers in similar situations.

Thus, the VW-Jones Day document seizure points to the need for some "low-tech" planning and management of relationships, such as advanced research, the nature of the engagement between client and lawyer, the lawyer's precise role as in-house counsel or outside counsel, conversations with clients at the time clients deliver documents, and other high-tech problems increasingly faced in the conduct of both domestic transactions with foreign cloud data storage and in cross-border representations. This "low-tech" planning and management remains an essential tool in whatever care the lawyer or law firm otherwise takes in securing valuable data and documents in the cloud—arguably beyond the "technical, physical, and administrative" components we normally associate with data security, but no less important.

V. Challenging "No-Notice" Government Warrants to Obtain Access to Data Stored in Clouds, and Extraterritorial Limits on the Effectiveness of Warrants Issued in the United States to Reach Data Stored Abroad

Turning now to issues that affect more specifically lawyers' use of cloud computing, lawyers should consider two different concerns raised by Microsoft relating to government access to stored data.

---

35 *Id.*

A. "No-Notice" or "Secret" Warrants Addressed to Cloud Providers

The first of these issues is whether the Electronic Communications Privacy Act (ECPA) allows "no-notice" or "secret" conditions in warrants that direct providers not to notify their customer indefinitely. Microsoft raised these issues in one of the highest-profile lawsuits related to cloud computing: its April 2016 facial challenge to the constitutionality of 18 U.S.C. §§ 2703 and 2705(b).[36] Microsoft is a "provider of electronic communications service or remote computing service," as ECPA defines those terms.[37] As such, section 2705(b) authorizes courts to order a provider "not to notify *any other person* of the existence of a legal demand for its customer's emails and documents" and to do so "for such period as the court deems appropriate."[38]

Among the issues Microsoft raised is who has standing to challenge warrants for production of stored communications—the person whose data is stored and being sought, or the cloud provider to whom the warrants are addressed.[39] As Microsoft's complaint alleges, the U.S. government uses secrecy orders under section 2705(b) to keep the cloud provider from informing its customers of the secret warrants, and the orders prohibit customer notifications for "unreasonably long (or even unlimited) periods of time."[40]

The issue of standing to challenge warrants and other process issued to third parties has been one of the major obstacles to maintenance of Fourth Amendment protections for data and documents since the Supreme Court's decisions in *United States v. Miller*[41] and *Smith v. Maryland.*[42] Prior to Microsoft's challenge, courts had held that Fourth Amendment protections may be asserted only by individuals, not vicariously by third parties—a category that covers Microsoft's role in this warrant challenge. The cloud and stored electronic communications generally complicate the assertion of clients' rights by clients, making it increasingly likely that this will continue to be challenged until resolved, and certainly until a more technology-suitable approach than the "third-party doctrine" from the 1970s is achieved through litigation or new legislation.

B. Extraterritorial Application of U.S. Warrants Seeking Access to Data Stored in Clouds Abroad

The second issue Microsoft and others have raised is whether warrants issued by the U.S. government are effective when seeking information stored solely outside the United States. In July 2016, the Second Circuit held that section 2703 of ECPA does not authorize

---

36 Complaint, Microsoft Corp. v. U.S. Dept. of Justice, ¶¶ 1 & 6, Case 2:16-cv-00538-JLR (W.D. Wash. Apr. 14, 2016). Although the 2016 complaint speaks only in terms of 18 U.S.C. § 2705(b) (which allows courts to impose indefinite or prolonged bans on notice to the targets of the warrants), commentators also mention 18 U.S.C. § 2703's "no-notice warrants" as being in issue. *See, e.g.,* Sarah E. Pugh, Comment, *Cloudy with a Chance of Abused Privacy Rights: Modifying Third-Party Fourth Amendment Standing Doctrine Post-Spokeo,* 66 Am. U. L. Rev. 971, 979 (2017).

37 Complaint, *supra* note 36, at ¶ 18.

38 *Id.*

39 *Id.* ¶ 9.

40 *Id.* ¶ 4.

41 425 U.S. 435 (1976).

42 442 U.S. 735 (1979).

courts to issue and enforce warrants for seizure of customer e-mails stored exclusively on foreign servers.[43] That court observed:

> Warrants traditionally carry territorial limitations: United States law enforcement officers may be directed by a court-issued warrant to seize items at locations in the United States and in United States-controlled areas, *see* Fed. R. Crim. P. 41(b), but their authority generally does not extend further.[44]

Officials of the European Union and the Government of Ireland, where the data in issue was stored at the time the warrant was issued, expressed vehement objections to the U.S. government's position on extraterritoriality. (The customer whose e-mails were being sought registered as a resident of Ireland.) Microsoft's position also received *amicus* support from dozens of members of the online communications industry. A majority of the states joined the government's side in this dispute in urging that certiorari be granted.[45]

The Supreme Court granted certiorari, but the core issue in Microsoft's dispute with the federal government was resolved on March 23, 2018, when Congress enacted and the President signed into law the Clarifying Lawful Overseas Use of Data Act (CLOUD Act).[46] The CLOUD Act amended 18 U.S.C. by adding:

> § 2713. Required preservation and disclosure of communications and records
>
> A provider of electronic communication service or remote computing service shall comply with the obligations of this chapter to preserve, backup, or disclose the contents of a wire or electronic communication and any record or other information pertaining to a customer or subscriber within such provider's possession, custody, or control, regardless of whether such communication, record, or other information is located within or outside of the United States.

The CLOUD Act also allows service providers to seek review of warrants to the extent that the individual is not a resident of the United States and compliance would subject the provider to "a material risk" of violating the laws of a foreign government."[47] The Supreme Court held on April 17, 2018, that the CLOUD Act rendered Microsoft's appeal moot.[48] At the very least, the CLOUD Act will require lawyers and law firms that use cloud computing to review and revise their policies and procedures to comport with its requirements.

A second dispute over extraterritoriality of ECPA warrants is pending. A magistrate judge presiding as a district court judge in the Third Circuit ordered Google in February 2017 to provide access because in that case, the invasion of privacy had occurred entirely

---

43 *In re* Warrant to Search a Certain E-Mail Account Controlled & Maintained by Microsoft Corp., 829 F. 3d 197, 201 (2d Cir. 2016).

44 *Id.*

45 Greg Stohr, *Microsoft Email-Access Fight with U.S. Gets Top Court Review,* BLOOMBERG.COM, Oct. 16, 2017, https://www.bloomberg.com/news/articles/2017-10-16/microsoft-email-access-fight-with-u-s-gets-supreme-court-review.

46 Pub. L. No. 115-141, div. V, 132 Stat. 348, 1213 (2018).

47 18 U.S.C. § 2703(h).

48 United States v. Microsoft Corp., 138 S. Ct. 1186 (2018) (remanding case to the Second Circuit with instructions first to vacate the district court's contempt finding against Microsoft and its denial of Microsoft's motion to quash, and then to direct the district court to dismiss the case as moot).

inside the United States, not the location at which the data was stored.[49] It is not clear what effect the CLOUD Act will have on Google's litigation.

VI. Other External Requirements on Lawyers and Law Firms Holding Electronic Data for Clients

Two more examples demonstrate additional challenges that lawyers and law firms may experience when they hold electronic data for clients. This Part IV describes these examples, which represent only some of the many issues—mostly "low-tech" issues—that exist above, beyond, and around the basic physical, administrative, and particularly technical aspects of securing data in clouds.

A. External Standards Applicable to Lawyers or Law Firms as Vendors to Clients in Specific Regulated Industries

Cybersecurity responsibilities applying to lawyers also come from outside the MRPC and the legal profession itself, for example from public regulations imposed on lawyers or law firms as "vendors" or "service providers" to regulated financial institutions, such as the DFS Cybersecurity Regulation, which became effective in 2017.[50] The regulation is not identical to earlier standards for third-party vendors, including lawyers and law firms, imposed by federal bank regulators, adding more complexity to how lawyers and law firms implement possibly conflicting requirements into their systems, policies, and procedures. Section 500.11(a) of the regulation speaks specifically to third-party service providers and provides that regulated entities must have written policies and procedures to ensure that service providers can secure information systems and nonpublic information, that they identify and manage risks associated with use of service providers, and that they periodically assess their service providers on the adequacy of their cybersecurity practices and the risks continued employment of them may present.

Moreover, section 500.11(b) requires due diligence and "contractual protections" between regulated entities and providers, including use of multifactor authentication, encryption to protect nonpublic information in transit and at rest, notice to the regulated entity in the event of a cybersecurity event affecting the regulated entity's information systems or nonpublic information held by the provider, and representations and warranties from the provider to the regulated entity that protect the latter.[51]

Like the MRPC, the DFS Cybersecurity Regulation specifies broad categories that regulated entities must address in their own compliance plans and that of their third-party service providers as well. It is, accordingly, more like a vessel or vase to be filled than a prescription of itself.

---

49 *See* Orin Kerr, *Google Must Turn Over Foreign-Stored Emails Pursuant to a Warrant, Court Rules,* Wash. Post, Feb. 3, 2017, https://www.washingtonpost.com/news/volokh-conspiracy/wp/2017/02/03/google-must-turn-over-foreign-stored-e-mails-pursuant-to-a-warrant-court-rules/.
50 NYS DFS Cybersecurity Regulation, *supra* note 8.
51 *Id.* § 500.11.

B. External Standards Applicable to Lawyers or Law Firms as Outside Counsel to Corporations Generally

Other externally imposed requirements are more like prescriptions than vessels. One such source of recent increases in lawyers' cybersecurity duties is the March 2017 *Model Information Protection and Security Controls for Outside Counsel Possessing Company Confidential Information* issued by the Association of Corporate Counsel (ACC).[52] The ACC called for lawyers and law firms performing services for corporate clients to conform to specific requirements relating to a host of subjects. The ACC maintains that the *Model Controls* document is "not intended to establish any industry standards for any purpose for either the company client or the outside vendor, including, but not limited to, contract, professional malpractice, or negligence."[53] The ACC's approach is sufficiently specific, and frankly daunting, to do precisely what it claims not to be doing. Moreover, the ACC's approach is likely to make it far more difficult for smaller firms and solo practitioners than for large firms to compete to provide services to corporate clients that adopt the white paper's approach because of the labor-intensive nature of the ACC's requirements.

The *Model Controls* broadly define the term "company confidential information" that its requirements seek to protect.[54] It also requires that outside counsel:

> have in place appropriate organizational and technical measures to protect company confidential information or other information of a similar nature against accidental or unlawful destruction, loss, alteration, unauthorized disclosure or access, and which provide a level of security appropriate to the risk represented by the processing and nature of the information to be protected.[55]

So far, this sounds like a prescription or requirement for physical, technical, and administrative controls such as the federal government imposed on providers of consumer financial services or consumer reporting agencies, as described earlier in this chapter.

For example, it requires encryption of information in transit, encryption of information at rest, and encryption of data stored on portable devices or transmitted over nonsecure communications channels—the latter two to be achieved in manners that meet U.S. Federal Information Processing Standard 140, Level 2 or equivalent industry standard.[56] There are detailed provisions for physical security protections.[57]

The most prescriptive of the *Model Controls* deals with system administration and network security, giving "examples" of industry standard safeguards such as ISO/IEC 27002:2005, NIST 800-44, Microsoft Security Hardening Guidelines, OWASP Guide to Building Secure Web Applications, and various Center for Internet Security Standards.[58] Additionally, the company may request that its outside counsel undergo the certification process for ISO 27001 and provide "evidence of certification when attained."[59] The *Model Controls* also seek outside counsel's "agreement" to conduct background screening of its

---

52 ACC Model Controls, *supra* note 9.
53 *Id.* at 1.
54 *Id.* at 2.
55 *Id.* at 2–3.
56 *Id.* at 5.
57 *Id.* at 7.
58 *Id.* at 9.
59 *Id.* at 10.

employees, subcontractors, and contingent workers,[60] and in countries in which it is possible to procure cyber insurance, to do so with minimum coverages of $10 million.[61]

Despite the ACC's disclaimer of any intention to create industry standards, the issuance of its *Model Controls* will create new challenges for larger and smaller providers of legal services to corporations that adhere to the ACC's guidance, with distinctly greater challenges to be imposed on smaller providers and solo practitioners. The ACC's guidance is more content-prescriptive than the MRPC.

C. Federal Regulations, Policies, or Guidance on Border Searches of Electronic Devices and Related Developments

What are a lawyer's ethical duties concerning protection of clients' confidential information prior to crossing the United States borders, and what are they during border-control searches and afterwards? This question arises because of the current ability of U.S. Customs and Border Patrol agents to search electronic devices at the entry points to the United States, and to detain the device or to save copies of its contents as well.

This Part IV.C. is intended to give readers a starting point for planning movement of devices such as mobile phones, tablets, laptops, and peripheral storage devices across the U.S. borders in advance, at the time of crossings, and following searches by border authorities in the United States and Canada.

On January 4, 2018, U.S. Customs and Border Patrol issued new directions for border searches of electronic devices.[62] The 2018 Directive governs all forms of electronic devices[63] and applies in both the outbound and inbound directions[64] and on a suspicionless basis. Arguably intended to be narrower than its predecessor Directive No. 3340-049,[65] the Directive explains that:

> The border search will include an examination of only the information that is resident upon the device and accessible through the device's operating system or through other software, tools, or applications. Officers may not intentionally use the device to access information that is solely stored remotely.[66]

It is worth considering two additional resources on how this revised Directive applies to devices carried across the borders of the United States and how it relates to lawyers' and law firms' duties under MRPC. First, the New York City Bar issued a formal opinion[67] that

---

60 *Id.*

61 *Id.*

62 CBP Directive No. 3340-049A, *supra* note 10.

63 *Id.* ¶ 3.2.

64 *Id.* ¶ 2.3.

65 U.S. Customs & Border Protection, CBP Directive No. 3340-049: Border Search of Electronic Devices Containing Information (Aug. 20, 2009), https://www.dhs.gov/xlibrary/assets/cbp_directive_3340-049.pdf.

66 CBP Directive No. 3340-049A, *supra* note 10, ¶ 5.1.2.

67 New York City Bar, Formal Op. 2017-5: An Attorney's Ethical Duties Regarding U.S. Border Searches of Electronic Devices Containing Clients' Confidential Information (reissued May 9, 2018), http://www.nycbar.org/member-and-career-services/committees/reports-listing/reports/detail/formal-opinion-2017-5-an-attorneys-ethical-duties-regarding-us-border-searches-of-electronic-devices-containing-clients-confidential-information.

further articulates expectations under the MRPC. The opinion addresses lawyers' ethical obligations at three points in time: before the attorney comes to the United States border, at the border, and after border agents review clients' confidential information that may have been stored in e-mails, texts, or documents on a device that the lawyer had in hand at the border.[68] Preborder obligations include reasonable efforts to prevent unauthorized access to clients' confidential information and implicate the lawyer's duty of competence to avoid disclosures.[69] At borders, the opinion counsels that lawyers may not comply with demands unless "reasonably necessary" under Rule 1.6(b)(6), which allows disclosures to "comply with 'law or court order.'"[70] The opinion also recommends that lawyers carry "proof of bar membership, such as an attorney ID card, when crossing a U.S. border."[71] Lastly, if the lawyer has had to disclose clients' confidential information during a border search, the opinion requires that the lawyer inform the client or clients of those disclosures pursuant to Rule 1.4.[72] The opinion also provides more details about lawyers' duties at each of these stages.[73]

The second document that will assist lawyers and law firms in evaluating how to meet their MRPC duties and deal with CBP Directive No. 3440-049A is the American Bar Association's January 2018 *Electronic Device Advisory for Mid-Year Meeting Attendees*.[74] The advisory specifically addresses MRPC 1.1 (competence), 1.6 (confidentiality), 5.1 and 5.3 (supervisory duties), and 1.4 (communication).[75] The advisory offers specific "measures" for "all legal professionals travelling to Canada for the Mid-Year Meeting," including minimizing the number of devices and the confidential information they may hold, buying a new device and minimizing the information it contains, identifying the types and locations of the devices you choose to carry over the border, and more.[76]

Additionally, the Canadian Border Security Agency has a written policy on inspections and searches at Canada's international borders.[77]

VII. Conclusion

The MRPC discussed in this chapter are stated in strict liability terms. This makes them major issues for lawyers and law firms that are victims of ransomware and malware incidents, of rogue employees that may steal or leak information pertaining to clients, or of other intrusions into client assets, regardless of how those assets came to the lawyer or firm, how they are stored and shared for work purposes, or whether a government is the party seeking access through legal process or surveillance. As well-composed and

---

68 *Id.* at 2.
69 *Id.* at 3.
70 *Id.*
71 *Id.*
72 *Id.*
73 *Id.* at 3–14.
74 Electronic Device Advisory 2018, *supra* note 11.
75 *Id.* at 3.
76 *Id.* at 6–7.
77 Canada Border Services Agency, Operational Bulletin PRG-2015-31, Examination of Digital Devices and Media at the Port of Entry (June 30, 2015), http://www.lexsage.com/documents/CBSA%20 Operational%20Bulletin%20PRG-2015-31%20Examination%20of%20Digital%20Devices%20and%20 Media%20at%20Port%20of%20Entry.pdf.

well-intended as it is, the MRPC leaves vague many important details about the scope of obligations it imposes. Lawyers attempting to fulfill the obligations imposed by the MRPC discussed in this chapter are like vessels or vases that are filled up using many outside and constantly expanding sources.

This chapter has mentioned a few possible sources that lawyers and law firms whose work is subject to the MRPC may find applicable. The sources are not restricted to technology solutions or even to the customary required trio of physical, administrative, and technical forms of data protection. Indeed, the "low-tech" issues described in this chapter are just as threatening to clients' assets as cyber attacks are in many respects. Thus, lawyers and law firms must remain attentive to new, as well as old-fashioned, reference points for what the MRPC requires. These new and old, domestic and foreign, technology and nontechnology issues described in this chapter as reference points "above, beyond, and around" the MRPC are intended to cause the profession to take a more holistic view of what the MRPC means for clients and for the lawyers and law firms who serve them. This holistic view would require lawyers' attention to technical standards to protecting data abroad—at a firm's offices or in a cloud—and knowledge of the risks from government agents or private persons that may differ when U.S. law is not the controlling law, or the only possible controlling law, on access.

What do these "low-tech" or "above, beyond, and around" sources of meaning suggest for future compliance by lawyers and law firms with the MRPC? Here are a few thoughts:

- As Microsoft argued in its 2016 action against the U.S. Department of Justice: "People do not give up their rights when they move their private information from physical storage to the cloud."[78] Thus, in addition to the physical, administrative, and technical features of cyber protection that lawyers and firms may employ, the "above, beyond, and around" aspects of taking a client's private information into the cloud requires more planning and knowledge of the legal rules that may govern access.
- Given the legal complexities in the more recent Microsoft warrant challenge, such as the ECPA provisions at 18 U.S.C. §§ 2703 and 2705(b), lawyers and law firms, as well as their clients, may not learn for extended periods of time that government agencies have been able to access cloud-stored information, or they may learn about it in a very public or inconvenient manner that will cause much consternation to the clients, lawyers, and firms. How will lawyers and law firms anticipate and manage these risks? How will they advise clients of these risks in advance in connection with choosing electronic data-sharing and cloud storage for a particular client or project?
- Some of the external standards described above prescribe the choices of lawyers and law firms more than others. For example, federal and state government regulations and policies, including the 2018 policy on border searches of electronic devices and regulations imposed on a pass-through basis from regulated entities to their third-party service providers, prescribe what lawyers and law firms must do to protect data. The ability of solo practitioners and smaller firms to meet these external regulatory requirements may be exceeded by their complexity, as the ACC's *Model Controls* demonstrate. Does this mean that corporations will tilt away from solo practitioners and smaller firms? It may well be.

---

78 Complaint, *supra* note 36, at ¶ 1.

- Finally, the complexities of managing the cybersecurity and other aspects of cloud usage—only some of which are discussed in this chapter—could cause some clients or their lawyers to move away from cloud usage back into more face-to-face, telephonic, or paper-based forms of communications and data storage. Will these alternatives be used only for the most sensitive types of client assets, such as communications that include trade secrets, technology, or merger or acquisition plans? Or could it become more generalized? Will "war rooms" for M&A deals be the norm again?

A movement away from cloud usage imposes different costs on clients, their counterparties in transactions, and the lawyers for both sides. As more persons are engaged in a deal, dispute, or negotiation, the value of data-sharing through clouds increases, and so do the risks that the perimeters protecting the data could be hacked. The balance between cloud usage and compliance with the MRPC then imposes costs that, like the sources of the contents of the MRPC "vessel," lawyers and law firms must evaluate from "above, beyond, and around." Additionally, a movement away or back from cloud computing raises more, not fewer, tasks to be managed by lawyers and law firms because it requires attention to more potential avenues of access to data belonging to clients or related to the lawyer or law firm's representation of the client—paper files, electronic files at rest, and electronic files in transmission. In the latter two categories, the data-protection efforts would have to cover cloud and noncloud storage and transmission.

The "above, beyond, and around" concerns presented in this chapter may be considered more low-tech than high-tech. With so much being written about cyber security, and so many resources being devoted to technology solutions to cybersecurity threats, it is possible to devote less thought and planning to risks grounded in other parts of the law or to more old-fashioned procedures developed for paper-based file management that may need to be revisited for their ability to protect clients' intellectual property assets and pending deals or strategic objectives. These concerns also are not likely to be issues that information-technology professionals who are not lawyers, however talented they may be, will have in mind as they focus on securing cyber assets of the lawyers, firms, and clients they serve. These are issues for lawyers themselves to manage.

Chapter 15

Mitigating Risk Through Cyberliability Insurance

By Edward R. Noriega, Nicole Sheth, and Harrison M. Covall[1]

Cyber security is a complex and ever-changing landscape. Additionally, the cyber risks associated with it present a myriad of unique challenges to organizations of all shapes and sizes. This chapter endeavors to show how one tool—cyberliability insurance—can be utilized as a shield against the economic impact of a cyber incident[2] and a proactive part of an organization's overall risk management strategy. Specifically, although this chapter will discuss cyberliability insurance writ large, it will pay particular attention to the role this sort of insurance can play with respect to an organization's use of cloud computing.

I. Introduction to Cyberliability

Data breaches pose an unprecedented threat to businesses worldwide. In its 2018 Cyber Claims Study, NetDiligence* found that the average total cost associated with breaches for the period 2013–2017 was $603,900, with a median cost of $34,000. Notably, for the purposes of this chapter, when a cloud computing vendor was involved in a breach, the average and median breach costs were $616,000 and $34,000 respectively.[3]

The need to be aware of the potential liability associated with cyber threats is no longer confined to the largest companies because businesses of all sizes have been targets of data breaches. Any company that utilizes the internet to interact with customers, store private data, or offer web-based services has significant cyberliability. Although all businesses face these threats, certain industries have emerged as top targets for nefarious actors. These industries include health care, retail, and financial institutions. Likewise, the government is a popular target.

Cyberliability has the potential to have an outsized impact on small- and mid-sized companies. In fact, NetDiligence* found that small- to medium-sized businesses—companies with less than $50M in revenue—are the most affected by cyber breaches. These companies often rely heavily on the internet to transact their business, thus exposing themselves to increased vulnerability, and often lack the resources and/or desire to adequately invest in cyber security. Although the sources of their cyberliability are similar to those faced by large companies, their ability to protect themselves against a data breach is significantly less.

---

1 Edward R. Noriega is a partner at Kaufman Borgeest & Ryan LLP and can be reached at enoriega@kbrlaw.com; Nicole Sheth is a partner and can be reached at nsheth@kbrlaw.com. Harrison M. Covall is an associate and can be reached at hcovall@kbrlaw.com.

2 We use the term "cyber incident" to generally describe events that negatively impact an organization's computer system. This is distinct from the term "data breach," which specifically refers to the unauthorized access to and/or exfiltration of information stored on an organization's computer system.

3 NetDiligence 2018 Cyber Claims Study (Nov. 7, 2018), https://netdiligence.com/wp-content/uploads/2018/11/2018-NetDiligence-Claims-Study_Version-1.0.pdf.

Cyberliability insurance is an asset to businesses of all sizes in that it protects against a total loss resulting from a data breach; however, cyberliability insurance can be particularly valuable to small- and mid-sized businesses because of its ability to be tailored to address the needs of individual businesses.

A. Evolving Threats

One of the most vexing challenges presented by cyber risks is that, as cybersecurity techniques improve to address present vulnerabilities, new threats are created to elude these security improvements. The so-called cyberattack industry is evolving every day and developing new exploits, attack vectors, and inexpensive software designed to steal or ransom valuable private data for profit. The cost imbalance between protecting an organization's computer system (expensive) and the tools through which to gain unauthorized access to it (inexpensive) present additional challenges. Some of these inexpensive tools have proven incredibly effective, including distributed denial of service attacks (DDoS), which have taken down entire swaths of the internet's backbone. Additionally, the growth in ransomware and extortionware continues to increase exponentially, representing the most straight-line monetization of digital threats. Further, nefarious actors have found success in targeting an organization's employees with manipulative messaging. These attacks, known as phishing or social-engineering attacks, have been among the most successful (and devastating) attack methods.

B. Challenges of Cloud Computing

Utilization of cloud computing is quickly becoming ubiquitous among businesses of all sizes. Driven by the potential for cost savings and efficiency, many companies are storing their data off-site on servers hosted and monitored by third-party vendors. Regardless of where the data is stored, however, these businesses must accept that there is always a risk of an attack and theft of their data. Similar to insuring against risks presented by hiring employees, maintaining premises, or indemnifying directors and officers, organizations would be wise to mitigate the risk presented by the use of cloud servers by purchasing cyberliability insurance to provide some level of assurance to the organization that, in the event of an cyber incident or data breach, they can guard against total loss.

The out-sourced,[4] decentralized nature of data on the cloud presents several potential points of increased liability.

1) **Encryption of data.** With the mobility of data in the cloud, encryption (or the lack thereof) is a key source of potential liability. Notably, there are several regulatory frameworks that impose encryption requirements on organizations. For example, although neither the Health Insurance Portability and Accountability Act (HIPAA) nor the European Union's General Data Protection Regulation (GDPR) explicitly require the encryption of data in every instance, properly encrypting data could shield an organization from liability under the statutes, whereas failing

---

4 Although certain large enterprises maintain their own cloud networks, the vast majority of organizations utilize third-party vendors. Regardless, similar challenges persist in cloud computing, whether the data is controlled by the company or not.

to encrypt data could expose the organization to increased liability. As encryption becomes more common, failing to encrypt data will increase the liability of an organization.

2) **Mobility of data/mobile devices.** One of the hallmarks of cloud storage is the ease of mobility of data. The ability to share data throughout an organization certainly has its value, but it also allows many avenues through which the network can be accessed by an unauthorized entity. Moreover, with the advent of mobile devices and the increased prevalence of "bring-your-own-device"[5] policies, there are even more potential access points available to nefarious actors.

3) **Constant monitoring/incident response.** The outsourced nature of cloud computing means that an organization is essentially putting the security of its data in the hands of another party. Thus, third-party liability can often arise from the cloud service provider's inability to properly protect the network and/or adequately respond to a cyber incident.

Cloud computing offers organizations a myriad of advantages; however, even though an organization may outsource the storage of its data, it still faces the same liability arising from a breach of its data that occurs at the cloud service provider as it would if the data were stored on its own internal systems. Moreover, due to the growth of companies using cloud computing to provide public-facing access to private-organization systems, there is an increased opportunity for direct attempts by bad actors to breach or shut down the hosting services. Ultimately, it will be the company to which the consumers provided their information that will be at risk if the information is lost or disclosed, and those companies ought to prepare for that possibility with appropriate insurance measures.

II. Value of Cyberliability Insurance

As the preceding shows, the economic consequences of any cyber incident, let alone a data breach, can be devastating for a company. This economic impact is felt even more acutely by small- and mid-sized organizations; however, despite these potential financial consequences, many organizations do not consider cyberliability insurance to be a necessity as they do with more traditional lines of insurance, such as commercial general liability (CGL) coverage, employment practices liability (EPL) coverage, directors and officers liability (D&O) coverage, or errors and omissions (E&O) coverage.

To illustrate this disconnect, another study conducted by the Ponemon Institute compared the decision-making process to purchase a traditional line of insurance—such as fire insurance—to the decision to purchase cyberliability insurance.[6] The authors explained that although the likelihood and financial impact of a data breach is far greater than that of a fire, companies see fire insurance as a "given," whereas they

---

5 A "bring-your-own-device" (BYOD) policy is a policy whereby a company encourages its employees to utilize their own devices (such as smart phones or laptops) at work and connect to the company's cloud network.

6 2017 Global Cyber Risk Transfer Comparison Report (Apr. 2017), http://www.aon.com/attachments/risk-services/cyber/2017-Global-Cyber-Risk-Transfer-Report-Final.pdf.

often remain unsure about committing resources to cyberliability insurance. To take this metaphor a step further, although a fire can certainly have devastating ramifications, the ways in which to mitigate the likelihood of a fire, the ways in which to respond to a fire, and the estimated damage a fire may cause are relatively predictable. Conversely, due to the evolving nature of cyber threats, there is significant variability as to a proper incident response and the potential losses stemming from a cyber incident or data breach. Thus, the liability stemming from cyber incidents or data breaches is much more difficult to anticipate than the liability addressed by traditional lines of insurance.

A. Overlap with Other Lines of Insurance

Cyberliability insurance typically guards against several types of cyber incidents, with different amounts and types of coverage available, all of which can be tailored to the specific needs of the purchasing organization. Most policies operate to provide coverage for two types of claims: first-party claims in which the insured organization has suffered some financial loss due to a cyber incident, and third-party claims in which a third party has asserted some claim against the insured organization based upon a cyber incident that occurred at the insured organization. Depending on the scenario, both coverages may be triggered to respond to the incident, although they place different obligations upon the insurance carrier. Additionally, cyberliability insurance policies offer a wide range of coverage for incident response services.

  Cyberliability typically works independently of other types of insurance purchased by an organization, which may include CGL coverage, EPL coverage, D&O coverage, or E&O coverage. Notably, organizations that have opted to forgo purchasing a stand-alone cyberliability policy have encountered adverse outcomes when they have attempted to tender a cyber claim under one of their existing insurance policies. For instance, a series of cases have found that a data breach may not be covered under a CGL policy due to the data breach failing to constitute a "publication" as defined by the policy.[7]

  The issue of whether coverage for cyber-specific losses will be afforded under policies other than stand-alone cyberliability policies is at the center of an emerging line of cases. These cases, which demonstrate the uncertainty of seeking cyber coverage under "traditional" insurance policies, address whether coverage for phishing attacks is covered under the "computer fraud" provisions of crime/fidelity insurance policies. As of June 2018, it appeared that a consensus was forming among courts that insurance policies that provided coverage for computer fraud would *not* provide coverage for phishing attacks unless such coverage was affirmatively granted. The general reasoning behind this rationale, which was utilized by both the Fifth and Ninth Circuits, was that although the at-issue transfer of funds from the insured to a nefarious third party was unauthorized, an authorized individual actually transmitted the funds. Thus, these courts held that affording coverage under the computer fraud provision of an insurance policy would be an overly broad reading of the policy's language due to the fact that the transfer of funds was

---

  7 *See, e.g.,* Zurich Am. Ins. v. Sony Corp. of Am., No. 651982/2011, 2014 N.Y. Misc. LEXIS 514 (Sup. Ct. Feb. 21, 2014); Recall Total Info. Mgmt. v. Fed. Ins. Co., 317 Conn. 46, 115 A.3d 458 (2015).

not "fraudulently caused" by a computer, but was instead transferred by an authorized individual.[8]

By July 2018, however, this consensus was thrown into turmoil. On July 6, 2018, the Second Circuit affirmed a lower court ruling which found coverage under a computer fraud provision of a "Federal Executive Protection" policy for an insured's fraudulent transfer of funds induced by a "spoofed" e-mail.[9] In *Medidata*, the Second Circuit determined that although the insured validly authorized the at-issue transfer of funds, the transfer was induced through the spoofed e-mail; thus, the spoofed e-mail (or phishing attack) was the "proximate cause" of the insured's losses.[10] Seven days later, on July 13, 2018, the Sixth Circuit relied on similar reasoning in reversing a lower court's decision and finding that a phishing attack constituted computer fraud (as defined by the insurance policy) that "directly caused" the insured's loss, thus triggering the policy's computer fraud coverage.[11]

Companies will continue to endeavor to utilize their computer systems to leverage consumer data and optimize their business operations; thus, the mechanisms protecting those computer systems must increase in robustness, and the insurance policies protecting this investment in computing must grow as well. As the foregoing demonstrates, seeking coverage for cyber-related losses under policies that do not expressly provide coverage for such losses is, at best, a risky proposition. Accordingly, organizations would be well-advised to purchase stand-alone cyberliability policies and/or seek affirmative grants of coverage for their cyber-related liability.

B. Cyberliability Coverages

At present, four general categories of cyberliability coverage are provided:

1) Liability arising out of a company's use of its computer system or its cloud vendor's failure to properly protect data;

---

8 *See* Pestmaster Servs. v. Travelers Cas. & Sur. Co. of Am., 656 F. App'x 332, 333 (9th Cir. 2016) (finding that "[b]ecause computers are used in almost every business transaction, reading this provision to cover all transfers that involve both a computer and fraud at some point in the transaction would convert this Crime Policy into a 'General Fraud' Policy"); *see also* Apache Corp. v. Great Am. Ins. Co., 662 F. App'x 252, 258 (5th Cir. 2016) (holding that "when the policy was issued in 2012, electronic communications were, as they are now, ubiquitous . . . [i]n short, few—if any—fraudulent schemes would not involve some form of computer-facilitated communication.") In *Pestmaster*, the fraudulent transfer of funds did not come from a phishing attack, but from a vendor who was authorized to access the insured's bank account in order to pay the insured's payroll taxes, yet kept the money for itself. Nevertheless, the reasoning of *Pestmaster* was relied upon in *Apache* to deny coverage for a phishing attack that caused an authorized individual to transfer funds to a nefarious third party.

9 *See* Medidata Sols. Inc. v. Fed. Ins. Co., 729 F. App'x 117 (2d Cir. 2018). A spoofed e-mail is an e-mail that has been disguised to appear to have been sent from an address from which it did not, in fact, originate.

10 *See id.* at 119 (finding that "[w]hile it is true that the Medidata employees themselves had to take action to effectuate the transfer, we do not see their actions as sufficient to sever the causal relationship between the spoofing attack and the losses incurred.").

11 *See* Am. Tooling Ctr., Inc. v. Travelers Cas. & Sur. Co. of Am., 895 F.3d 455, 462, 463 (6th Cir. 2018) (explaining that the "chain of events that was precipitated by the fraudulent emails and led to the wire transfers involved multiple internal actions at [the Insured] . . . [t]hus the computer fraud 'directly caused' [the insured's] 'direct loss.'").

2) Incident response coverage for costs incurred by the insured organization to respond to a cyber incident; these often include IT forensic investigation, public-relations costs, customer notification, and credit monitoring;
3) Regulatory fines/penalties imposed by regulatory agencies; and
4) Credit card industry penalties, including card reissuance costs.

One of the most distinct features of cyberliability insurance is the lack of uniformity among policies. Thus, although these categories of coverage are found in most cyberliability policies, the extent of their coverage varies. These types of coverage are usually offered on a first-party and third-party basis.

There are also specific coverages that are often included in cyberliability policies:

- **Multimedia coverage.** Some media or other content produced and published by the insured organization has violated the privacy of another party, or has been defamatory, or has been negligently relied upon and is now the basis for a suit. Intellectual property rights, including copyright, patent, and trademark infringement, may be covered under this type of coverage, as well as liability related to the insured's advertising activities.
- **Privacy or security coverage.** An organization's cybersecurity apparatus failed to prevent a third party from accessing the private data held by the organization, and the disclosure either has harmed the individual or entity whose information it was, or has triggered certain regulatory obligations. This type of action can include both breaches of security that do not lead to subsequent privacy breaches (typically known as unauthorized access) and privacy breaches resulting in the exfiltration of private data.
- **Technology services and products coverage.** When technology services or technology products are offered to others for a fee and they fail to operate as expected or promised, the consumers who purchased those services/products often file a lawsuit against the service provider, seeking repayment and reimbursement for any damages the customer suffered as a result. This coverage is available for technology services or products provided/sold by the insured, but it does not cover services performed *for* the insured.
- **Business interruption coverage.** When a cyber incident causes an insured's computer system to operate improperly—or fail to operate at all—the financial losses resulting from the interruption in service would be covered. The loss suffered from such an incident is typically calculated by comparing the difference between the insured's typical business income to that which it accrued during the incident. It is important to note that coverage is usually available only for a specified time period. This time period, which is defined in the policy, is meant to give the insured organization a reasonable timeframe from the discovery of the incident to restore its service to its typical form. Although first-party business interruption coverage has become common, third-party coverage—contingent business interruption—is also often available. Contingent business interruption coverage is especially valuable in the cloud context. Specifically, it covers losses suffered due to a business operation interruption caused by a network that is not under the control of the insured (i.e., a network operated by a third-party cloud service provider).
- **Cyberextortion coverage.** If an insured's computer system is infected with ransomware (a software program that renders a computer system inoperable unless

payment is made by the insured to unlock the system), this coverage would provide payment of the ransom in addition to other remediation services. This type of coverage has become increasingly common as the prevalence of ransomware attacks has increased.

- **Data asset restoration coverage.** Although reimbursement for financial losses caused by a cyber incident is important, often the cost to restore the affected data can be just as burdensome. Thus, data asset restoration coverage would cover the cost incurred by the insured to recover/repair the data assets that were affected by the cyber incident/data breach.

- **Public-relations coverage.** If an insured has suffered a data breach, the negative publicity associated with the breach may have a bigger impact than the costs of the breach itself. Accordingly, this coverage would allow the insured organization to hire a public-relations firm to assist in the strategy and delivery of the company's public response to a cyber incident or data breach.

- **Phishing/social-engineering fraud/wire transfer fraud coverage.** As previously discussed, there has been an increase in both the quantity and sophistication of phishing attacks targeting companies. Accordingly, this coverage would provide an affirmative grant of coverage for claims arising from loss caused by such an attack. This coverage often includes data restoration and public-relations components as well.

C. Triggers of Coverage

1. Triggers for First-Party Coverage

Typically, first-party claims require indemnification of losses stemming from a cyber incident in addition to costs incurred to remediate the incident. Covered remediation services usually include the retaining of investigatory firms to determine the extent of the damage, legal counsel to advise the insured organization, and potentially a breach coach to coordinate the response and guide the organization through any notification process that is mandated. Coverage may also exist in the event that the incident has created some negative media attention, and public-relations professionals may be called in to respond if the organization's reputation is at stake.

First-party events typically take the following forms:

- **Data security/privacy incident.** Some number of private customer, employee, or company records are lost or stolen as the result of an intrusion into the organization's system, social engineering, or a lost or stolen device with access to private files or the files themselves on the device.

- **Digital asset protection/business interruption.** An incident (whether from an attacker or an accident) renders digital assets lost and/or stops the normal operations of the business. Examples include ransomware, distributed denial of service attacks, and attacks on storage infrastructure by a third party.

- **Interruption at a third-party cloud service provider.** Cyberliability insurance can also protect an insured organization against a cyber incident that affects its records stored by a third-party cloud service provider. Cyberliability insurance would generally still be effective in mitigating these losses because the cyber incident would occur on servers *maintained for the benefit of the insured organization, if not literally by it.* Coverage would likely be afforded for loss resulting from the attack or loss of records. It should be noted that not all policies provide coverage for data or computer systems that are not directly controlled by the insured organization (discussed further in Part III); thus, organizations must always be vigilant in their search for the cyberliability insurance policy that fits their needs.

2. Triggers of Third-Party Coverage

Third-party events are generally triggered by a demand or lawsuit resulting from a cyber incident that is brought against the insured organization by a third party. These cyber incidents include situations where some group or individual private data was lost, and that group or individual sues or demands compensation from the organization that suffered the cyber incident. Responding to these claims often involves assigning defense counsel to respond to allegations made against the insured organization, as well as retaining investigative firms to determine what type of breach or incident occurred.

D. Value of Cyberliability Coverage for Cloud Computing

Cyber incidents affecting cloud computing often trigger both first- and third-party coverage. Specifically, in terms of first-party coverage for cloud service providers, consumers who have had their private data exfiltrated from the servers of the cloud service provider may seek damages from the provider for failure to adequately safeguard the data and prevent its unauthorized access. Some types of data, including health data and payment card data, have special rules and regulations that require a heighted level of maintenance of an entity's cyber security and proscribe statutory penalties in the event that those standards are not properly met. Specifically, HIPAA and the Health Information Technology for Clinical and Economic Health Act (HITECH) have codified rules that are intended to enhance patient privacy by requiring entities that maintain or transmit patient information—known as "covered entities" and "business associates" under HIPAA—to adhere to certain cybersecurity protocols. Moreover, these statutes (and similar statutes implemented at the state level) provide individuals with certain rights regarding their health information while also allowing the government to enforce the heightened standards and requirements through fines and other penal actions.

   Third-party coverage also may provide protection for cloud service providers that are facing an inquiry, complaint, or investigation from a federal, state, or administrative agency related to their collection of private information. This coverage is similar to the other third-party coverages in that defense counsel will be assigned, and the insurance carrier will assist in obtaining a resolution of the regulatory action.

   Further, in the event a cloud service provider is providing public-facing services hosted on its cloud storage system, these services may constitute "technology services and products" that are insurable under the organization's cyberliability insurance policy. If such coverage exists, the cloud service provider would be protected against a portion of the losses sought by its customers who were negatively impacted by the provider's service failing to operate as required or promised.

E. Insurance as a Risk Management Tool

One of the most unique—and valuable—aspects of cyberliability insurance is the inclusion of risk management services into the insuring agreement. Premised on other lines of insurance that have incorporated aspects of risk management into their policies, such as EPL insurance, cyberliability policies offer a wide range of tools that can be utilized by the insured as a part of its overall risk management strategy.

Most cyberliability policies will include incident response services. These services, which are meant to assist the insured in mitigating losses associated with a covered cyber incident, are often offered to the insured as part of a prearranged package. The insureds are either given the option to select incident response vendors from a preapproved list, or they may be required to use specified vendors. The prenegotiated nature of these services provide the insureds, and the insurance carriers, the ability to control costs and better assess the overall cost of a cyber incident.

In addition to incident response services, many cyberliability policies are beginning to offer proactive risk management tools. For instance, some policies provide "avoidance" tools such as complementary security assessments, helplines, and cybersecurity consulting.

In all, cyberliability insurance is a vital part of an organization's overall risk management strategy. The services offered by many cyberliability insurance policies not only provide insureds the ability to mitigate losses caused by cyber incidents, but also require the insureds to at least contemplate how they would handle a cyber incident.

III. Limits on Coverage

Insurance policies operate by defining the type of events or claims that trigger coverage under the specific insuring agreements of the policy. Events or claims that do not trigger any insuring agreement of the policy will not trigger any coverage. Further, events or claims that do appear to trigger coverage may still be excluded through a variety of exclusions, definitions, and legal concepts that allow insurance carriers to prepare for the amount of risk they insure while also adequately pricing that risk. Some types of policies (like D&O insurance) provide coverage for nearly all tendered incidents and winnow down the coverage available for those incidents through an extensive use of policy exclusions. Other policies (such as EPL coverage) use specific, enumerated types of claims or wrongful acts to trigger coverage, typically none of which are designed to encompass cyber security failures.

As opposed to the types of insurance policies (like D&O policies) that tend to have an expansive definition of the type of "wrongful acts" that trigger coverage, cyberliability policies often have specific insuring agreements that categorically list the types of incidents, events, and claims that trigger coverage pursuant to the policy. In addition to these specific, delineated triggering events, cyberliability insurance policies typically utilize fairly robust lists of exclusions that serve to narrow coverage further and carve out claims and events frequently covered by other lines of insurance. For example, cyberliability policies will typically exclude coverage for property damage as well as employment-related claims made against the insured organization because such claims are expected to be covered by CGL and EPL policies, respectively.

A. General Limitations on Coverage

Cyberliability policies also share many limiting terms and definitions with other types of policies commonly purchased by organizations. Specifically, coverage will be limited with respect to incidents that take place before the relevant policy period, incidents of which the organization had notice before the policy period, and incidents in which a past, present, or future employee, director, or officer or subsidiary of the organization makes a claim against the insured organization.

Similarly, cyberliability insurance policies tend not to provide coverage for intentionally performed acts, including deliberate breaches of contract, criminal acts, or other willful acts that ultimately lead to the incident, damages, or claim asserted by a third party. Typical cyberliability policies also do not provide coverage for liability with which the insured organization would not otherwise be burdened, but which the insured organization agreed to take on as part of a contract.

B. Limitations on Coverage That May Impact Cloud Computing

1. Wear and Tear, Maintenance, and Nonfinal Software Exclusion

Cyberliability policies typically do not cover losses that result from the ordinary "wear and tear" of digital hardware, the failure to properly maintain computers and servers, and issues arising from computer software and hardware that are not finished or properly tested. This means that although a cyber incident may otherwise be covered under the insured organization's cyberliability policy, if the cyber incident is a product of one of the foregoing circumstances, coverage will not be available. These exclusions generally reflect the expectation that basic maintenance should be performed on the systems being used (to the extent possible) and that the insured organization is taking steps to ensure that its computer system is running appropriate software that will allow the system to function properly and will adequately protect against unauthorized access to the data stored on the system.

Given that many organizations store their data on cloud servers not owned or operated by the insured organization, the exclusions found in the organization's policy may be more relevant than the bases for coverage. Specifically, as previously explained, although an organization may store its data on a third-party server, it nevertheless retains liability relative to the protection of its data. Thus, a cloud service provider's failure to properly maintain its systems may cause the insured organization to lose the ability to access insurance coverage it would otherwise be afforded. Accordingly, it is incumbent upon organizations to ensure that their cloud service providers have an understanding of the kinds of routine maintenance and safeguards that must be in place in order to provide a stable and consistent hosting environment. Further, cloud service providers should provide sufficient information to their customers about the systems where data is stored so that the organizations purchasing the cloud services can rely on the fact that the cloud service provider will adequately protect their data (and not expose the organizations to increased liability).

2. "On Behalf Of" Policy Language

To the extent that such a thing exists, "traditional" cyberliability insurance policies were meant to provide coverage for losses resulting from cyber incidents occurring on the insured organization's computer system. These early cyberliability policies did not contemplate that an insured organization would outsource significant portions of their daily computing and data storage to outside vendors. In other words, cloud computing as a service provided to organizations to store data or host applications is not what cyberliability insurance policies have been historically designed to cover.

In addition to not accounting for the outsourcing of data, these early cyberliability policies also assumed that the computer systems they covered were controlled, managed, and operated onsite by the organization, and that they were used solely for the organization's benefit. However, with the use of cloud computing services offered by third parties who provide only a portion of their hardware's storage, the same considerations of control, maintenance, and purpose of the insured organization's hardware and software no longer apply. Therefore, organizations using cloud computing services must be confident that the policy language they are purchasing includes an understanding that coverage should be afforded to hardware and software not controlled by, or solely servicing, that organization.

In order to account for this recent business operation trend, cyberliability insurance policies have begun to include language that affords coverage for third-party entities that store and maintain data "on behalf of" the insured organization. The inclusion of this language extends coverage from the organization's computer system (typically operated and maintained onsite and housing the entirety of the digital operations of the business) to computer systems operated and maintained on behalf of the organization by cloud service providers. This language allows for incidents affecting the cloud system, whether they are a cyber attack, system failure, or result from the services hosted on the cloud system, to be covered under the same policy that would otherwise provide coverage for the insured organization's onsite systems.

3. Reporting Time for Incidents

As previously discussed, cloud computing offers innumerable advantages for those organizations that utilize it; however, the outsourced and decentralized nature of cloud computing presents several challenges to organizations that endeavor to protect their data. Specifically, by outsourcing the monitoring of their data, there may be a potential delay in the organization becoming aware of a data breach that occurs on the third-party's system, having major implications on the coverage provided to the organization by a cyberliability insurance policy.

Traditionally, an insured organization must report incidents that are covered under an insurance policy to the insurance carrier within a specified amount of time. These time-sensitive reporting requirements are meant to allow the insurance carrier to effectively carry out its duties as prescribed by the insurance policy. Failing to timely report an incident can prejudice the defense of the insured or the collection of evidence by the insurance carrier and thereby potentially expose the organization—and the insurance carrier—to excessive and unnecessary risk. Thus, if an insured organization suffers an otherwise covered event, but does not notify its insurance carrier in the timeframe proscribed by the insurance policy, the insurance carrier has basis to disclaim coverage for the event.

This restriction becomes more important when considering the statutorily imposed time constraints relative to data breaches. Given that there are additional notification requirements resulting from the loss of private data, it becomes more incumbent upon organizations to promptly report the incident to their insurance carrier to have breach counsel and a forensic investigation firm assigned to determine the extent of the loss as well as what laws must be complied with and in what timeframe. Failing to timely tender the matter may result in the loss of coverage for some or all fees related to the breach response, or expose the organization to federal or state fines or investigations if the organization fails to comply with the applicable reporting laws.

Accordingly, when the insured organization is utilizing cloud services, it must be aware of these requirements. Moreover, organizations should work with their cloud service provider to ensure that protocols are in place to timely notify the insured organization of a data breach affecting its data that occurred on the cloud service provider's system.

IV. Selecting the Right Policy

Determining the correct amount of coverage to purchase can be a daunting challenge for any organization. Not all companies have the resources for the highest level of cyberliability protection; however, no company is immune from cyber threats. Thus, in order to determine the appropriate amount of coverage, organizations must consider several factors including: (1) the size of the organization—its revenue, number of employees, and its various business activities; (2) the size of its digital operation—the number of records stored, the number anticipated to be stored, and the scope of any digital services offered; (3) the industry in which it operates; and (4) the potential for an overlap of existing liability coverage with cyberliability coverage. Negotiating for policy coverage often comes down to the ultimate limits of liability and how much of a self-insured retention the policy will have before coverage obligations are placed upon the insurance carrier.

A. Organization Size/Makeup

The first issue an organization should consider when determining the proper cyberliability policy is in relation to the size of the organization, both in terms of the total revenue of the organization and the number of personnel working within it. In addition to these typical benchmarks of "size," the organization should consider how its digital operation (both internally and externally) accounts for its total value. For instance, a construction company may generate considerable revenue and may employ a vast number of people, but its digital operation may not contribute significantly to the company's stability or long-term growth. By contrast, a technology start-up may have minimal revenue and few employees, but its digital operations are integral to its longevity. Accordingly, the technology start-up may be wise to invest more of its scarce resources into a cyberliability insurance policy, whereas the construction company may opt for a less robust policy.

It should be noted that although an organization may initially appear to have a limited digital footprint, cyberliability coverage can also extend to an organization's local computer networks in addition to larger cloud services. In this vein, organizations should remember to take both into account when considering the need for, and ultimately the amount of, cyberliability insurance.

B. Stored Data

As digital operations grow larger and more complex, organizations must determine not only the sum total of their digital operations, but also the total number of stored digital records (which may encompass employee records, customer records, and private business records). They must also anticipate the potential growth in the total number of records stored over the upcoming year. Projecting the amount of data stored by the company is important for coverage because basing the amount of coverage obtained on records stored at the start of coverage may lead to purchasing coverage that will ultimately provide much less coverage per record as the number of records increases.

Additionally, organizations should take into account the services they offer to the public via cloud computing and audit the usage data generated therefrom. This can provide some information on the scale of the service's total usage, which should inform the total amount of coverage necessary should the service fail to properly operate, become the source of some exploit leading to infiltration and exfiltrated data, or otherwise become the source of some claim or demand. Knowing the size of the potential class of users as well as the extent to which they use the service should provide some metric for determining the total potential exposure faced by the organization that should be insured via cyberliability coverage.

C. Type of Industry

As previously discussed, there are certain industries that are bigger targets for data breaches than others. Moreover, certain industries may be governed by particularly onerous regulatory frameworks with respect to data security. Thus, the industry in which an organization operates has a significant impact on determining the appropriate cyberliability insurance policy.

Notably, the health care and financial services industries have been among the most targeted for cyber attacks. There are many reasons for this, but the most prominent one is that the information stored by organizations in these industries is particularly valuable on the black market. Although the types and sizes of organizations in these industries may vary, the increased threat they face remains the same. Accordingly, an organization in these industries that may not have the internal resources needed to create a robust cybersecurity apparatus may want to invest in heightened cyberliability insurance.

D. Potential for Coverage Overlap

Most organizations have the various insurance coverage policies previously discussed in this chapter to insure against risks that might lead to loss. Although these other coverages do not cover the same risks as cyberliability insurance, there are likely to be some overlapping areas that should factor into consideration of the amount of coverage sought. Specifically, D&O coverage commonly provides an expansive definition of "wrongful act" that triggers coverage, upon which exclusions may operate to limit or eliminate coverage. Accordingly, there are areas that may create coverage for both types of policies. Additionally, E&O coverage may provide some overlap, especially if the E&O coverage is for some specialized service provided by the organization that involves its computer system, cloud computing system, or other technological capacity. These potential overlaps might provide some degree of extra coverage in the event of an incident and should be carefully considered when seeking coverage.

V. Choosing the Best Policy

In the last few years, the options for cyberliability policies have expanded tremendously, allowing organizations seeking coverage the opportunity to acquire tailored solutions for their unique risk profiles. However, with the proliferation of insurance carriers offering cyberliability coverage, organizations must carefully determine how to find the policy that is the best fit for them. After considering the different types of coverage laid out in Part II, the various limits on coverage noted in Part III, and the amounts of coverage that may be necessary in Part IV, the choice may be clearer, or it may require additional investigation into the slight differences among available policies. This part will endeavor to separate the more nuanced distinctions among policies that may otherwise appear to provide similar coverage.

The primary difference among cyberliability policies is the range of cyber incidents they cover and the remediation services provided under the policy. These distinctions are reflected in the premiums charged (higher rates usually correlating to more robust coverages and services), as well as the amounts required to be paid as a self-insured retention and the maximum limits available for each time an incident is reported.

As such, it is vitally important that any organization searching for cyberliability coverage looks to maximize the amount of relevant coverage needed with favorable retention and premium rates.

A. Data Privacy Coverage Differences

Different policies have different approaches on how to address the liability resulting from data breaches. Additionally, policies differ in regards to the limits of liability that are available to remediate cyber incidents and whether the policy will deem fines and/or penalties as covered. Traditional lines of insurance do not cover fines and penalties because covering them would effectively incentivize bad behavior on the part of the insured by removing the punishment of the offending organizations. However, because most first-party events dealing with data breaches carry risk of fines levied by governmental and administrative authorities, coverage for fines and penalties can be sought and is more freely given in the cyberliability context. Organizations that operate in industries with specific cyber-related regulations (health care, retail) should prioritize selecting a policy with this type of coverage.

Policies also differ in what types of remediation costs will be covered. These costs include IT forensics to determine the extent of a data breach, and funds to redress customers or employees whose data was stolen (notification costs, credit monitoring, identity protection, etc.). Another important consideration for many organizations is whether "crisis management" is a covered remediation service. Specifically, given the exigent nature of a data breach, public-relations firms or other crisis management services may be needed. This type of coverage is incredibly valuable for all companies, especially those that are well-known or rely on the public's trust. After all, there is no monetary value that can be put on a company's diminishment in public perception.

The types of data that can be covered are also subject to change depending on the policy language. Data is often broken into categories such as individual's (often customer's) private data, corporate data, and data in nondigital formats. Different policies may require the purchase of endorsements to extend coverage to different formats or to other specific types of data. Thus, an organization should ensure that all of the particular types of data it stores will be covered by the purchased policy.

B. Other Important Differences for Cloud Computing Coverage

As discussed previously, cyberliability policies offer coverage beyond the protection of data. Depending on the business operations of a cloud service provider, it may be wise to seek coverage beyond that of data security. For instance, if the company offers cloud services that relate to advertising, multimedia coverage (see Part II) may be valuable. Notably, cloud service providers may want to consider intellectual property coverage (although coverage may excluded for patent infringement or misappropriation of trade secret claims). Lastly, as discussed previously, many policies limit coverage to the so-called named insured, who is the primary entity purchasing coverage. Some policies extend coverage by default to other types of entities that relate to the insured organization; however, those companies utilizing a cloud service provider should ensure that their coverage extends to data stored on the third-party system.

VI. Best Practices

When considering the need for cyberliability insurance, the question is not "if" an organization's computer system will be attacked; the question is "when" and "how bad will it be." As such, properly insuring against such a loss is a priority for all businesses engaged in the collection of data. As demonstrated in Part V, there is great diversity in available offerings of cyberliability insurance, and tailoring a policy to any specific needs should be a priority. However, before the search for the correct policy can be completed, there are some steps that an organization should complete first:

1) Organizations looking for coverage should perform a complete audit of their cybersecurity practices and protocols because most carriers will seek this information. As a result of the audit, organizations may consider creating new password procedures, access restrictions, or other security-hardening measures before applying for coverage. This will not only improve data security practices and the overall enterprise risk-management of the organization, but it will assist the investigation efforts in the event that there is a cyber incident and allow investigators to more efficiently diagnose the cause and ramifications of the incident.

2) Prior to applying for coverage, organizations should also perform an audit of all prior cyber incidents that have occurred because if it is determined that they had awareness prior to purchasing coverage of an otherwise covered incident, that incident will be disclaimed by the insurance carrier. These type of incidents may include a prior ransomware attack for which the organization paid the ransom, legal threats made related to services provided by cloud servers, or data backup problems previously reported by their cloud service provider.

3) When comparing policies and coverages, organizations should consider the form their cloud computing usage will take. If they intend to offer public-facing services and support, they should look into policies that contain third-party coverages in order to protect them from suits levied against them. If the organization is primarily using the cloud servers to store data, it should focus more on coverage for downtime, business interruption, and loss of data in the event the hosting company suffers an attack or accident causing loss of data or the access to it.

4) Organizations should audit the total amount of personal information they presently have and how much they expect to acquire when determining how much coverage to obtain. Policies are updated yearly, and the size of the organizations' data stores may grow exponentially in that time. Companies should consider whether their total coverage limits will be able to fully compensate them in the case of catastrophic loss of data or access. Although most policies will not put organizations in a better place after an incident than where they were before, the organization should ensure that the policy chosen will put them in at least as good a position as they were preincident.

VII. Conclusion

As the internet and computerized devices have become ubiquitous, so too have cyber threats and vulnerabilities. This parallel trajectory—continually improving technological capabilities being mirrored by continually evolving cyber-attack vectors—is particularly evident in the use of cloud computing. While cloud computing affords great benefits for both commercial and personal purposes, the ever-increasing reliance on its capabilities creates the potential for enormous liability. As such, cyberliability insurance is no longer an ancillary protection sought by a certain segment of businesses, but is instead an integral part of a company's risk management portfolio. While the cyberliability needs of an organization may vary, the need for protection against the economic impact of cyber risks is universal.

Index